The United States
in World Affairs

1960

The
United States
in
World Affairs

1960

Richard P. Stebbins

Vintage Books
A DIVISION OF RANDOM HOUSE
New York

The Council on Foreign Relations is a non-profit institution
devoted to study of the international aspects of American
political, economic and strategic problems. It takes no stand,
expressed or implied, on American policy.

The authors of books published under the auspices of the
Council are responsible for their statements of fact and expressions of opinion. The Council is responsible only for
determining that they should be presented to the public.

For information, address Council on Foreign
Relations, 58 East 68th Street, New York 21

Published as a Vintage Book by arrangement
with the Council on Foreign Relations

VINTAGE BOOKS
are published by ALFRED A. KNOPF, INC.
and RANDOM HOUSE, INC.

First Vintage Edition, September, 1961

Manufactured in the United States of America

PREFACE

THE AIM of this volume is to present a concise record and interpretation of the international activities of the United States during the calendar year 1960. Continuing the series of annual surveys of American foreign policy initiated by the Council on Foreign Relations in 1931, it thus rounds out a period of three decades broken only by the war years 1941-1944.

The increase in the international responsibilities of the United States during this thirty-year period has added appreciably to the difficulty of bringing the whole range of American foreign relations within the compass of a single annual volume. Each of the eight chapters that compose the present narrative could all too easily have been expanded to book length. The temptation to do so has been resisted in the belief that specialists and thoughtful citizens will still find use for a condensed account which presents the essential facts with just enough background and comment to indicate their underlying significance.

In no sense is the volume to be regarded as an official or semiofficial statement of governmental views, nor does it purport in any way to reflect the opinions of the Council on Foreign Relations. The author's principal concern as a member of the Council staff has been to present the story in an objective and nonpartisan way and to maintain so far as possible the professional standards that distinguish the Council's publications. Much of the documentation on which the narrative is based will be found in the parallel Council on Foreign Relations volume, *Documents on American Foreign Relations, 1960,* references to which have been included side by side with the citations of such standard authorities as the *Department of State*

Bulletin, the *United Nations Review, The New York Times,* and *The Current Digest of the Soviet Press.*

As in past years, the author owes much to the encouragement and support of Dr. Henry M. Wriston, of the members of the Council's Committee on Studies, and of Hamilton Fish Armstrong, George S. Franklin, Jr., William Henderson, Philip E. Mosely, and other colleagues at the Harold Pratt House. John C. Campbell generously found time to read and comment on the entire manuscript, and several other readers made valuable suggestions on individual chapters. Elaine P. Adam has extended her beneficent influence to all phases of the work. Others who have made an indispensable contribution include Donald Wasson, Librarian of the Council, Janet Rigney, Assistant Librarian, and the members of the Library staff; John Kotselas, Production and Promotion Manager; Joseph Cucolo; E. D. Weldon of the American Geographical Society, who prepared the maps; and the admirable technicians of American Book-Stratford Press, Inc. The steadfast cooperation of William Wyck in all matters involving the physical environment of the project will long be gratefully remembered. Special thanks are due also to Dr. Gerald Stourzh, Director, and Maria Schenk of the Austrian Society for Foreign Policy for the courtesy which enabled the author to continue work on the volume during a protracted sojourn abroad.

For permission to reprint cartoons the Council extends its thanks to Herbert L. Block and to *The Hartford Times, The Louisville Times, The Minneapolis Tribune,* the Register and Tribune Syndicate, the *St. Louis Post-Dispatch,* and the *San Francisco Chronicle. The New York Times* has kindly authorized the use of a number of direct quotations which are identified by footnote references.

While deeply appreciative of the assistance provided him from so many directions, the author retains the usual personal responsibility for the entire volume.

R. P. S.

February 1961

CONTENTS

MAPS

CARTOONS

INTRODUCING 1960

NINETEEN HUNDRED AND SIXTY will be remembered as
the year when an American U-2 aircraft was shot down on
a secret photographic mission over the heart of the Soviet
Union; when President Dwight D. Eisenhower journeyed
to Paris for a Big Four "summit conference" which was
prevented from meeting by the anger of Nikita S. Khrushchev; when new flames burst from the unextinguished
ashes of the "cold war," scorching the hope of East-West
political accommodation and igniting fresh blazes in Africa, Latin America, and Southeast Asia; when Japanese
street mobs prevented an American President from visiting their capital; when eighteen formerly colonial countries achieved independence, and seventeen of them were
admitted to the United Nations; France became a member
of the "atomic club"; Premier Khrushchev waved his shoe
at the United Nations General Assembly; and the American people wrote "Finis" to eight years of Republican
leadership, entrusting their future to Senator John F.
Kennedy and the Democratic administration which would
take office on January 20, 1961.

While the significance of these events was variously assessed in different parts of the world, the revived antagonism between the Communist and Western powers was
generally conceded decisive importance both for the peoples immediately concerned and for the world-wide movement of international affairs. In one sense, the failure
of the Paris summit meeting and the evaporation of the

so-called "spirit of Camp David" merely returned the relations of East and West to the unsatisfactory condition that had prevailed before Khrushchev's first visit to the United States in 1959. Even if the summit conference had taken place, there is no evidence that the Soviet Union was prepared to settle any of the outstanding diplomatic issues in a manner at all compatible with Western interests. After its breakdown, the possibility of mutual annihilation continued to act as a powerful, if scarcely infallible, deterrent to the initiation of major hostilities by either side. The Soviet Government, while flaunting its determination to conquer the world for Communist-style "socialism," continued to assert its belief in "peaceful coexistence" rather than war as the most expedient means of doing so. Within a few months of the Paris debacle, Khrushchev was talking once again of the necessity for negotiations at the highest level, and seeking a channel of communication with the incoming American administration.

At the same time, the failure of the Paris meeting spelled the loss of what might have been a promising opportunity to begin the process of East-West accommodation which many observers believed to be the only alternative to an eventual nuclear catastrophe. The Soviet Union's rupture of negotiations on disarmament shortly after the Paris meeting condemned the world to a continuation of the armaments race, unchecked except for the voluntary suspension of nuclear weapons tests that had been observed by the United States, Great Britain, and, presumably, the Soviet Union since the fall of 1958. Although these three powers continued their negotiations looking toward a formal suspension of nuclear weapons testing under international control, the lack of agreement on pertinent issues and the lack of reliable information about what the Soviet Union was actually doing created strong pressures for an early resumption of underground nuclear testing by the United States. Meanwhile the success of the French in developing their own atomic devices emphasized the probability that such weapons would soon become available to Communist China and, perhaps, to other countries not wholly friendly to the West.

* * * * *

Already the United States and the Soviet Union were engaged in a life-and-death competition to maintain and strengthen their respective armed forces and incorporate into their weapons systems the long-range missiles that were now becoming available to both sides. In 1960, many though not all observers felt that the advantage in this competition was tending increasingly to shift away from the United States and in favor of the Soviet Union. Though the United States was generally conceded to possess an "adequate margin of deterrence" for the immediate future, the U.S.S.R. was credited in some American quarters with the capability of achieving a pronounced numerical superiority in long-range missiles within the next two or three years. This advantage might, indeed, be offset at least in part by a continuing American superiority in long-range bombers and by the coming of age of America's seaborne "Polaris" intermediate-range missile. The first two units in a prospective fleet of Polaris-carrying nuclear submarines actually put to sea in the latter part of 1960. Yet the bare possibility that the United States might fall behind in the over-all military race provided some observers with an additional reason for uneasiness over the lack of any progress toward general arms control.

The United States fared rather better in the competitive exploration of outer space during 1960, conclusively demonstrating its superiority to the U.S.S.R. in at least some important phases of space enterprise. Neither power had fully solved as yet the problems of manned space flight, though both expected to do so in the relatively near future. The principal Soviet achievement of the year, made possible by the greatly superior thrust of Soviet rockets, was the orbiting on August 19 of a five-ton "spacecraft" containing two dogs and other animals which were safely returned to earth the following day. The United States, while failing in several attempts to send a rocket around the moon, placed a wide variety of smaller, highly instrumented space satellites in orbit and developed a reliable technique for retrieving a space capsule after its return to the atmosphere. Some of the American satellites, like "Echo" and "Courier," pointed the way to a vast improvement in electronic communications; others, like "Tiros" and "Midas," could provide photographic information on meteorological conditions and, potentially, on military developments in other countries. This was another field of endeavor that cried out for some form of international regulation, particularly as regards its military aspects. But although the United States had advanced a variety of proposals aimed at keeping the existing power rivalries from intruding into outer space, the U.S.S.R. continued throughout 1960 to evade serious negotiations on the subject.

*   *   *   *   *

Khrushchev and the other authorized spokesmen of world Communism never disguised the fact that the overriding objective of their policy was to make possible the eventual prevalence of the Communist system throughout the world. Their unremitting efforts to expand the frontiers of Communism dominated the day-to-day course of international relations in 1960 as in earlier years. No new area was definitively included within the Communist orbit in 1960; still less did any country ruled by Communism abandon the Communist bloc. West Berlin, with the support of the United States and its Western allies, continued to withstand the psychological and administrative pressures to which it had been subjected since late 1958. Iraq achieved at least a temporary stabilization in which the powers of the local Communists, who had threatened to become predominant in 1959, were severely curbed.

But these setbacks to Communist aims were compensated by a pronounced growth of Communist influence in several other areas. By creating an atmosphere of acute international crisis and consistently backing the most extreme proponents of the new African nationalism, the U.S.S.R. secured a definite if slippery foothold in the new Republic of the Congo as well as strengthening its ties with Guinea, Ghana, Morocco, and several other African states. Both Communist China and the U.S.S.R. intensified their association with the insurgent "National Liberation Front" that was fighting the French in Algeria. Of more immediate concern to most Americans was a growing Communist ascendancy in nearby Cuba, whose revolutionary government increasingly developed the characteristics of a Communist satellite, flouted and vilified the United States at every opportunity, and acted as a center for the promotion of subversive and pro-Communist influences throughout the Americas.

Still another country that trembled on the brink of Communist conquest was Laos in Southeast Asia, where a complicated interplay of neutral, pro-Communist and anti-Communist tendencies had resolved itself by December into a small-scale civil war in which one party was openly supported by the United States, the other by the Soviet Union and the Far Eastern Communist regimes of North Vietnam and Communist China. The latter power, whose hostility to the United States was even more unqualified than that of the Soviet Union, attempted no armed adventures of its own during 1960, but openly dissented from the Khrushchev doctrine of "peaceful coexistence" and vigorously defended the use of force in promoting Communist aims. On this and related ideological points its leaders frankly disagreed with the U.S.S.R., and there were other signs of coolness between these two major powers of the Communist camp. But both agreed in proclaiming their dedication to Communist world conquest and in identifying the United States as the principal obstacle to their ambitions—or, as they phrased it, as "an enemy of the peoples of the whole world." [1]

* * * * *

That the future development of this global contest between Communist and non-Communist forces would be profoundly influenced by the attitude of the countries of Asia and Africa became increasingly evident throughout 1960. Already these countries represented an influential factor on the world scene, a kind of unofficial balance wheel or "third force" between the Communist and Western camps. "As I see it," British Prime Minister Harold Macmillan observed early in the year, "the great issue in this second half of the twentieth century is whether the uncommitted peoples of Asia and Africa will swing to the East or the West." [2] The pertinence of this comment was repeatedly emphasized by subsequent developments in the Congo and elsewhere—developments which, moreover, found a significant number of African and Asian governments inclining regularly toward an Eastern rather than a Western position.

This tendency was not to be explained by any inherent preference for Communism. To most African and Asian leaders, the abstract merits of East and West, of Communism and democracy, were less important than the attitudes adopted by the rival great powers on the questions to which they themselves ascribed greatest importance. The chief desiderata of international politics, from the orthodox Asian-African standpoint, were (1) the preservation of world peace, even at the price of substantial concessions by one or the other power bloc; (2) the promotion of economic development and higher living standards in Asian and African countries, by whatever methods would contribute most efficaciously to the prestige of their leaders and the self-respect of their peoples; and (3) the elimination of "colonialism" and racial discrimination, especially by white people, in Asia, Africa, and wherever else those evils might be practiced. Much of the success of

Communist policy in recent years could be credited to the
skill with which the Communist governments had seemed
to associate themselves with these deep-seated aspirations,
to which some or all of the Western powers had often
found themselves in seeming opposition despite their genuine concern for peace and their broad commitment to the
elimination of poverty and exploitation.

Though the issues of peace, economic development, and
colonialism all stood close to the center of international
concern in 1960, the colonial issue perhaps outranked even
the other two in a year when so many formerly dependent
peoples were emerging into independent statehood and
when the nationalist struggle against French rule in Algeria was reaching its climax. (Most Asians and Africans
showed far less concern with the plight of Communist-
dominated peoples in Europe or even in Asia.) Colonialism, however, was an issue on which the United States
had found it peculiarly difficult to take a clear-cut stand.
Its attitude was congenitally divided between sympathy
for the independence movement and the necessity of cooperating with allies in Europe—who, in some instances,
had been decidedly reluctant to part with their colonial empires. Americans, moreover, had some doubts about
the wisdom of granting immediate independence to people who had not been adequately prepared for its burdens, and these doubts were heightened by the chaotic
situation that developed in the new Republic of the
Congo immediately upon the cessation of Belgian responsibility on June 30, 1960. Thus the American stand on the
various aspects of the colonial issue that required international attention in 1960 fell far short of the demands of
most Asian and African governments, even though it also
failed to give complete satisfaction to such "colonial"
countries as Belgium, France, and Portugal.

* * * * *

The colonial issue was one of a number of factors that
disturbed the alliance of the Western, anti-Communist

powers in this year of intensified Communist challenge. In part, the difficulties of the Western coalition in 1960 reflected the success of past American programs aimed at restoring the strength and vitality of its allies. It was perhaps a healthy sign that the United States no longer dominated Western policy as it had sometimes been accused of doing in the past. But there were also elements of weakness within the Western community that arose from causes only remotely, if at all, related to United States policy. France's political stability, military power, and sense of solidarity with its allies were chronically impaired by the war in Algeria and, to some extent at least, by the temperament of its political leadership. Belgium experienced a major economic and psychological blow in the loss of the Congo. Portugal's devotion to the North Atlantic alliance was severely qualified by discontent over allied attitudes concerning the Portuguese territories in Africa. Among the other sources of division and disunity within the NATO family were widespread fear and jealousy of the rising power of Western Germany; suspicion and hostility among the German Federal Republic, Great Britain, and France; doubts about the wisdom of President Charles de Gaulle's insistence on a French atomic striking force and a larger French voice in European and global affairs; misgivings about Prime Minister Macmillan's unflagging pursuit of a summit conference; a deep division on commercial policy between the six nations of the European Economic Community and the seven members of the European Free Trade Association.

There was also apparent in certain allied countries, both in Europe and elsewhere, a revulsion against American defense policies and, more generally, against the whole concept of the use of nuclear weapons in the defense of the non-Communist world. This revulsion became especially noticeable after the U-2 incident, which vividly recalled to popular attention the grave and continuing dangers of the East-West military confrontation. In Japan, the protests of a violent if limited section of the public very nearly led to the repudiation of a new security treaty with the United States, and did necessitate the last-minute cancellation of President Eisenhower's proposed visit. In Great Britain, the so-called Campaign for Nuclear Disarmament conducted a persistent agitation against official British as well as American defense policies, decried the use of British bases by American nuclear-armed bombers, and led the widespread popular outcry that followed a grant of British facilities for the use of American Polaris submarines. Though clearly a minority movement, the neutralist current in Great Britain was powerful enough to impose its views at least temporarily as the official doctrine of the Labor opposition party.

There were other countries allied with the United States in which pro-American or pro-Western governments were actually overthrown in 1960, a further indication that American policy might not be as firmly anchored in popular sentiment abroad as would have been desirable. In Turkey and Korea, the issues involved in these upsets were mainly domestic, and the more or less authoritarian regimes that had functioned in those countries were replaced by new but still pro-Western leadership. In the Korean case, at least, the change of regime was not unwelcome to the United States. In Laos, on the contrary, the military coup carried out by Captain Kong Le on August 9 substituted a definitely neutralist regime for the previous American-supported government and started a chain of events which by the end of the year had reached a stage of acute crisis. Two other national leaders who had been more or less closely identified with American policy, President Ngo Dinh Diem of the Republic of Vietnam and Emperor Haile Selassie of Ethiopia, were also the victims of attempted coups in 1960 but managed to regain their positions by facing down the resistance of dissatisfied military elements.

Still more unfavorable from the point of view of the United States was the rift within the inter-American system that followed the emergence of the Castro government in Cuba and its unabashed acceptance of Soviet and Chinese Communist support. Khrushchev's patronage of the Castro regime and his offers to defend Cuba with Soviet rockets in case of United States "aggression" represented an open challenge to the Monroe Doctrine and to established inter-American principles. The Cuban leaders' attempts to export their particular brand of social revolution to other countries in Latin America was as gross a breach of the inter-American tradition as were their repeated attempts to indict the United States before the United Nations—for offenses which, moreover, were almost wholly imaginary. The prevalent poverty and social unrest in Latin America nevertheless assured the Castro movement of widespread popular sympathy and caused other American governments to hesitate about joining the United States in effective measures to discipline or even rebuke the Cuban regime.

The United Nations, too, showed signs of lessened effectiveness as a protection for Western interests and a means of checking Communist expansion. Ironically, this trend became most evident at the very moment when United States acceptance of and reliance upon the United Nations had reached what was perhaps an all-time peak. Yet the admission to membership of seventeen formerly colonial territories could hardly fail to accentuate the neutralist, if not outright anti-Western, tendencies that had become apparent in the world organization in recent years. The conduct of the United Nations operation in the Congo, though by no means impeccable from a Western point of view, infuriated the U.S.S.R. to such a degree that Khrushchev utilized his visit to New York in the autumn to launch a full-scale attack on Secretary-General Dag Hammarskjold and the institution of the Secretariat. Although the Soviet attitude won little immediate support among the Asian and African countries, its continuance could cripple the one United Nations organ that had hitherto displayed a consistent capacity for effective action.

*   *   *   *   *

Behind the shifting political and military patterns that characterized the surface of international politics lay the deeper question of the degree of effort, expenditure, and imagination which the major "cold war" contenders were devoting to the pursuit of their very different international aims. The U.S.S.R., with a gross national product about half that of the United States, was already believed to be spending about as much as its rival for defense purposes, while its combined outlays for economic aid, informational and cultural activities, and similar purposes were also approaching parity with those of the United States. Since the Soviet economy was growing at approximately twice as fast a rate as the American economy, it could thus be anticipated that within a few years the U.S.S.R.'s total expenditure for international purposes might substantially exceed that of the United States,[3] while by 1970 the over-all economic gap between the two countries might be dangerously narrowed. The proper course of action for the United States in these circumstances was a subject of intense debate during the autumn election campaign. Statements by the successful presidential candidate indicated that the incoming Democratic administration would give high priority to trying to promote more rapid economic growth at home and contemplated somewhat increased outlays for defense, economic aid, and other international programs.

The importance of providing a more substantial measure of economic and technical assistance to the developing countries overseas was acknowledged in practically all responsible non-Communist quarters. Humanitarian, political, and economic considerations all seemed to demand a more sustained effort to assist the developing countries in providing for their rapidly expanding populations, to match the world-wide Communist economic offensive, and to create a broader market for the products of the industrialized West.

A limitation on any expansion of American activities in this field had, however, lately come to the fore in the shape of a chronic deficit in the nation's balance of international payments. Simply stated, the United States had for several years past been spending considerably more abroad for imports, foreign aid and investment, military forces and bases, tourism, etc. than other countries had been spending in the United States. Such a condition, which produced an alarming decline in the nation's stock of monetary gold during 1960, militated rather strongly against any pronounced expansion in overseas aid by the United States itself; and through 1960, at least, other industrialized countries were slow to act on American suggestions that they increase their own foreign aid outlays and eliminate the restrictions against American trade which some of them still maintained.

The manifest alarm occasioned by the balance-of-payments situation somewhat dimmed the popular image of the United States as the world's strongest and most resourceful economic power. It also clouded to some extent the future of the Western defense arrangements that centered in the North Atlantic Treaty Organization. By late 1960, efforts to halt the dollar drain had led to restrictions by the United States on the stationing of dependents with the American armed forces overseas; and there were official intimations that the United States might even be compelled to bring home a part of its troops deployed in Europe unless the situation improved. In conjunction with certain American suggestions looking toward the establishment of a missile-submarine force under NATO auspices, these warnings helped to revive the old suspicion in Europe that the United States was losing interest in the attempt to maintain a NATO "shield force" capable of resisting a Soviet attack by land. Such suspicions, if unchecked in 1961, could lead to an increase in neutralist sentiment in Europe and weaken the Western diplomatic position whenever negotiations with the U.S.S.R. resumed.

*   *   *   *   *

This recapitulation of some of the major themes that run through the following chapters may suggest that the net effect of international developments in 1960 was a grave impairment of the world position of the United States and an uninterrupted series of triumphs for its enemies. Such a conclusion would be greatly exaggerated, since the year brought many gains as well as losses from the American point of view. Nevertheless the over-all impression is undeniably one of slow erosion in the national position, and of growing world indifference to the values with which the United States had hitherto been associated. The appeals to mass hysteria of a Fidel Castro or a Patrice Lumumba did not make for the kind of humane and liberal international order the United States and its principal partners had sought to bring into being. Ten more years like 1960 would leave America and the free world in a critical if not a hopeless position.

At the same time, it is important to realize that while 1960 inflicted needless tragedy and suffering on many thousands of human beings, it witnessed no irretrievable political disaster of the kind that had occurred in certain earlier postwar years. Cuba, Laos, the Congo might still be capable of rescue, however dark the immediate prospect. If the United States and its partners had thus far been playing a losing game, their peoples retained the capacity for recovering themselves and resuming the initiative if they could be brought to realize the potential seriousness of their situation and the penalties of indifference. There were qualities in human nature that would continue to sustain the cause of freedom if they could be shown how to operate.

Dean Rusk, the former State Department official and foundation director who was selected to fill the office of Secretary of State in the incoming administration, offered what may have been the most balanced short comment on the situation of the United States at this grave political turning point:

"Senator Kennedy has called upon all of us to help him take hold of the great problems which now face us in the world about us. We are in a period of rapid and revolutionary change, as peoples in many parts of the world are striking out on new courses for themselves. But America at its best can be a confident America, and we need not be afraid of changes which arise out of hopes and aspirations which we, ourselves, share with other peoples in many parts of the world. This great country of ours is not like the cork that is tossed on the waves over which we have no control. Our enormous capacity to act imposes upon us a responsibility to make history, and to take a large part in the shaping of events.

"We are fortunate to have the leadership of President Kennedy, but he will need the full and united support of the American people." [4]

CHAPTER ONE

FOREIGN POLICY
THROUGH AMERICAN EYES

AMERICANS ARE known throughout the world as an optimistic people, and the national mood as 1960 began did
not belie this reputation. For most of the 179 million
people of the United States, the new year and decade which
opened on January 1 held forth the promise of a measure
of national and individual fulfillment exceeding anything
in past experience. Within the preceding two years, the
nation had largely recovered the sense of equilibrium and
self-confidence which it had seemed in danger of losing
for a few weeks in the autumn of 1957, when the first
Soviet "Sputniks" had suddenly pointed the way into the
new realm of outer space and demonstrated the scientific
and technological prowess of the country long recognized
as America's most formidable and determined rival. Since
that time, the progress of the United States' own missile
and space programs had been sufficiently spectacular to
assuage any momentary feelings of inferiority. The economic recession which had set in during that same autumn
of 1957 and persisted through most of 1958 had likewise
given way in recent months to a new upsurge of prosperity.
Production and trade had surpassed their former levels,
unemployment had been confined within what were
known as tolerable limits, and the imminent settlement of
a prolonged strike in the steel industry was expected to

clear the way for a record national output of as much as
$500 billion in 1960.

Even more gratifying in many ways was the waning of
the threat of war that had seemed to be implicit in the
postwar East-West rivalry and had been brought to the
forefront of public awareness by Premier Khrushchev's
demand of November 1958 for fundamental changes in the
status of West Berlin, that unique outpost of the Western
world 110 miles inside the Iron Curtain. Since Khrushchev's conversations with President Eisenhower at Camp
David in the fall of 1959, the Berlin question and other
matters of East-West dispute had been temporarily put "on
ice" to await a meeting of the leaders of the "Big Four"
governments that was now scheduled to begin in Paris
on May 16. Thereafter, President Eisenhower was expected to pay a visit to the Soviet Union which might be
expected to consolidate further the incipient improvement
in East-West relations.

1. AGENDA FOR 1960

It is true that these seemingly abundant grounds for
optimism were open to important qualifications. Some of
these were plainly pointed out by President Eisenhower
in the annual State of the Union message which he delivered to Congress on January 7, 1960.[1] In a divided world
in which both sides were possessed of "unbelievably de-
structive weapons," the President warned, the possibility
of "mutual annihilation" must always remain the pre-emi-
nent fact which "colors everything we say, plan and do."
Nevertheless, Mr. Eisenhower conceded, "recent Soviet
deportment and pronouncements suggest the possible opening of a somewhat less strained period in the relationships
between the Soviet Union and the rest of the world." The
United States, the President emphasized, would not permit
itself "to be misled by pleasant promises until they are
tested by performance"; but it was equally determined "to
approach this apparently new opportunity with the utmost

seriousness," losing no opportunity "to break the calamitous cycle of frustrations and crises which, if unchecked, could spiral into nuclear disaster; the ultimate insanity." It would be idle to expect "sudden and revolutionary results" from our attempts to arrive at a more tolerable relationship with the Soviet Union, Mr. Eisenhower warned. Yet it was clearly essential that we go on trying, for only by doing so could we hope to realize the potentialities of the dawning technological age, with its capacity not only for human destruction but also for making "poverty and human misery obsolete." "If our unremitting efforts for dependable peace begin to attain some success," the President promised, "we can surely become participants in creating an age characterized by justice and rising levels of human well-being."

The quest for dependable methods of establishing "peace with justice" in the world had long been recognized as the preeminent responsibility of the American Government. But for President Eisenhower, as for most Americans, this quest involved considerably more than a mere willingness to try to get along with the Soviet Union and negotiate agreements on the major issues of international affairs. Three elements, in particular, were regarded by the President and his advisers as indispensable components of any effective American policy for preserving peace and protecting the other values to whose support the United States had committed itself.

The first and most fundamental of these obligations was that of ensuring that powerful military forces were maintained by the United States and its allies in Europe and Asia for the purpose of deterring any attempt by the Communist powers to further their expansionist ambitions by military aggression. Second, and equally compelling in Mr. Eisenhower's eyes, was the duty of the United States, as the mainstay of the free world coalition, to husband its own strength and resources and pursue "sound" fiscal and budgetary policies aimed at restraining inflation, protecting the balance of payments, and avoiding the temptation to resort to deficit financing. Finally, the President attached fundamental importance to the obligation which the United States had assumed to provide assistance to a large number of friendly governments, not merely to enable them to maintain a more effective military posture but also to help them promote a more rapid rate of economic development and afford their people a realistic hope of improving their material circumstances. The importance of this last endeavor, particularly as it affected the countries of Asia, Africa, and Latin America, had been increasingly stressed in the past four of five years as the U.S.S.R. and the other Communist states had broadened their own appeal and unfolded their own more modest but highly publicized assistance schemes in newly independent and developing countries.

The attempt to combine these sometimes conflicting requirements in a coherent national policy was a perpetual challenge to American policy-makers and budgetary experts. The difficulties involved were all the greater because the conditions under which the broad principles had to be applied were constantly changing. Military affairs, in particular, had for years been in a continual state of flux as the result of the advent of successive generations of new weapons, most recently the intermediate- and long-range ballistic missiles which by the beginning of 1960 were already beginning to supersede manned aircraft for certain purposes. Missiles might well become the decisive weapons of the 1960's, and it was a source of uneasiness to quite a number of Americans that this was a field in which the Soviet Union was known to have gained at least an initial lead over the United States. Some American observers predicted the development of an extremely dangerous "missile gap" during the next few years. The United States, they asserted, might be on the point of losing the relative safety it had enjoyed thus far, thanks mainly to the deterrent power of the nuclear-armed bombers in its Strategic Air Command. President Eisenhower, however, had minimized the danger of any such "missile gap," either present or potential. In his opinion, the "enormous" American defense power already in existence and planned provided a sufficient guarantee that no hostile nation would venture to carry out a major attack on the United States and its allies, even though theoretically in a position to do so.

Being especially desirous to produce a substantial budgetary surplus during his last year in office, the President had strongly resisted the demands of the military services and their congressional friends for an increase in defense appropriations for the new fiscal year starting July 1, 1960. Even before 1959 was over he had let it be known that he intended to keep expenditures and new appropriations for "major national security" programs at about their existing levels. These programs, which included foreign military assistance and atomic energy development as well as the regular Department of Defense budget of just under $41 billion, would aggregate somewhere between $45 and $46 billion—an amount that represented over 57 per cent of the government's total budgetary expenditures, though well under one-tenth of the nation's anticipated total production during the period in question.

In the field of economic and technical assistance to friendly nations, the President likewise envisaged no very great expansion over current outlays, despite the growth of the competing Communist economic aid programs and the vivid impressions of human need which he himself had brought back from a recent visit to India, Pakistan, and other developing countries. Expenditures under this head were expected to remain at a level of somewhat less than $2 billion in the next fiscal year. Although he stressed America's obligation to contribute its share to raising levels of economic well-being in the free world, the President's recommendations to Congress in the economic field were primarily noteworthy for their emphasis on the need for cooperative endeavor between the United States and its increasingly prosperous partners in Western Europe and Japan. In recent months the administration had become openly disturbed by the adverse trend in the balance of international payments, which had been interpreted as a sign that the United States had been carrying a disproportionate share of the free world's economic burdens and must lose no time in transferring a part of the load to other shoulders. This preoccupation was to remain throughout the year as a potent influence on the shaping of American policy in economic and even military affairs.

Several other leading concerns of contemporary international policy were touched upon in the President's State of the Union message and in his subsequent messages on the budget [2] and the Mutual Security Program.[3] Among them were the promise and the perils inherent in man's growing penetration of outer space; the challenge of the independence movement in colonial and formerly colonial areas, which had brought twenty new nations into being since World War II and was expected to bring still others to birth in 1960; the world-wide revolt against racial discrimination in all its forms, an area in which American domestic and international preoccupations overlapped; the importance of strengthening the rule of law in international affairs and of enhancing the stature of the International Court of Justice. Knowing that the American scene would be increasingly dominated in the coming months by the approaching presidential election, Mr. Eisenhower particularly appealed to the Democratic-controlled Congress to help set an example of constructive collaboration between the executive and legislative branches. This, too, he implied, could be an important factor in the all-embracing ideological competition with Communism in which the nation found itself involved.

"We must make clear our peaceful intentions, our aspirations for a better world," the President insisted once again as he sought to chart America's course for the year ahead. He himself had only recently returned from a memorable journey, explicitly dedicated to this end, which had carried him to no fewer than eleven countries in Europe, Asia, and Africa and had quickened his sense of the importance of extending a helping hand to peoples that were trying to overcome a heritage of poverty and ignorance. During his final year in office, Mr. Eisenhower planned a further extension of his efforts in the field of "personal diplomacy" by visits to Latin America and the Far East, in addition to the critical journeys to Paris for the summit conference and to the Soviet Union for discussions with Premier Khrushchev. Unforeseen events, however, were to force a number of changes in this program and to suggest that the comparative optimism prevailing in the United States in the first weeks of 1960 had taken insufficient account of some important factors bearing upon America's world position.

2. DEMOCRACY AND "PEACEFUL COMPETITION"

Though apparently quite acceptable to the average citizen, the Eisenhower administration's general approach to international policy had always had critics as well as defenders among those Americans who professed a special interest in world affairs. At one extreme, a dwindling but determined band of "isolationists" continued to tax the national leadership with "softness" to Communism and subordination of American interests to the whims of a more or less imaginary "international community" or "free world." At the other extreme, a handful of Communists and fellow-travelers and a larger number of well-intentioned idealists dissented from the policy of armed vigilance toward the Communist bloc, deplored the skepticism of the government in regard to Khrushchev's professions of peaceful intentions, and deprecated the refusal to embrace on his own terms the Soviet leader's repeated offers of "peaceful coexistence."

Still other Americans, while fully conceding the specious nature of the Communist "peaceful coexistence" propaganda, reproached the administration with an unduly rigid attitude in such matters as the negotiations for a suspension of nuclear weapons tests or the recurrent question of the recognition of Communist China. Finally, a substantial segment of American opinion maintained that the national government, though thoroughly justified in its resistance to Communist designs throughout the world, had been guilty of underestimating the strength and scope of the Communist challenge and had failed to provide the leadership the nation required if it was to meet the challenge successfully.

This last group of critics, partly though by no means exclusively associated with the Democratic party, could find unlimited ammunition in the recent record of Soviet achievements in such fields as rocketry and space penetration, general economic development, and scientific and technical education. They could point to various authoritative statements by Khrushchev and other Communist spokesmen which indicated that Moscow's basic objective was nothing less than to "overtake and surpass" the United States as the world's leading industrial power, and to attract the "uncommitted" nations—and ultimately the whole of humanity—to its side by demonstrating that "socialism," as they called it, had infinitely more to offer than did the "outmoded" capitalist order supposedly upheld by the United States. It was an undisputed fact that the Soviet economy in recent years had been expanding at a much more rapid rate than that of its chief rival. Khrushchev had been bold—or rash—enough to designate the year 1970 as the latest date for outstripping the United States in both total and per capita output.[4] The U.S.S.R. and its satellites, moreover, had already embarked on a fairly substantial program of "trade and aid" operations in selected countries of the "less developed" group, and there had been signs that some of the newer Asian and African states —Guinea was a favorite example—were not insensitive to the attractions of the Soviet model even in the ordering of their internal affairs.

In the military field, meanwhile, the U.S.S.R. with its long-range rockets and its well-equipped conventional forces had admittedly reached a position in which it could neutralize, even if it could not necessarily overwhelm, the deterrent-retaliatory power of the United States. The United States and the West were constantly being faced with new evidence of Soviet military progress. Addressing the Supreme Soviet of the U.S.S.R. on January 14, 1960, Khrushchev announced that in view of the rapid growth of its rocket power, the U.S.S.R. intended to continue its progressive release of men from the colors and order a one-third reduction in the size of its standing military forces. Gradual demobilization over the next year or two, Khrushchev said, would bring the Soviet forces down to a level of 2,423,000 men, slightly less than the contemplated 2,489,000-man strength of the American armed forces. Although this adjustment was characteristically described as a further step in the Soviet "peace" campaign, Khrushchev made clear that it involved a further modernization, rather than a reduction, of the U.S.S.R.'s over-all military might.[5]

Further evidence of Soviet rocket prowess came to world attention a week later, January 21, when Moscow announced that a "ballistic multistage rocket," ostensibly designed for peaceful space missions, had been fired experimentally over a 12,500-kilometer (7,762-mile) course across the central Pacific and landed less than two kilometers from its target. The United States had thus far advanced no comparable claims for its own ballistic missiles, although President Eisenhower had reported that the "Atlas" intercontinental missile, the only long-range missile currently in at least nominal operational status, had displayed remarkable accuracy at ranges of over 5,000 miles. On May 20, however, the United States was able to announce the successful test of an Atlas missile over a 9,000-mile course.

Whatever the precise merit of Soviet claims in this or that field, the U.S.S.R. was plainly becoming a more and more formidable competitor in every branch of military, economic, scientific and technological endeavor. Ever since "Sputnik," some people in the United States had been asking themselves whether this country should not put forward a similar effort to develop its over-all potential as a means of meeting the many-sided Soviet challenge. Numerous reports by expert panels in the past two or three years had pointed up shortcomings in the national performance and recommended a wide variety of remedial measures in military affairs, in the promotion of economic growth, in the expansion of aid to less developed countries, in the promotion of educational and cultural exchanges, and so on. Among the most widely publicized of these analyses had been a series of reports issued by the Rockefeller Brothers Fund which had recommended, among other things, a \$3 billion annual increase in defense expenditure and an economic growth rate of 5 per cent a year, substantially above the figure attained in recent years.[6]

The difficulty with such prescriptions was that, however desirable they might appear in the abstract, they almost invariably called for increased financial outlays in the public sector and for increased intervention by the government in the normal life of the nation. They thus collided head-on with the political and economic philosophy espoused by the President and by at least the more traditionally minded elements of the party he headed. President Eisenhower had long ago set his face against allowing America to become a "garrison state," and tended to look upon any major intensification of governmental activity in response to the Soviet challenge as a dangerous step in that direction.

Mr. Eisenhower personally felt no sense of defeatism in face of Soviet achievements, he assured a news conference on February 3, 1960. Naturally, dictatorships often displayed remarkable efficiency, but it was his opinion that "our people ought to have greater faith in their own system." "We have a free enterprise," the President philosophized. "We place above all other values our own individual freedoms and rights, and we believe, moreover, that the operation of such a system in the long run produces more, not only more happiness, more satisfaction and pride in our people, but also more goods, more wealth." Unlike the Soviet Union, Mr. Eisenhower insisted, "we are talking of a democracy we hope is an enduring form of government. We are, therefore, trying to do these things at the same time we keep these values." Furthermore, the President added, "I believe that there is just as much of the seeds of self-destruction in the Communist system as they claim is in ours." [7]

Whether this faith in inherited democratic values would represent a sufficient response to the challenge of Soviet "peaceful competition" in the 1960's was to remain a subject of lively controversy throughout the year, and would emerge as one of the leading themes in the presidential campaign. Some influential observers continued to feel that in the absence of a stronger lead from Washington, the current trend of American society would remain fundamentally out of tune with the rising demands of the world situation. Not only was the resistance to racial equality in the United States coming to seem more and more of an anachronism (and a diplomatic embarrassment) at a time when so many nonwhite peoples in Africa and elsewhere were gaining full control of their own affairs. Too large a share of America's national wealth and energies, it was frequently asserted, was being channeled into what one writer had called "the affluent society." "It is every man for himself, and the Nation take what is left," was the characteristic complaint of Senator James W. Fulbright, the Chairman of the Foreign Relations Committee,[8] whose view was by no means an isolated one.

President Eisenhower himself conceded the need for serious thought about these matters in early February when he directed his new Commission on National Goals, a group of distinguished private citizens which would be headed by Dr. Henry M. Wriston as chairman, to try to "identify the great issues of our generation" and formulate a broad outline of national objectives for the next decade and more. "It is no wonder," the President wrote, "that a nation so recently thrust into a position of world leadership is sometimes bewildered by its new role." The commission, he suggested, would have an opportunity "to sound a call for greatness to a resolute people, in the best tradition of our founding fathers." [9]

3. SOME SHATTERED ILLUSIONS

The debate on the scope and quality of America's response to the Soviet challenge hinged partly on technical details of military capability and economics, and partly on broader arguments from the realm of social and political philosophy. But meanwhile a succession of events had been occurring in overseas theaters which cast doubt on some of the practical assumptions of American policy as well. Much of this policy, it began to appear, had been built on rather shaky foundations. Some Americans who watched the development of their country's foreign relations during the first six or seven months of 1960 were driven to admit that they and their countrymen had taken too much for granted about the strength and solidity of the American alliance system, about the prospects for reducing the threat of a collision with the Soviet Union, even, perhaps, about the integrity of their own government in some aspects of its relationships with other nations. Nothing that transpired during this period was necessarily irreparable from the standpoint of America's fundamental interests and objectives. But the United States was compelled during these months to swallow some unprecedented affronts and to see some favorite illusions go up in smoke. By midsummer the nation was entering a period of trouble and danger that contrasted sharply with the agreeable expectations on which the year had opened.

That there was internal weakness and instability in some of the forty-two non-Communist nations with which the United States had linked itself in bilateral or multilateral defense alliances was known to every informed observer. To remedy such weaknesses before they become dangerous was one of the main purposes of the Mutual Security Program, the overriding aim of which was to strengthen the free world's ability to resist the threat of

Communist aggression or subversion. But the events of early 1960 revealed a degree of political unsteadiness in several countries long associated with the United States—unrelated, in most instances, to any immediate Communist threat—which raised a question whether the United States had even yet paid sufficient attention to securing the political foundations of its alliance system.

The newly established Fifth French Republic, to take the most prominent example, passed through a veritable life-and-death crisis in the last days of January 1960 as the result of resistance to President de Gaulle's Algerian policy on the part of European civilian and army elements in that territory. In the end, the French President's personality proved just strong enough to overawe the dissidents and avert the prospect of a civil war which would have had to be waged against the very forces that had helped raise him to power twenty months earlier.

Only three months later, President Syngman Rhee of the Republic of Korea, long regarded as one of the firmest allies of the United States, was forced to resign amid a howling tempest of opposition stirred up by his own authoritarian methods of government. In May, a similar protest movement in Turkey resulted in the removal of two other strongly anti-Communist though authoritarian figures, Premier Adnan Menderes and President Celal Bayar, by a revolutionary committee of army officers. Korea and Turkey were countries in which the democratic virtues extolled by President Eisenhower had thus far been practiced only intermittently.

The new Korean and Turkish governments lost no time in affirming their anti-Communist principles and their complete loyalty to existing alliances. Conceivably the two countries might ultimately prove stronger allies than they had been in the past. But meanwhile serious trouble had also been brewing in the immediate vicinity of the United States, where the revolutionary Cuban government of Fidel Castro was displaying not only an unbridled hostility to this country but also a disturbing readiness to place itself in a position of dependence on the Communist bloc. In some of the countries of South America, too, President Eisenhower in the course of his late winter tour was to be made vividly aware that there were depths of hostility as well as friendship for the United States.[10] Every indication of a negative trend in the affairs of the American Republics, as in Europe and Asia, served as grist to the Communist propaganda mill and encouraged the Soviet leadership to reckon on the eventual destruction of American influence in the non-Communist world.

Of much more crushing impact, both for the United States and for the world at large, were the events that preceded and followed the convoking of the Paris summit conference on May 16. Premier Khrushchev, whose tone had become increasingly intransigent as this momentous date approached, alarmed and astounded the entire world on May 5 with the dramatic assertion that the United States had actually been trying to "wreck" the conference in advance by committing "aggressive acts"—specifically, by dispatching American aircraft on unauthorized flights over the Soviet Union. Citing two such incursions, on April 9 and May 1, he further claimed that the second plane had actually been shot down over Soviet territory.

The United States, which had already announced the disappearance of a high-flying U-2 aircraft ostensibly engaged on a weather research mission in the Middle East, initially took the line that if the plane had in fact entered the U.S.S.R. the intrusion must have been accidental. Khrushchev, however, disclosed on May 7 that the destroyed aircraft, allegedly shot down far inside the Soviet Union, had been found to contain numerous items of "espionage equipment" and that the pilot himself had been captured and freely admitted having been engaged on a photoreconnaissance mission that was to have taken him straight across the U.S.S.R. from Pakistan to Norway.[11]

After some tergiversation in Washington, Secretary of State Christian A. Herter conceded the substantial accuracy of this version in a formal statement of May 9. As part of its efforts to guard against surprise attack, he explained, the United States had for some years—apparently since 1956—been carrying out "extensive aerial surveillance [of the U.S.S.R.] by unarmed aircraft, normally of a peripheral character but on occasion by penetration." [12] Khrushchev had said that he did not believe that the President himself could have known of these intrusions; but Mr. Eisenhower at his news conference on May 11 not only took personal responsibility for the flights—though it appeared that he had not authorized this particular one—but intimated that however distasteful such intelligence-gathering activities might be, the safety of the free world made them indispensable.[13]

Had the Soviet leaders wished the summit conference to succeed, they could presumably have found ways to smooth the matter over even at this stage. They might, for instance, have contented themselves with the highly damaging impression created throughout the world by the circumstances under which this closely guarded and undeniably risky American activity had been brought to light. Nothing that the United States could say about the U.S.S.R.'s own espionage activities, or about the repeated Soviet rejection of international measures to guard against surprise attack, could offset the effect of Washington's enforced admission that it had resorted to so unusual a venture. While there was some disagreement among experts as to whether the flights were technically contrary to international law, they were clearly contrary to custom and, most observers felt, to prudence and diplomatic propriety.

For Soviet purposes, however, it was not enough to have put the United States spectacularly in the wrong in the eyes of world opinion. On the contrary, the U.S.S.R. chose to exploit the issue in such a way as to engender an atmosphere of acute international crisis; to justify repeated threats of retaliation against the United States and any of its allies who cooperated in such flights; and, perhaps most serious of all, to prevent the summit conference from coming to grips with the momentous issues it had been called to discuss. When the Big Four statesmen assembled in Paris on May 16, Khrushchev flatly refused to proceed unless the United States explicitly condemned and canceled all flights of this nature and brought the "guilty" to strict account. Whether or not the United States accepted these conditions, he added, it would be quite impossible under present circumstances to proceed with the program for President Eisenhower's visit to the U.S.S.R., set for the middle of June. The Soviet people, he explained, would not be able to receive the President with fitting "cordiality." [14]

Mr. Eisenhower had already planned to announce the suspension of the U-2 flights as soon as the conference convened. Yet he could not realistically have been expected to humiliate himself in the way that Khrushchev demanded. Such an "ultimatum," he felt, could only be regarded as aimed at "sabotaging this meeting on which so much of the hopes of the world rested." Attempts by Premier Macmillan and President de Gaulle to moderate the Soviet leader's stand proved unavailing. Khrushchev had never been harsher. The only crumb of comfort for the West was that on his departure from Paris he took no immediate steps to aggravate the threatening Berlin situation. He several times expressed the hope of another attempt at a summit conference in six or eight months—in other words, after America's presidential elections. With President Eisenhower, he made clear, he had no desire to engage in further contacts, preferring to keep him as an object of ridicule and mock commiseration in future speeches and press conferences.

Thus disintegrated the last vestiges of the "spirit of Camp David" initiated by the Eisenhower-Khrushchev talks a scant eight months earlier. East-West tension had revived in all its former acuteness, and was to go on mounting through the summer. Most observers took the view that the U-2 incident had been the pretext rather than the cause of the sudden turnabout in Soviet behavior. But this reflection did not make the facts any less distressing to those who had hoped for a lasting improvement in East-West relations.

Meanwhile the United States was compelled to suffer a fresh and bitter humiliation in the cancellation of President Eisenhower's proposed visit to Japan in celebration of the hundredth anniversary of American-Japanese relations. Originally intended as a sequel to the now canceled Soviet trip, the President's mission to the Far East had been rescheduled in such a way as to take him via Alaska to the Philippines, Taiwan, Okinawa, Japan (where he was to arrive on June 19), and Korea. The high point of the trip was intended to be the solemnization of the new "equal" relationship between Japan and the United States under a revised treaty of mutual cooperation and security, one that embodied substantial advantages to the Japanese as compared with earlier arrangements. Since its conclusion early in the year, however, the treaty had stirred unexpectedly violent resistance on the part of Japanese leftist and neutralist elements, both Communist and non-Communist.

As the date of Mr. Eisenhower's arrival approached, the demonstrations in Tokyo against the treaty and against the President's visit assumed such threatening proportions that Premier Nobusuke Kishi was reluctantly driven to the conclusion that his government would be unable to guarantee the President's safety. Mr. Eisenhower was already in the Philippines when news came on June 16 that the visit could not take place. The treaty itself was saved, despite tumultuous opposition, and went into effect a week later.[15] But once again the free world's most prominent statesman had been prevented, under the most unpalatable circumstances, from pursuing his plan to acquaint all nations with America's devotion to "peace and friendship in freedom."

4. AN ANXIOUS SUMMER

Even in an ordinary year, such a series of rebuffs would have caused grave misgivings at home and touched off an intensive effort to assess responsibilities. With the political campaign approaching, the temptation to find fault with the recent management of American policy was held in check only by a general desire not to create additional difficulties for the President and Secretary Herter at a time of unmistakable national danger. Even so, most members of the Senate Foreign Relations Committee concluded after a detailed investigation of the U-2 incident that the affair had been gravely mishandled by most of those concerned, even if it could not be proved responsible for the breakdown at the summit.[16]

But what the United States had experienced hitherto was scarcely to be compared with the shocks that awaited it during the next few weeks as the U.S.S.R. proceeded to implement the new "tough" line on which it had evidently settled either before or, at latest, immediately after the summit collapse. While faithful in the main to Khrushchev's undertaking to do nothing immediately to aggravate the Berlin situation, Moscow now unfolded a wide-ranging diplomatic offensive which raised the tension in Soviet-American relations to an alarming degree and introduced the Soviet Union for the first time as a dangerous contender in the affairs of Africa and, worse still, in those of the Western Hemisphere.[17] The matter of the U-2 incident was promptly referred to the Security Council of the United Nations with a demand—rejected by seven votes to two, with two abstentions—that that body condemn American intelligence flights over the territory of other states and request their immediate discontinuance.[18] Not long afterward, the Soviet Government cut one of the few remaining threads of peaceful negotiation between East and West by walking out of the ten-nation disarmament discussions at Geneva, leaving the conference on sus-

pending nuclear weapons tests as the only active forum
of East-West interchange.[19]

In addition to intruding its policy into new fields of
action, notably in Cuba and in the newborn Congo Republic, the U.S.S.R. continued its efforts to capitalize on
the U-2 incident by constant propaganda, by generating
an artificial spy mania, and by attempting to create new
incidents on a more or less similar pattern. On July 11,
Khrushchev histrionically announced the shooting down
of a second American plane, this one an Air Force RB-47
which, according to the Soviet leader, had violated Soviet
territory near the Arctic Circle. The United States insisted, on the contrary, that in this instance the aircraft in
question had never come within thirty miles of Soviet territory. According to the statement of Ambassador Henry
Cabot Lodge to the Security Council, Soviet fighter planes
had tried, without success, to force it into the Soviet
air space. Once again the U.S.S.R. failed to obtain a
Security Council condemnation of the United States, although it was able to veto on July 26 an American proposal for an impartial investigation.[20] It also denied all
official access to the two surviving crew members of the
RB-47 as well as the pilot of the U-2, Francis G. Powers,
who was subjected to a propaganda show trial in late August, pleaded guilty of violating Soviet territory for purposes of intelligence gathering, and was sentenced to ten
years' "deprivation of liberty."

By the middle of July the condition of world politics
had thus deteriorated to an alarming degree. While Prime
Minister Macmillan wrote to Khrushchev of the anxieties
inspired by recent Soviet behavior, Secretary Herter conferred with the President at Newport and was unofficially
described as warning Mr. Eisenhower that the free world
might well be facing dangers of the gravest sort. This
was the atmosphere in which the two American political
parties were called upon to hold their presidential nominating conventions and to continue the running debate

about whether the nation might not need to increase its exertions in the defense field and related areas.

The Democrats, who had just finished nominating Senator John F. Kennedy as their presidential candidate, said flatly that it did. It was they who had been insisting all along that the United States had been lulled to sleep by a complacent leadership. According to the Democratic party's "basic platform," America's very first task under a new administration would be to "restore our national strength—military, political, economic, and moral," and to "recast our military capacity in order to provide forces and weapons of a diversity, balance, and mobility sufficient in quantity and quality to deter both limited and general aggressions." [21] This was to be an essential feature of the "New Frontier" program on which Senator Kennedy and Senator Lyndon B. Johnson, his vice-presidential running mate, proposed to base their campaign.

The situation in the Republican camp was more complicated because President Eisenhower had so often said that American defense power already met the requirements of either general or limited war. Vice-President Richard M. Nixon, the prospective Republican nominee, was understandably reluctant to suggest that Mr. Eisenhower had misjudged the situation in his own field. On the other hand, Governor Nelson A. Rockefeller of New York, who at one time had himself aspired to the Republican nomination, had been exerting strong pressure to buttress the Republican platform with some of the ideas already put forward in the reports of the Rockefeller Brothers Fund. A pre-convention meeting between Messrs. Nixon and Rockefeller on July 23 produced an unlooked-for agreement between the two men which went a considerable distance toward the acceptance of Governor Rockefeller's standpoint. According to Mr. Rockefeller's phraseology, both agreed that "the growing vigor and aggressiveness of communism demands new and profound effort and action in all areas of American life"; that "the vital need of our foreign policy is new political creativity";

that a variety of "new efforts" were required in the sphere of national defense; and that "the United States can afford and must provide the increased expenditures" needed to implement an adequate defense program.[22] These statements, which deviated sharply from what had been the accepted Republican view, found a somewhat muted echo in the official platform adopted at Chicago shortly before Mr. Nixon was swept to the nomination.

Though President Eisenhower was described as less than enthusiastic about the Nixon-Rockefeller agreement, he was as well aware as anyone that the world situation had drastically altered since the submission of his own defense estimates at the beginning of the year. As early as April, before the summit conference, he had authorized a speed-up in the missile program in order to confront any threatened "missile gap" with additional Atlas and Polaris missiles at a somewhat earlier date than previously scheduled.[23] Congress, in passing the regular Defense Department appropriation bill for the 1960-61 fiscal year, had added an extra $662 million to the presidential estimates, bringing total funds available (exclusive of appropriations for military construction) to just under $40 billion ($39,-996,608,000). The administration, however, had indicated initially that most of this added money would not be used.

When Congress reconvened after the political conventions, the President made known in a special message of August 8 that he still had no plans to increase defense spending in any substantial way, despite the recent "intensification of Communist truculence." He did reveal, however, that certain practical military measures had already been ordered within the framework of the existing program: deployment of additional aircraft carriers to the Sixth Fleet in the Mediterranean and the Seventh Fleet in the Pacific; steps to increase the operational readiness of the Strategic Air Command and the ground forces; and an expansion of certain long-range programs, particularly those relating to the Polaris missile system. In the same message the President asked congressional ap-

proval of a new $600 million aid program for Latin Amer-
ica and a $100 million increase in Mutual Security funds
to deal with emergency situations such as the one that
currently existed in the Congo.[24]

Mr. Eisenhower's comments on the defense program
were received with marked coolness by the Democratic
majority in Congress. That defense policy nevertheless
failed to emerge as a major issue in the following weeks
was due not so much to the President's renewed assurances
about the adequacy of existing arrangements as it was to
a series of remarkable current accomplishments in the
missile and space field. The 9,000-mile Atlas missile test
in May had been followed on July 20 by the first test-firing
of two Polaris missiles from the nuclear submarine *George
Washington,* which was expected to become operational
within the next few months. On August 30 there was a
5,000-mile test-firing of a Titan missile, also scheduled for
operational status within a year. At the moment, the
United States had only eight or nine Atlas missiles in
operational status, but the successful development of the
Polaris and Titan, as well as the progress of work on the
solid fuel Minuteman, now scheduled for operational
readiness in 1962, suggested that the position would in fact
be considerably improved within the next year or two.

In the space realm, meanwhile, the United States within
a period of some twenty-four hours on August 11-12 succeeded in orbiting the first balloon-type communications
satellite (Echo I), recovered the first instrument capsule
ejected from a satellite (Discoverer XIV), and broke the
world's altitude record for manned aircraft as the X-15
"rocket ship" climbed to a height of 131,000 feet. Such
achievements, coming on top of earlier successes in orbiting a Tiros weather satellite and a Midas "missile defense
alarm" satellite, helped to offset the effect of concurrent
Soviet space achievements and reduce the feeling of uneasiness engendered by recent international events.

Congress had gone home before it became generally
known that whatever the current state of development of

America's long-range missiles, the construction of bases from which to fire them had fallen several months behind schedule. But here, too, many of the existing difficulties were ironed out before the end of the year, and steps were also taken to use some of the extra funds appropriated by Congress to expedite the development of the B-70 supersonic bomber, a project which was of great interest to the Air Force but had been assigned a very low priority in the original program for the year.

In other respects the post-convention session of Congress was somewhat unsatisfactory to everyone concerned. The endorsement of President Eisenhower's Latin American aid program (subject to later appropriation of the actual funds) proved decidedly helpful to the United States in dealing with a critical series of inter-American conferences which took place in August and September and reached important decisions in both the political and economic fields. On the other hand, Congress failed to support the administration in its plea for special legislation enabling it to discontinue sugar purchases from the Dominican Republic in accordance with another important recommendation of the Organization of American States.[25] Despite the Democratic platform's endorsement of "the world revolution of rising expectations for a better life," the Democratic-controlled Congress also reduced the regular Mutual Security appropriation for military and economic assistance to a level that the President and his aides found tragically inadequate.[26] Perhaps the most positive legislative accomplishment of these weeks was the Senate's approval, by a majority of 66-21, of the twelve-nation Antarctic Treaty negotiated on American initiative in late 1959. This action could be viewed as an important step toward a more peaceful international order at some time in the future, even if it seemed sadly out of harmony with the confused and turbulent present.[27]

5. MUTUAL SECURITY AND ECONOMIC DEVELOPMENT

In the years since World War II, assistance to other non-Communist nations in the military and economic fields had gradually come to be recognized as an activity no less essential, though considerably less costly, than the maintenance of America's own defense power. The principal vehicle for such assistance, aside from the loans extended directly by the Export-Import Bank out of its recently augmented capital of $7 billion, was the program of grants and loans carried out under the authority of the Mutual Security Act. This complicated piece of legislation was revised each year in order to establish conditions and financial guidelines for the coming fiscal period.

As already noted, considerations relating to the budget and particularly to the balance of international payments had placed a severe limitation on United States foreign aid programs within the past year or two. It was later revealed that net foreign aid of all kinds made available by the United States in the fiscal year ending June 30, 1960 actually fell to the lowest level since World War II. The outlays during that twelve-month period amounted altogether to $2,003 million for military aid and $2,073 million for economic aid, or a total of $4,076 million, including Export-Import Bank loans—or $4,156 million if a contribution of $80 million to the International Bank was included. These figures could be compared with an average outlay of about $5 billion during the postwar period as a whole.[28]

In its plans for the new fiscal year which would begin July 1, 1960, the administration had contemplated no major increase in this level of expenditure, but laid heavy emphasis on the need for a more cooperative type of mutual security effort in which the other industrialized nations should assume a much more prominent role. The time had come, it repeatedly asserted, for the other Western nations and Japan to join their efforts with those of the United States in promoting economic growth and higher living standards in the less developed countries.

The contribution which other industrialized countries of the free world had been making to this end was already significant. In the six years 1954-59, the State Department calculated, these countries had actually expended approximately $5.9 billion in bilateral economic assistance to less developed countries. The comparable figure for the United States was a little over $12 billion, while the countries of the Soviet bloc, it was estimated, had allocated (though not necessarily expended) something less than $3 billion for similar purposes.[29] These figures did not include the aid provided by the Western nations through such instrumentalities as the United Nations technical assistance program and the International Bank for Reconstruction and Development, which by the end of 1959 had disbursed a total of almost $3.6 billion in 249 loans in fifty-one countries.[30]

In 1958, the United States had moved to increase the flow of aid through multilateral channels by proposing an expansion of the authorized capital of the International Bank from $10 billion to $21 billion. This increase had now been carried out. Another recent initiative in the field of multilateral aid had been the drafting, again at the suggestion of the United States, of plans for an International Development Association to be administered as an affiliate of the International Bank and provide financing on easier terms for certain development projects. In response to a special message from the President, Congress approved United States membership in this organization early in 1960 and subsequently appropriated $73,666,700 as the first installment of a United States contribution which was ultimately expected to reach $320 million.[31] Formal establishment of the I.D.A. took place in September. A similar institution for the American Republics, the Inter-American Development Bank, had been approved by Congress in 1959 and was able to start operations late in 1960.[32] Also during 1960, the United States was the prime mover in the planning of a new twenty-nation body, the Organization for Economic Cooperation and Development

(O.E.C.D.), which was designed to harmonize and coordinate the efforts of the principal Western nations in this and other fields of international economic policy.[33]

But even if the resources of the free world as a whole could be more effectively mobilized for the task of economic development, the need would clearly remain for a substantial American contribution through the Mutual Security Program. According to Paul G. Hoffman, the American Managing Director of the United Nations Special Fund, assistance to less developed countries had been running at a rate of something like $4 billion a year from all sources during the 1950's but ought to be stepped up to $7 billion annually in the 1960's.[34] Other authorities took a similar view, and urged a sharp expansion in outlays by the United States as well as other countries. In addition to its economic aid expenditures, moreover, the United States was committed to carry forward a substantial military aid program which, though regarded with limited sympathy in some congressional quarters and in some important non-Communist countries, was regarded by the Pentagon and the White House as an essential supplement to the defense efforts being made by allied and friendly countries in NATO and in various parts of the world outside of NATO's orbit.

In preparing his detailed estimate of requirements for the Mutual Security Program in fiscal year 1961, President Eisenhower had originally anticipated a need for new funds in the amount of $4,175,000,000, about one-tenth the amount envisaged for the United States' own defense program. Two billion dollars, or almost half of the total Mutual Security request, was intended for purely military assistance, the balance of $2,175,000,000 being distributed among so-called defense support ($724 million), the Development Loan Fund ($700 million), technical cooperation, and various other programs of a nonmilitary character.

Though this was the first time since 1957 that the President's annual request had exceeded the $4 billion level, the reason was not to be found in any expansion of economic aid plans. On the economic side, the program actually turned out to be a bit more modest than the one submitted the year before. The reason for the increase was an upward revision in the request for military assistance, in line with the recommendations of a special committee headed by General William H. Draper which had surveyed the military aid operation in 1959. The intention, President Eisenhower explained in his annual Mutual Security message,[35] was not to increase the nation's proportionate contribution to the collective defense, but to ensure that deliveries of military equipment to allied countries in Europe and Asia would continue at or near existing levels.

As always, Congress found sufficient reasons for skepticism about both the military and economic phases of the program to undertake substantial reductions in these figures. The Mutual Security authorization bill adopted in May left intact the $2 billion for military assistance, but trimmed the over-all total to $4,086,300,000 by reductions in defense support and other nonmilitary categories. The actual appropriation bill, action on which was not completed until late August, reduced the total further to $3,722,350,000, including a reduction of the military assistance item to $1.8 billion and of defense support to $610 million.[36] Since the over-all appropriation also included the extra $100 million for contingencies which the President had requested in his message of August 8, the net reduction as compared with Mr. Eisenhower's requests was $100 million larger than it appeared.

These drastic reductions, the President warned, "would sharply curtail support indispensable to the defense of allies now under intensified Soviet pressure and deny aid urgently needed by other friendly nations struggling under the gravest difficulties to make progress in freedom." [37] Though unable to reverse the determination of congressional leaders, the administration did later secure an extra $65 million in Mutual Security funds as part of a supplemental appropriations bill,[38] thus raising the aggregate new funds available for 1960-61 to $3,787,350,000.

As already mentioned, Congress also authorized at rather short notice a special $600 million aid program for Latin America,[39] leaving the matter of actually appropriating the funds for later consideration.

While no detailed analysis of the effect of these congressional cuts was made available, it could be noted that the total Mutual Security appropriation was still substantially higher than the $3,225,813,000 appropriated for fiscal 1960. The most disheartening feature from the standpoint of economic aid advocates was the comparatively small appropriation for the Development Loan Fund, which had won recognition over the past two or three years as one of the most important elements in the Mutual Security Program.[40] From the $700 million recommended by the President, the Development Loan Fund was once again reduced to the same $550 million level which had prevailed in the two preceding years—not much more than half of the $1 billion which had sometimes been spoken of as the ideal figure. Among the more positive features of the new Mutual Security Act was the endorsement of a United States contribution to a $1 billion "package plan" which had been devised by the International Bank for development of the Indus Basin as a contribution to improved relations between India and Pakistan.[41] Legislative authority was also provided for the establishment by the State Department of a Center for Cultural and Technical Interchange Between East and West in Hawaii and the drafting of plans for a similar Western Hemisphere center in Puerto Rico.

6. INVESTMENT, TRADE, AND THE BALANCE OF PAYMENTS

The history of the 1960 Mutual Security legislation showed clearly that neither the administration nor Congress was prepared to give overseas development aid the high priority demanded for it by a growing number of international affairs specialists. The administration, for all its insistence on the importance of the Mutual Security effort, had never thought of the Development Loan Fund and the other phases of the program as playing more than a subsidiary role in the economic development process. The basic responsibility for improving the conditions of life in underdeveloped areas, the President and other administration spokesmen had repeatedly emphasized, lay with the peoples of the developing countries themselves. Their job was to mobilize their own resources and talents to the greatest extent possible, relying on the outside world only for those forms of capital and "knowhow" that could not be provided locally. Outside assistance, the administration had further maintained, should normally take the form not of public grants or loans but of private capital invested by those business enterprises that saw a chance for profitable operations and, presumably, were best qualified to provide the necessary training in up-to-date technical methods. Governmental assistance, whether extended directly or through international instrumentalities, should be confined to those tasks which for one reason or another private investment was unable or unwilling to undertake.

In spite of the unconcealed hostility of many of the developing countries toward Western private enterprise as they had known it in the past, the United States Government had been laboring for years to secure more wholehearted acceptance of this view not only by countries in need of foreign capital but also by a larger number of American business firms. Partly, no doubt, as a result of official encouragement, the outflow of American private capital to foreign countries had substantially increased in recent years, from an average of just over $1 billion a year in the 1953-55 period to approximately $2¼ billion (net) in 1959.[42] Though very unevenly distributed from a geographical viewpoint and not always directed into the most beneficial activities from the recipient countries' point of view, this form of investment did represent a substantial part of the total United States contribution to economic growth abroad. Up to about the middle of 1959, there had been considerable talk in Washington of a need for legislative and other measures to promote a further increase in overseas private investment as one means of meeting the ever-increasing demand for development capital in the less developed countries. Since that time, however, the subject had been thrust somewhat into the background by more pressing considerations.

The most important new factor in the situation had been the administration's acute concern over the recently enlarged deficit in the nation's balance of international payments, the over-all tabulation of its financial transactions with the rest of the world. In contrast to the comparatively small annual deficits registered through most of the postwar period, the United States sustained a balance-of-payments deficit of $3.6 billion in 1958 and another of $3.8 billion in 1959. During those two years, in other words, it paid out to other nations for a variety of purposes approximately $7.4 billion more than it took in from them.[43] The resultant increase in foreign holdings of United States gold and dollars had been quite advantageous to some of the other non-Communist countries and had helped to promote an unusual degree of stability in the international monetary field. It was generally recognized, however, that such a trend could not be allowed to continue without inviting serious consequences to the United States and to many of its economic associates.

The most conspicuous reason for the enlarged deficit as it had developed up to this time had been a rather sharp decline in United States exports, attributable in large measure to the economic revival of the other industrialized countries in Western Europe and Japan and their increased ability to compete with the United States in world markets. Throughout most of the postwar period, United States foreign economic policy had sought to promote this very development in order to hasten the time when the principal allied countries would be able to stand on their own feet economically. But once this objective had been realized, official attention was compelled to shift to the more immediate problem of safeguarding the United States' own economic position and assuring it the opportunity to compete on equal terms with its increasingly prosperous associates. In addition to the export-import balance, financial authorities in Washington had been impelled to examine other elements in the balance of payments—foreign aid, private investment abroad, overseas military expenditures, and the like—which also contributed their share to the deficit and might be in need of curtailment if the difficulties continued. These were among the most important considerations behind the new American emphasis on cooperative effort in the field of economic assistance. They also helped to account for occasional rumors indicating that the United States might be contemplating a gradual reduction in the military forces it maintained abroad.

Whatever readjustments might have to be made in response to these novel conditions, it was clearly desirable to avoid measures that would be inconsistent with the interests of allied countries or with the broad policy of economic expansion to which the United States had generally adhered thus far. In the field of foreign trade, for example, it would be much better for the United States and its friends abroad if the present difficulty were resolved by measures to expand American exports, rather than by adopting the alternative course of restricting imports and thus risking a reversal of the over-all growth in world trade which had occurred in recent years. The administration did not regard the situation as one that called for special measures aimed at stimulating over-all economic growth at home and thus, presumably, improving the competitive position of the entire economy. It had, however, established a requirement that loans from the D.L.F. must in most instances be spent within the United States. It also attached great importance to a new program for the direct promotion of American exports which was outlined by the President in a special message to Congress on March 17, 1960.

Drawn up by an interagency task force, this program contemplated a variety of governmental measures designed to assist and encourage an export drive by private business through increased informational and promotional activities, expanded participation in international trade fairs, and similar measures. Its chief novelty was a plan to offer new guarantees in connection with certain short-term trade credits made available by the Export-Import Bank.[44] In addition, the government now promised to intensify its long-standing effort to eliminate the restrictions against American exports which were still being maintained, though on a reduced scale, by a large number of non-Communist countries.[45] In its contacts with the European Economic Community and the European Free Trade Association, the new multinational economic organizations in Western Europe, the United States showed special vigilance in trying to hold discrimination against American trade to a minimum.[46]

Even before some of these measures could be put in execution, the export situation had begun to improve markedly. Exports, indeed, had shown some signs of reviving as early as the middle of 1959. By September 1960, the Department of Commerce could report "encouraging indications that the vitality of U.S. exporters is beginning to chip away at our international payments deficit." Merchandise exports during the first half of 1960, it was noted, had reached an annual seasonally adjusted rate of nearly $19 billion, a 15 per cent increase over the corresponding period of 1959. Imports, in contrast, were up only 6 per cent, to an annual rate of $15½ billion. Although a continuation of these trends would obviously mean a much larger trade surplus than in the preceding year, an over-all balance-of-payments deficit of $2.5 to $3 billion still seemed likely, and American officials took the view that much greater efforts would be required in the next year or two if a reasonable equilibrium was to be restored.[47] Already, however, such international financial authorities as Per Jacobsson, Managing Director of the

International Monetary Fund, were hailing the improvement achieved so far as "more than anyone could have foreseen." [48] If there were signs of renewed slackness in the American business picture as autumn began, Mr. Jacobsson agreed with Secretary of the Treasury Robert B. Anderson in ascribing them to a momentary hesitation due to the abatement of inflationary pressures, not to any threat of renewed recession.[49]

The future trend of American business and of the payments situation would go far to determine whether the United States could continue to rely primarily on the growth of exports to solve its balance-of-payments problem or would feel compelled to resort to other measures, such as a reduction in overseas spending or the introduction of restrictive commercial policies aimed at protecting American business against its foreign competitors. The acid test of American intentions in the trade field would come early in 1961 when a long-awaited tariff conference of the General Agreement on Tariffs and Trade (GATT), which began its meetings at Geneva on September 1, 1960, reached the stage of concrete bargaining on the basis of the tariff-cutting powers entrusted to the administration under the Trade Agreements Extension Act of 1958.[50] Since that law was passed there had been a marked resurgence of protectionist sentiment in some sections of the American economy, most noticeably in the textile field, where labor as well as industrial leaders were showing extreme sensitivity to an influx of cheap fabrics and garments from Japan, Hong Kong, and elsewhere.

In certain other fields, such as aviation, the government was already under heavy pressure from industry sources to limit the access of foreign competitors to the American market. A refusal of additional landing rights sought by K.L.M., the Netherlands national airline, had already caused sharp resentment on the part of one allied country.[51] In the main, however, the United States had thus far adhered with reasonable consistency to its proclaimed intention of trying to solve its economic problems in concert with, rather than in opposition to, its non-Communist partners.

Another branch of foreign economic policy which involved some risk of friction with allied nations, although it was not directly related to the balance-of-payments issue, had to do with the disposal of the vast quantities of surplus food and fiber produced by the American agricultural economy under the traditional price support system. Since Congress ignored the President's requests for legislation aimed at bringing farm production more nearly into line with demand, 1960 went by without any new attack on the basic aspects of this long-standing problem. There was, however, a noticeable increase in official emphasis on the constructive use of surplus agricultural commodities to relieve distress and promote economic development abroad where this could be done without disrupting world markets or causing undue difficulty for other food exporting nations.[52] The largest single contract drawn up under the Agricultural Trade Development and Assistance Act —a four-year commitment to supply India with wheat and rice to a value equivalent to $1,276 million in Indian rupees—was concluded in May.[53] As a further extension of the "food for peace" concept, the outlines of a program for the allocation of American and other food surpluses through the Food and Agriculture Organization were drafted during the summer for submission to the United Nations at the autumn session of the General Assembly.[54]

7. THE UNITED NATIONS ASSEMBLY AND THE ELECTION

All Americans had known that the autumn of 1960 would be largely dominated by the give-and-take of the presidential election campaign. This year, however, novel events were to compete for world attention with the travels and speeches of the two candidates and their running mates. For the first time in the history of the United Nations, the General Assembly of the world organization had felt able to schedule its annual session in New York at the very time the campaign would be in progress. But no one could have foreseen at the time this decision was made that the 1960 meeting of the Assembly would produce an international sensation of a kind that for several weeks would overshadow the campaign itself.

The reason for this unexpected development was the decision of Premier Khrushchev to pay a second visit to the United States in the guise of chief Soviet delegate to the United Nations Assembly, a position in which the Soviet leader had obviously perceived a unique opportunity for prosecuting the Soviet offensive against the non-Communist world under the tattered but still vivid banners of "peaceful coexistence." Though fully aware that he could no longer be a welcome guest in the United States after the events of the spring and summer, the Soviet leader not only proposed to take full advantage of his rights and privileges under the United Nations headquarters agreement but did his best to turn the occasion into a new kind of "summit conference" by encouraging the attendance of as many other heads of state and government as were willing to come. As a result of these efforts, a surprised and somewhat unwilling New York found itself playing host during late September and early October not only to Khrushchev and his principal associates from Eastern Europe, but also to such world-famous leaders as President Tito of Yugoslavia, President Gamal Abdel Nasser of the United Arab Republic, Premier Fidel Castro of Cuba, Prime Minister Jawaharlal Nehru of India, Prime Minister Macmillan of Great Britain, and a host of secondary notabilities, including the heads of some dozen new states in Africa.

The simultaneous presence of so many controversial figures in a city of numerous minority groups and strong political passions created a grave security problem and produced a number of embarrassing incidents which were quickly turned to account in quarters unfriendly to the United States. Four of the visitors—Premier Khrushchev, Communist chief János Kádár of Hungary, Premier

Mehmet Shehu of Albania, and Premier Castro—were required with certain exceptions to remain on Manhattan Island.[55] President Tito and President Abdel Nasser were subjected to no such restrictions, although the former was annoyed by the activities of anti-Communist pickets near his official residence. But anti-Communist and anti-Castro pickets were indefatigably active all over New York. In conjunction with the massive police formations thought necessary for the visitors' protection, these hostile demonstrations lent some weight to Khrushchev's assertion in the General Assembly that it would be better for the United Nations to remove itself from American soil.[56]

Such thoughts were incidental to the large political issues that dominated the early weeks of the Assembly. The first of these was precipitated by Khrushchev's open attempt to subvert the procedures of the United Nations through a calculated course of bad behavior in the Assembly chamber and, more important, through a concentrated assault on the institution of the Secretariat and on the person of Secretary-General Dag Hammarskjold, whose handling of the crisis in the Congo had earned him the execration of the Soviet bloc. This opening attack in what might prove to be a long-range Soviet campaign against the United Nations was vigorously resisted by Ambassador James J. Wadsworth of the United States. (Ambassador Lodge had meanwhile become the Republican vice-presidential candidate.) Initially, at least, it gained little support among the Asian and African states which were beginning to hold the balance of power in the Assembly.[57]

But there was another, perhaps equally important issue on which the United States position proved rather less in harmony with Asian and African views. From the moment of their arrival in New York, Marshal Tito, Prime Minister Nehru, and other neutral leaders let it be known that one of their principal aims was to bring about a meeting between President Eisenhower and Premier Khrushchev in the hope of healing the rift opened up by the U-2 incident. Khrushchev himself gave no open encouragement to these efforts, but it fell to Mr. Eisenhower to quench the neutrals' hopes with a statement of October 2 in which he set forth the reasons why he did not feel that such a meeting could be useful in the circumstances created by Soviet policy.[58] The disappointment of the neutral leaders was great and unconcealed. Equally undisguised was their tendency to blame the United States rather than the Soviet Union for the impasse that had developed between East and West.

The importance of this episode was magnified by the rapidly growing prominence of the neutral countries, and of the Asian and African countries generally, both in the United Nations and on the wider international scene. Sixteen new African states were actually admitted to the United Nations during this one session of the Assembly. Some observers professed to regard the whole session as a contest between the U.S.S.R. and the United States for the allegiance of the newer countries—a contest, moreover, in which the U.S.S.R., in the person of Khrushchev, was generally felt to be exerting itself far more effectively than was the United States. While President Eisenhower came to New York to address the Assembly early in the session [59] and held brief meetings with Messrs. Tito, Nehru, Abdel Nasser, and Macmillan among others, Khrushchev participated regularly in the Assembly's work for several weeks and was in daily contact with a much wider group of political leaders. The psychological balance was only partially redressed by the cordiality which prevailed at a White House reception held on October 14 for the delegation heads of sixteen newly admitted United Nations members, all of whom subsequently went on a government-sponsored tour of the United States.[60]

That there would be room for increased vigor and imagination in the conduct of American foreign policy in the coming years was repeatedly recognized during these weeks by both of America's presidential candidates. For Senator Kennedy as for Vice-President Nixon, foreign policy was indisputably the dominant issue in the cam-

paign, and they and their running mates returned to the
subject repeatedly in their speeches as well as in the four
television debates which provided the principal novelty
of the contest. Concerning the current state of American
foreign relations there was a remarkable difference between the two aspirants. Mr. Nixon, as heir to the Eisenhower record, professed to find matters in excellent shape
as the end of Mr. Eisenhower's term approached. "Communist prestige in the world," he said on October 7, "is at
an all-time low and American prestige is at an all-time
high." [61] Yet Mr. Kennedy, supported by a considerable
body of independent testimony,[62] took a diametrically
opposite view and maintained that heroic efforts would be
needed to restore America's shaken military, economic, and
political position. Mr. Nixon himself did not by any means
deny that greater exertion would be called for in some
fields, and it seemed obvious to most observers that which-
ever was elected, the new generation of political leadership
that was now coming to the fore would impart a new and
in some ways more dynamic "style" to American international action.

Major changes in the substance of American foreign
policy appeared less likely on the basis of the campaign
discussion, which found the two candidates and their
running mates agreeing to a surprising extent on almost
all of the essentials.[63] In contrast to other recent presidential contests, there was relatively little discussion of the
meaning and obligations of "bipartisanship." Yet the most
significant feature of the campaign may well have been its
revelation of the extent to which American foreign policy
had in fact become a bipartisan enterprise. The main outlines of the national policy as it had developed since World
War II were unequivocally endorsed on both sides. The
only basic question between them appeared to be which
individual, and which party, was best qualified to build on
the foundations already laid, to meet the continuing threat
of Soviet Communism, and to pursue the unremitting

search for peace, justice, and freedom for America and the world.

Differences of detail were naturally made to seem important as the campaign progressed. Mr. Nixon was more convinced than Mr. Kennedy about the necessity of defending the Chinese offshore islands of Quemoy and Matsu; [64] Mr. Kennedy shocked Mr. Nixon and others by his call for national support of the "non-Batista democratic anti-Castro forces" in exile and in Cuba that were trying to overthrow the Castro regime.[65] Halfway through the campaign, Mr. Nixon retreated a little from his past insistence on the need to eliminate the restrictions affecting American participation in the International Court of Justice.[66] But there was no basic question of "isolationism" versus "internationalism" in this campaign, because both candidates were thoroughly "international" in outlook. There was no debate about "liberation" versus "containment," because it was tacitly conceded by both candidates that liberation of the Communist-dominated peoples was an ideal and a hope rather than an immediate policy objective.[67] There was no question of "Europe first" or "Asia first," because both realized that Europe and Asia were alike essential. Nor did either question that Africa and Latin America would be increasingly important to the United States in years to come.

So far as foreign policy was concerned, the question thus resolved itself largely into a choice between the two candidates' personal and intellectual qualities. Many voters were undoubtedly impressed by the forty-seven-year-old Mr. Nixon's claim to be the more experienced and levelheaded of the two candidates; many refused to be swayed by his characterization of his forty-three-year-old opponent as an impetuous juvenile who tended to "shoot from the hip." For the average voter, foreign policy considerations were perhaps less important than the two candidates' social and religious backgrounds (Mr. Kennedy was the second Roman Catholic to run for the Presidency) and their positions on civil rights, the economy, and other domestic issues.

When the ballots were counted on November 8 and the following days, the Kennedy-Johnson victory turned out to have been achieved by one of the narrowest margins in history. The popular vote, according to practically complete returns, amounted to 34,221,463 to 34,108,582. (The electoral vote was divided 303 to 219, with fifteen unpledged Southern votes going to Senator Harry F. Byrd of Virginia.) Democratic majorities in House and Senate were also somewhat reduced as compared with those in the Eighty-Sixth Congress, although the new President could look forward to working with a Congress dominated by his own party as President Eisenhower had been unable to do for the past six years. It was Vice-President Nixon who characterized the over-all result as a "striking and eloquent example of the stability of our constitutional system and of the proud tradition of the American people of developing, respecting and honoring institutions of self-government." "In our campaigns," the defeated candidate emphasized, "no matter how hard-fought they may be, no matter how close the election may turn out to be, those who lose accept the verdict, and support those who win." [68]

8. A FORWARD LOOK

The rhythm of American political life involves an unavoidable period of uncertainty between the election of a new President in November and his inauguration in January. The outgoing administration retains the outward attributes of power, but loses some of its capacity for making long-range decisions; the President-elect has neither the knowledge nor the authority to establish policy for the period ahead. However great the desire on both sides to ease the process of transition—and President Eisenhower, Senator Kennedy, and their aides omitted no step that could contribute to this end [69]—the Government is unavoidably gripped at such times by a kind of semi-paralysis in which its actions are likely to fall short of their full effect for the simple reason that no one can be sure how far the incoming administration will sustain them.

Yet the world situation does not remain static, and the United States was faced with many issues during the last weeks of 1960 on which its constitutional leaders were obliged to take positions even at the risk of tying the hands of their successors. The situation in the Congo, though temporarily stabilized by action of the United Nations, remained precarious in the extreme and daily threatened to degenerate into a new scramble for position by outside powers. The Algerian problem had been approaching one of those recurrent climaxes in which the United States would be forced to choose between the claims of its French ally and those of the African and Asian nations whose respect and friendship it wished to retain. New threats to stability had appeared in the Caribbean and South America as the Castro government increasingly revealed itself as the focus of a revolutionary movement of continental scope. In Southeast Asia, Laos had teetered for weeks on the brink of civil war and possible outside intervention. All these were matters which the Eisenhower administration was forced to meet to the best of its ability, even as it prepared to hand over the reins to a new set of drivers.[70]

Equally urgent and not less disquieting were the economic trends that had appeared while the electoral campaign was in progress. By autumn, the boom conditions prevailing in the United States at the beginning of 1960 had definitely disappeared. The economy as a whole was heading for a record gross product of $503.2 billion. But production had fallen off since midyear, unemployment had widened, and some independent observers had joined with Democratic campaign orators in asking whether the country might not be heading into another full-scale recession.

Admittedly the foreign trade picture was better than it had been in many months. The figures through October showed an export surplus of $5 billion at annual rates and suggested that exports for the year as a whole might even surpass the previous record set in 1957. Later figures set the total of merchandise exports for the full year at nearly $19.6 billion, slightly above the 1957 peak.[71]

But this improvement failed to exert the expected favorable effect on the balance of payments. On the contrary, a disparity in interest rates between prosperous Europe and the not-so-prosperous United States had produced a substantial outflow of short-term capital during the third quarter of the year which helped to widen the over-all balance-of-payments deficit to an annual rate of $4⅓ billion.[72] This phenomenon was accompanied by a sharp decline in the United States monetary gold stock, which dwindled in the course of the year from $19.4 billion to $17.8 billion.[73] In the third week of October a speculative flurry in London occasioned a sharp though temporary rise in the price of gold and accentuated fears of an incipient flight from the dollar. Although the run on gold was checked, the balance-of-payments deficit for the full year 1960 was ultimately reckoned at $3.8 billion, approximately the same as in 1959.

Some authorities continued to insist that these difficulties were essentially temporary in character, but Secretary of the Treasury Anderson and President Eisenhower regarded them rather as a product of deep structural maladjustments that called for equally profound remedies. Though most of the basic decisions in this field would obviously have to be left to the next administration, some immediate action was felt to be indispensable. On November 16, accordingly, the President issued a series of directives aimed at reducing governmental expenditure overseas as promptly as possible through a variety of dollar-saving measures which, it was hoped, might amount to as much as $1 billion annually. The most important steps were a shift of foreign aid and other types of procurement to American sources of supply wherever possible, and a gradual reduction in the number of military dependents overseas from a current 484,000 to 200,000.[74] A few days later, Secretary Anderson and Under-Secretary of State Douglas Dillon were sent on a special mission to Bonn in the hope of inducing the German Federal Republic to take over much of the financial support of the American forces deployed in its territory. The failure of the Germans to accede to this request [75] was followed by intimations in Washington that the United States would not shrink from even so drastic a step as a withdrawal of some of its military forces from Europe if this proved necessary to protect "the integrity of the dollar."

Such statements were read without enthusiasm in the Department of Defense, where the order to reduce dependents had been accepted with great reluctance and with many warnings about the effect on service morale, not to mention the civilian populations in such sensitive areas as West Berlin. From a larger point of view, such expedients would clearly do nothing to elevate the national prestige which had been so much talked about during the campaign. Very little was happening in the United States in these closing weeks of 1960 that could assist in projecting the image of a strong and confident power before the world. The Polaris submarine *George Washington* did, indeed, become operational on schedule, the *Patrick Henry* followed it to sea on December 30, and there was talk of assigning a number of these mobile missile carriers to operate under NATO command.[76] There were also further successes in retrieving the capsules ejected by Discoverer satellites. But the Mercury man-in-space program underwent a pair of further setbacks, and December brought the sixth successive American failure to send a rocket around the moon. Violence in New Orleans and elsewhere over the school integration program represented a further liability in the eyes of much of the world.

On the other hand, the progress of Senator Kennedy and his advisers in putting together the new administration was followed with interest and good hope in many nations. The new foreign policy executives—Dean Rusk as Secre-

"PRESTIGE"

York in *The Louisville Times*

tary of State, Chester W. Bowles as Under-Secretary, and Adlai E. Stevenson as Permanent Representative to the United Nations, with a "key role" in policy-making—inspired general if not undiluted approval in the free world. Europeans, though a little fearful that American interest might be shifting too much to other parts of the world, regarded Mr. Dillon's appointment to the Treasury as an encouraging intimation that future concern for the dollar would be tempered by a full awareness of diplomatic factors.

The full capacities of the new Kennedy "team"—and of the permanent government departments on which it would depend—would plainly be needed in coping with the vital national and international problems that were piling up as the date of Mr. Kennedy's inauguaration approached. Among the most urgent, apart from the staffing of governmental and ambassadorial posts, would be the recasting of national defense policies which Mr. Kennedy had promised during the campaign. This would require far-reaching decisions about the organization of the Defense Department and the armed services, the allotment of funds for missiles, aircraft, and conventional forces, and the use of nuclear weapons within the NATO alliance. Of special importance in this connection would be the question of whether, and how soon, to resume the program of nuclear weapons tests which had been suspended since October 31, 1958 in the hope—thus far delusive—of a controlled no-testing agreement with the Russians. This, in turn, would require a judgment as to the current prospects of coming to any understanding with the U.S.S.R., and, particularly, on the wisdom of agreeing to the summit meeting for which Khrushchev had again begun to agitate on the apparent, if unwarranted, assumption that President Kennedy might prove more yielding than President Eisenhower had been.

Behind these immediate issues of foreign policy lay a more general question about the aims and direction of the American democracy, the relative responsibility of the leadership and the individual citizen, in the new period of American history that was now opening. A crystallization of recent national thought on these matters had lately become available in the long-awaited report of President Eisenhower's Commission on National Goals.[77] Admitting frankly that the nation and its historical ideas stood in "grave danger" and could be rescued only by "extraordinary personal responsibility, sustained effort, and sacrifice" on the part of every American, this document outlined the many tasks to which Americans would have to devote themselves at home and abroad if the promise held forth to the world by the Declaration of Independence was still to be redeemed amid the adverse circumstances of the 1960's.

"Man has never been an island unto himself," this important analysis concluded. "The shores of his concern have expanded from his neighborhood to his nation, and from his nation to his world. Free men have always known the necessity for responsibilty. A basic goal for each American is to achieve a sense of responsibility as broad as his worldwide concerns and as compelling as the dangers and opportunities he confronts."

CHAPTER TWO

THE SOVIET BLOC
AND EAST-WEST RELATIONS

THE SOVIET UNION needed no Commission on National Goals to identify its long-term objectives as the 1960's began. The long-term objectives of the U.S.S.R. had been set forth once and for all in the writings of Lenin and had been reaffirmed many times by his successors, J. V. Stalin and N. S. Khrushchev. The ultimate goal of Soviet policy, to which the entire life of the Soviet Union and its satellites had been consistently subordinated, had been proclaimed again and again to be nothing less than the extension of the Communist system to the whole of human society. This large ambition had been reiterated too often, and on too high authority, to admit of reasonable doubt as to its genuineness. The only reasonable questions to which it gave rise were how vigorously the Soviet leaders intended to pursue it, what means they intended to employ, and what risks they were prepared to run in the hope of hastening its realization.

9. THE STRATEGY OF "PEACEFUL COEXISTENCE"

In this respect there had been important changes since the accession of Khrushchev to the direction of Soviet affairs in the mid-1950's. Where Lenin and presumably Stalin had anticipated that the natural opposition to Soviet aims on the part of the "imperialist" powers could be over-

GOOD NEWS

Long in *The Minneapolis Tribune*

come only by war, Khrushchev had been arguing since 1956 that the growth of the "socialist camp" and the emergence of a large number of other countries more or less sympathetic to the Soviet Union had brought about a fundamental shift in the world balance of forces, thus opening up the possibility that the triumph of "socialism," as he preferred to call it, could be brought about without any fighting at all. If war did occur, Khrushchev insisted, it would be the fault of the "imperialists"; and, though this would be a tremendous tragedy for everyone concerned, it was the "imperialists" who would suffer most. Khrushchev's own stated preference, however, was to establish the relations between the two camps on a basis of "peaceful coexistence" or "peaceful competition"—a state of affairs in which neither side would attack the other, but in which the "socialist camp" headed by the Soviet Union would be left free to demonstrate its inherent superiority to "capitalism" and thus gradually draw the rest of the world to its side. While this would obviously be a much gentler process than the "series of frightful collisions" foreseen by Lenin, the ultimate result would be the same.

In his elucidations of this theme Khrushchev had always insisted that notwithstanding the new possibility of a peaceful Communist victory, the U.S.S.R. and the "socialist camp" must keep up their armed strength in order to deal a "decisive rebuff" to the "imperialists" if the latter were after all so foolhardy as to attack. In spite of announced reductions of 2,140,000 in the past five years, by Khrushchev's own figures the Soviet military establishment at the beginning of 1960 still counted 3,623,000 men in uniform as well as large aggregations of tanks, airplanes, submarines, and more recently missiles or rockets. Americans and other non-Communist peoples who had listened to Soviet predictions of their own political demise could not be sure whether this formidable array of military power was intended only for the protection of the Soviet camp, as Khrushchev claimed, or whether the Soviet leaders had thoughts of loosing it against the United States and its partners at some opportune moment.

Quite possibly the Soviet leaders may have felt similar uncertainties about the substantial military establishments maintained by the United States and its Western allies, including the German Federal Republic. The existence of these mutually opposed forces, each of them embodying incalculable powers of destruction, would have been a serious impediment to trustful relations between the two groups even if Moscow had concealed its hope of eventually liquidating the "imperialist" camp. The terms of the problem were not materially altered by the surprising development that took place on January 14, 1960, when Khrushchev announced that the U.S.S.R. intended to reduce its armed forces by a further 1,200,000 men within the next two years and to assign the demobilized recruits to productive labor. Although he urged the Western powers to follow the Soviet example and thus help to alleviate the international arms race, Khrushchev emphasized at the same time that the proposed reduction would in no way impair the U.S.S.R.'s fighting power. On the contrary, he said, the fire power of the Soviet armed forces in terms of quality would actually "increase many times over." [1]

Whether or not Soviet military preparedness had any sinister purpose beyond that of a kind of "insurance policy" against a Western attack, it clearly formed part of a broad pattern whose various elements were closely correlated with the over-all aims of Soviet policy. Each phase of Soviet activity, military, economic, cultural, and diplomatic, played a recognizable part in the Kremlin's grand design of strengthening the Soviet Union's position on the world scene and weakening the position of its "imperialist" opponents.

On the economic front, the drive to overtake and surpass the United States as the world's leading industrial power provided the inspiration both of the U.S.S.R.'s new Seven-Year Plan for 1959-65 and of the long-range, fifteen-to twenty-year development program of which it formed a part. "And we are firmly convinced," Khrushchev affirmed once again in his January 14 address, "that in the peaceful economic competition of the two systems, the more progressive and virile socialist system will emerge victorious." [2]

Scientific and technological advance, including the exploration of outer space with rockets and satellites, was an integral part of this effort, although it also represented an essential contribution to the maintenance and expansion of Soviet military potential. Not less central to Soviet purposes was the elaborate program of economic and cultural penetration of newly independent and less developed countries which the U.S.S.R. had undertaken of late years in conjunction with such Communist-ruled "satellite" states as Czechoslovakia, East Germany, and Poland. An identical objective inspired Moscow's widely ramifying activities in the field of cultural, technical, and educational interchange with Communist, neutral, and Western nations.

Soviet diplomatic activities, too, were unmistakably directed toward the basic objective of improving the U.S.S.R.'s global military and political position and undermining that of its non-Communist opponents. It is true that the declared objective of Soviet diplomacy, as of most other Soviet activities, was not so much to damage the "imperialist" powers as simply to strengthen the cause of world peace. But "peace," in Soviet usage, was synonymous with the interests of the Soviet Union. In its pursuit of this fundamental aim, the U.S.S.R. had labored year in and year out to turn world opinion against the policies of the West, had supported virtually every anti-Western or anti-United States movement in Asia, Africa, and Latin America, and had used every opportunity to try to foment suspicion and mutual hostility among the Western nations themselves. Much of its diplomatic effort had aimed directly at undermining the Western military position (and its support by public opinion) by agitating for the liquidation of American military bases overseas, the withdrawal of American forces from Europe, the abandonment of West Germany's rearmament, the dissolution of NATO, and its replacement by an all-European security system more or less openly dependent on Soviet sufferance.[3]

In November, 1958, the Soviet assault on the Western

defense system in Europe had moved into a new phase with the sudden demand that the Western powers withdraw from the positions in Berlin which they had taken up at the end of the war in agreement with the U.S.S.R. itself. Capitulation to such a demand, Moscow must have reasoned, would be a natural prelude to the collapse of the allied position in Germany and perhaps throughout Western Europe. Although the Western powers and the people of West Berlin had thus far refused to give in to Soviet and East German threats and pressure, the matter was not yet settled and was scheduled to come up again at the summit conference in May 1960.

In the disarmament field, meanwhile, the U.S.S.R. had recently put forward another of its characteristic proposals for sweeping measures of disarmament—the latest one had called for "general and complete" disarmament within four years—without any clear-cut provisions for inspection and control such as would ensure that the measures agreed upon were really carried out. The West, in other words, was invited to disarm without any reliable assurance that the U.S.S.R. would do the same. This proposal, fantastic as it might sound, was shortly to be taken up, together with such alternative suggestions as might be advanced by the Western powers, at a special ten-nation disarmament conference which would be meeting in Geneva in March.

Western authorities did not exclude the possibility that the U.S.S.R. would really like to arrive at some kind of disarmament agreement with the object of lessening the danger of war, gaining some strategic or political advantage, or simply lightening its military budget and releasing more resources for nonmilitary purposes. Thus far, however, Moscow had refused to contemplate any measure of inspection and control sufficiently precise to enable the West to reduce its own armaments with any confidence. As in the related question of a possible international agreement suspending nuclear weapons tests, about which negotiations had been going on in Geneva since October 1958, the Soviet Government thus far had found it more advantageous to condemn the Western attitude than to modify its own approach in a way that might really make agreement possible.

Although there were times when Moscow's over-all strategy appeared decidedly effective in its impact on world public opinion, it was subject to a number of practical limitations, quite aside from the unwillingness of the Western governments to fall in with Soviet designs. Khrushchev's methods of operation were not without critics within the Soviet ruling group itself. The advocates of a more militant policy such as had prevailed in Stalin's time might still be in a position to reassert themselves unless Khrushchev could prove that "peaceful coexistence" was really capable of producing worthwhile results. Also to be taken into account was the attitude of the Soviet population, which, though it had certainly displayed no disloyal tendencies of late years, was plainly interested in bettering its material circumstances and might be disinclined to make great sacrifices or run great risks for so abstract a cause as the international triumph of "socialism."

Finally, there were the problems of the Eastern European countries, docile at present but always a potential source of unrest, and, above all, the problem of Communist China, an increasingly weighty and to some extent incalculable force in Communist affairs. Mao Tse-tung and his associates in Peking had not always seen the development of international relations in precisely the same light as the men in the Kremlin. Khrushchev, while he repeatedly denied that there were any significant differences between the two Communist powers, had already found it necessary to warn the Chinese leaders rather sharply against the risks of provoking a clash with the "imperialist" camp.[4] In his own future dealings with the "imperialists," the Soviet leader would have to bear in mind that the day was coming, perhaps within the next few years, when Communist China would have its own atomic weapons and might be even less inclined to accept guidance from Moscow than it had been in the past.

10. NEGOTIATIONS ON NUCLEAR WEAPONS TESTS

Western observers who thought they detected an unavowed rivalry between the U.S.S.R. and Communist China often expressed the view that Moscow should welcome an international agreement to outlaw the testing of nuclear weapons if only because it might help to prevent the Peking government from acquiring a nuclear capability. Admittedly, a no-testing agreement confined to the U.S.S.R., Great Britain, and the United States, the three powers which had been negotiating on the subject since 1958, might not deter the Chinese Communists from developing nuclear weapons on their own account. France had certainly not been deterred by these negotiations from carrying out the national atomic development program which was crowned by the detonation of two French nuclear devices in the Sahara early in 1960. All the same, it was argued, the U.S.S.R. shared with the principal Western powers an obvious interest in preventing the spread of atomic weapons to other countries. Some thought that this consideration might even help it to overcome its traditional aversion to measures of inspection and control on its own territory.

The U.S.S.R., in fact, was already on record as firmly opposing the testing of nuclear weapons by any of the great powers. As with so many other aspects of Soviet policy, however, Americans had not been able to determine how far, if at all, its attitude was inspired by genuine concern for easing international tension and limiting the release of harmful fission products, and how far it aimed simply at preventing the Western powers, especially the United States, from perfecting their own atomic armament. In any event, neither the United States, Great Britain, nor, so far as was known, the U.S.S.R. had actually carried out any nuclear weapons tests since November 3, 1958. To that extent, at least, a truce already prevailed in one important branch of the international arms race. Yet the tripartite negotiations which had been initiated at that time with a view toward agreement on a formal, permanent ban on nuclear testing had proceeded so slowly that the United States had given notice at the end of 1959 that it must reserve the right to resume its own test program at any time.[5] Although Great Britain took the position that it would not carry out any tests while the Geneva negotiations were going on, the Russians had already made clear that they too reserved the right to resume testing if either of the Western powers did so.

If the motives of Soviet participation in the Geneva talks had been open to varied interpretations, the attitude of the United States was also not entirely without ambivalence. There were important differences of opinion within the American Government as to whether a ban on nuclear testing was really desirable, even if it could be negotiated. Influential figures in the Defense Department, the Atomic Energy Commission, and the Congress entertained serious doubts on this point. Research and development on new types of atomic weapons, particularly in the smaller categories, was much more important to the United States, according to this view, than any advantages to be gained from a "no-testing" treaty with the U.S.S.R. Such tests as might be needed for this purpose, it was emphasized, could be carried out underground or at high altitudes, and would thus produce no radioactive fallout. But President Eisenhower had thus far supported the opposite view, maintained by the State Department and by some influential members of Congress, that it was essential to keep trying for agreement with the U.S.S.R. and to avoid antagonizing world opinion by a premature resumption of testing. After all, it was argued, the Geneva negotiators had managed in a little over two years' time to agree on a preamble, seventeen articles, and an annex to the proposed treaty.[6] Was there not at least a chance that they would eventually succeed in producing a finished document?

While the approach of each of the parties to the Geneva negotiations was influenced by a variety of extraneous considerations, most of the technical obstacles to agreement had to do with the familiar question of inspection and control. The negotiators at Geneva had long since agreed that there must be a control system to supervise adherence to the treaty, and that its basis should be the network of some 180 control posts first outlined by scientific representatives of the three countries in 1958. Disagreement centered around such questions as where the control posts should be situated, who should staff them, what rights of inspection and investigation should be allowed to the mobile teams which were expected to operate under the central control authority, and how this authority itself should arrive at its decisions. On all such questions the American delegation headed by James J. Wadsworth had sought wide powers for the control organization, while the Soviet group had endeavored to limit its activities and its authority at every turn. Ostensibly the Soviet attitude was motivated by anxiety lest the control organization and its personnel engage in "espionage." Americans could not help suspecting, however, that Moscow might be trying to weaken the organization so that it would be in a position to carry out tests clandestinely after the treaty went into effect.

While these larger questions remained unsettled, the Geneva discussions in recent months had focused mainly on the problem of detecting underground nuclear tests and especially on the problem of distinguishing such tests from natural disturbances. American scientists held that nuclear explosions which produced a seismological reading of 4.75 or more—equivalent to an explosive force of 20,000 tons of TNT, or approximately the size of the first atomic bomb—could be satisfactorily identified at a distance. Smaller ones, however, would have to be investigated on the spot to determine whether they were caused by nuclear explosions or by earthquakes. But Soviet representatives disagreed with this analysis and discounted the need for local inspection. The British, who frequently tried to mediate between the American and Soviet viewpoints, had suggested that the difficulty might be bypassed by declaring a temporary "moratorium" on small-scale underground tests while proceeding with the conclusion of a binding treaty covering other types of tests.

In an attempt to clarify the discussion and take at least partial account of Soviet and British views, the United States on February 11, 1960 introduced at Geneva a new proposal in which the problem of small underground tests was reserved for special treatment—though not the kind of special treatment favored by the other two powers. According to the American plan, there would be an immediate ban on nuclear weapons tests in the atmosphere, in the oceans, and "in those regions in space where effective controls can now be agreed." Also banned immediately would be all underground tests which could be monitored with existing technical means—i.e., those above the "threshold" of 4.75. For smaller underground tests, the American plan envisaged a joint program of research and experimentation aimed at developing an effective monitoring procedure so that these tests could be brought under the ban at a later date.[7]

What the American proposal did *not* provide for was an actual moratorium on the smaller tests pending the time when a monitoring system might be perfected. It was left to the U.S.S.R. to exploit this omission in a rival proposal, put forward on March 19, which accepted the idea of a joint research program but insisted that there must be a moratorium on small tests, as well as a complete ban on large ones, while the research program was being carried out.[8] The Soviet plan, in other words, would stop *all* tests while the research program was going forward—a period estimated by the Soviets as of four or five years' duration. During that period, if the Soviet proposal was accepted, the United States would be prevented from carrying out tests, but would have no assurance that the U.S.S.R. was living up to the terms of the moratorium.

Whatever its shortcomings, this was practically the first indication that the U.S.S.R. might settle for something less than an immediate and unconditional ban on tests of all

kinds. To Prime Minister Macmillan, the Soviet proposal
was of such importance that he arranged to fly to the
United States at short notice in hopes of persuading the
President to authorize a further modification in the American position. Concluding their conference at Camp David
on March 29, the American and British leaders announced
that they would now be agreeable to proclaiming a voluntary moratorium on tests below the "threshold" of 4.75
as soon as a treaty outlawing larger tests had been concluded and signed and arrangements had been completed
for a coordinated research program.[9] Although the United
States still declined to accept a moratorium before the
other questions in dispute had been resolved, the Soviet
negotiators responded favorably to the new plan. Agreement was shortly reached to schedule a preliminary conference of scientific representatives to discuss a research
program.

But even this limited concession on President Eisenhower's part had aroused strong misgivings among those
in the United States who doubted the wisdom of any test-
ban treaty. Some prominent members of the American
scientific community had by now reached the conclusion
that the whole control system as envisaged at Geneva on
the basis of the scientific knowledge of 1958 was fundamentally inadequate.[10] The attitude of members of the
Joint Congressional Atomic Energy Committee raised
doubt as to whether a treaty negotiated on that basis would
be ratified even if the administration signed it.

No final resolution of this issue was expected before the
summit conference. On May 7, however, the White House
announced that the United States, as part of its own research and development program looking to an improved
detection and identification system for underground tests
(Project Vela), was already preparing to carry out a series
of underground detonations involving both high explosive
and, in certain cases, nuclear explosions.[11] Although the
President subsequently emphasized that no testing of nuclear weapons was involved,[12] the fact that the United

States was planning at this moment to conduct any kind of nuclear explosions at all proved somewhat disturbing to world opinion, already seriously shaken as a result of the U-2 incident. Under the circumstances it was not surprising that the U.S.S.R. was soon denouncing the new plan as additional evidence of what it was now beginning to call the "perfidy" of United States policy.

11. DISARMAMENT AGAIN

Suspension of nuclear weapons tests was the only aspect of disarmament which had been under negotiation among the great powers since the autumn of 1957, when the U.S.S.R., flushed with the success of its first Sputniks and intercontinental missiles, had announced its withdrawal from participation in the United Nations Disarmament Commission. Since that time, new complications had entered the disarmament picture with the increasing prominence of missiles and rockets in the defense establishments of both major power groups. Both sides agreed, however, that disarmament remained the most urgent problem facing mankind, and in the course of 1959 it had been decided to resume the discussion in a special ten-nation negotiating group, established outside the United Nations, which would be constituted on a basis of numerical "parity" with a membership of five Communist and five Western states.[13]

This group would be something of a novelty not only in its composition but also in the scope of the problems it would be negotiating about. As had happened so often in the past, the Russians had seized the initiative in advance of the discussions with the dramatic plan for "general and complete disarmament" within a period of four years which Khrushchev had laid before the United Nations Assembly on September 18, 1959.[14] Although the objective of total disarmament had hitherto been regarded as somewhat utopian in informed Western circles, the effectiveness of Khrushchev's sweeping proposal as a propaganda gesture had been obvious from the first. This was all the more true because the Soviet leader's statements suggested at least a possibility that the traditional Soviet resistance to effective inspection and control might be weakening. The Western powers were thus compelled to treat the plan as a serious one and to see whether they could not adjust their own positions in such a way as to produce something equally attractive and better suited to the protection of non-Communist interests. The commitment to set their sights on nothing less than "general and complete disarmament" had been underlined by the inclusion of this phrase in a resolution unanimously adopted by the General Assembly later in its 1959 session.[15] No one could doubt that Khrushchev's proposal was destined to provide the basis of Communist strategy at the coming ten-nation conference, now scheduled to open at Geneva on March 15, 1960. The nominally independent delegations of Communist-ruled Bulgaria, Czechoslovakia, Poland, and Rumania could be trusted to share the Soviet point of view in every essential respect. The five Western governments which were to participate—the United States, Great Britain, France, Italy, and Canada—found it considerably less easy to arrive at a unified position. The situation of the United States had been particularly difficult because a special committee set up in July 1959 to draft a new American disarmament policy had not come up with an acceptable negotiating position, and the problem had to be attacked practically from scratch in the early weeks of 1960. Total disarmament of the sort Khrushchev was now proposing had not thus far been considered in Washington as a particularly feasible objective, however desirable it might be in the abstract. What the United States had sought was the more modest goal of a *limitation* of armaments, under effective inspection and control, which would tend to reduce the fury of the arms race and at the same time ensure that no single power or group obtained an undue advantage over its competitors. Complete disarmament, as Secretary Herter pointed out in a preliminary statement of American views on February 18, 1960,[16] could lead directly to anarchy unless other means were available to ensure that international law and order were maintained after national armaments were abolished.

What the United States now proposed to recommend, accordingly, was a two-phased program embracing, in the first stage, measures to reduce the immediate risk of war and thus create conditions for "progressive, gradual, and balanced reductions in national military forces"; and, in the second phase, a development of international law and of international machinery, including international armed forces, which would be capable of maintaining the peace while national forces were being further reduced or eliminated. Among specific measures to be taken in the first phase, Mr. Herter mentioned particularly the need for safeguards against surprise attack and against the promiscuous spread of nuclear weapons.

If these American views were to have a significant impact at Geneva, they would first have to be reconciled with those of the other Western governments, particularly Britain and France. British Foreign Secretary Selwyn Lloyd had already submitted a comprehensive, three-stage disarmament plan at the last session of the General Assembly,[17] and it was a comparatively simple matter to add to it the Herter plan for international peace-keeping machinery. The French attitude presented greater difficulty, since France, unlike its two partners, was disinclined to envisage any limitations on atomic weapons at a time when its own atomic weapons program was still in its initial stages. The place to begin, in the French view, was not with the nuclear weapons themselves but with the missiles and other carriers designed to deliver them on target—a procedure by no means acceptable to the American government. In spite of these interallied differences, experts from the five Western governments managed to put together an agreed "working paper," setting forth general principles of disarmament, which was released on the eve of the ten-nation meeting.[18]

Vague though it proved to be on certain points where the Western governments had found it impossible to reach full agreement, this document was firm and forthright in its insistence that progress toward general disarmament must proceed "by balanced, phased, and safeguarded agreements" and must at every stage be "observed and verified by an appropriate international organization." The West, in other words, stood solidly on its past contention that disarmament was possible only on a basis of effective inspection and control. But the U.S.S.R., despite Khrushchev's loose talk of the preceding autumn, still showed no great interest in disarmament under these conditions. Even before the Western position had been officially explained by Frederick M. Eaton of the United States and the other Western delegation chiefs, the Soviet press had begun to misrepresent the Western position as a demand for "control without disarmament." This slogan was to be repeated *ad nauseam* in the coming months. The West, according to Soviet delegate V. A. Zorin and his Communist colleagues, was trying to put the cart before the horse. The way to begin, they insisted, was to agree that there was really going to be complete and general disarmament. Such details as control could be discussed afterward.

Despite their apparent rejection of the fundamental feature of the Western plan, the Communists conducted their argument with sufficient skill to convince a large part of the world, including President Eisenhower,[19] that this time they genuinely wanted at least "a degree of disarmament." Details of the Khrushchev plan were manipulated with surprising dexterity. When the West complained that the Communists were paying too much attention to eliminating American bases and too little to eliminating nuclear weapons, the latter subject was promptly moved to the head of their priority list. Even on the critical question of inspection and control, a prospect was held open that the Communist side would agree to quite substantial measures if only the Western powers would first commit themselves to the over-all objective. Controls, the Communists intimated, would be set up progressively as the various disarmament steps were actually carried out. What they could not accept was that controls should be set up in advance of disarmament. "Dive in," they seemed to say, "and we will let water into the pool as soon as you are off the springboard."

Since the Western delegates showed no inclination whatever to accept this invitation, the principal effect of the new, "balanced" membership in the committee was simply to enable the Communist side to make as many speeches as the West. This advantage was put to good use as the discussions began more and more to degenerate into the kind of propaganda contest which was already familiar from earlier disarmament conferences. As the talks went on, details of the various new proposals on either side began to seem less significant from the standpoint of advancing disarmament than from that of impressing world opinion. This was a game in which the Communists had long since demonstrated their superiority. Particularly effective as a political warfare move was the introduction on April 11 of a Soviet text which reiterated the demand for complete disarmament in four years and, in addition, called upon each of the powers possessing nuclear weapons to "solemnly declare that they will not be the first to use such weapons." [20] The Western powers, whose whole defense strategy in recent years had been based on the use of nuclear weapons from the outset of any major conflict, could not possibly take such a pledge; but it was a little embarrassing to have to decline it under these particular circumstances.

By the end of April, when the conference adjourned to await the discussions at the summit, it was evident to the West that no real progress could be made unless Khrushchev directed his representatives to modify their position substantially when the talks resumed. Khrushchev, on his side, could not fail to perceive that the West had no intention of swallowing his own proposal for "disarmament before control." As in the discussions on nuclear weapons tests, the Western powers—especially the United States—felt it necessary to insist on control because without it they could not be sure the U.S.S.R. would live up to its commitments. The U.S.S.R., on the contrary, insisted that this position was totally unjustified and could only be prompted by the desire to pry into Soviet military secrets.

12. THE DEBATE ON BERLIN

If Khrushchev's recent efforts to promote a "relaxation of tension" had been aimed at reducing Western resistance to Soviet diplomatic proposals, they could not be said to have produced any great result as yet in so far as armament problems were concerned. From Moscow's viewpoint, this did not necessarily mean that the effort had been wasted. If the West refused to fall in with Soviet disarmament proposals, the U.S.S.R. could always convince a good many people that the fault lay with the West rather than with the Soviet Union. Real disarmament was a matter on which the Soviet leaders apparently felt that they could afford to wait.

There was less patience in Moscow about the Soviet drive to expel the Western powers from Berlin and establish the Western sectors of the former German capital as an unprotected "free city." The problem raised by the Soviet note of November 27, 1958 to the United States, Great Britain, and France [21] was both more pressing and more dangerous than those currently under discussion in Geneva. It was more pressing because Khrushchev had heavily committed his own prestige and that of his government to the objective of loosening the Western grip on this critical position within a limited period of time. It was more dangerous because, while no one thought of going to war over the disarmament question, both sides had recognized quite clearly that war over Berlin was a definite possibility unless the issue could be satisfactorily resolved by diplomatic means.

Past attempts to arrive at a negotiated solution of the

Berlin problem, and of the wider German problem of which it formed a part, had not proved especially fruitful. The Foreign Ministers of the four occupying powers —the United States, Great Britain, France, and the U.S.S.R.—had discussed the matter at Geneva for a total of nine weeks in the spring and summer of 1959 without arriving at any definite conclusion. The Western powers had urged that the Berlin problem be dealt with as part of a comprehensive plan for the reunification of Germany through free, all-German elections. The U.S.S.R., however, had refused to countenance such a procedure and insisted instead on the conclusion of a German peace treaty, of a sort that would tend to strengthen the Communist position in Germany and would also include a settlement of the Berlin problem in accordance with Soviet desires. Thereafter there had been some inconclusive discussion of an "interim" plan for Berlin whereby the Western powers might make certain limited concessions on the understanding that their occupation rights in the city would be respected for a period of years.[22] But there had been no final agreement at Geneva, and President Eisenhower and Premier Khrushchev in their subsequent discussion at Camp David had agreed only that the negotiations, while not subject to any fixed time limit, "should not be prolonged indefinitely." [23]

The Camp David formula had sounded quite reassuring in the optimistic climate of September 1959. It began to sound less reassuring as the time for the summit conference approached and Khrushchev began to intimate that he was still very much in earnest about the need for a radical solution of the Berlin problem and, indeed, the whole German question. The existing situation in Germany, Khrushchev asserted once again in his major report to the Supreme Soviet on January 14, 1960, was a standing threat to peace. He could not speak harshly enough of the "militarist" and "revanchist" tendencies that were allegedly being fostered in the Western-oriented German Federal Republic under the government of Chancellor

Konrad Adenauer. The U.S.S.R., Khrushchev recalled, had long been urging the conclusion of a German peace treaty applicable to both the German Federal Republic in the west and the Communist-ruled "German Democratic Republic" in the east. But its proposals to this end had been persistently rejected. If this attitude continued, the Soviet leader warned, the U.S.S.R. and its friends would have no alternative but to sign a separate peace treaty with East Germany, "with all the attendant implications." [24]

Interpreted in the light of past Soviet pronouncements, this statement meant that the U.S.S.R. would still prefer to settle the entire German question at one stroke in a way that would sever West Germany's links with the Western alliance and reopen it to Soviet influence. Failing this, it was prepared to turn over full authority in Eastern Germany to the East German Communists, allowing them to handle the Berlin matter and all other current questions directly with the Western occupation powers. Since the Western powers were dependent on the land and air routes across East Germany to supply their garrisons in Berlin, they would find it extremely difficult under these conditions to avoid recognizing the East German government as the legitimate authority in East Germany. True, such a step would directly contradict their past attitude and reflect adversely on the political position of their West German ally. Yet if they refused to deal with the East Germans, the latter would be in a position to create all kinds of difficulties for them, even to barring their military convoys and interrupting their communications with West Berlin. And if the Western powers resorted to force in trying to maintain their rights against East German interference, Khrushchev had warned repeatedly in the past that the "German Democratic Republic" would be supported by the U.S.S.R. and the entire "Socialist camp." The solidarity of the Communist bloc on this and all other current East-West issues was soon afterward reaffirmed in a declaration of the Communist satellite governments, issued in Moscow on February 4 in the name of the Soviet-sponsored Warsaw Treaty Organization.[25]

In attempting to meet this rather ominous line of argument, the Western powers had been handicapped from the beginning by two main factors. First, they could not fail to realize that short of unleashing a full-scale nuclear war, they were not very favorably situated for defending their position in Berlin by military means if that were to become necessary. Second, they had experienced great difficulty in harmonizing their views as to the most effective means of maintaining their interests on the diplomatic plane. Temporarily submerged during the Foreign Ministers' conference in 1959, these difficulties were now reemerging as the Western governments attempted to agree on a common position to be defended at the forthcoming summit meeting.

All of the Western allies agreed that the rights of the Western powers and the freedom of West Berlin's population must be maintained. They disagreed rather widely as to how this was to be done. The British contended that the only reasonable procedure was to try to arrive at an "interim" solution of the Berlin problem on somewhat the same basis as had been discussed the summer before. Chancellor Adenauer, on the other hand, insisted on an attitude of maximum firmness, urged retraction of the limited concessions considered in 1959, and, in fact, strongly opposed negotiating about Berlin at all except in the framework of wider plans for settling the whole German problem in accordance with Western ideas. In this controversy it was the United States that tended to be in the middle, with France inclining somewhat toward the German viewpoint. Congenitally suspicious of the British, Chancellor Adenauer paid a special visit to Washington in mid-March to urge his views on President Eisenhower,[26] who managed to soothe the German statesman's anxiety temporarily without necessarily closing the door to negotiations on an interim plan. The differences of approach among the allied powers were further evidenced by their treatment of various current policy questions in Germany, among them an American plan (ultimately shelved on instructions from the President) to assert what was regarded as an allied right by carrying out certain military flights at high altitudes in the air corridors leading to Berlin.

In the meantime Khrushchev had been agitating the Berlin issue in a series of public pronouncements which tended to grow more thunderous as the summit drew nearer. In Indonesia, where he spent several days in the late winter, he stated flatly on February 29 that the signature of a Soviet peace treaty with East Germany would mean the immediate cancellation of all allied rights in East Germany, including Berlin.[27] A month later, on a visit to France which seemed openly aimed at dividing that country from its allies, he warned repeatedly of the dangers of West German "militarism" and again stated that a separate East German peace would deprive the Western powers of all their occupation rights—a thesis that the State Department promptly declared to be wholly untenable on legal grounds.[28]

But the Soviet leader miscalculated if he expected these tactics to result in a weakening of the Western position in advance of the summit conference. Secretary Herter, in a speech of April 4, strongly reaffirmed the determination of the Western powers not only "to protect the freedom and security of the people of West Berlin" but also to defend their point of view in other East-West matters.[29] Under-Secretary Dillon, addressing a labor conference on world affairs in New York on April 20, was even sharper. Khrushchev had been "skating on very thin ice" in his recent statements, Mr. Dillon said. The Soviet leader and his associates, he warned, "will be profoundly disillusioned if they assume that we will bow to threats or that we will accept their distorted picture of the German problem as a factual premise upon which to negotiate." [30]

Khrushchev's reply, delivered at Baku in Soviet Azerbaijan on April 25, was nothing if not defiant. The Dillon speech, he said, "just reeks of the 'cold war' spirit." Mr.

Dillon's remarks, like those of Secretary Herter, impressed him as only too typical of the "one-sided" attitude that some of the Western leaders had been adopting in relation to disarmament and nuclear weapons tests as well as Berlin and Germany. He himself, Khrushchev insisted, was approaching the Paris conference "with the most sincere intentions" to try to improve the international atmosphere and do everything to try to reach mutual understanding with the Western leaders. Nevertheless, he strongly reaffirmed the Soviet point of view on all matters currently under discussion, renewed the threat to conclude a separate peace with East Germany if the Western powers rejected a "concerted solution," and reiterated that in this event the Western occupation rights in Berlin would disappear. He also stated once again that if the Western allies thought of trying to maintain their position in Berlin by force, he must warn "such hotheads . . . that this force will be countered with the force of the other side." [31] These were scarcely the words of a man who expected to gain his ends by compromise or friendly conversation around a table.

13. EXPLOSION AT THE SUMMIT

This was the state of affairs when the luckless flight of the U-2 photoreconnaissance plane over the U.S.S.R. on May 1 initiated the dramatic chain of events that culminated sixteen days later in Khrushchev's abrupt breakup of the summit conference before there could be any discussion of the important issues dividing East and West. This startling development, briefly sketched in the preceding chapter,[32] has been explained in diametrically opposite ways. According to the Soviet version, the action of the United States in resorting to aerial espionage at a moment of such delicacy demonstrated Washington's fundamental lack of interest in East-West accommodation, the worthlessness of the personal relationship established between Premier Khrushchev and President Eisenhower, and the futility of any attempt to carry on high-level negotiations until there was a fundamental change in the attitude of the American Government. In the official United States view, on the other hand, Khrushchev had concluded even before the interception of the U-2 that the firmness of the Western powers left him no hope of achieving a diplomatic success in Paris. Accordingly, it is argued, he merely seized upon the U-2 incident as a pretext for breaking up the conference in the most dramatic manner possible and casting the entire responsibility on the United States.[33]

While no final verdict is possible in the absence of trustworthy evidence from the Soviet side, it is obvious that the Soviet Government must at some point have reached the conclusion that it had more to gain (or less to lose) from breaking up the conference than from allowing it to proceed. Otherwise it would have refrained from forcing the rupture which Khrushchev appeared determined to bring about from the moment he arrived in Paris. This conclusion does not, of course, exclude the possibility that the U-2 incident may have caused genuine shock and dismay in high Soviet quarters and caused the Kremlin to adopt a more uncompromising stand than it would otherwise have done. The morbid sensitivity of the Soviet authorities about espionage in general and about aerial espionage in particular had already been demonstrated by a dozen or so earlier air incidents in the neighborhood of the Soviet borders, as well as by years of discussion in various disarmament bodies. To the Soviet mind, the flight of the U-2 might well have come as confirmation of the sinister intent habitually ascribed to American proposals for "open skies," "mutual aerial inspection," and effective control of other phases of disarmament. Washington's initial lack of candor in relation to the U-2 could have done nothing to relieve such misgivings, especially among people who were themselves in the habit of resorting to every form of trickery and deceit in order to gain access to the secrets of their opponents.

The U-2 incident may also have had its embarrassing

aspects from the standpoint of Soviet internal affairs. In reporting the matter to the Supreme Soviet, Khrushchev virtually admitted that until recently the U.S.S.R.'s anti-aircraft defenses had not been good enough to intercept and shoot down high-flying intruders. Even now, not everyone was convinced by his claim that the U-2 had been downed by rocket fire while flying at or near its maximum altitude. Some of the evidence released by the United States would indicate that it was not. And if an unarmed U-2 could penetrate Soviet air space, the Soviet man in the street might reason, other aircraft carrying atomic and hydrogen bombs could perhaps do the same.

Even more delicate was the possible impact of the affair on Khrushchev's relationships with his supposed critics in the Soviet ruling group and, perhaps, in Communist China and other parts of the Communist world. The Soviet Premier had staked a great deal on his policy of "peaceful coexistence," "relaxation of tensions," and the establishment of a personal entente with President Eisenhower. His initial statements about the U-2 gave the impression that he hoped the President would help to preserve this relationship by disclaiming any personal knowledge of the flights and throwing the blame on his subordinates. Once Mr. Eisenhower had assumed personal responsibility, it would have been doubly difficult for Khrushchev to continue to justify a policy for which some of his associates had apparently never had much sympathy. Western observers were soon pointing to bits of evidence which suggested that Khrushchev had lost a good deal of his freedom of action in the conduct of foreign affairs and was perhaps being forced by his associates to adopt an even more intransigent line than he himself would normally have taken.

Khrushchev's behavior at Paris tended to support the impression that he was now acting as the spokesman, rather than the fountainhead, of Soviet policy. The long and bitter tirade of May 16 in which he demanded President Eisenhower's apology for the U-2 as a precondition of any four-power meeting [34] bore all the earmarks of having been composed in Moscow some days before. It was noticed by Western observers at the Elysée Palace, where the summit meetings had been scheduled to take place, that the Soviet Premier now paid unwonted deference to Marshal Rodion Y. Malinovsky, the grim-faced Defense Minister who had accompanied him and Foreign Minister Andrei A. Gromyko to Paris. According to former Ambassador Charles E. Bohlen of the American delegation, Khrushchev actually stated in the conference room that his stand "was a matter that involved deeply the internal politics of the Soviet Union." [35] In any case, his position was clear: he would not allow the conference to meet unless the United States, in the person of President Eisenhower, would publicly humiliate itself in a manner without precedent in recent international history.

Such was the truculence of Khrushchev's behavior during these days that it was difficult to exclude the possibility that Moscow might be on the point of scrapping the whole idea of "peaceful competition" and preparing for a military solution of the East-West impasse. News of a world-wide test alert of the American military forces, ordered from Paris by Secretary of Defense Thomas H. Gates, Jr. on the night of May 15-16, accentuated the feeling that war might not be far distant. Although Khrushchev took the position that a summit meeting might be held in six to eight months and that the conferences on disarmament and nuclear weapons tests should not be interrupted,[36] his violent rages nullified the limited reassurance conveyed by his words. He gave the impression of a man who had lost not only his self-control but his sense of proportion. It was comforting to the United States at such a moment that Prime Minister Macmillan and President de Gaulle, greatly though they too deplored the situation that had developed, unwaveringly supported the President in his refusal to bow to Khrushchev's exorbitant demands.

Not until Khrushchev had withdrawn from Paris and gone to East Berlin to confer with the leaders of the "German Democratic Republic" did the pattern of Soviet intentions for the immediate future begin to clarify. To the great relief of the West and the evident disappointment of the East German Communists, the Soviet Premier made known on May 20 that he was still not ready to carry out the oft-repeated threat to conclude a peace treaty with East Germany. In spite of everything that had happened, he told a Communist rally, it was worthwhile to wait "a little longer"—though not "endlessly"—for an agreed solution of the German problem. "The existing situation," he said, "will apparently have to be preserved till the heads of government meeting, which, it is to be hoped, will take place in six or eight months." In the meantime, Khrushchev stated, the U.S.S.R. did not intend to "do anything that might aggravate the international situation and bring it back to the worst times of the cold war." On the contrary, it meant to "do everything necessary, just as before, toward improving the international situation." [37]

Although the basic policy of "peaceful coexistence" was thus reaffirmed, its pursuit in the coming months was to be characterized by a degree of harshness that would make it very difficult to distinguish from what Khrushchev called "the worst times of the cold war." Whether the change of tone that began in Paris was consistent with the long-term advantage of the Soviet Union would take some time to determine. Although the U-2 incident had unquestionably damaged the United States in the eyes of allied and neutral countries, the disappointment and dismay occasioned by Khrushchev's performance in Paris undoubtedly went far to even the scales. Soviet threats of retaliation against countries that cooperated in American "spy flights" had caused some alarm in Norway, Pakistan, and other countries more remote from the U-2's projected itinerary. Yet the very vehemence of these threats—combined with President Eisenhower's announcement in Paris that the flights had already been discontinued—contributed in some measure to swing opinion in favor of the United States. The moderate tone of President Eisenhower's May 25 report to the American people, in which he proposed to submit a new "open skies" plan for United Nations consideration,[38] may have contributed further to restoring America's shaken position in world esteem.

Some indication of this revulsion of opinion was afforded by the debate in the United Nations Security Council which took place late in May as the result of Moscow's determination to seek a formal condemnation of the United States in connection with the U-2 affair. The demand for an immediate cessation of "incursions by United States aircraft into the territory of other states" already seemed a trifle anachronistic in view of the announced suspension of the U-2 program and the recent disclosure that the United States now had at its disposal a much more sophisticated intelligence tool in the Tiros and Midas photographic satellites. Gromyko's anti-American diatribes in New York added nothing substantial to the Soviet case. The United States, in contrast, was afforded an opportunity to document its charge that the U.S.S.R. was by far the worse offender in the matter of espionage. Of the eleven members of the Security Council, only the U.S.S.R. and Poland voted on May 26 to condemn the U-2 flights as "aggressive acts." [39] Two other countries, Ceylon and Tunisia, abstained, while five voted for rejection of the Soviet resolution. As an alternative the Council adopted next day (with the U.S.S.R. and Poland abstaining) an expression of regret for the failure of the summit conference and an appeal to the major governments to avoid provocative acts and urgently seek a peaceful solution of their difficulties.[40]

14. COLD WAR OR COEXISTENCE?

To a normal vision, the actions of the Soviet Government during the next three months reflected little of the spirit of moderation recommended by the Security Council. The campaign against American "espionage" was continued at a high and even dangerous pitch; negotiations on disarmament were broken off; an air of tension was maintained in relation to Berlin; Communist activity was stepped up in Japan, Italy, and other non-Communist countries; important new "cold war" fronts were opened in Cuba and in the Congo; the Western powers and the United Nations were subjected to heavy doses of Soviet pressure and obstructionism. Yet at the very time when Khrushchev was superintending this intensified offensive against what he called the "forces of imperialism," he was also conducting a protracted battle within the Soviet bloc on behalf of his own ideas of "peaceful coexistence" and the continued possibility of a Communist victory over the West without war.

This effort to justify the fundamental principles of recent Communist strategy appears to have been largely successful so far as the satellite governments in Eastern Europe were concerned. In June, a meeting of Communist leaders at Bucharest heard Khrushchev make an eloquent defense of his doctrine and thereafter issued a declaration (dated June 24) which generally reaffirmed earlier statements on the coexistence policy.[41] With respect to Communist China, however, Khrushchev would seem to have failed utterly to win acceptance of his views. A representative of the Chinese Communist party did, indeed, subscribe his name to the Bucharest document; but subsequent authoritative utterances from Peking displayed an astonishing contempt for Khrushchev's theories. The only way to get rid of "imperialism," Chinese Communist sources insisted, was to fight it; nor did Peking agree in the least with Khrushchev's suggestion that the "ruling class" in "capitalist" countries might allow itself to be dislodged by peaceful means. Before long a first-class ideological debate was raging in the Soviet and Chinese Communist press—a debate regarded by many as merely the surface manifestation of a profounder clash of interests between the two leading Communist powers.[42]

There was no sign whatever during these months that the U.S.S.R. was disposed to seek a better understanding with the West, whatever the difficulties it might be having with its own ally. The Soviet Government showed almost as little regard for the feelings of other Western countries as it did for those of the United States. One of the earliest and most alarming manifestations of the new Soviet mood was a statement by Marshal Malinovsky on May 30, subsequently endorsed by Khrushchev, to the effect that as a result of the U-2 incident, Soviet rocket forces had already received orders "to strike at any base from which a plane might fly to violate the territory of the Soviet Union or the Socialist countries." [43] The U.S.S.R., in other words, would not content itself in future with shooting down an intruding plane; it would retaliate directly against the country from which the plane had taken off. Since such retaliation would not improbably result in counteraction by the West, it looked as though the decision for war or peace might rest henceforth in the hands of a subordinate Soviet commander. Given the suspension of the U-2 flights, such warnings might have seemed entirely unnecessary. Nevertheless they helped to maintain a feeling of uneasiness in some allied countries. In Japan, they helped to swell the opposition to the new United States-Japanese security treaty and may have played a part in the popular commotions that necessitated the cancellation of President Eisenhower's visit.

In its treatment of the case of the American RB-47 aircraft shot down over the Barents Sea on July 1, the U.S.S.R. was only too obviously concerned to accentuate this prevalent sense of anxiety. As already noted,[44] the United States insisted that the RB-47, unlike the U-2, was not an espionage plane and in fact had not come near Soviet territory. Although these statements were perhaps a trifle less readily accepted than would have been true at an earlier date, a majority of the Security Council again refused to vote a condemnation of the United States such as the U.S.S.R. demanded at a series of meetings that began July 22. This time even Ceylon and Tunisia voted against the Soviet draft resolution, which was defeated on

July 26 by a vote of two in favor and nine opposed.[45] Nor did the U.S.S.R. entirely redress the balance when it proceeded to veto two alternative resolutions, aimed respectively at submitting the affair to impartial investigation and at providing Red Cross assistance for the two American crewmen who were being held incommunicado in the Soviet Union.[46]

Undeterred by this setback, the U.S.S.R. gave notice that it would carry both the U-2 and RB-47 cases before the General Assembly at its autumn session. As Soviet-American relations continued to deteriorate, the United States took the initiative on July 14 in postponing until a more favorable time the opening of long-awaited negotiations for an American-Soviet air transport agreement, and on July 22 expelled a Soviet diplomat on espionage charges.[47] The U.S.S.R., on its side, kept the spy fever alive by repeated warnings to the Soviet public against the possibly nefarious intentions of American exchange students and tourists; by expelling a United States air attaché and an economic attaché for alleged spying; [48] by strenuous complaints about the "buzzing" of Soviet vessels on the high seas by American aircraft; [49] and by preparations for the propaganda trial of U-2 pilot Francis Powers, which was so arranged as to serve the dual purpose of refreshing the memory of the U-2 incident and, perhaps, reassuring Soviet citizens about the state of their defenses.[50] Mr. Powers had scarcely begun his ten-year sentence, imposed on August 19, when the U.S.S.R. created a new sensation by producing two defecting employees of the United States National Security Agency, who disclosed purported details of American espionage procedures at a Moscow press conference.[51]

While they contributed their share to the revival of international tension, these events would perhaps seem less important in retrospect than the concurrent developments involving Cuba and the Congo, which must be reserved for detailed treatment in later chapters.[52] Nor were their implications as serious from most points of view as those that seemed to flow from Moscow's abrupt torpedoing of the ten-nation disarmament conference on June 27.

One of the earliest Soviet moves after the breakup of the summit conference had been the ostentatious release on June 2 of another new disarmament plan, one that purported to meet the demands of the Western powers "half way," in preparation for the resumption of the ten-nation talks on June 7.[53] Its principal novelty, apparently designed to appeal primarily to France, was an offer to begin the disarmament process by the destruction of missiles and other means of delivery for nuclear weapons—though only on condition that other countries (meaning primarily the United States) would immediately give up their military bases abroad and repatriate their troops. The American delegation could find little merit in this plan, which seemed to retain most if not all the objectionable features of earlier Soviet proposals. Still, the gesture had come at a moment when the world was eager to believe that international conditions were not as bad as they seemed, and the United States thus found itself under heavy pressure to show a similar measure of flexibility. Mr. Eaton therefore returned to Washington and won assent to a revised United States proposal which, though it involved no fundamental departure from the past American position, incorporated a few minor adjustments designed "to provide a fresh basis for advancing the negotiations." [54]

There was no time to discuss this proposal in any detail with the other Western delegations. As matters fell out, it could not even be laid before the full conference, since those responsible for Soviet strategy had by now decided to break up the disarmament meeting just as they had broken up the summit conference. On June 27, the Polish chairman forestalled the tabling of the American plan by bringing the proceedings of the conference to an abrupt halt, refusing even to allow the Western delegates to register their protests.[55] Western obstruction, Khrushchev asserted the same day in lengthy communications to the interested governments, had rendered further meetings useless. The only proper course, according to him, was to refer the matter back to the United Nations Assembly at its forthcoming regular session.[56]

In American eyes, this drastic move could mean only one thing: Moscow, for the present at least, had no interest in serious disarmament negotiations and preferred to treat disarmament exclusively as a propaganda issue. While vigorously condemning the Soviet attitude, Washington refused to allow the matter to rest until the autumn as Khrushchev had proposed. Overcoming the reluctance of its allies, which feared a threatened boycott by the Communist states and possibly some of the neutrals, it pressed instead for an early meeting of the eighty-two-nation United Nations Disarmament Commission.[57] This body convened for three days on August 16-18, listened to a new United States proposal to begin diverting fissionable material from military to peaceful uses, and thereafter adopted a noncontroversial resolution favoring an early resumption of disarmament negotiations.[58] Though even the Soviet Union voted in favor of this text, Moscow gave no evidence of having modified its objections to the effective inspection and control which were still regarded by the Western powers as the only acceptable basis for disarmament.

In the midst of this excitement, the Geneva negotiations on the suspension of nuclear weapons tests had continued with just enough flexibility on both the Soviet and American sides to sustain the hope that they might ultimately lead to an agreement. If none of the important questions at issue had actually been resolved in recent weeks, certain differences had been narrowed and a number of technical definitions had been agreed upon. Although the meeting of scientists on the outlines of a research program had turned out disappointingly, the United States had continued to defer the start of "Project Vela" in the hope that the U.S.S.R. could still be persuaded to come in on a joint research effort. But meanwhile the agitation within the

United States for a resumption of nuclear weapons testing had not abated, and President Eisenhower indicated
on August 10 that in view of the "disappointing and discouraging" record at Geneva, the point might soon be
reached when "we have to take care of ourselves." The
only positive assurance Mr. Eisenhower could give in relation to this last surviving hope of early East-West agreement was that he did not intend to authorize further
nuclear testing in the atmosphere.[59]

15. IDEOLOGICAL AND ECONOMIC COMPETITION

If Khrushchev's own statements were to be believed,
these political differences between East and West represented only the surface of international affairs. The substance, in Khrushchev's view, consisted not in the direct
clashes of interest between the two blocs, sharp as these occasionally were, but in the underlying struggle between
the "socialist" and "capitalist" systems to demonstrate
their superiority and gain the allegiance of the uncommitted countries and ultimately of all mankind. Both in
the period of "relaxation of tensions" that preceded the
summit conference and in the hectic months that followed it, the actions of the Soviet Government reflected
the fundamental importance assigned to this contest in
every phase of Soviet policy. Each diplomatic move revealed, by its style even more than by its substance, the
determination to draw advantages for the U.S.S.R. from
the universal craving for peace and the almost equally
widespread revulsion against Western "colonialism." In
its world-wide propaganda operations, its programs of educational and cultural exchange, its far-flung trade relationships and its increasingly comprehensive schemes of
economic and technical assistance, Moscow plainly aimed
at the same fundamental objective of expanding its influence, winning acceptance for its ideas, and gradually
eliminating Western influence from one key area after
another.

Since the launching of Sputnik I in late 1957, accomplishments in the field of outer space research had represented one of the most potent elements in this long-term drive to convince the world of "socialist" preeminence. Although the U.S.S.R. was no longer alone in pioneering the empty reaches of space—in number and variety, the American space vehicles in orbit considerably exceeded those of Soviet origin throughout 1960—Moscow continued to exploit to good effect the advantages provided by the superior thrust of its rockets as well as the greater resonance of its propaganda. The firing of two experimental "space" rockets into the Central Pacific in January [60] was followed in early July by two more such flights, each allegedly for distances of over 8,000 miles. If these ostensibly peaceful feats appeared to have a significant military connotation as well, the "peaceful" element was clearly uppermost in the launching of a so-called "space ship," weighing nearly five tons and carrying a dummy space man, which was placed in orbit the day before the scheduled opening of the summit conference. On August 19 this achievement was topped in its turn by the launching of "Spacecraft II," with a passenger list that included two dogs and smaller animals which were claimed to have been safely returned to earth after twenty-four hours in orbit. Observers around the world began to brace themselves for an announcement from Moscow of the first human flight beyond the earth's atmosphere. But no such announcement came in 1960.

While these accomplishments and expectations were being trumpeted abroad by a propaganda apparatus that commanded facilities and resources far beyond those developed by Western countries, the U.S.S.R. continued to implement the far-reaching program of educational and cultural exchanges, involving both individuals and specialized groups, on which it apparently counted to develop over the years a growing appreciation of the Soviet way of life in countries that had not experienced it directly. The emphasis in these activities continued to be directed mainly, though by no means exclusively, to the Soviet-oriented and less developed, non-Western countries on which Moscow obviously counted to turn the world balance in its favor.

Khrushchev himself undertook an important role in these efforts with a journey to India, Burma, Indonesia, and Afghanistan during February and March in which he apparently sought—though with less than complete success —to obliterate the memory of President Eisenhower's Asian visit in December 1959.[61] In the course of his stay in Indonesia the Soviet leader promised President Sukarno a new development credit of $250 million and also announced plans for the establishment in Moscow of a "University of Friendship of Peoples" especially designed for students from Asian, African, and Latin American countries. Although there were occasional indications that Asian and African students already in the U.S.S.R. were not always satisfied with the treatment they received, the opening of the "Friendship University" later in the year testified once again to the importance Moscow attached to gaining an intellectual ascendancy among younger people in the developing countries.

The principal Western nations also had their place in Soviet exchange programs, and Khrushchev said several times that the exchanges of artists, technicians, and students agreed upon with the United States in 1958 should go forward despite the deterioration of political relations that followed the U-2 incident and the summit breakdown. Though Washington could claim no very spectacular results for the exchanges carried out thus far, it was reluctant to close this small aperture in the "Iron Curtain" and was strongly in favor of carrying forward the agreed program. It also made no attempt to discourage private American visits to the U.S.S.R., despite the difficulties encountered by some American travelers as a result of the intensified "spy mania" that developed during the summer.

Economic relations between the Soviet bloc and the outside world were also regarded in Moscow as an essential instrument for the advancement of over-all Soviet policy. The scope of these relations had been growing steadily through the later 1950's, and the increase in Soviet industrial and agricultural production provided a promising basis for their continued expansion in the 1960's. Although Communist foreign economic policy was governed at least in part by the normal economic objectives of securing materials and commodities needed by the Soviet bloc, it plainly revealed the additional motive of winning footholds in the non-Soviet world which could be used in support of Communist political aims. At times there had even been indications that the U.S.S.R. was engaging in a kind of economic warfare against selected free world countries by such measures as the unloading of excess raw materials at prices which disrupted free world markets and caused damage to competing suppliers.[62] In the main, however, both the U.S.S.R. and the other Communist countries took care to give their economic activities a "businesslike" appearance even at times when their political attitude was most menacing.

While the U.S.S.R. and its Communist associates had for years displayed keen interest in expanding their trade with the industrialized countries of the West, their most noteworthy advances in the economic field had indisputably been achieved in relations with the "less developed" Asian and African countries. Trade with the Western nations, though it had grown remarkably in recent years— even the United States reported a larger volume of exchanges with the U.S.S.R. in 1959 than in any previous year since 1950 [63]—was limited by the long-standing Western embargo on "strategic" shipments to the Communist bloc, by a lack of suitable financing, and by the frequent inability of the Communist countries to deliver the type of goods desired in the West. Most of the less developed countries, on the other hand, were hungry for basic industrial goods of a kind that Communist states like Czechoslovakia, Poland, or the "German Democratic Republic" could readily supply. They often had unmarketable surpluses of agricultural and industrial raw materials that could be offered in exchange. They had few political inhibitions about dealing with Communist nations, and they could generally count on an understanding attitude in regard to such matters as credits and terms of repayment. Although there had been cases in which one or another Communist country had failed to meet its commitments satisfactorily, the total trade turnover between the Soviet bloc (including Communist China) and the less developed countries was estimated to have increased by no less than 143 per cent between 1954 and 1958, from $871 million to $2.1 billion. Of this latter figure, the U.S.S.R. itself accounted for $676 million, the European satellites for $1,036 million, and Communist China for $409 million.[64]

If the U.S.S.R. had thus far lagged behind its satellites in trade relations with the less developed countries, it led the field in the equally important matter of grants and credits—especially credits—for economic development. While its motivations were believed in the West to be the opposite of those professed by the Western powers, assistance to less developed countries had come to play as important a role in over-all Communist policy as it did in that of the West. The volume of Communist aid, though still substantially below that made available from Western sources, had nevertheless been gradually increasing ever since 1954 and had reached a level of $1 billion a year in 1958 and 1959. Of the estimated total of about $3.8 billion which had been allocated by April 1960 (including some $800 million for military assistance to selected countries), the U.S.S.R. had provided $2.9 billion, its satellites $740 million, and Communist China $180 million. The bulk of this aid had been concentrated in substantial credits on favorable repayment terms to a few key countries, principally India, Afghanistan, the United Arab Republic, Iraq, and Indonesia.[65]

During the first eight months of 1960 the U.S.S.R. extended these commitments by authorizing important new credits to the U.A.R., to Indonesia, and to India, which had been granted a $375 million credit toward its third five-year plan in 1959 and accepted a new credit of 500 million rubles ($125 million at the unrealistic official exchange rate) in August 1960. In February Moscow also achieved its most spectacular penetration of the Western Hemisphere to date through a pair of agreements with Cuba that provided for a $100 million long-term credit plus a five-year commitment to purchase a million tons a year of Cuban sugar. In August, Ghana was added to the list of Soviet aid recipients. Communist Outer Mongolia was awarded a 615 million ruble development credit in September.[66] Significantly, most of these agreements provided for the services of Soviet technical experts in carrying out the development projects to be undertaken under their terms. Quite possibly the 6,500 Soviet bloc technicians who had already been at work in twenty-two of the less developed countries during the second half of 1959 would eventually be found to have been even more effective missionaries for the Communist cause than the explosive Mr. Khrushchev.

16. REUNION IN NEW YORK

In walking out of the ten-nation disarmament meetings on June 27, the U.S.S.R. had taken the position that the discussion of disarmament should now be returned to the United Nations General Assembly at its regular autumn session. When the United States proposed instead that the matter should be referred directly to the Disarmament Commission, Moscow did not back down but put forward a dramatic variation of its idea. The General Assembly was still the place, it insisted in a communication of August 1; but no ordinary session of the Assembly would really suffice for deliberations on so important a theme. To bring the discussion "to the proper level," according to this new Soviet view, the heads of government of the United Nations member states, particularly those with the greatest military power, should be invited to participate directly in the Assembly's work.[67]

This novel proposal was bound to arouse interest if only because it suggested a departure from Khrushchev's previous refusal to meet again with President Eisenhower. True, the idea of a "summit conference" involving eighty-two members of the United Nations could not commend itself to a realistic mind as a good way to make progress on disarmament. But while the United States and the other Western powers persisted in the plan to convoke the Disarmament Commission, Khrushchev held tenaciously to his own idea. No one, after all, could prevent him from going to the United Nations himself, whether or not the other heads of government wished to do so. The leaders of the Eastern European satellite states would naturally be ready to accompany him, and it soon turned out that only a little persuasion on his part was needed to induce a number of prominent neutral leaders to do likewise. Their example in turn was presently followed by many in the Western world, including Prime Minister Macmillan. By Soviet initiative, the Assembly session was thus given the appearance of at least a partial "summit" despite the coolness of the United States and various other governments to Khrushchev's original project. By the time the Assembly was ready to convene on September 20, only President de Gaulle appeared to be making a special point of staying away.

While setting the stage for this new act in the East-West drama and awaiting developments in the Congo, the Caribbean, and the interminable negotiations on nuclear weapons testing, the Soviet leader had also undertaken to stir renewed anxiety about the status of Berlin. During a visit to Austria early in July, he had voiced serious objections to a plan of the West German Bundestag to hold an autumn session in West Berlin in accordance with a custom established some years earlier. A suggestion that the U.S.S.R. might choose this delicate moment to unleash the East Germans was enough to touch off a prolonged and anxious debate in the German Federal Republic and the West, a debate which went on through the summer and ultimately resulted in an indefinite postponement of the proposed meeting.

In the meantime the East German authorities were beginning to introduce various new restrictions on travel to and from Berlin, principally by West Germans, thus raising once again the question of how Western rights in the city were going to be protected if the East insisted on overriding them. The angry notes exchanged at military and governmental levels [68] could not resolve the serious practical issue posed by these East German "salami tactics," as they were called by Willy Brandt, the Governing Mayor of West Berlin. If such encroachments were allowed to go unchallenged, they could lead in time to the complete isolation or strangulation of West Berlin. Yet if the West attempted any drastic retaliation, such as a suspension of trade between East and West Germany, there was always a possibility that the East might respond with stronger measures of its own, conceivably even a full blockade of the city.

These developments in the Berlin problem were only a reminder to the Germans and the Western governments of the insecurity of their position in the former German capital. They played no particular part in the new offensive against the West which Khrushchev opened up on his appearance in New York, and brought to a climax in a dramatic address to the General Assembly on September 23.[69] His evident objective in this forum was to impress the representatives of the neutralist group, particularly those from Asia and Africa. Combining vehement denunciation of American and Western policies with praise of "peaceful coexistence" on the Soviet pattern, he also introduced several novelties into his line of attack, among them a new and slightly modified set of disarmament proposals [70] and a plan to expand the ten-nation disarmament committee through the addition of five neutral states.[71] The attack on the world position of the West was also substantially broadened by the submission for the Assembly's approval of a special declaration calling in the most uncompromising terms for the "complete and final liquidation of the colonial regime." [72] Even more important, Khrushchev for the first time struck heavily at the United Nations itself by demanding the ouster of Secretary-General Hammarskjold and the remodeling of the Secretariat in such a way that it could no longer act in a manner unacceptable to the U.S.S.R.[73]

The scope and fury of this offensive did not discourage those neutral leaders who felt that Khrushchev's presence in New York presented an excellent opportunity to restore his broken contact with President Eisenhower and renew the seemingly peaceful trend in world affairs that had prevailed before the U-2 incident and the summit meeting. Mr. Eisenhower, it was true, had carefully avoided the Soviet leader on the occasion of his own address to the Assembly on September 22, in which he had offered certain new suggestions on disarmament and stressed the urgency of an agreement on outer space.[74] But Khrushchev had managed to convey the impression that he would not refuse a meeting if the President asked for it. Thus, without consulting the United States, a group of the most prominent neutral leaders—President Tito, Prime Minister Nehru, President Abdel Nasser, President Sukarno, and President Kwame Nkrumah of Ghana—prepared a formal resolution requesting an Eisenhower-Khrushchev meeting and presented it for the approval of the General Assembly.[75]

This move, which seemed likely to roll up an enthusiastic vote in the Assembly, was highly unwelcome to the United States. It was not certain that Khrushchev himself desired a meeting; but the Soviet leader must have gloated at the neutrals' discomfiture when the President, after a conference with Prime Minister Macmillan and Prime Minister R. G. Menzies of Australia, wrote to them on October 2 that he could not accept their suggestion. Soviet behavior thus far, he pointed out, had given him no reason to suppose that such an encounter would be useful.[76] Having allowed Mr. Eisenhower to take the responsibility of declining a meeting, Khrushchev wrote the neutral leaders next day that he could not meet the President in any case unless the latter was now ready to condemn the U-2 flights.[77] The disappointed neutrals thus had to content themselves with a general resolution in favor of a reduction of world tensions which was unanimously adopted by the Assembly a fortnight later.[78]

The question of a renewal of East-West contacts at the highest level did not end here, however. Prime Minister Macmillan had been as interested in investigating the prospects along this line as he had been in ensuring that Khrushchev's speeches in the Assembly were effectively answered on behalf of the West. His own address to the Assembly on September 29, which was interrupted on two occasions by shouts from the Soviet delegation chief, won general acclaim as a firm but temperate reply to Khrushchev's oratorical excesses.[79] His private talks with the Soviet leader on this and subsequent days had the further effect of renewing the discussion of a Big Four, as distinguished from a Big Two, meeting sometime after the American election.

As a result of these discussions, Khrushchev asserted at a news conference on October 7 that the Prime Minister had actually "assured" him that there would be a summit conference on Berlin and Germany shortly after January 20. The British, although they promptly denied that there had been any such "positive assurance," did not deny that Mr. Macmillan strongly favored the idea. Khrushchev himself indicated that he wanted two things. He wanted a summit conference on Berlin and Germany as soon as possible after the new American President was inaugurated; and he also wanted a special session of the General Assembly on disarmament, to be held not later than April 1961, preferably in Europe. If there was to be a summit conference shortly after the election, he added, the U.S.S.R. would "keep [its] word" about preserving the *status quo* in Berlin in the meantime. On the other hand, he repeated, if the West showed no desire to reach agreement, there would be a separate peace treaty with East Germany, and the "occupation regime" in West Berlin would be terminated.[80]

Neither Vice-President Nixon nor Senator Kennedy had thus far given any indication that he would be available to participate in a summit conference if he were elected. On the contrary, both candidates took the line that the failure at Paris had demonstrated once again the wisdom of avoiding such meetings unless the road to agreement had been carefully paved by diplomatic exchanges at lower levels.[81] Some observers nevertheless expressed the opinion that Khrushchev had it in his power to force a summit meeting at his own convenience simply by tightening the screws on Berlin. This was essentially the technique he had used in the past, before the Camp David meeting; and there seemed no reason to suppose that he would shrink from using it again, despite his current disclaimers of any intention to use "threats" or "force" in connection with the Berlin question.[82]

In any event, one of the main effects of Khrushchev's activities in New York was to revive the faltering hope of an eventual East-West understanding, and to encourage the somewhat dubious impression that agreement would be easier to reach after President Eisenhower had left the scene. This accomplishment, together with his effective cultivation of such neutralist or anti-American leaders as President Abdel Nasser, President Nkrumah, and Premier Castro, overshadowed in some ways Khrushchev's rather mixed achievement in regard to the regular business of the General Assembly, where he encountered a number of parliamentary defeats as well as registering some significant victories.[83] By opening a door to contact with the next American President, Khrushchev no doubt hoped not only to improve his standing in some of the non-Communist lands but also to strengthen his position in the increasingly intense ideological battle that was still raging within the Communist camp.

17. THE STRUGGLE GOES ON

We have already observed that Khrushchev's highly personal approach to the conduct of East-West relations could by no means claim the undivided support of the Soviet bloc or even, it would seem, the Communist hierarchy within the Soviet Union. Communist China, in particular, had continued even after the Bucharest meeting to espouse a much more militant revolutionary line, and openly challenged Khrushchev's views on such crucial issues as the possibility of a "socialist" victory without war.[84] While most of the other Communist parties had thus far appeared to take Khrushchev's side in the controversy, a few of them, including those of Eastern Germany and especially Albania, had shown signs of leaning toward the Chinese view. These matters were now to be threshed out in a much more fundamental way than had been possible at Bucharest by representatives of all of the Communist parties, to the number of some eighty-one, which were sending delegates to Moscow for the celebration on November 7 of the forty-third anniversary of the Bolshevik Revolution. The Chinese People's Republic was to be represented by chief of state Liu Shao-chi, who stood second only to Chairman Mao Tse-tung as an authority in ideological matters.

That this gathering happened to occur at the moment of the American election was, of course, purely fortuitous; nor did the American campaign reveal as great an interest in these internal Communist controversies as might have been expected from a country that only eight years earlier had proclaimed the principle of peaceful liberation of the nations enslaved by Communism. Liberation of the Soviet satellite countries was no longer a primary issue of American politics. Experience in the Hungarian revolt of 1956 had convinced most Americans that liberation without war was unlikely to take place in the foreseeable future, and the United States had accordingly continued the quiet but profound readjustment in its political and psychological attitude toward the Communist world which had been in progress ever since 1953.

President Eisenhower did, indeed, carry out the past instructions of the Congress by proclaiming a "Captive Nations Week" in 1960 as he had done in 1959; [85] but his statements on the subject made it clear that liberation was now regarded more as an ideal than as a practical objective. Although the goals of 1952 were "as yet unachieved," he told a Polish-American group on September 30, 1960, this did not mean "that anyone must give up hope." Liberation remained "a tenet in the faith of every right-thinking American," he emphasized, and the nation must "keep faithful to that ideal of freedom, well realizing that freedom and peace are in the long run indivisible." [86] Since neither presidential candidate dissented from this view in any fundamental way, the subject played no major part in the 1960 campaign. Senator Kennedy did offer a number of suggestions for establishing closer relations with the "Iron Curtain" countries, particularly Poland, in the hope of reducing their dependence on the Soviet bloc; but he strongly deprecated any rash promises to the peoples of Eastern Europe, and emphasized the wholly peaceful and evolutionary character of his recommendations. Vice-President Nixon promised that if elected he would visit each of the Eastern European countries to remind the world that their peoples would one day be "delivered out of bondage," but he too disclaimed any intention of trying to arouse revolutionary movements which, under the circumstances, would be bound to fail. [87]

The idea of encouraging a greater sense of independence within the Soviet bloc countries, especially Poland, was not in itself new. Ever since 1956 the United States had been attempting to apply such a policy in Poland, mainly by assisting the regime of Wladyslaw Gomulka with small credits and surplus food deals and by encouraging cultural and intellectual exchanges with the Polish people. A new $60 million farm surplus agreement had been concluded as recently as July 21, 1960 in the wake of a settlement of United States financial claims against Poland.[88] In the course of his subsequent visit to the United Nations, Mr. Gomulka alone among the Soviet bloc leaders was received by Secretary Herter—though not by the President, as he had apparently hoped—and arrangements were made for a new concession involving the restoration of the most-favored-nation treatment of Polish imports which had been revoked by the United States in 1951.[89] Such measures had had no visible effect on Poland's official allegiance to the Soviet bloc, but were considered useful as a means of keeping open the channels of communication with a nation that had not forgotten its historical ties with the United States.

In its contacts with other Soviet-bloc countries, the United States had also seemed to be working toward a gradual normalization of relations, if not toward anything approaching cordiality. The prohibition on American travel to Hungary was lifted early in the year,[90] and, although the United States insisted as usual that the continued defiance of the United Nations by the Kádár regime and the U.S.S.R. be brought to the attention of the General Assembly, the substance of the Hungarian question did not come up for debate during the 1960 part of the session.[91] Diplomatic relations with Bulgaria, severed in 1950, were restored in March pursuant to a decision made in 1959. With Rumania there was an agreement on the settlement of financial claims, followed toward the end of the year by the decision to institute a small cultural exchange program on the United States-Soviet model.[92]

Yugoslavia, of course, was no longer identified with the Soviet bloc and enjoyed a very satisfactory relationship with the United States, notwithstanding the tendency of Marshal Tito's government to take a contrary position on most important international issues. Although Tito and Khrushchev managed an appearance of cordiality during their visit to New York, Yugoslavia did not participate in the subsequent meeting of Communist party representatives, and remained an outcast in the eyes of the rest of the Communist world. In trade and economic matters, the Belgrade regime had for some years been gravitating toward closer participation in the free world economic system that centered in the General Agreement on Tariffs and Trade (GATT). Continued movement in this direction was assured by the announcement on December 27 of a series of credits from Western sources to enable Yugoslavia to carry out a program of monetary and trade reforms within the framework of a new five-year plan which was to start in 1961. Of the total projected assistance of $275 million, the International Monetary Fund planned to provide $75 million, Western European governments and banks $100 million, and the United States $100 million from the Export-Import Bank, the Development Loan Fund, and the Mutual Security Program.[93]

The failure of the Eastern European problem to emerge as a prominent issue in United States-Soviet relations during 1960 may have afforded some encouragement to Premier Khrushchev in his renewed attempt to justify his theories and methods before the Communist party chiefs assembled in Moscow. That he was anxious to obtain an opportunity of giving the methods of "peaceful coexistence" another trial seemed very evident from his reaction to the news of Senator Kennedy's election just as the ideological discussions were about to get under way. In earlier comments on the election campaign, the Soviet leader had expressed some personal dislike of Vice-President Nixon but had insisted on his fundamental indifference as to the outcome. "A pair of boots," he had called the two candidates, in allusion to their supposedly equal addiction to the policies of "cold war" and "positions of strength." But once Senator Kennedy's election was assured, Khrushchev lost no time in sending off a most cordial message (to which the Senator returned a polite if noncommittal reply),[94] while the Soviet press and diplomats began to intimate that the

American people, having had the "good sense" to repudiate the "Eisenhower policies," had cleared the way for a new effort to establish peace on a solid basis.

In accordance with this view that things might change once Senator Kennedy was inaugurated—an assumption that surely found no basis in the Senator's own statements —Soviet diplomacy gave evidence during the late autumn of a disinclination to force any of the pending issues while the Eisenhower administration remained in office. There were no important new threats on Berlin, and the virulence of the attacks on the German Federal Republic abated. A note of moderation appeared in Moscow's encouragement of the Castro government in Cuba.[95] The disarmament question was left for the moment in the hands of the United Nations, where a full dozen resolutions were under discussion in the Political Committee, though only three of them—urging continued suspension of nuclear weapons tests and opposing the spread of nuclear weapons —were finally approved before the year-end recess.[96] At Geneva, where the conference on the suspension of nuclear weapons tests had recently reached agreement on an annex setting forth the privileges and immunities of the proposed control organization,[97] the delegates marked time for a few weeks longer and then adjourned on December 5 to await the views of the Kennedy administration. Senator Kennedy had promised "one last great effort" to reach agreement before ordering a resumption of underground tests.[98]

But if all this looked like a reversion to the kind of policy that had prevailed before the U-2 and the summit, it was by no means certain as yet that it represented more than a temporary interlude. Throughout these weeks the representatives of the eighty-one Communist parties were meeting behind closed doors, and with minimal publicity. After their adjournment on December 1, it required several days more to draft the 20,000-word declaration that was to embody the fruit of their deliberations. And the declaration, when it finally appeared on December 6,[99] was nothing if not circumspect in its endorsement of Khrushchev's views. "Yes, but"—such was its general position on the policy of "peaceful coexistence," on the possibility of "socialist" victory without war, on the possibility of non-violent revolutions, and on all the other points in controversy. What the document seemed to represent was a skillfully worded compromise between the Soviet (Khrushchev) and Chinese viewpoints, one that nominally endorsed the former but at the same time virtually nullified it with reservations and qualifications. Just who got the best of the compromise was a matter for debate among experts. The Chinese, at least, seemed clearly determined to go their own way, even though for form's sake they had paid lip service to the rival thesis.

About at least one thing, however, the declaration was unequivocal. This was the assertion that "socialism" was winning its battle for the world and that the time had come for an intensified struggle—described, of course, as a struggle for "peace"—against the "imperialist" camp and especially against the United States. "United States imperialism" said the declaration, "is the chief bulwark of world reaction and . . . has become an enemy of the peoples of the whole world. . . . The broadest possible united front of peace supporters, fighters against the imperialist policy of aggression and war inspired by U.S. imperialism, is essential to preserve world peace." Such language, repeated in somewhat muted form in an "Appeal to the Peoples of the World" that was shortly issued in the name of the eighty-one Communist parties,[100] did not suggest that Communists in general were animated by any overwhelming desire for an understanding with the new American administration. Some American students of Communist affairs found themselves wondering more and more about the position of Khrushchev himself, the one ardent advocate of negotiations with the West. Had he really been speaking for the Soviet Union, or only for himself?

At all events, the tone of the declaration suggested a strong probability that the United States and its allies would face an intensified challenge in the coming months, and one that would probably not be confined to the economic and psychological arena. The economic and psychological battle was still going forward, of course. Although the U.S.S.R.'s only satellite launching during these weeks turned out to be a partial failure, Moscow had scored one important psychological point on November 11 by announcing plans for an arbitrary revaluation of the Soviet ruble from $0.25 to $1.11, effective at the beginning of 1961. This move would actually involve a sharp reduction in the gold content of the ruble; but its natural effect would be to raise the Soviet monetary unit in popular esteem at a moment when the United States was displaying real alarm about its own gold outflow and the future of the dollar.[101]

The U.S.S.R. also made several new moves on the economic aid front during these weeks, including a $47,-770,000 loan to North Vietnam, a promise of increased assistance to Cuba, and the offer of a $150 million credit to Bolivia. But December also brought ominous signs of a "tougher" diplomatic attitude in the Congo, in Latin America and in Laos, where something approaching a major crisis had developed by mid-December and where the U.S.S.R. was openly intervening by the end of the month.[102] It was true that Khrushchev continued to show a keen desire for contact with the next American President, notwithstanding the skepticism about "summit diplomacy" attributed both to Mr. Kennedy and to Dean Rusk, the prospective Secretary of State. By New Year's Eve, the Soviet leader was even offering to forget about the U-2 incident.[103] Yet even if 1961 was to bring a renewal of discussions at the highest level, the Communist world had once again made clear beyond the possibility of doubt that its true aim was not just an understanding with the "imperialist camp," but its total defeat—a defeat that would remove the last obstacle to what was regarded in Communist circles as the inevitable, world-wide triumph of Communist "socialism."

CHAPTER THREE

THE WESTERN COMMUNITY

IN THE DECADE and more that had elapsed since the conclusion of the North Atlantic Treaty, Americans had lived through some lively debates about the importance of Europe to America, and Europeans had engaged in a good deal of discussion about the importance of the United States to them. As the 1960's began, such arguments about the fundamental necessity of the Atlantic partnership seemed at least temporarily to have subsided. Since Sputnik and, more particularly, since the opening of Khrushchev's campaign against free Berlin in late 1958, majority opinion throughout the "Atlantic Community"—in the United States and Canada, in Britain and on the Continent, in Greece and Turkey at the eastern end of the Mediterranean—had tended to view the association of the Western nations with renewed attachment. Awkward and inconvenient though it might be at times, it seemed too necessary to all its members to be challenged in any basic way. Outside of the pro-Communist and neutralist circles that were still influential in a few Western countries, political discussion within the Western family hinged not so much on the acceptability of the Western association as on the possibility of improving it, neutralizing its possible dangers, and making it into a more effective instrument for promoting common interests while safeguarding the national interests of its individual members.

18. WESTERN PROBLEM AREAS

That there was ample room for improvement of existing arrangements in the military, economic, and political fields was nowhere questioned, however vehemently men might disagree about what exactly needed to be done. The Soviet threat which had brought NATO into being in 1949 might still persist, but its form had plainly altered almost beyond recognition. Other developments of the past few years had all but outmoded some of the original conceptions of the NATO association. The progressive shift from conventional to nuclear weapons, and from aircraft to missiles, had revolutionized the bases of military strategy and was widely felt to require a fundamental rethinking of the military problems involved in defending the North Atlantic area. In many minds it had raised a question as to whether the United States might not eventually decide to withdraw the substantial forces it had been maintaining on the European Continent—currently reckoned at five divisions and three armored units—and rely primarily on its home-based and seaborne missiles to deter any Soviet attack that might be threatened in the future against either Western Europe or North America.

Despite signs of uneasiness in Washington about the increased balance-of-payments deficit and the large expenditures involved in keeping its forces overseas, such a move did not appear by any means imminent in early 1960. At the moment, the United States appeared more interested in stiffening the NATO defense system in Western Europe with nuclear weapons and intermediate-range missiles which might help to hold the Russians in check until America's long-range missile capability had been further developed. Yet although virtually no one in the United States now talked of "writing off" Western Europe, the possibility of an eventual American withdrawal inevitably played a role in the long-range calculations of European statesmen. In the meantime, there was a question about the degree of real protection afforded by American bombers and missiles at a time when the U.S.S.R. already appeared to be in a position to loose its own nuclear-armed missiles at American cities. If American efforts to deter a Soviet attack in Europe involved a risk of the destruction of Washington or New York, there might be at least a theoretical possibility that the United States would decide at the last moment to keep its deterrent forces from going into action—or that the U.S.S.R. might gamble on its doing so. Some people in Europe had suggested that under these circumstances it would be better for the Europeans to have a nuclear deterrent capability of their own which could, if necessary, be employed independently of the United States. Others had merely been strengthened in their aversion to all nuclear weapons as a matter of principle.

The changes of the past decade in economic relations between the United States and its European associates had been equally momentous. No one could any longer claim that the once war-devastated countries of Western Europe required further American help in restoring their economic life. If anything, the shoe was now on the other foot: the United States was looking squarely to its European partners to assist in coping with the budgetary, trade, and balance-of-payments problems that had begun to trouble it so severely within the past year or so. The time had come, Washington now insisted, for the revitalized countries of Western Europe to assume a larger share of the burdens of collective defense, to expand their hitherto rather limited assistance to less developed countries, and to open their markets to American goods on a genuinely nondiscriminatory basis. Because of its anxiety to ensure a fair deal for American exporters, Washington had been observing with particular attention of late the development of the new regional economic organizations that had emerged in Western Europe, the six-nation European Economic Community or "common market" established by France, Western Germany, Italy, and the Benelux group, and the seven-nation European Free Trade Association which was being set up in answer to it by Great Britain and six continental nations.

The dramatic material recovery of Western Europe had naturally brought with it a tendency on the part of European governments to pay a somewhat reduced deference to United States views in political matters. This trend had been startlingly illustrated as far back as the Suez crisis of 1956. Increasing independence of the United States did not mean, however, that the other Western countries had drawn closer together in their own political viewpoints. Despite years of emphasis on the ideals of European unity, radical divergencies of outlook persisted even within the non-Communist section of the Western family. While the essential freedom that permitted and even encouraged such differences was undoubtedly one of the chief glories of the West, its results were often inconvenient and sometimes even dangerous at a time when the whole Western community was under continuous pressure from the Soviet bloc and, to an increasing extent, from the Asian and African countries as well. Not only between the various Western countries but even within individual countries, the most varied attitudes prevailed on all the great questions of the day: on policy toward the Soviet Union, on colonialism and the independence movement in African countries, on defense policy and nuclear weapons, on intra-European organization, on the proper role and position of some of the Western countries themselves.

A central element in many of the current problems of the Western world was the attitude of France under the new leadership established by General de Gaulle in 1958. From an over-all Western viewpoint, the substitution of a strong presidential regime for the unstable interplay of French parties that had prevailed under the Fourth Republic had thus far seemed to create almost as many problems as it solved. French cabinets were no longer being toppled at the rate of three or four a year, and the increase in political stability had been accompanied by a remarkable improvement in economic conditions. The new French

President had not, however, succeeded as yet in halting the five-year-old war in Algeria, which represented a serious military, political, and moral handicap not only to France but to the entire Western community; nor had he been able to overcome the related differences among Frenchmen which on two occasions, in May 1958 and in January 1960, came close to plunging the country into civil war.

At the same time, President de Gaulle's determination to restore his country to an independent role in world affairs placed him in direct opposition to the prevailing movement toward a closer integration of Western military, economic, and political efforts. France's new chief executive insisted on his country's right to develop an independent nuclear capability, claimed equality with the United States and Britain in the formulation of global policy, demanded maximum autonomy for the French military forces in NATO, and, while nominally accepting for France the obligations of membership in the six-nation European Economic Community, had rejected the "supranational" concept which was supposed to be one of that organization's main features. If the close personal relationship he had established with Chancellor Adenauer had helped to attenuate the historic Franco-German enmity, it had also contributed to the rather strained relations between Great Britain and the continental bloc which was finding its clearest expression at the moment in the rivalry between the Common Market and the Free Trade Area.

But France was by no means the West's only problem nation. The German Federal Republic had always presented special problems for Western policy, partly because of its unusual position as a former enemy country and partly because of the dangers resulting from the division of Germany and the direct exposure of Western Germany to Communist pressures of many kinds. The current threat to Berlin had served to highlight both the inherent perils of the German situation and the important role of the Federal Republic as a bastion of the West—a role that was becoming ever more vital as the German military forces built toward their twelve-division target.

But although West German support of the alliance had undoubtedly been as steady as that of any of the member states, Germany's unenviable record in the Hitler period had not been forgotten in Great Britain and other neighboring countries. A flurry of anti-Semitic and pro-Nazi activity which took place within the Federal Republic in late 1959 and early 1960 aroused misgivings in many Western quarters and provided new arguments for the unremitting Soviet propaganda campaign on the theme of reviving German militarism and Nazism. Chancellor Adenauer's efforts to convince allied nations that such phenomena had no roots in the new Germany were in no way assisted by the disclosure early in 1960 that representatives of the Bonn government had been quietly investigating the possibility of establishing German training and supply bases in Spain. Though it was recognized that the German forces had a legitimate need for certain military facilities outside the restricted territory of the Federal Republic, the secretive manner in which they had been sought caused a setback to the acceptance of Western Germany as a full and equal partner of the other Western nations.

The relations between Great Britain and the German Federal Republic had been particularly lacking in cordiality in recent years. Wartime memories, economic and commercial rivalries, differing views on the Soviet problem, and personal factors all played a part in the coolness that normally prevailed between Bonn and London.

The United States, too, occasionally seemed less than enthusiastic about the British attitude in world politics, notwithstanding the traditional intimacy between the two governments and the personal friendship between President Eisenhower and Prime Minister Macmillan. With no other country except Canada was the United States so closely linked in defense matters. The vital role assumed by the British defense forces in Western strategy was fully acknowledged in Washington. So was the firmly pro-

American attitude of the Prime Minister and Foreign Secretary Lloyd. On the other hand, the eagerness of the British leaders to find a basis for accommodation with the U.S.S.R. often led them to take positions that from an American standpoint seemed inconvenient and even ill-advised. Americans could not rid themselves of the feeling that there was a goodly share of wishful thinking in the British approach to East-West problems.

Whatever the attitude of the British Government, more-over, it was well known in Washington that a substantial section of British opinion was highly critical of the Western reliance on nuclear weapons, of the growing rearmament of Germany, and of the use of British bases by American nuclear-armed bombers. The Labor party, the only likely alternative to the existing Conservative government, was veering in the direction of outright condemnation of existing Western defense arrangements. Nor were American policy-makers at all happy about the split between Britain and the major continental powers which had helped to bring about the formation of the two rival trade blocs and might lead, if some pessimistic predictions were realized, to a major economic conflict within the Western family at the very time when all of the Western nations needed to pool their energies in response to the massive challenge of Soviet "competitive coexistence."

19. E.E.C., E.F.T.A., AND O.E.C.D.

The threatened division of Western Europe into rival trade blocs was not an entirely new development. It might better be described as the latest phase in a conflict between two different attitudes or conceptions regarding the future of Europe which had been apparent throughout the process of European economic recovery and growing cooperation over the past dozen years.

On one side of the argument were those who looked beyond the immediate tasks of economic and military collaboration in Western Europe to the formation of a close

European union which would eventually extend into all fields of public life and might culminate in the establishment of a supranational European federation or "United States of Europe." The chief embodiment of this conception, now somewhat weakened by the attitude of the de Gaulle government, was the association of France, West Germany, Italy, Belgium, the Netherlands, and Luxembourg, the six nations which had joined in forming the European Coal and Steel Community (E.C.S.C.), the European Atomic Energy Community (Euratom), and the European Economic Community (E.E.C.) or Common Market established pursuant to the Rome treaties of March 25, 1957.

In the opposite camp were those countries, headed by Great Britain, whose governments tended to favor a much more limited type of intra-European cooperation, rejected membership in a political federation, and had felt unable or unwilling to participate in a common market of the type that their friends of "the Six" were now forming. Confronted with a possible loss of export markets within the Common Market area, the so-called "Outer Seven" countries—Great Britain, Norway, Denmark, Sweden, Portugal, Switzerland, and Austria—had decided in 1959 to form a European Free Trade Association (E.F.T.A.) and had drawn up an appropriate convention which was initialed in Stockholm on November 20, 1959 and went into effect May 3, 1960.[1] The E.F.T.A. arrangement resembled the Common Market in that it provided for the gradual elimination of internal tariff barriers among the members of the association. Unlike the Common Market, it would have no common external tariff but would leave each member free to preserve its existing tariff arrangements affecting outside countries. Great Britain, for example, could maintain the system of imperial preference that had long existed within the Commonwealth.

The E.F.T.A. members had not particularly liked the idea of cutting themselves off from their neighbors of the Six by setting up a rival trading association. Most of them had preferred to think of their action not as a final step toward the division of Europe, but rather as a necessary step toward reaching a new understanding with the Six and establishing some kind of all-European free trade area of a kind that all parties could accept. The various measures involved in setting up the two organizations had nevertheless occasioned a great deal of mutual suspicion and much talk of supposed ulterior motives, accentuated to some extent by the differences among France, Western Germany, and Great Britain on policy toward the U.S.S.R. and on various other matters unrelated to the East-West problem. Thus a development that might from one point of view have looked like a promising growth of international cooperation actually took place in a climate of deteriorating political relations which by the end of 1959 could be regarded as a genuine threat to the interests of the Western community as a whole.

As a long-time advocate of European unity, the United States had avoided taking a definite stand on these issues except to warn both sides that it would look with disfavor on any arrangement that violated the rules of the General Agreement on Tariffs and Trade (GATT) and placed American exporters at an unfair disadvantage. Although Washington had appeared to feel a certain partiality for the Common Market because of what were assumed to be its greater political potentialities, it made no attempt to bring any influence to bear in the matter until late 1959, when the situation had already reached a somewhat threatening stage and when the United States itself had become seriously alarmed about its balance-of-payments deficit. A series of consultations carried out in Europe by Under-Secretary Dillon in preparation for the Western "summit" meeting in December 1959 was followed early in 1960 by a major American initiative, inspired by the twofold aim of heading off the threatened trade clash and relieving the American balance of payments by enlisting greater European participation in aid to less developed countries.

Among the essential features of the so-called "Dillon

plan" was a modification of the United States' own relationship with its European partners in such a way as to permit the discussion of common economic problems in a Western rather than a purely European framework. This was to be accomplished by the reorganization or, possibly, the replacement of the eighteen-nation Organization for European Economic Cooperation (O.E.E.C.), a group to which both the Six and the Seven belonged and in which the United States and Canada participated as associate members. In the revised organization it was contemplated that the United States and Canada would become full members, thus dramatizing the broadened scope of current Western economic preoccupations.

The forum to which the Dillon plan was officially presented was a so-called "Special Economic Committee," representing twelve O.E.E.C. participants and the European Economic Community, which met in Paris on January 12-13, 1960. What Mr. Dillon proposed, and the committee approved with minor changes, was the establishment of a series of *ad hoc* study groups to examine (1) the relationship between E.E.C. and E.F.T.A.; (2) the question of aid to underdeveloped areas; and (3) a reorganization of the O.E.E.C. in such a way as to equip it for the new tasks of the 1960's and to permit full participation by the United States and Canada. Mr. Dillon's intimation that the United States would be willing to consider full membership in the O.E.E.C. or its successor organization was the clearest indication of the importance Washington now attached to securing action on the other two problems.[2]

Since the American proposals called for study rather than for immediate action, there was no serious impediment to putting them into effect. A Development Assistance Group, representing eight European nations plus the United States, Japan, and the E.E.C. Commission, met in Washington in March and held two further meetings later in the year to discuss means of increasing the flow of development aid to less developed countries.[3] Since the question of a redistribution of aid burdens did not figure officially in its agenda, its main accomplishments presumably lay in the field of mutual education.

The problem of reorganizing the O.E.E.C. was entrusted to a committee of four "wise men"—Ambassador W. Randolph Burgess was the American member—who presently produced the blueprint of a twenty-nation "Organization for Economic Cooperation and Development" (O.E.C.D.), equipped, like the O.E.E.C., with both a secretary-general and a council of ministers. (The words "Atlantic" and "Western" were carefully excluded from the name of the proposed organization out of consideration for those O.E.E.C. members which did not participate in NATO). Discussed at an intergovernmental conference in May and subsequently revised by a new working group, the O.E.C.D. project was subjected to further modifications at a ministerial-level meeting in Paris on July 22-23, and was then handed on to a preparatory committee with instructions to submit a final text for approval before the end of the year. The most evident concern of the United States throughout these proceedings was to guard against the new organization's being given such extensive powers, especially in the trade field, as to prejudice its acceptability to the American Congress.[4]

On the more pressing issue of the rival trade blocs, the hope of avoiding a clash between E.E.C. and E.F.T.A. was only partially realized. All parties had now been made aware of the importance attached by the United States to an adjustment between the two blocs—an adjustment which, American spokesmen continued to emphasize, must be fully consistent with the multilateral and nondiscriminatory principles of the GATT organization. But the twenty-nation "Committee on Trade Problems" which met in Paris to consider the issue on March 29-30 found the situation severely complicated as the result of a new plan which had been developed in E.E.C.—supported more or less warmly by the United States, but strongly resented by the E.F.T.A. group—to accelerate the movement of the

Six toward a common tariff by making a very substantial new adjustment in tariff rates as early as July 1, 1960.

After some rather acrimonious discussions, the E.E.C. decided to spread the adjustment over a somewhat longer period, and the situation was further eased by agreements between the two blocs to keep on talking and to try to deal with the most acute problems on a commodity-by-commodity basis. Certain statements made in Great Britain in the wake of the summit conference improved the atmosphere to some extent by suggesting a willingness on Britain's part to consider at least a degree of association with the Six in future. But no long-range solution was in sight by July 1, when an initial 10 per cent reduction in internal tariffs by E.F.T.A. and a second 10 per cent cut by E.E.C. (the first had been made on January 1, 1959) carried Europe a long step further toward actual economic separation.[5] Any real rapprochement between the two groups, it appeared, would require a stronger impulse than either the Dillon plan or the recent failure of the summit conference had supplied.

20. DEFENDING THE NORTH ATLANTIC AREA

The economic problems of Western Europe were an inescapable concern of every member of the proposed O.E.C.D., not excluding the politically neutral governments of Austria, Ireland, Sweden, and Switzerland. The military defense of Western Europe and the "North Atlantic area," in contrast, rested essentially on the narrower basis of the fifteen NATO members and Spain, a country that did not belong to the Western alliance but nevertheless played an essential role in Western defense through the presence on its territory of some of the most important of America's overseas air and naval bases.

Through most of the 1950's the key to an effective discharge of NATO's defense responsibilities had been held to lie in the building up of a powerful "shield force" on the European Continent, as a direct protection to NATO's

TOGETHERNESS

Mauldin in the *St. Louis Post-Dispatch*

continental members and an essential counterpart of the nuclear deterrent forces maintained by the United States and Great Britain. Superimposed on this problem since the opening of the missile age in 1957 had been the attempt to reinforce the deterrent power of the alliance through the introduction of nuclear weapons into the "shield force" and the stationing of intermediate-range ballistic missiles in Britain and on the Continent.

The advent of the de Gaulle government in 1958 had complicated these endeavors because of the French President's demand for an equal voice in Western strategy, his insistence on greater military autonomy for France, his withdrawal of the French fleet from NATO control, his refusal to accept the placement of nuclear-armed missiles on French soil unless France was given a veto on their use, and his objections to French participation in an integrated air defense system for Western Europe. Though not the only power that insisted on having its own way in important fields of NATO activity, France under its new President had been by all odds the most conspicuous and the most systematic.

Symbolic of the French attitude had been General de Gaulle's determination that France should develop its own nuclear weapons and eventually possess its own atomic striking force. As a nuclear power, the French leader apparently reasoned, France would not only be less dependent on its allies but would gain increased influence and bargaining power within the alliance. Among other, more intangible advantages, it might have a better chance of inducing the United States to share its own atomic secrets with France, as was being done with Great Britain and to a lesser extent with several other NATO countries.

The critical step in the French program was successfully taken—to the extreme annoyance of several African governments—with the detonation of two French atomic devices in the Sahara on February 13 and April 1, 1960. But although France thus won recognition as the fourth member of the world's "atomic club," hitherto limited to the United

States, Britain, and the U.S.S.R., it soon became evident that this achievement was not regarded in authoritative American quarters as a sufficient reason for relaxing the restrictions imposed by Congress on the transfer of nuclear equipment and technology to other countries.

President de Gaulle himself paid a long-deferred visit to Washington late in April, and was doubtless informed that the whole question of equipping NATO with up-to-date nuclear armaments had been under discussion within the American Government without, as yet, reaching any clear-cut resolution. In February, President Eisenhower had indicated that he personally would favor a change in the atomic energy law that would enable the United States to supply trusted allies with atomic information and even weapons of those types already available to the Russians; [6] but his statement had produced a strongly adverse reaction on the part of leading congressmen and other Americans opposed to the further spread of nuclear weapons. Among the cogent objections that had been raised was the likelihood that the U.S.S.R. might try to counter such a plan by handing out nuclear weapons to its own allies in the Warsaw Pact. The same objection had been raised in connection with a recent plan attributed to General Lauris Norstad, NATO's Supreme Commander in Europe, which involved the formation within NATO of an international "task force" equipped with atomic weapons.[7] For the moment, there thus appeared to be no prospect of an early change in the existing system whereby NATO forces in Europe received training in some phases of nuclear combat while the actual weapons, together with much of the pertinent information concerning them, remained under the exclusive control of the United States.

A similar principle applied to the nuclear-armed intermediate-range missiles which were in process of being set up at bases in Great Britain, Italy, and Turkey as an answer to the U.S.S.R.'s long-range missiles. By early 1960 it was being said that at least one of the four "Thor" missile bases in the United Kingdom and one of the two

"Jupiter" bases in Italy had reached operational status, the nuclear warheads remaining in American custody unless and until needed. Originally conceived primarily as a stopgap arrangement pending the development of American long-range missiles based in the United States, it now appeared that American I.R.B.M.'s based in Europe would represent an important element in the Western deterrent for some time to come. In April the British Government announced that it had decided to abandon the development for military purposes of the British "Blue Streak" missile, relying instead on American-built "Polaris" missiles and, at a later stage, on the air-launched American "Skybolt." The rapid development of the Polaris, which was expected to become operational in the United States Navy in the fall of 1960 but could also be fired from mobile launching platforms on land, had enabled the United States to intimate to its allies that within the next two or three years it could make quantities of these missiles available for deployment under NATO auspices in such countries as Italy, Belgium or the Netherlands, and perhaps Western Germany and France.[8] There had also been talk of supplementing the land-based missile system with a fleet of American Polaris-armed submarines stationed in European waters.

To the extent that they involved Great Britain, France, or Germany, such projects would continue to run up against special political problems—in the British case, the widespread opposition to the basing of nuclear weapons in the United Kingdom; in the French, General de Gaulle's insistence on ultimate control over the employment of any missiles set up in French territory; and in the case of Germany, the opposition to West German rearmament, particularly nuclear rearmament, which continued to exist on both sides of the "Iron Curtain." The furor created by Bonn's quest for logistics bases in Spain did not provide the most favorable atmosphere for consideration of any new measures that would tend to convert the Federal Republic into a nuclear power. In the midst of its preoccupation with the Berlin problem and the U-2 incident, the Soviet Government found time during the spring to issue a stream of notes and statements protesting NATO's alleged plans to arm the "West German revenge-seekers" with atomic weapons and missiles. Though Soviet objections presumably had no effect on the development of the allied plans, which were still highly tentative in any case, they played an important part in Moscow's unremitting efforts to mislead world opinion about the real sources of the tension in Europe.

Despite the gradual trend toward a greater concentration of nuclear and missile power in Europe, North America would obviously remain the center of the Western defense system for a long time to come. Nothing that was done in Western Europe would be of much avail if the United States and Canada were put out of action by a Soviet missile attack. The defense of North America was not only a formal obligation under the terms of the North Atlantic Treaty but a vital concern of all NATO nations, scarcely less important than the defense of their own territories.

In the absence of an effective means of anti-missile defense, the deterrence of a Soviet attack on North America in the next few years could be expected to rest primarily on the capacity for prompt retaliation by the United States against the Soviet Union. We have already noted that there were varying opinions as to the prospects of maintaining such a capacity as the Soviet missile inventory increased.[9] The elaborate continental defense arrangements already in existence as a joint project of the United States and Canada were designed primarily to deal with an attack by manned aircraft, and would have at best a very limited usefulness in the event of a missile attack. About the best that could be hoped for in the latter eventuality would be to get sufficiently prompt notice of an attack so that the retaliatory forces could be ordered into immediate action rather than waiting to be destroyed on the ground.

This, presumably, was the essential purpose of the new

Ballistic Missile Early Warning System (BMEWS), with its huge radar installations at Thule, Greenland, at Clear, Alaska, and at Fylingdales Moor, Yorkshire, which was currently being set up by the United States with the cooperation of Denmark and the United Kingdom. The inauguration of the Thule station in the fall of 1960 and of the Clear station sometime in 1961 was expected to provide upward of fifteen minutes' notice of the approach of hostile missiles, a margin that *might* prove critically significant to the defense of North America and, indirectly, of the entire Western world.

21. WESTERN POLITICS BEFORE THE SUMMIT

With all its shortcomings, cooperation among the Western nations in economic and military matters went far beyond anything they had known in the period before the Marshall Plan and the establishment of NATO. In political affairs, too, experience in NATO and the discipline of years of negotiation with the U.S.S.R. had brought the principal Western governments to a degree of unity on many essential matters which was all the more remarkable in view of the differing interests and preconceptions with which they had started out. Such unity, it is true, was seldom complete even in questions involving the Russians, and was much less evident in relation to those problems that concerned only the Western family or their relations in the non-Communist world.

Great Britain, Belgium, France, the Netherlands, and Portugal, all of which administered important overseas territories, naturally took a somewhat different view of "colonial" issues from that of countries like Greece or Norway which had no responsibilities in this field. Occasionally, moreover, there had been sharp clashes of interest and policy between individual members of the Western family. Iceland and Great Britain had been at odds for some time over the question of fishing rights in waters off the Icelandic coast, a matter of economic importance to both countries which hinged in part on a disputed point of international law that two successive United Nations conferences had been unable to resolve.[10] A quarrel about the future of Cyprus which had caused much bad blood among Great Britain, Greece, and Turkey had been settled early in 1959 by an agreement to give that British-held island the status of an independent republic. But the implementation of this plan, originally scheduled to go into effect on February 19, 1960, had been delayed by further arguments about the size and status of the military bases which Great Britain proposed to retain in Cyprus with the consent of its new government. Still another source of dissension among Western nations, this one involving the relations of a NATO member with one of Europe's politically neutral states, was an increasingly embittered quarrel between Austria and Italy about the status of the German-speaking population in Italy's Trentino-Alto Adige region.

Such differences were hardly of a nature to lead to active hostilities under the conditions of the postwar world. From the standpoint of larger Western interests, their main importance lay in the possibility that they might lead to a weakening of solidarity and even a drift toward neutralism on the part of allies that felt their interests unfairly neglected. It was well known that Moscow relied in part on the quarrels of its adversaries to destroy the unity of the free world, and the Western cause could ill afford the loss of such small but strategic countries as Iceland or Greece, both of which had for years been the objects of special attention in Moscow. In the main, however, the Soviet Government employed more direct methods of creating division in the West. More than by taking sides in the conflicts between Western governments, it normally concentrated on trying to stir up disagreement between the Western governments and their own peoples by appealing to the pacifist, antimilitarist, neutralist, anti-German and anti-American tendencies in European opinion and calling on the peoples of Western Europe to ensure "peace" by repudiating the misguided policies of their accredited leaders.

For every phase of the official Western policy in Europe, the U.S.S.R. and its Communist satellites had managed to devise an alternative program of the sort that would be likely to appeal to disaffected elements in the West and, if accepted, would materially advance the interests of the Soviet Union. To counter the Western plan for the reunification of Germany on the basis of free all-German elections, they had produced their program for a German peace settlement plus a merger of the two parts of Germany —a merger in which the Communist structure of the "German Democratic Republic" would be preserved intact and the Communists would have a good chance of taking over West Germany as well. As a substitute for the Western defense structure developed under NATO, they had repeatedly suggested the establishment of an all-European security system, a nonagression pact between the NATO and Warsaw Pact nations, and an agreement on a zone in Central Europe from which nuclear weapons would be excluded. The last two offers, which were by no means unfavorably regarded in some non-Communist Western circles, were explicitly reaffirmed in the February 4 declaration of the Warsaw Treaty states, which had the further effect of putting the whole of Soviet-dominated Eastern Europe behind Khrushchev's current demands relating to Berlin and Germany.[11]

In the economic field, it had been a familiar Soviet tactic to advocate the formation of some kind of all-European economic organization to take the place of the existing Western organizations and of the Communist countries' Council of Economic Mutual Assistance (Comecon). No one was particularly surprised, therefore, when the Russians in April 1960 took advantage of a meeting of the United Nations Economic Commission for Europe— the one all-European economic body in which both Communist and Western nations *did* participate—to suggest that the U.S.S.R. might join the projected Organization for Economic Cooperation and Development and thus help to rescue the cause of economic cooperation from the deleterious influence of political blocs. Although this proposal and an accompanying plan for a conference of Eastern and Western trade ministers were declined by the Western governments on technical grounds,[12] the Soviet initiative testified once again to the fertility of the Communist imagination in devising expedients which, on superficial examination, might easily appear more desirable than the ones they were intended to replace.

These manifestations of what was intended to look like a cooperative spirit on the part of the U.S.S.R. were not without an effect on European popular opinion during the spring of 1960. Like the threats and bluster in which Khrushchev indulged on his visit to France in late March and early April, they helped to encourage those Europeans who felt that Western policy was on the wrong track, and accentuated the difficulties of the Western governments in devising a unified policy on disarmament and the other East-West matters that were already under negotiation in Geneva or might be expected to come up at the summit conference in Paris.[13]

These were matters that concerned not only the nations directly involved but the Western family as a whole, and considerable efforts were made to ensure that any proposals put forward on behalf of the West would have at least the official backing of the entire NATO group. After approval by the Foreign Ministers, the Western position papers on Berlin and on disarmament were scrupulously gone over with the permanent NATO Council in Paris, and a final review of the prospects for the summit was expected to be the principal item of business at the regular ministerial meeting of the NATO Council which had been scheduled to take place in Istanbul on May 2-4.

It so happened that Turkey at this moment was in the midst of the political convulsions that were to lead a few weeks later to the overthrow of the Menderes government.[14] Premier Menderes himself, who had declared martial law in Ankara and Istanbul a day or two before, was thus prevented from attending the most important international meeting which had yet taken place on Turkish soil. Although this state of affairs threw an odd light on conditions in the country that had served as NATO's eastern anchor ever since its admission to the alliance in 1952, the delegates in the heavily guarded meeting room in Istanbul found enough to occupy them for the moment in the report of the American, British, and French Foreign Ministers on their final pre-summit deliberations.

The official communiqué that closed the Istanbul meeting [15] reported that the Council had found itself in "entire agreement with the common positions" of the Big Three—a formula that glossed over the nonacceptance by the United States and Britain of certain French ideas relating to disarmament and to a possible summit understanding on policy toward underdeveloped countries. In addition, the Council endorsed the broad disarmament proposals submitted to the ten-nation conference at Geneva, reaffirmed the solidarity of the other NATO countries with the German Federal Republic, and reiterated their determination to protect the freedom of the people of West Berlin. After acknowledging with particular appreciation a message from President Eisenhower which emphasized the long-term nature of the United States commitment to NATO,[16] the delegates dispersed a few hours before Khrushchev's initial disclosures concerning the U-2 flight destroyed even the limited optimism about the prospects of an East-West *détente* that had prevailed during the meeting.

22. WESTERN POLITICS AFTER THE SUMMIT

The momentous events that began with the U-2 incident and the breakup of the summit conference affected attitudes and policies within the Western community in somewhat contradictory ways. On the one hand, the circumstances surrounding the U-2 flight and the fiasco at the summit unquestionably damaged the United States in the eyes of its Western associates and caused a certain amount of popular revulsion against the American approach to world politics. President de Gaulle's public characterization of the U-2 mission as "at the least ill-timed" [17] was among the more charitable judgments on the episode. The subsequent refusal of Khrushchev to have anything further to do with President Eisenhower automatically destroyed the latter's potentialities as a negotiator with the U.S.S.R., while the prospect of a lessening in American initiative during the presidential campaign tended further to reduce the influence of American counsels within the alliance.

On the other hand, the violence of Khrushchev's behavior in Paris and the accompanying revival of acute international tension dispelled a good many of the comfortable illusions that had prevailed of late regarding the prospect for a lasting amelioration in East-West relations. In the atmosphere created by Khrushchev's rages and Malinovsky's threats of rocket retaliation, nuclear war had once again to be regarded as a practical possibility of today or tomorrow rather than a merely theoretical menace at some time in the future. Though Khrushchev continued, like the Western leaders, to insist on his determination to work for improvement in the international climate, the pattern of Soviet activity showed conclusively that the U.S.S.R. was in no mood for compromise at present and did not shrink from threatening violent action in Africa, in the Caribbean, or wherever else its ambitions were challenged.

These broad reactions to the Paris experience interacted with local circumstances in the individual Western countries to produce highly varied results. In Great Britain, the most noticeable trend was a strengthening of the unofficial opposition to current Western defense policies and particularly to the basing of American aircraft and missiles on British soil. The commotion that followed the shooting down on July 1 of the American RB-47, which had taken off from a British base, forced Prime Minister Macmillan to seek a special guarantee from President Eisenhower that Great Britain would be consulted in advance of any further flights that might operate close enough to Soviet territory to be considered "provocative." [18] After his return from the United States in October, the Prime Minister announced a revision of the relevant Anglo-American agreement along lines which nominally satisfied the British demand for consultation, although they left open the question of whether or not Great Britain could actually exercise a "veto" on American flights of which it might disapprove.[19]

The events of the summer also gave a further impetus to the Campaign for Nuclear Disarmament and to the pacifist wing of the Labor party, which by October had mustered sufficient strength to override the party leadership and commit the opposition, on paper at least, to a policy of unilateral renunciation of nuclear weapons and termination of American base rights. But party leader Hugh Gaitskell made known his determination to fight for a reversal of this decision; and Prime Minister Macmillan, who had brought the Earl of Home to the Foreign Office as part of a cabinet reshuffle in which Selwyn Lloyd became Chancellor of the Exchequer, was not deterred from authorizing still a further development in Britain's defense association with the United States.

At the beginning of November, the Prime Minister disclosed the conclusion of a new agreement with Washington whereby the United States was granted a Polaris submarine support base at Holy Loch in the Firth of Clyde. Once again, there was a certain vagueness about how much control the British would be able to exercise over American use of the base. According to the British Government's understanding, there would be "the fullest possible previous consultation" before any vessel based at Holy Loch engaged in belligerent action.[20] But the storm of opposition which this announcement provoked in the United Kingdom demonstrated once again the extreme sensitivity of large sections of the British public, irrespective of political party, about the possibility that their country might some day be destroyed as a result of American actions based on Britain but unauthorized by the British Government. It was small wonder that Mr. Macmillan continued to pursue so assiduously the hope of an arrangement with the Russians which would reduce the likelihood of hostilities breaking out.

Canada's outlook, too, was affected in some degree by the U-2 incident and related events. In view of their close association with the United States in defense matters and their direct exposure to Soviet attack by bombers or missiles, Canadians were bound to be especially sensitive to any development that heightened international tension and threatened to lead to violence. Aside from a tendency to find fault with American actions vis-à-vis the U.S.S.R., there was also marked discontent in Canada over some phases of the Canadian-American defense relationship; and there was real anxiety about a growth in unemployment which was attributed in large part to the renewed slackness of business conditions in the United States. Former External Affairs Minister Lester B. Pearson, leader of the opposition and once an outstanding proponent of close ties with the United States, was perhaps the most eloquent critic of contemporary American attitudes and policies; but there were also signs of a more independent stand on the part of Howard C. Green, the current foreign affairs chief, and the Canadian delegation to the United Nations Assembly. A more positive note in Canadian-American relations was the conclusion, after many years of American hesitation, of a preliminary agreement on cooperative development of the water resources of the Columbia River Basin.[21]

In the German Federal Republic the political tendencies that followed the summit breakdown were at least superficially of an opposite kind. Chancellor Adenauer's government had never shown much faith in the possibility of accommodation with the Russians, and had greatly preferred the relative security afforded by the Western alliance. This stand now seemed to command even wider political support than in the past, notwithstanding a continuous barrage of Soviet complaints (and fabrications) regarding the supposed plan to equip the Federal Republic with nuclear missiles.[22] Reviewing its program in preparation for the 1961 parliamentary elections, the Social Democratic party, hitherto the principal focus of opposition to the Adenauer policies, decided in July to repudiate its quasi-neutralistic stand of the past and announce a foreign policy based on full acceptance and support of NATO. The coming election thus seemed likely to raise no major questions of principle in so far as Germany's increasingly important contribution to Western defense was concerned.

France, too, showed no signs of wavering in its fundamental attachment to the Western cause. As always, however, the nature of France's participation in Western enterprises was rendered decidedly problematical by a combination of internal and diplomatic factors. French moderate opinion, heavily preoccupied with the Algerian problem, had been growing increasingly restive and was beginning for the first time to engage in open criticism of the de Gaulle regime for its failure to put an end to the war in Algeria and for its somewhat authoritarian procedures at home. If M. de Gaulle's personal popularity in France remained largely intact, Premier Michel Debré and his ministry now confronted rising opposition from several directions. There was considerable resistance to the government's $2 billion program for developing an independent nuclear striking force, which was pushed through a highly reluctant parliament during the late autumn. Of even graver import was a resurgence of right-wing and military opposition to M. de Gaulle's plans for self-determination in Algeria, which were felt by many to invite the possibility of a new revolt by French settler groups. As a hedge against a possible renewal of the attempt to upset the government, plans were announced late in the year to submit the main features of the Algerian program to the judgment of the entire electorate in France and

Algeria in a referendum which was eventually scheduled to take place in France on January 8, 1961.[23]

Another aspect of current French policy that caused some anxiety to Frenchmen as well as outsiders was the individualistic attitude adopted by the French Government in relation to European and NATO affairs—not to mention the United Nations, to whose deliberations France officially displayed an indifference verging on contempt. So far as President de Gaulle was concerned, the over-all result of the summit conference and related events would seem to have been a strengthened conviction that France's destiny must be worked out on a national and not on any collective basis. The United States, he seems to have concluded, was bound to reduce its participation in European affairs in future. Such a prospect made it the more urgent to work toward a reordering of the Western association, particularly on the Continent, which would place the emphasis on national rather than collective efforts and in which France would assume the prominent role that had been denied it hitherto.

Thus it was France that undertook the one important diplomatic initiative of the post-summit period in Europe and gave the main impetus to a new round of intra-European consultations which began with an invitation from President de Gaulle to Chancellor Adenauer to visit Paris at the end of July. These consultations were described by a German spokesman as "a Western effort to overcome the political vacuum after the summit conference"—language that was widely interpreted as a reference to an absence of American leadership as the United States recovered from the summit experience and moved into its electoral campaign. For the French President, the objective was more precise. What he apparently sought was to find a way of doing without the United States and restoring the preeminence of national, as distinguished from supranational, authority both in the organization of Europe and in the Western alliance as a whole.

The nominal objective of the complicated plan which

President de Gaulle outlined to Chancellor Adenauer was simply to improve coordination of policy among the continental European nations through a system of political, economic, and military secretariats. But unlike the existing executive commissions of the six-nation communities, these new bodies would have little authority of their own. Closely controlled by the national governments, they would in effect represent a step away from unity, not toward it. Such at least was the conclusion of most of those familiar with the plan. In addition, General de Gaulle envisaged a reform of NATO along lines which would enlarge its area of responsibility to include the French possessions overseas, would increase the role of France in setting over-all NATO policy, and would substitute reliance on national forces for the current principle of military "integration." [24]

The reception of this plan was the reverse of enthusiastic. To Chancellor Adenauer and to most of the other continental statesmen with whom the matter was discussed in the following weeks, its full implementation seemed likely to undo much that had already been achieved within the existing six-nation community. Even more serious, it threatened to weaken NATO by deepening the division between Great Britain and the Continent and very possibly alienating the United States as well, thus bringing about the very withdrawal of the Americans from Europe that M. de Gaulle appeared to anticipate. No one felt like turning down the proposal outright, but reservations were expressed on every hand.

One of Dr. Adenauer's first moves after hearing of the project was to schedule a conference with Prime Minister Macmillan, in whose political judgment he had not always appeared to repose great confidence in the past. The de Gaulle plan placed matters in a different perspective, and the Prime Minister's visit to Bonn on August 10-11 produced both an immediate improvement in the atmosphere of Anglo-German relations and an agreement to make a new try at resolving the E.E.C.-E.F.T.A. impasse. As discussion of the de Gaulle project continued through the summer, Secretary Herter joined the chorus of those who were saying that military integration in NATO must be preserved at all costs.[25] The kind of role that the United States itself would be playing in NATO in future would, of course, be conditioned by a variety of unknown factors, some of which might be clearer by the time the Ministerial Council of the alliance was ready to hold its regular meeting in December.

Among the other countries of Western Europe, the repercussions of the summit experience tended to lose themselves amid the complicated interplay of domestic politics. In Italy, the strongly pro-Western Christian Democratic cabinet which Premier Antonio Segni had formed in February was brought down in July amid a wave of Communist demonstrations and street fighting that was startlingly reminiscent of the dangerous days of 1947. Some observers linked this outburst of disorder to the new harshness of Soviet policy, and pointed to the similar manifestations that had recently occurred in Japan.[26] Others, perhaps better informed, explained the disturbances as a reaction to the growing self-confidence of Italy's internal neo-Fascist movement. In any event, the net result of the crisis was a sharper realization among non-Communist Italians of the dangers of political factionalism, and an agreement was negotiated among the center parties to provide the necessary parliamentary support to a new Christian Democratic cabinet under Amintore Fanfani.

It would be too much to speak of a post-summit growth of neutralism in Norway, Denmark, and Iceland, NATO's Scandinavian members. But there is little doubt that Norway's state of mind was somewhat adversely affected by its involuntary association with the U-2 flight (the pilot had expected to descend at Bodo in northern Norway) and by Moscow's subsequent threats of rocket retaliation in case of a repetition. Denmark, whose King and Queen made a state visit to the United States in October,[27] held a parliamentary election on November 15 which eliminated the Communist party from representation but markedly strengthened the position of the neutralist Socialist Peoples party, whose leader had formerly headed the Danish Communists but had adopted a "Titoist" line since the crushing of the Hungarian revolt in 1956. In Iceland, enthusiasm for NATO was already at low ebb because of a variety of factors, among which the fisheries quarrel with Great Britain was perhaps the most prominent. However, London's renewed attempt to straighten out this vexatious question through bilateral negotiations prevented the occurrence of further incidents in the "fishing war" during the balance of the year.

Belgium, though relatively little affected by the U-2 and the summit, was extremely hard hit during these months by the untoward developments in the Congo, in which it suddenly found itself the object of widespread opprobrium and complained bitterly of lack of support by its allies. Although the government of Premier Gaston Eyskens indicated that the financial losses sustained in the Congo would necessitate some reduction in Belgium's contribution to Western defense, the most serious effects of the Congo disaster were experienced within Belgium itself. By late December, a new "austerity" bill designed to make good the economic consequences of the summer's events had touched off major protest strikes, led by the Socialist trade-unions, which seriously disrupted the country's internal life for weeks on end.

Portugal, too, was less than satisfied with the attitude of its allies on the various questions relating to the Portuguese overseas empire which were bringing it into conflict with the anticolonial bloc in the United Nations.[28] But there was also a happier development in the field of colonial relationships, the successful conclusion of the negotiations on the British bases in Cyprus. With this last obstacle to Cypriote independence removed, Cyprus made its bow on August 16 as an independent republic, provisionally attached to the British Commonwealth and committed by Archbishop Makarios, its new President, to an "independent" foreign policy. Five weeks later Cyprus became a member of the United Nations. Although its new status precluded membership in NATO, the attitude of its delegation at the United Nations Assembly suggested a determination to remain on friendly terms with the West.

Europe's other neutral or noncommitted countries, particularly Austria and Finland, did not escape the effects of the recent upheaval in East-West relations. Premier Khrushchev utilized a state visit to Austria at the beginning of July for a series of violent denunciations of Chancellor Adenauer and the West, interspersed with warnings to the Austrians to exclude pro-Western tendencies from their foreign policy. Public reaction to these admonitions was by no means sympathetic, however, and it was Under-Secretary Dillon who won the warm applause of the Austrians a few days later with a Vienna speech in which he assured them that the way they conducted their neutrality was their own business.[29] The United States did not, however, encourage Austria's announced determination to take its quarrel with Italy over the South Tyrol before the United Nations Assembly; nor did it support Austria's later request to that body to recommend negotiations between the two parties on the basis of the Austrian version of the dispute. Instead, the American delegation favored the compromise plan by which the Assembly eventually decided to urge a renewal of negotiations without taking any stand on the merits of the issue.[30]

When Khrushchev visited Finland at the beginning of September he employed a much softer tone than he had used in Austria, although he did not disguise his interest in building up the position of Finnish President U. K. Kekkonen as one non-Communist politician who enjoyed Moscow's confidence and approval. As a proof of his friendly sentiments toward the Finns, Khrushchev even intimated that he would not object to Finnish membership in the European Free Trade Association if satisfactory arrangements could be made for the protection of Soviet

commercial interests in relation to Finland. This understanding was confirmed on the occasion of Mr. Kekkonen's
return visit to Moscow in November.[31] Other E.F.T.A.
members, fearing that Finland might be compelled to act
as an entering wedge for Soviet influence within their association, reacted somewhat doubtfully to the prospect of
a Finnish bid for admission.

23. NEW PROSPECTS IN WASHINGTON

Throughout these months the European public had
paid a good deal of attention to the electoral campaign in
the United States, which, though it seemed unlikely to
portend any drastic revolution in American foreign policy, was at least thought likely to clarify United States
intentions on the principal international problems of the
immediate future. The expressions of satisfaction that
greeted the news of Senator Kennedy's election could be
attributed partly to the favorable impression created by
the Democratic candidate's campaign speeches and partly
to mere relief at the ending of a period of uncertainty.
The misgivings aroused in France by Mr. Kennedy's past
utterances on the Algerian problem had been largely al-
layed in the course of the campaign by his expressions of
regard for France as a member of the Western family.
Chancellor Adenauer had recovered from his initial
doubts as to whether the Senator from Massachusetts
could be relied upon to stand firm on the problems of
Germany and Berlin. Prime Minister Macmillan hoped
that the warm relations he had established with President
Eisenhower could be continued with his successor. After
the months of comparative inactivity that had followed
the summit breakdown, the prospect of more youthful and
energetic direction of American policy was not unwelcome
either in England or on the Continent.

With production and general prosperity at record
heights in most countries of Western Europe, it had not
yet been generally realized that the rich and powerful

United States was beginning to encounter serious economic and financial problems of its own, problems which could actually lead to a curtailment of its role in Europe unless means of alleviating them were promptly found. European financial institutions had already taken a number of unobtrusive steps to assist the United States with its current balance-of-payments difficulties. But it was not until President Eisenhower's order of November 16 for a reduction in overseas spending and in the number of military dependents abroad [32] that the average European became aware that the problem was one that could affect his own pocketbook and daily life. The presence of the American forces and their families might have been an irritant from some points of view, but many communities would acutely feel their loss.

The order of November 16 was shortly followed by the dispatch of Secretary of the Treasury Anderson and Under-Secretary of State Dillon to the German Federal Republic with the well-advertised objective of trying to persuade that country, which had a large surplus in its own balance of payments, to relieve the United States of a substantial part of the cost of maintaining its troops in Germany. Although the West German authorities offered to assist in subsidiary ways, including an expansion of aid to less developed countries, they quite refused to meet Secretary Anderson's request for a contribution of $600 million in the form of military support costs. Opinions differed as to how far this negative outcome could be attributed to inept diplomacy and how far it might reflect the exigencies of German internal politics as the opening of Germany's 1961 election campaign approached. The mission's most impressive result was the accompanying intimation that the United States might even feel compelled to withdraw some of its troops from the NATO "shield force" unless its allies were able to help in curbing the dollar drain.[33]

Enlistment of outside help in meeting America's overseas financial commitments had, of course, been one of the two principal motivations of the "Dillon plan" of January 1960, the other being the need to try to reconcile the economic policy conflict between the Six and the Seven. Very little of a practical nature had been accomplished as yet toward realizing either of these objectives. There was still no agreed Western policy on the apportionment or administration of aid to less developed countries, and, despite the somewhat warmer attitude of the British, nothing had yet come of the efforts to bridge the gap between E.E.C. and E.F.T.A. Both of these organizations raised problems for the United States which seemed especially relevant at the moment because of the balance-of-payments situation. Although the six-nation area of the E.E.C. was proving an attractive field of investment for American businessmen, Washington was concerned lest the proposed common external tariff, which would begin to be put into effect on January 1, 1961, should operate in such a way as to keep out American exports, particularly agricultural exports. A not dissimilar issue was raised by the decision of the seven E.F.T.A. countries to proceed with their own program of internal tariff adjustment. Aspects of these problems were touched upon, though in no very conclusive manner, at the regular autumn session of the GATT Contracting Parties in Geneva.[34]

A more convenient forum for the discussion of Western trade and economic problems might soon be available with the completion of the convention establishing the twenty-nation Organization for Economic Cooperation and Development (O.E.C.D.). Under-Secretary Dillon headed a new American delegation to Paris for a two-day ministerial meeting on the subject in mid-December, and the convention was formally signed on December 14, although it would not go into force unless ratified by at least fifteen of the twenty signatories.[35] As envisaged in the original American plan, the convention provided for consultation and cooperation among the twenty prospective O.E.C.D. nations with a view to promoting economic progress in the member states, sound economic expansion in developing countries, and general expansion of world trade. Provision was made for a Council, representing all the participating governments, which would operate by "mutual agreement," and for an executive organ which would be headed by Dr. Thorkil Kristensen of Denmark as Secretary-General. But the broadening of the organization through the inclusion of the United States and Canada was counterbalanced in some measure by a restriction of its functions and responsibilities as compared with those of the O.E.E.C., particularly in the trade field. Assuming that the convention proved acceptable to Congress, it would remain for the future to show how far the United States intended to make the new organization an effective instrument.

24. WHAT NEXT FOR NATO?

The warnings from Washington about a possible reduction of American troops in Europe came at a moment when NATO military affairs were already in a state of some uncertainty. Apart from the confusion engendered by President de Gaulle's latest initiative, the whole question of the role of nuclear weapons in Western defense had been made more urgent by the deterioration of East-West relations and the progress of France's drive to achieve an independent nuclear capability. This was an issue on which the United States seemed likely to have to take some stand even before the new administration took office.

Some other long-standing problems within the NATO association had been resolved during these months despite the handicaps imposed by governmental policy. A marked improvement in military teamwork within the alliance was evidenced by the far-flung land, sea and air exercises that took place over most of the North Atlantic area during the latter part of September; and a compromise on the military level was expected to alleviate substantially the difficulties occasioned by France's independent stand in the matter of integrated air defenses. As part of this same arrangement, the United States had undertaken to provide training in the use of nuclear weapons to French troops in Germany and, in addition, had consented to place its own forces in Germany directly under NATO command.[36] Late in the year it was disclosed that the British air defense forces were also being placed under NATO command.[37] The problem of additional training areas for the new German army had also been partially resolved by the assignment of certain areas in France for the use of German troops—a step whose political significance was certainly not to be underrated. The designation of the German General Adolf Heusinger to head the NATO Military Committee in Washington was a further reminder of the key role that the Federal Republic now played in the defense of the West. But the question of NATO armament, in contrast, was still wholly unresolved.

That there was a military need for wider use of nuclear weapons and missiles in Western defense was generally agreed in authoritative NATO quarters, although there was also an opposing school of thought which held that any attempt to use nuclear weapons in Europe would have disastrous consequences and that the great need was for stronger conventional forces. Even if the necessity for basing the defense of Europe on nuclear weapons was conceded, however, and even if the weapons were available, there still remained the question of who was to control them and who was to have authority to order their use in case of necessity. Up to this time, all nuclear weapons actually placed at the disposal of the alliance had remained under American control, with the understanding that they would be fired only by agreement between the American authorities and NATO—or by agreement between the United States and Great Britain in the case of the Thor missiles stationed in that country. Any departure from this arrangement, so far as weapons of American origin were concerned, would mean in effect that the United States would be giving up the final control it had hitherto exercised over its own nuclear armory. We have already observed the disfavor with which such a prospect was regarded in some influential Washington quarters.

On the other hand, so long as no nuclear weapon could be discharged without the consent of the United States, the European members of the alliance would have no absolute guarantee that the weapons would be available in a crisis. Far from being in too much haste to employ its nuclear weapons, the United States might just possibly refuse to let them be used at all. This had been the principal argument behind the agitation for a "European nuclear deterrent" that would enable Europe to act in its own defense even if the United States refused to join. The issue had now been brought to a head by General de Gaulle's plan for an independent French nuclear striking force. This project had few supporters outside M. de Gaulle's own government. NATO quarters were dismayed at the idea of a French nuclear force acting independently of NATO command. Chancellor Adenauer, among others, glimpsed a horrifying possibility that other Western countries, including his own, would sooner or later demand the right to imitate France's example. Yet the French program was plainly going to be put into effect unless some alternative was found.

A variety of plans had been drawn up in the endeavor to provide an answer to NATO's requirements without the risk of NATO's members embarking on an atomic arms race. General Norstad had produced a plan for a "NATO deterrent" which, in addition to removing much of the justification for the French project, would be designed to assure the alliance a more direct role in nuclear defense and to quiet any fear that the United States might leave Europe in the lurch. The essence of the Norstad proposal involved the establishment within NATO of a "multilateral atomic authority" which would control the nuclear components of NATO weapons systems, make NATO a "fourth atomic power," and assure "an equal voice in the control of the particular pool of forces which could be established as essential to the direct defence of

Europe." [38] This NATO deterrent could presumably be brought into play only with the consent of all fifteen NATO members. The British, who had their own nuclear deterrent and were unenthusiastic about the Norstad plan, referred with some sarcasm to "fifteen fingers on the trigger."

A rather similar plan had been developed in the United States and was under discussion between the State and Defense departments with a view to possible presentation at the forthcoming NATO Council meeting. There was, however, a serious political obstacle in so far as the United States was concerned. All of the plans under discussion involved the transfer of American weapons to other hands; yet none of them had been approved as yet by any of the relevant political authorities in Washington. This was a matter in which the decisive voice would clearly have to rest with President-elect Kennedy rather than with anyone in the outgoing administration. Undoubtedly the Joint Congressional Committee on Atomic Energy would also have a word to say about any nuclear sharing within the alliance. But with the NATO Council about to meet in Paris, the United States was under considerable pressure to indicate at least provisionally where it expected to stand.

The American delegation to the NATO meeting, which consisted of Secretary of State Herter, Secretary of the Treasury Anderson, and Defense Secretary Gates, had another matter to lay before NATO which occupied an even larger place in the thinking of the outgoing administration. Before Secretary Herter left for Paris, it would appear that he was instructed by the President to take the opportunity of bringing up once again the problem of the American balance of payments and to dispel any doubt that unless the United States got more help from its allies, it would have to consider a "material redeployment" of its forces away from Europe. [39] As spokesman of an administration that would be leaving office in little more than a month, Secretary Herter may have undertaken this assignment with a certain reluctance. When the Council met on December 16, he tempered the blow as best he might by insisting that even if such a redeployment did become necessary, the United States did not intend to "lower its flag" in Europe.[40] He also assured the Council that the United States had no intention of withdrawing from the NATO area the nuclear weapons made available to the alliance under existing arrangements.[41]

Nevertheless, the Secretary of State's remarks amounted to a confirmation that the United States was thinking of withdrawing at least a part of its troops from the NATO shield force. This intimation naturally affected the reception of Mr. Herter's announcement on the proposed NATO nuclear deterrent. Put forward as a "concept" rather than a proposal, his suggestions unavoidably reflected the prevailing uncertainty about the attitude of the next administration and of Congress. At the same time, they tended to strengthen the impression that the United States was beginning to deemphasize the idea of trying to defend Europe on the ground. What Mr. Herter's "concept" involved was a multilateral, medium-range ballistic missile force which would presumably operate under NATO and would consist of two main elements: (1) five Polaris submarines with eighty missiles, to be given to NATO by the United States by the end of 1963; and (2) 100 additional Polaris or Pershing missiles, also, apparently, for deployment at sea, which would be sold rather than given by the United States at a cost of some $1 million apiece. Both parts of the plan would apparently be conditional on the conclusion of an agreement governing political control of the weapons.[42]

Though this was undoubtedly the most important suggestion of a military character that had been laid before the alliance since the original American offer of intermediate-range ballistic missiles in 1957, it did not constitute a firm proposal; and the Council, though obviously unenthusiastic, could take no immediate position on it. Officially the matter was assigned to the permanent NATO

Council representatives for study with a view to further discussion at the next ministerial meeting, to be held in Oslo in May 1961. By that date the views of the incoming American administration might be better known. In the meantime the Council observed that it was also important to strengthen the shield force and to maintain a proper balance of nuclear and conventional strength so that there should be no misunderstanding of NATO's determination and ability to resist aggression by any "appropriate and necessary" means.[43]

No other major decisions were taken by the Council before its adjournment on December 18, although there was some rather tense discussion of the question of political coordination within the alliance. Secretary-General Paul-Henri Spaak made no secret of his dissatisfaction with NATO's record in this respect. Complaints were heard from Belgium and Portugal, among others, about what seemed to them the lukewarm support provided by allied governments on colonial issues before the United Nations. France may or may not have informed its allies that another nuclear device of "limited power" was going to be tested in the Sahara on December 27. But if none of the basic questions of the Western association had been resolved at this last NATO meeting of the Eisenhower administration, the stage had at least been set for a new attempt to grapple with them once the change of government in the United States had been accomplished. The question in everyone's mind was how far the United States intended to reassert the positive leadership it had given the alliance throughout most of its first decade.

CHAPTER FOUR

THE YEAR OF AFRICA

THAT 1960 would be a year of special importance in the political history of Africa had been foreseen as early as the winter of 1949-1950, when the General Assembly of the United Nations had determined that Libya should become independent by 1952 and that the barren and thinly populated territory of Somaliland should achieve a like status after a preparatory period of ten years under Italian trusteeship.[1] But it would have been extremely difficult to foresee at that time the rapidity of the political evolution that was to take place in Africa in the following decade. In the course of the 1950's not only Libya but five other states, Tunisia, Morocco, the Sudan, Ghana, and Guinea, achieved recognition as fully independent countries. Numbers of other dependent areas moved rapidly toward the same goal. By the end of the decade it had become evident that 1960 would see the birth of at least as many independent states as had come to birth in all the years since 1945. In terms of population, the "class of 1960" would greatly overshadow the combined strength of all its predecessors.[2]

25. THE ROAD TO INDEPENDENCE

The rapid disappearance of the "colonial system" from large parts of Africa during these years could be attributed to two main factors. One was the rising pressure for independence on the part of many of the indigenous African

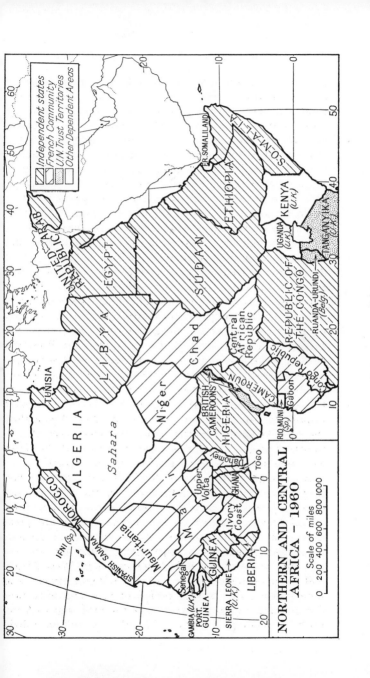

NORTHERN AND CENTRAL
AFRICA – 1960

Scale of miles
0 200 400 600 800 1000

Independent states
French Community
U.N Trust Territories
Other Dependent Areas

MOROCCO
IFNI (Sp.)
SPANISH SAHARA
ALGERIA
TUNISIA
LIBYA
UNITED ARAB REPUBLIC
EGYPT
Sahara
Mauritanie
Mali
Senegal
GAMBIA (U.K.)
PORT. GUINEA
GUINEA
SIERRA LEONE (U.K.)
LIBERIA
Ivory Coast
Upper Volta
GHANA
TOGO
Dahomey
Niger
NIGERIA
BRITISH CAMEROONS
Chad
CAMEROUN
Central African Republic
SUDAN
ETHIOPIA
FR. SOMALILAND
SOMALIA
UGANDA (U.K.)
KENYA (U.K.)
TANGANYIKA (U.K.)
RUANDA-URUNDI (Belg.)
REPUBLIC OF THE CONGO
Congo Republic
Gabon
RIO MUNI (Sp.)

peoples, a pressure that was vigorously encouraged by already independent countries in Africa and Asia, by the propaganda of the Soviet Union and other Communist states, and, to at least a limited extent, by the historical example (if not always by the direct intention) of the United States. The other factor was a growing disinclination on the part of Great Britain, and to a lesser extent of France and Belgium, to resist the pressure for independence once it had reached a level of intensity at which it could be contained only at the cost of considerable trouble, expense, bloodshed, and international unpopularity.

There were wide variations in the attitudes of these and certain other European powers that still held territory in Africa. Not infrequently the attitude of the same power varied from one African territory to another. France, which had been willing to fight a bitter and prolonged war to keep Algeria under French control, had made virtually no effort to prevent the departure of Guinea from the French Community in 1958. The government of President de Gaulle was now engaged in eliminating the last vestiges of compulsion from France's relations with its other dependencies in West and Equatorial Africa. Great Britain, for equally understandable reasons, had been much more prompt to free its "black" colonies in West Africa than the East African territories which included areas of substantial European settlement, although most of the latter were now plainly setting out along the same path.

Because of the rapidity with which basic attitudes had been changing both in Africa and in the metropolitan countries, the prospects for independence in any individual African territory no longer depended in any great degree on the preparedness of the indigenous African population to manage its own affairs. Some African peoples, like those of the British territories in West Africa, had been consciously prepared for self-government and independence over a long period of time and were now demonstrating their ability to take the final step with impressive smoothness. Others, like the 13 million inhab-

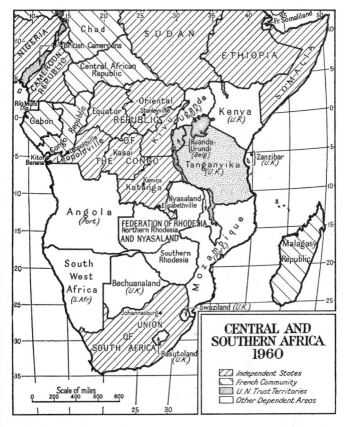

CENTRAL AND
SOUTHERN AFRICA
1960

Independent States
French Community
U. N. Trust Territories
Other Dependent Areas

itants of the Belgian Congo, had been systematically denied all access to higher education and political training and were now suddenly confronted with the prospect of shifting for themselves in a world about whose realities most of them had only the vaguest and most inaccurate notions.

Among the countries that were definitely scheduled to become independent in 1960, three were United Nations Trust Territories and, as such, had benefited by at least some rudimentary training in the techniques of politics and administration. The French-administered trust territory of the Cameroons actually achieved its independence on the first day of 1960 under the name of Republic of Cameroun. Its pro-French administration appeared to outsiders to have about an even chance of surviving the disorders fomented within the country by dissatisfied politicians and unruly tribal elements. The trust territory of French-administered Togoland likewise entered the ranks of independent states on April 27, 1960 as the Republic of Togo—again under a leadership friendly to the West, although determined, like the governments of most new African states, to steer clear of involvement in international political quarrels. Somaliland, in turn, said goodbye to its Italian administrators on July 1, 1960 and made its bow as the Republic of Somalia. Its first official action was to include within its boundaries the adjacent territory of former British Somaliland, an almost equally impoverished area which Great Britain had made independent five days earlier as a contribution to a projected union of all the Somali peoples. This action was observed with some misgivings by authorities in adjacent Ethiopia, French Somaliland, and Kenya, all of which had some reason to expect that they too might soon be faced with Somali territorial claims.

Once these ceremonies had been carried out, there remained only three United Nations trust territories on the entire continent of Africa. One of them, Cameroons under British administration, was expected to disappear soon after February 11, 1961, when United Nations plebiscites were to be held in the territory's northern and southern sections to determine whether their inhabitants preferred absorption in the adjacent Cameroun Republic or annexation to an independent Nigeria.[3] The other two were also moving rapidly toward a new and presumably independent status. Belgian-administered Ruanda-Urundi, which adjoined the huge territory of the Congo, would be intimately affected by the course of developments in that colony but seemed a not improbable candidate for independence in 1961. Tanganyika, extending eastward to the Indian Ocean, remained under British administration for the moment, but had already been promised full self-government in 1960 and confidently expected independence within the next four or five years at most. Julius Nyerere, leader of the Tanganyika African National Union, had already earned recognition as an African statesman whose perspective extended well beyond the confines of his own territory.

While the preparation of the various trust territories for self-government and independence had gone forward under the direct authority and encouragement of the United Nations, the world organization had had no direct responsibility for the larger and more important of the African countries that stood on the threshold of independence as 1960 began. The 36 million inhabitants of British Nigeria, the giant among Britain's West African territories, had been promised their independence for October 1, 1960 under a federal regime which had already certified its intention of remaining within the Commonwealth of Nations. Nigeria would thus be following the pattern already established by Ghana, the former British colony of the Gold Coast, which Prime Minister Kwame Nkrumah had led to independence in 1957. There was, however, some reason to believe that Nigeria's new government, headed by Sir Abubukar Tafawa Balewa, would prove somewhat more respectful of the British constitutional tradition, and somewhat less radical in matters of African nationalism and relations with the Communist bloc, than Ghana had become under Dr. Nkrumah's dynamic leadership. Still another British West African territory, the colony of Sierra Leone, was hoping for independence within the next two years and succeeded early in 1960 in persuading the British Colonial Office to set a date of April 27, 1961.

That Belgium's great colony of the Congo should become independent in the foreseeable future had until recently been anticipated by no one, least of all by the

Congolese themselves. It was only within the past year that the Belgian Government had been impelled to start thinking along these lines as the result of an outburst of African political unrest at the beginning of 1959 and a proliferation of "independence" parties during the following months. Despite the seeming inability of Congolese nationalist leaders to agree on a clear-cut program for the future of the territory, pressure for drastic change had become so intense that a round-table conference on the subject had been scheduled to meet in Brussels in January 1960. The result of this meeting, which took place amid conditions of disorder that might have served as a warning against further precipitate action, was a decision to speed up the formation of an indigenous administration, based on parliamentary elections in the best European tradition, so that the Congo could become independent on June 30, 1960. The question of the internal structure of the new state, and of the nature of the links with Belgium on which the mother country fondly counted to protect its economic investment, was left to future adjustment. As will be seen, the lack of a consensus on these matters was to become a source of infinite trouble before independence was many days old.[4]

It remains to speak of the French Community, that other great block of sub-Saharan colonial territory which consisted of the former French colonies of West and Equatorial Africa (minus Guinea) together with the Malagasy Republic on the Island of Madagascar. Conceived in 1958 primarily as a means of holding these important territories within the French orbit, the Community had evolved within a year or so into what amounted to an instrumentality for promoting them to virtual independence. "It is necessary to know," President de Gaulle observed, "when the time has come—and it has come—to recognize the right of all to self-determination, to trust them in principle and even to expect all of them to contribute in turn to the welfare of humanity."[5]

This essentially liberal principle had been much easier

to apply in "black" Africa than it had been in Algeria. As early as the beginning of 1960, France had signified its readiness to enter into negotiations with as many of the Community's eleven autonomous republics as might desire it with a view to granting them full sovereignty, including the right of separate diplomatic representation. Before the end of 1960, all of them would have availed themselves of this opportunity and one, the Republic of Mali (formerly Soudan), would have gone further and virtually severed its ties with the French Community. The others, General de Gaulle obviously hoped, would be guided in their future relations with France by the spirit of a Malagasy proverb: "One should not push away the boat which has enabled one to cross the river." [6]

26. COLONIAL AND RACIAL CONFLICT

Most if not all of the African states that were now winning independence were beset by serious internal problems which might, under other circumstances, have raised graver doubts about their ability to shift for themselves in a world that generally showed little mercy to the weak and inexperienced. Social, economic, and educational inadequacies, an almost universal lack of trained administrators, the prevalence of tribal enmities, personal rivalries, and irredentist ambitions affecting neighboring states were all the more dangerous under the conditions of 1960 because of the rapid growth of Communist interest in Africa and the boldness with which the U.S.S.R., its satellites, and even Communist China were beginning to try to manipulate African developments for their own benefit. The initial handicaps under which the newly independent African states were entering the world arena represented a grave challenge both to the new African leaders and to the imagination and generosity of those outside powers that wanted their efforts to be successful.

Up to the moment when the Belgian Congo became independent on June 30, 1960, however, the world's anxieties had focused less on the uncertain prospects of the new states than on the troubles already plaguing a considerable number of African territories where nationalist demands had encountered more serious resistance on the part of the dominant European "colonial" elements. The desire of intelligent Africans to improve their socio-economic and political status was often matched by an equal determination on the part of the European ruling groups to maintain intact the privileged positions they had acquired during the age of colonialism.

African nationalism, intermixed as it was with tribal, racial, religious, and ideological factors of many kinds, was a highly complex phenomenon with an infinite number of local variations. The forms, objectives, and intensity of the nationalist struggle in the different African territories varied accordingly, running the entire gamut from the five-year-old civil war in Algeria to the sporadic demonstrations which were understood to have occurred within the closely guarded confines of Portuguese Angola and Mozambique. A particularly explosive situation had been developing within the past two or three years in the Central African Federation of Rhodesia and Nyasaland. Even more dangerous conditions prevailed in that historic citadel of "white supremacy," the Union of South Africa.

The conflict in Algeria, which will require more detailed discussion later in this chapter, strongly engaged the emotions of politically conscious Africans throughout the continent. It thus served as one of the main unifying factors of the new African nationalism, however limited the ethnic and cultural affinities between the North African Muslims and the peoples of sub-Saharan Africa who had now become the principal standard-bearers of the African independence movement. There was little patience in Africa with the official French claim that Algeria was not, after all, a colony but a part of the French homeland; there was strong resentment of France's refusal to accept the Algerian "provisional government" established under Ferhat Abbas in 1958 as legitimate spokesman of the Algerian people. Many Africans were highly skeptical about the value of President de Gaulle's promise of September 16, 1959 to allow the Algerians to choose their own future after the present military conflict had been ended and the country had been pacified.[7] The hostility of most Europeans in Algeria to General de Gaulle's concept, demonstrated once again by a resort to the barricades in open defiance of the Paris government in late January 1960, indicated how formidable were the barriers that stood between the 10½ million Muslim Algerians and the right of self-determination that General de Gaulle had promised them.

In parts of British East and Central Africa a similar constellation of forces could be made out, in spite of manifold differences in race and in geographic, climatic, and political conditions. In Kenya and in the Central African Federation, dominant European minorities were striving desperately to hold their own in the face of rising African self-assertiveness and rather lukewarm support from the home government in London. The racial and political issues in Kenya, where there was also a substantial Asian minority, were thrashed out in some detail in January and February 1960 at a constitutional conference in London at which the British Colonial Secretary, Ian Macleod, put forward a program of constitutional change involving the introduction of wider African representation and increased self-government responsibilities as a step toward eventual independence. Denounced by white extremists as "the death blow to the European community in Kenya," the plan was equally disappointing to Africans like Tom Mboya, the most prominent of Kenya's nationalist leaders during the later 1950's. Mr. Mboya's goal was nothing less than "immediate independence based on one man, one vote." [8]

The situation in the Central African Federation, the loose union of Southern Rhodesia, Northern Rhodesia, and Nyasaland which had been established in 1953, was even more complicated because of differing racial and political conditions within the three individual units. Here the chief issue was whether the Federation as a whole should become an independent member of the Commonwealth under predominantly white rule, as advocated by the federal government under Sir Roy Welensky, or whether some other course was dictated by the interests of the African populations, especially in Northern Rhodesia and Nyasaland, where the whites were a tiny minority and African hostility to the Federation was intense and widespread. This complicated problem was to be reviewed during 1960 by a special commission under Viscount Monckton. In the meantime Prime Minister Macmillan, in the course of a January tour of Commonwealth countries in Africa, caused grave disappointment in pro-Federation circles by declaring that Great Britain could not consider according dominion status to the Federation unless this was the clear desire of its peoples—and unless Northern Rhodesia and Nyasaland were granted responsible self-government based on the will of the people of all races.[9]

This bold dissent from the principle of white supremacy within the Federation tended to confirm the impression that the attitude of the British Government had been undergoing a considerable readjustment in response to the rapid evolution of African affairs, supplemented, perhaps, by pressure from India, Ghana, and other non-white members of the Commonwealth. This impression was confirmed by the courageous speech on African affairs which Mr. Macmillan delivered on February 3 before the most unsympathetic audience he could have found, the parliament of the Union of South Africa. "The wind of change is blowing through the continent," the British Prime Minister declared. ". . . The growth of national consciousness in Africa is a political fact and we must accept it as such. I sincerely believe that if we cannot do so, we may imperil the precarious balance of East and West on which the peace of the world depends." To leave no doubt that he was thinking specifically of South Africa's official policy of racial segregation or *apartheid,* Mr. Macmillan went on to say that there were aspects of South African policy which Great Britain could not support "without being false to our own deep convictions about the political destinies of free men, to which in our own territories we are trying to give effect." [10]

The practice of *apartheid* in the Union of South Africa was a long-standing international as well as a national issue, the subject of a large number of critical resolutions which had been adopted by the United Nations General Assembly but ignored by the South African Government. Some weeks after Mr. Macmillan's visit, the question of South African racial policies took on a hitherto unknown acuteness as the result of mass resistance by Africans to the enforcement of the "pass laws" traditionally employed by the Union Government as one means of enforcing the segregation policy. Protest demonstrations which broke out in Sharpeville and other South African towns on March 21 were met by stern police repression in which some seventy-two Africans were killed and 184 wounded. This virtual massacre was instantly condemned in many countries, including the United States, where the "tragic loss of life" was publicly regretted by the State Department [11] in a noteworthy departure from that agency's normal practice of avoiding comment on South African internal affairs. Reactions in most parts of the world were even sharper. Twenty-eight African and Asian nations went so far as to demand an urgent meeting of the United Nations Security Council to consider a situation which, according to their contention, actually constituted a danger to international peace and security.

Although the validity of this assertion could not be proved, the continued disorder in South Africa during late March was enough to convince most interested governments that a discussion by the Security Council would be in order. Ambassador Henry Cabot Lodge, the United States representative, not only supported the request for a debate but spoke forcefully in behalf of a proposed resolution submitted by Ecuador which deplored the attitude of the South African Government, called upon it once again to change its policies, and requested the Secretary-General to consult with it about arrangements which "would adequately help in upholding the purposes and principles of the Charter." [12] Great Britain and France, which had expressed doubts about the propriety of Security Council action, abstained from voting, but the resolution was adopted on April 1 by a vote of nine in favor and none opposed. South Africa, though insisting that the United Nations had no proper concern in the matter, nevertheless agreed to hold a discussion with Secretary-General Hammarskjold at a later date. The continuing ferment within the Union, where mass arrests were taking place and where a white South African shortly afterward attempted to assassinate Prime Minister Hendrik F. Verwoerd, ensured that the matter would still be current whenever Mr. Hammarskjold was able to make the trip.

27. AFRICA IN WORLD POLITICS

Mr. Lodge's vigorous participation in the Security Council debate was one of many signs that the United States, like the United Kingdom, was gradually adjusting its policies in Africa in a way that tended to bring them into closer harmony with indigenous African sentiment, even at the risk of cooler relations with a traditionally friendly government like that of the South African Union. In part this readjustment represented a natural response to the rapid evolution of the African political and economic picture, which had already produced a heightened emphasis on African affairs in Washington and the appearance of a growing number of American diplomatic, economic, and cultural representatives on the local African scene.[13] Aside from the influence of a national tradition in which the principles of equality and independence had occupied a central place, it was fully realized in Washington that the emergence of new African states was altering the distribution of political power in the world, especially in the

United Nations, in a manner that made it increasingly imperative to pay attention to African attitudes. If these factors were not enough, there was also the growing Communist interest in Africa and the evident determination of the Communist states to make the most of the opportunities that were opening up for the advancement of their own program. Washington, too, was becoming increasingly convinced that Africa might hold the key to what Prime Minister Macmillan had called "the precarious balance of East and West."

In the gradual expansion of its African activities the United States faced two important hazards. One was the danger of unduly offending its traditional allies in Europe, several of which still had important interests in Africa and were not entirely immune to the suspicion that the United States might be trying to supplant them for its own benefit. The other was the extreme sensitivity of the new African governments about any move that could be viewed as an infringement of their sovereignty or an attempt to draw them into the "cold war." The policies of the established African governments—Liberia, Ghana, and Guinea in the west, Morocco, Tunisia, and Libya in the north, the Sudan and Ethiopia in the east—varied widely, yet all were committed in one degree or another to stay clear of great power rivalries and pursue a policy of "independence," "noninvolvement," or "positive neutrality." In 1957, the United States had made a tentative effort to line up a number of these countries in support of its anti-Communist position in international affairs.[14] The attempt had not been a notable success, and present American endeavors were limited for the most part to trying to persuade the Africans that they should in fact stay neutral and independent rather than veering toward the Communist side.

This change of emphasis had not occurred any too soon. A realistic observer of African developments over the preceding two or three years could hardly escape the conclusion that the over-all political trend in the newer states had been one of increasing dissociation from the West and, in some cases, increasing tolerance or even benevolence toward the Soviet Union and the Communist world. The initially pro-Western attitude of Morocco and Tunisia, the two African countries which President Eisenhower had included in his tricontinental tour of December 1959, had been severely shaken by their discontent with the attitude of France in Algeria and elsewhere. Tunisia, which had vainly urged an early settlement of the Algerian conflict in order to forestall the possibility of Communist infiltration of the "provisional government," was at loggerheads with France over a number of other issues and was pressing the French with growing impatience to evacuate their naval base at Bizerte. Morocco had already persuaded the United States to relinquish all its strategic bases in the country by the end of 1963, and had now set itself to secure the withdrawal of all French and Spanish military forces still in the country. It was also engaged in controversy with France and Spain over conflicting territorial claims in the Sahara. If it had not yet formed serious ties with the Communist world, the potentiality was there.

In West Africa, meanwhile, the Communist bloc had already won an important foothold in the new state of Guinea, where President Sékou Touré's concept of neutrality had an "Eastern" tinge at least as pronounced as the "Western" orientation hitherto maintained by Tunisian President Habib Bourguiba. Ghana, too, had appeared to be leaning increasingly toward the Soviet bloc in international policy. (It had also incurred the distrust of some of its African neighbors, especially Togoland, as the possible exponent of a new "black imperialism.") Emperor Haile Selassie of Ethiopia, dissatisfied with the assistance his government had received from the United States and greatly upset by the possibility of a Somali irredentist movement directed at his country's southeastern frontier, had gone to Moscow in the summer of 1959 and accepted a Soviet economic development credit of $100 million, the largest such bounty yet extended to an African country.

If such developments suggested a gradual shift of African sympathies in the direction of the Communist bloc, it was not because the new African governments had any special love for the Communist powers or wanted to imitate the Communist pattern in their own territories. Guinea was the only African state whose internal arrangements seemed at least partly based on a Communist model, with all power in the hands of a ruling party that controlled the machinery of government at all levels. Many of the new African leaders professed a belief in centralized, one-party, authoritarian rule and insisted that Western-type democracy was unsuited to African conditions; but all of them were emphatic in disclaiming Communist ties. Confident of their ability to avoid entrapment by Communist wiles, they were glad to profit by the apparent generosity of the Communist states and did not worry too much about possible ulterior motives. If the U.S.S.R. and its satellites displayed more flexibility than the United States in meeting their requests for economic assistance—and, in the case of Guinea and later Morocco, military assistance as well—they saw no reason not to take advantage of it.

Possibly even more important from the African point of view was the eagerness of the Communist governments to associate themselves, in a far more unequivocal manner than the United States had found possible, with the strong emotional drives that were shared by most politically conscious Africans. Moscow and its satellites were as vociferous as the Africans themselves in denouncing Western colonialism, racial discrimination, exploitation of every kind. Their proclaimed objectives were identical with those of the Africans: liberation of dependent areas, protection of the independence and sovereignty of the new states, economic assistance with no strings attached, trade and peaceful cooperation between large and small countries. That these were regarded by Communists merely as means to an end—the world-wide triumph of Communist "socialism"—was a point that aroused no particular alarm in Africa.

It was perhaps no wonder that African politicians, for all the "seriousness, devotion and intelligence" for which Secretary-General Hammarskjold commended them on his return from an African tour in January 1960,[15] were sometimes inclined to take Communist declarations of solidarity at face value. Familiar as they were with the seamy side of Western colonialism, they could know little of the realities behind the Soviet propaganda line. The U.S.S.R., they frequently pointed out, had no colonies in Africa. Why should they refuse to accept its support against the West, which did? The fact that France, Great Britain, Belgium, Portugal, and Spain still ruled over large African populations colored the African reaction to every step taken by the Western governments. An illustration was the extremely hostile reaction of the African governments to France's nuclear weapons tests in the Sahara, a reaction in no way mitigated by the fact that the tests had been so arranged as to eliminate any possibility of harmful fallout.

The principal result of Mr. Hammarskjold's African mission—the first of several he would be obliged to undertake during the year—was a clearer focusing of Western attention on the economic and technical help that was going to be needed in increasing measure if the new African countries were to survive as independent states. In spite of the rapid development of African resources in recent years, Mr. Hammarskjold pointed out, "most of the African countries, and in particular those south of the Sahara with their large subsistence sectors, are still among the poorest of the world in terms of money income. . . . As in all other countries in a similar stage of development, industrialization in Africa is impeded by the lack of basic technical skills, of power, transport, and other basic facilities, of social services and in general of that economic and social infrastructure without which investment is inhibited. . . . It is essential that African economic growth acquire sufficient momentum to match the pace of political change. The early period of independence may in this respect prove decisive." [16]

This was a matter on which the United States Government saw completely eye to eye with the Secretary-General and with most of the new African leaders. Even if the Soviet Union had managed to seize an important initial advantage, the United States could still make a significant impact in the field of long-range economic development. As Julius Nyerere put it, the United States might have "missed the boat" of the African freedom movement, but could still catch "the economic and development boat." [17]

Although Washington hoped that Western European countries would continue to carry the main burden of economic assistance in Africa, President Eisenhower gave unusual emphasis to African requirements in his Mutual Security message for 1960-61. In addition to a moderate increase in regular technical assistance, he proposed a special allocation of $20 million to initiate a program of education and training in Africa south of the Sahara.[18] While the United States had developed no plans for spectacular credits of the type favored by the Soviet Union, it could point out that the Export-Import Bank had already financed transactions with Africa to a total of some $240 million, and that African projects supported by the Development Loan Fund had already come to over $64 million.[19] As the largest contributor to the economic programs of the United Nations, the United States could also claim some of the credit for the expanding activities being undertaken through that organization and its recently established Economic Commission for Africa. As in some other parts of the world, however, it might require an even stronger impetus if the dimensions of American and international assistance were to be expanded in a manner truly commensurate with African requirements.

28. THE ALGERIAN HEMORRHAGE

This lengthy catalog of African problems may be concluded with a few words on the war in Algeria, potentially one of the most explosive of all the issues Africa had presented to the international community. There is no need to emphasize the tragic character of this conflict which had already claimed perhaps 160,000 lives,[20] exacted an incalculable toll in human suffering, diverted a French army of up to 500,000 from the defense of Europe, caused deep and painful fissures within the French body politic, and inhibited France and its allies from reaching any deeper understanding with the new nations of Asia and Africa. The political and psychological burden which the war imposed on France and the West had grown heavier each year as the prospects for ending the bloodshed continued to recede and the harsh methods employed by the French Army began to receive as much publicity as the ruthless terrorism to which the insurgents had resorted from the very beginning.

The only mitigating circumstance about the Algerian conflict from a Western standpoint was the fact that it had so far been kept insulated from the larger East-West struggle. The leaders of the Algerian National Liberation Front (F.L.N.) or "Provisional Government" were not Communists themselves, and their movement—unlike the Vietminh insurrection which had caused France such heavy losses in Indochina—had not thus far been significantly infiltrated by Communists or subordinated to Communist global strategy. The reluctance of the insurgent leaders to put themselves in pawn to the Communist powers was a relative and perhaps temporary thing, however. President Bourguiba of Tunisia had warned for years that the rebels would "turn East" whenever they concluded that there was no hope of achieving Algerian independence in agreement with France and within the Western family.

Hope of a negotiated solution which would keep Algeria within the Western world had by no means disappeared at the begining of 1960. Theoretically, the offer of self-determination which General de Gaulle had put forward on September 16, 1959, and which the United States had promptly endorsed,[21] provided a wholly reasonable basis for settlement. In practice, however, it was only very partially acceptable to the F.L.N. and was not acceptable at all to the extremist European elements in Algeria who insisted that Algeria must remain French under all circumstances. The position of this latter group, though supported by a part of the French Army in Algeria, was seriously if not irremediably weakened as the result of its unsuccessful insurrection against the Paris government at the end of January 1960. In an impressive display of his personal authority, President de Gaulle at the height of the crisis explicitly reaffirmed the self-determination policy, "the only policy that is worthy of France," in the dramatic broadcast that preceded the collapse of the revolt.[22]

There remained, however, the equally difficult problem of reaching an agreement with the "provisional government" on a cease-fire and a procedure for exercising the right of self-determination. The F.L.N. leaders, while accepting self-determination "in principle," had insisted from the outset that they could not lay down their arms as General de Gaulle had asked without strong guarantees that the position they had gained in the course of the fighting would be protected pending the holding of a referendum. If a referendum was to be held, they wanted to be reasonably sure of winning it. Their confidence in the French Government had never been great, and they had been seriously disturbed by an intimation in General de Gaulle's speech that he expected to entrust arrangements for the referendum to the French Army. Although both Paris and the provisional government appeared to be moderating their positions somewhat in the wake of the Algiers insurrection, a behind-the-scenes attempt to arrange for peace talks fell through.

By early March, when General de Gaulle paid a visit to Algeria to explain his position to the French Army, the French President was once again predicting a long war and insisting that the only way to end it was by a clear-cut military victory. At the same time, General de Gaulle indicated more clearly than hitherto his belief that the ultimate solution for Algeria could be neither the complete integration with France demanded by the defeated partisans of *"Algérie française"* nor the complete independence sought by the rebels. The result of the self-determination process, he predicted on March 5, would be the choice of a middle course—some form of French-Algerian association which might be summed up in the formula, "an Algerian Algeria tied to France." [23]

Although the insurgents publicly took the position that General de Gaulle had slammed the door on a negotiated peace, they took care to keep open the possibility of renewed contact with the French Government. Even Khrushchev, who was seeking French favor during this pre-summit period in the hope of drawing France away from its allies, allowed himself to say an approving word for M. de Gaulle's self-determination policy when he came to Paris at the end of March.[24] But it was never quite easy to know exactly what M. de Gaulle's policy involved. Premier Michel Debré, speaking in Algiers on April 12, said flatly that France would never "abandon" Algeria and confirmed the widespread impression that if the Algerians seceded from France, their territory would be partitioned so that the French population could remain on French soil.[25] Yet when President Eisenhower asked M. de Gaulle in Washington a fortnight later whether his position had "hardened" or changed, he was assured that the policy still stood as enunciated on September 16, 1959. "On that basis," Mr. Eisenhower responded, in a comment that was to be bitterly resented throughout North Africa, "just as I did in September 1959, I [endorse] what you [are] doing and wish you well in its progress." [26]

Meanwhile the war continued, more people were being killed and maimed, more vexatious incidents were occurring on the frontiers of Tunisia and Morocco. A new chance for peace talks seemed nevertheless to open up as the result of the excellent showing made by supporters of General de Gaulle's program in the departmental elections held in Algeria on May 30. A solution was never closer, General de Gaulle asserted on June 14; and he renewed his invitation to the insurgents to join in seeking an honorable end to the fighting. This time the provisional government from its seat in Tunis agreed that President Ferhat Abbas should go to France as head of a delegation to meet the French President, and two F.L.N. emissaries were sent ahead to settle the details. But the preliminary talks with French representatives, held at Melun, near Paris, on June 25-29, produced no semblance of agreement about the status and facilities to be accorded the Algerian delegates. On July 4, the provisional government announced that it saw no point in continuing the discussion unless the French were prepared to adopt a more reasonable attitude.[27]

From this time on the insurgents gave the impression that they had practically lost hope of achieving a settlement through negotiations with France. As the time for the United Nations General Assembly meeting approached and the F.L.N. prepared to step up the campaign of terrorism in Algeria that normally preceded each annual session, a new political strategy was elaborated for use in the coming debate. Self-determination as defined by France had become a meaningless concept, the provisional government declared on August 22. France was nullifying a sound principle by refusing to negotiate about the necessary conditions and guarantees for "a free consultation of the Algerian people." Under these conditions, the provisional government asserted, the proposed consultation of the Algerian peoples should not take place under French auspices at all. Instead, it should take the form of "a referendum organized and controlled by the United Nations."[28]

The idea of a United Nations referendum could be trusted to appeal to a large number of Asian and African countries, and might very well win the endorsement of the General Assembly as a whole. Yet such a procedure was the very last thing that France was likely to permit in its Algerian territories. In his news conference on September 5, President de Gaulle said plainly that France would not be bound by any decision the United Nations might take in reference to Algeria. Algeria, he insisted, was a French problem in which the world organization had no right to interfere.[29] Pointing to the encouraging progress which he said was already being made in the economic and social development of Algeria under the so-called Constantine plan announced in 1958, the French leader reiterated his own stand on self-determination, repeating several times in the following days that the insurgents had only to "lay aside the knife" for peace talks to begin.

In the meantime the insurgents, who had for some months been showing increasing impatience not only with France but also with what they considered the pro-French attitude of the United States, appeared at long last to have resolved upon that "turn to the East" which had always loomed in the background of the conflict. Ferhat Abbas, hitherto regarded as one of the most "Western" of the insurgents leaders, spent several days in Communist China in late September, returning by way of the Soviet Union and apparently receiving encouragement and promises of support in both countries. Communist China was already on record as a supporter of the F.L.N., and the U.S.S.R., though it had previously backed the de Gaulle program for Algeria, now altered its position to the extent of granting the F.L.N. "*de facto* recognition" and promising it both material assistance and political support. In New York, where President Eisenhower avoided reference to Algeria in his September 22 address to the General Assembly, Khrushchev cited the Algerian conflict as a classic illustration of the evils of "colonialism" and spent hours with the unofficial F.L.N. delegates.[30] Conceivably the F.L.N. was merely exerting psychological pressure on the West. But if the Communist governments had finally decided to give the insurrection their full support, the situation in Algeria could easily become even more dangerous than the one that had already developed in the former Belgian Congo.

29. CRISIS IN THE CONGO

(1) *The Origins*

History affords no parallel to the tumultuous experience that centered in the Republic of the Congo in the months that followed the emergence of that large and populous country from Belgian rule on June 30, 1960. The ensuing crisis—still unresolved in most respects at the end of the year—brought the East-West struggle for the first time directly into the heart of Africa, confronted the United Nations with the most difficult assignment in its fifteen-year history, and offered a frightening display of the consequences to which independence could lead in a nation psychologically and politically unprepared for it. All of the parties involved, including the Belgians,[31] agreed that the government in Brussels had made a grave error in denying the Congolese the training and experience they would need to operate their country when the levers of control were suddenly placed in their hands. The breakdown of authority which began to occur even before the new Congolese government took office on June 30 not only threatened to undo the material achievements of three-quarters of a century of Belgian rule but created a vacuum which inevitably drew both great and small powers to the scene and made the Congo a battleground of their competing interests.

In trying to grasp the events of this complex period it is helpful to recognize at the outset that the Congo situation involved a number of separate conflicts which intertwined at various levels. At the root of the situation was a clash between the elementary principles of liberty and authority, or of discipline and license, among the Congolese peoples themselves. Large numbers of Belgium's former subjects unquestionably viewed the coming of independence as an invitation to cast off all restraints and turn their pent-up energies against their former masters, against hereditary enemies in other tribal groups, and, indeed, against law and order generally. This understandable, if lamentable, misconception was largely responsible for the mutiny in the Congolese *Force publique* or military police on July 6 which led to a return of Belgian military forces and precipitated the need for outside intervention. It helps to explain the terrorism and looting that prevailed in large areas of the Congo for several weeks after independence, and played its part in a recrudescence of intertribal warfare that continued for a much longer period. It also supplied much of the emotional force behind the drive on the part of the new Congolese leaders to oust the Belgians from the positions of influence the latter had hoped to retain under a treaty of friendship and collaboration signed (though not ratified) on the day before independence became effective on June 30. To say this is not, of course, to deny the probability that some Belgians tried hard to protect their threatened interests by back-door maneuvers amid the chaos that followed the breakdown of Congolese authority.

Superimposed upon this play of elemental forces was a struggle for power among the Congolese political leaders, one that tended to take the form of a constitutional conflict between the advocates of a centralized Congolese state and the partisans of a decentralized federal system which would allow more scope for provincial and tribal interests. Epitomizing the clash of political principles was the personal enmity between Patrice Lumumba, a fanatical "centralist" who was generally regarded in other parts of Africa as the most authentic exponent of Congolese nationalism, and Joseph Kasavubu, the representative of a more localized tribal constituency in the lower Congo region, who had upheld the federalist principle in the pre-independence negotiations with Belgium but subsequently relapsed into seeming inactivity, allowing his rival a virtually free hand in the first two months after independence. The compromise arrangement whereby M. Lumumba was initially made Prime Minister while M. Kasavubu became Chief of State proved no more effective in resolving the constitutional dilemma than it did in assuaging the personal rivalry between the two leaders.

Nor did M. Kasavubu necessarily see eye to eye with the other prominent opponents of M. Lumumba and of the centralized regime for which he stood. One of these was Moise Tshombe, premier of the rich southeastern province of Katanga, who declared his territory independent of the central government at Leopoldville as early as July 11 and was promptly, if inaccurately, denounced by M. Lumumba and his partisans in and outside of the Congo as a Belgian "stooge." Still a third exponent of federalist or separatist tendencies was Albert Kalonji of Kasai Province, who later set up a rather shadowy independent regime in the south Kasai regions adjacent to M. Tshombe's domain.

The topmost layer of conflict was that of the international forces that were drawn into the struggle as the result of the obvious inability of the Congolese regime to maintain order and protect life and property, either European or Congolese. By general consent, the initial responsibility for making good the deficiencies of the Leopoldville government was entrusted to the United Nations, to which the new Congolese authorities themselves appealed on July 11 and the following days for military assistance in reorganizing the country's rebellious armed forces. But the effectiveness of United Nations action was to be vitiated from the first by a radical difference of opinion as to its real purpose.

To many outsiders, including most Americans, it seemed that the prime task of the international organization must be to reestablish order, protect helpless Europeans, and assist the local Congolese authorities in providing essential services. But the central Congolese government, which for practical purposes meant M. Lumumba, had quite different views. In requesting United Nations military assistance, M. Lumumba's government took care to specify that its purpose was *not* to restore the internal situation in the Congo, but rather to protect the Congo against the "act of aggression" allegedly perpetrated by the Belgian metropolitan troops who had returned to the country to protect the European population.[32] What M. Lumumba wanted, as subsequent events made clear, was an international instrument that would help him consolidate his own power by (1) curbing his unruly troops, (2) driving out the Belgian forces, and (3) eventually restoring the authority of the central government in Katanga and other outlying parts of the country.

In this concept of the United Nations role M. Lumumba could count on the sympathy of most African governments and also on the full support of the Soviet Union, which had obviously perceived in the Congo situation an unprecedented opportunity for the pursuit of its own standard policy of backing the extreme "anticolonial" elements and using them as an entering wedge for Soviet influence. Even before the Security Council could meet to consider M. Lumumba's initial request for help, Moscow had begun to accuse Belgium and the other Western powers of "unleashing armed aggression" in the Congo. Simultaneously M. Lumumba, an avowed neutralist although presumably no Communist, began to intimate that if he did not obtain satisfaction from the United Nations he would turn "elsewhere" for help. Not many days had passed before M. Lumumba was making it clear that when he said "elsewhere" he was thinking especially of the Soviet Union. The U.S.S.R. on its side was shouting "Hands off the Congo!" and threatening to take "resolute measures" to defend Congolese integrity against its alleged enemies. In the already tense atmosphere that followed the summit breakdown and the RB-47 incident, it was difficult to dismiss the possibility that the U.S.S.R. might make good its threat and create a situation in which the Western powers would be forced to act vigorously unless they were willing to let the Congo go by default.

The United States had already declined an invitation to send some of its own troops to the Congo, and for obvious reasons was anxious that the Russians should not do so either. Whatever needed to be done there, in the

American view, ought without question to be done under international auspices. There had been cases in the past, notably in the Suez crisis of 1956, when timely action by the United Nations had sufficed to quiet a threatening local situation and avert a possible conflict among the great powers. Secretary-General Hammarskjold, recalling the United Nations Emergency Force which had been sent to the Middle East in 1956 and was still on duty in the Suez area, had already indicated that he would be ready to organize another United Nations "peace force," made up predominantly of African contingents, for service in the Congo.

Thus when the Security Council met to consider the Congolese request on July 13, the United States was de-lighted to support a resolution proposed by Tunisia which authorized the Secretary-General to provide the Congo with "such military assistance" as might be necessary until the Congolese national security forces were in a position to do their job. Because of the urgency of the situation, Ambassador Lodge raised no objection to a further para-graph in the resolution which called on Belgium to with-draw its own troops from the Congo. Pressure on Belgium might seem to Americans a trifle gratuitous at this stage, but it was clearly considered important by the African and Asian states, and Belgium had anounced in any case that its troops would be withdrawn upon the introduction of United Nations forces. Although China, France, and Great Britain abstained when the resolution came to a vote early on July 14, the U.S.S.R. as well as the United States cast affirmative votes and the resolution was adopted by an official tally of 8 to 0.[33] It was possible to infer from the Soviet stand that Moscow, too, preferred not to get too deeply involved in the Congo situation in spite of its clamorous support of the Lumumba government.

In the succeeding days the United States cooperated wholeheartedly in the United Nations' new effort to im-provise an international force that would be capable at one and the same time of carrying out a difficult technical assignment and of avoiding any justified cause for complaint or intervention by an outside power. United States aircraft provided the bulk of the airlift of men and equipment required to build up a force which by July 20 already numbered about 3,500 officers and men from Ethiopia, Ghana, Morocco, and Tunisia, with others expected from Guinea, the Federation of Mali, Sweden, and Ireland.[34] Command of the force, for which Mr. Hammarskjold had set an initial target of about 10,000 men but which would ultimately grow to nearly twice that number, was entrusted to Major-General Carl Carlsson von Horn, the Swedish commander of the United Nations Truce Supervision Organization in Palestine. In common with various other governments and with units of the United Nations and the specialized agencies, the United States also helped out with emergency food shipments to the Congo and supported a wide variety of supplementary United Nations measures undertaken on the authority of the Secretary-General with the aim of averting a complete breakdown in civilian services and public health conditions.[35]

The principal difficulty at this stage was that it would inevitably take some time for ONUC, as the United Nations Operation in the Congo was called from its French initials, to restore a sufficient measure of public security throughout the country to permit the Belgian troops to be withdrawn. Yet M. Lumumba and his government had continued to insist that the Belgians must leave immediately and unconditionally. So had most of the independent African states, and so had the Soviet Union. By July 17, M. Lumumba was threatening to call in "Soviet Russian troops" if the Belgians were not gone within seventy-two hours; and statements from the U.S.S.R. encouraged the impression that Moscow would be only too ready to oblige. This, of course, was precisely the situation that the United Nations action had been intended to avert—at least in the eyes of the United States. When the Security Council reconvened on Soviet request on July 20, Ambassador

Lodge gave his Soviet opposite a clear though diplomatic warning that the United States would be opposed to unilateral intervention from any quarter. "With other United Nations members," he said, "we will do whatever may be necessary to prevent the intrusion of any military forces not requested by the United Nations." [36] Secretary Herter said the same thing at greater length at his July 21 news conference.[37]

Although Soviet delegate V. V. Kuznetsov retorted that his country would not be "bullied," he was dissuaded from pressing his initial demand that Belgium withdraw from the Congo within three days. Even the African states found this time limit somewhat unreasonable. Nevertheless the resolution drafted by Ceylon and Tunisia and unanimously adopted by the Council early on July 22 included an admonition to Belgium to withdraw "speedily," together with an endorsement of the efforts being made by the Secretary-General and a request to "all States" to refrain from actions prejudicial to law and order, to the authority of the Congo government, or to the integrity and independence of the Congolese state.[38] Belgium, which had been deeply shocked by the plight of many of its nationals in the Congo, was more than a little annoyed at this renewed pressure but indicated that the process of withdrawal had already begun and would be completed—with certain exceptions—within a reasonable time.

(2) Removing the Belgians

While the Security Council was in session, Premier Lumumba had been on his way to the United States to explain his point of view at United Nations headquarters and in Washington. His cordial reception in the American capital irritated the Belgians but produced no lasting modification of the Congolese Premier's attitude or methods of doing business. Secretary Herter assured the visitor that the United States was prepared to meet "its fair share" of the Congo's needs for technical and financial assistance. But he emphasized that it would act only through the United Nations, in which, he said, it had "placed its confidence . . . regarding all these matters." [39]

A more important journey was that of Secretary-General Hammarskjold to the Congo for a personal survey of the United Nations activities developed in recent days under the supervision of his personal representative, Dr. Ralph J. Bunche. The most thorny problem confronting the United Nations at the moment concerned those Congolese areas where the Belgians had indicated that they planned to remain even after their troops were withdrawn from other parts of the Congo in compliance with the Security Council resolutions. These areas comprised (1) the three military bases of Kitona, Banana, and Kamina, which Belgium claimed the right to occupy under the terms of the Belgian-Congolese friendship treaty; and (2) the entire area of Katanga Province, which, as already noted, had declared its independence of the Congo a fortnight earlier.

Katanga, the center of the copper mining industry, had been the Congo's wealthiest province. In contrast to the conditions prevailing elsewhere in the country, M. Tshombe's regime had not only succeeded in preserving law and order but seemed willing to continue working in close cooperation with the local Belgians. For their part the Belgians appeared more than willing to cooperate with him. If Katanga succeeded in maintaining its independence, Belgium would have a good chance of preserving its most important economic asset in the Congo. But to Premier Lumumba and his supporters this was an intolerable prospect. Katanga might be important to the Belgians, but it was indispensable to the new Congolese state. In the eyes of the Leopoldville government, M. Tshombe's Belgian-supported regime had no validity whatsoever. It was essential, Leopoldville insisted, that the Belgians be expelled and the authority of the central government restored without delay throughout the country.

This was a point of view with which the United Nations

found it difficult to disagree. The Security Council resolutions had said plainly that Belgium must withdraw from "the territory of the Republic of the Congo." They had made no exception for Katanga or any other area. The U.S.S.R. was threatening "resolute measures" if the United Nations failed to do its duty. On the other hand, M. Tshombe had said several times that he wanted no United Nations troops in Katanga. In fact, he intimated, he would resist them by force if they tried to enter.

After several days of intense negotiation in Brussels and Leopoldville, Mr. Hammarskjold on August 2 was able to announce what seemed a satisfactory compromise. United Nations forces, he said, would start entering Katanga to relieve the Belgian troops on August 6; but they would maintain strict neutrality so far as the political conflict between M. Tshombe and M. Lumumba was concerned. This, however, was not good enough for M. Tshombe. Intervention by the United Nations, he declared, would constitute "aggression" and would be resisted accordingly. By August 5 the Secretary-General had been driven to the conclusion that M. Tshombe meant business, that the United Nations could not enter Katanga except by the use of force, and that the only course open to him was to appeal to the Security Council for new instructions.

This unexpected reversal on Mr. Hammarskjold's part was bitterly denounced by M. Lumumba, by the U.S.S.R., and by several of the African states. M. Lumumba, who was having some difficulty in maintaining his own footing amid the shifting sands of Congolese politics, intimated that it might be as well for the United Nations to get out of the Congo altogether. The U.S.S.R., increasingly critical of Mr. Hammarskjold's alleged subservience to the "imperialists," suggested that troops of "other countries" should go to the Congo if the United Nations forces were unable to perform their mission. President Nkrumah said that Ghanaian troops would be quite willing to drive the Belgians out of the Congo, with or without a United Nations mandate. Guinea took a similar line.

Such pressures had never been known to impair the Secretary-General's capacity for cool and measured analysis. "The problem facing the Congo is one of peace or war —and not only in the Congo," he told the Security Council when it reconvened in New York on August 8 to hear his first-hand report. Mr. Hammarskjold did not spare criticism of any of the parties involved. It was of the first urgency, he said, to find a solution that would get the Belgians out and enable the Congolese people to determine both their internal arrangements and their international political orientation—and, he added, to do so without the intrusion of foreign elements which "might get conflicts extraneous to the African world introduced on the continent."

The U.S.S.R., as usual, had a drastic solution to offer— an order to the Secretary-General to "take resolute measures without hesitating to use any means" to get the Belgian troops out of the Congo. Ambassador Lodge agreed, though in more temperate language, that "the time has come for Belgian withdrawal [from Katanga] at the earliest moment under arrangements to be worked out by the Secretary-General for the preservation of law and order." Once again it was Tunisia and Ceylon who drafted the necessary resolution. Its essential paragraphs called on Belgium to withdraw its troops from Katanga immediately; insisted, for M. Tshombe's benefit, on the necessity of the entry of the United Nations force into Katanga; but assured the Katanga leader that the force "will not be a party to or in any way intervene in or be used to influence the outcome of any internal conflict, constitutional or otherwise." It would, in other words, confine itself to taking over from the Belgians and would not involve itself in the internal conflict between the Congolese and Katanga governments. This text the Council approved early on August 9 by a vote of 9 to 0. The U.S.S.R. refrained from casting a veto but abstained, together with Poland, in obvious discontent at the failure of the Council to take a stronger line.[40]

The resolution of August 9 represented the beginning of the end of the crisis so far as the evacuation of Belgian troops was concerned. Mr. Hammarskjold returned to the Congo and, after further tense negotiations with M. Tshombe, secured the latter's agreement to the entry of United Nations forces. The Secretary-General personally led the first group of 220 Swedish troops into Katanga on August 12. By this time even the most recalcitrant among the Belgians had realized that this phase of the game was over, both in Katanga and elsewhere. By the end of August all Belgian combat troops had either left the Congo or were waiting to depart as soon as transport was available. All that remained of a Belgian army of 20,000 were 1,500 technicians at the Kamina and Kitona bases whose presence was felt by Mr. Hammarskjold himself to be necessary for the support of the local economy.

(3) *Lumumba vs. Kasavubu*

Up to this time the United Nations had been acting at least nominally as an agent of the central Congolese government, in line with the latter's requests to the Security Council. Not only had it obtained the withdrawal of the Belgian forces within a matter of two months or less; it had also undertaken the systematic retraining of the Congolese military forces and had launched a vast program of technical and administrative assistance designed to ward off the ever-present possibility that the country might relapse into complete chaos.[41] But the uneasy partnership between the United Nations and the Leopoldville government which had made these things possible was now nearing its end. The next phase of the crisis was to be dominated not by cooperation but by conflict between the United Nations and M. Lumumba. While the United Nations continued its desperate effort to maintain stability in the Congo, M. Lumumba, supported by the U.S.S.R. and to a somewhat variable degree by other African states, appeared to be doing his best to make the performance of this task impossible.

The Congolese Premier had been in no way satisfied with the neutral position adopted by the United Nations in his quarrel with M. Tshombe. What he wanted was not neutrality, but help in bringing M. Tshombe to book; and he continued to threaten that if the United Nations would not provide it, he would seek assistance elsewhere. The Congolese people and government had lost confidence in Mr. Hammarskjold, M. Lumumba asserted on August 15. If the Secretary-General was to continue in charge, he suggested, his actions should be supervised by a watchdog group of Asian and African nations to make sure that he was not evading his duty. The idea that Asian and African nations had a special responsibility for overseeing developments in the Congo was to prove quite popular among the Asian and African delegations in New York.

There were signs, however, that M. Lumumba's political support within the Congo was beginning to dwindle as his dependence on Communist support and advice become more evident. The Congolese Premier also gave the impression of an increasing reliance on xenophobe and racist tendencies to support his battle with the United Nations. He became inaccessible to Dr. Bunche, the world organization's ranking representative. On August 19, he went so far as to demand the withdrawal of all white troops from the United Nations force. This demand was dropped the next day, presumably on the advice of Tunisia and other African states which were beginning to be disturbed by the Congolese leader's unbridled fanaticism. But there were ugly incidents involving the manhandling of Canadian and other United Nations troops. Late in August, eight United States Air Force men were severely beaten by Congolese military personnel who claimed to have mistaken them for "Belgian parachutists."

If difficulties of this kind were to be thrown in its way, the whole United Nations effort in the Congo might have to be reconsidered, Mr. Hammarskjold told the Security Council on August 21. Though he clearly did not favor the establishment of a "watchdog group" such as M. Lumumba had proposed and the U.S.S.R. was now formally urging, the Secretary-General said he did plan to set up an informal advisory committee of those countries, by this time fifteen in number, which were contributing units to the United Nations force. Since all but three of these were Asian and African states, such an arrangement would ensure that Asian and African views were adequately and continuously represented at United Nations headquarters. Another move that might help to soothe M. Lumumba's anxieties was the announcement that the American Dr. Bunche would be replaced by Rajeshwar Dayal of India as the Secretary-General's personal representative. All the non-Communist members of the Security Council voiced strong support of the Secretary-General's position, and the U.S.S.R. withdrew its proposal for the establishment of a watchdog group. "This is no time to be looking for fly specks," Mr. Lodge observed after he had refuted the criticisms of the Soviet representative and warned the U.S.S.R. to stop toying with its idea of sending Soviet "volunteers" to the Congo. "We are embarked on a great adventure. Let us all get behind this project and put our shoulders to the wheel." [42]

In the course of the next four weeks the Congo situation was to reach a pitch of confusion exceeding anything imagined thus far.[43] While representatives of the independent African states were meeting in Leopoldville and casting about for ways to "calm down Lumumba," that leader was preparing to undertake a military campaign aimed at reconquering M. Kalonji's so-called "Mining State" in South Kasai and using the territory as a jumping-off place for an invasion of Katanga. Intertribal hostilities had meanwhile broken out on a large scale in both areas; M. Tshombe was denouncing the United Nations for failing to quell his enemies of the Baluba tribe; Mr. Hammarskjold was pressing the Belgians to complete the evacuation of Katanga and other areas; and, perhaps most dangerous of all from the American standpoint, the U.S.S.R. and Czechoslovakia were sending in large numbers of technicians, establishing large diplomatic missions in the capital, and obviously working at top speed to secure a permanent foothold.

Among other questionable activities, it was learned that the U.S.S.R. had supplied certain aircraft and other military equipment directly to M. Lumumba for use against his internal foes—a procedure in no way consistent with the objectives of the Security Council resolutions. President Eisenhower himself emphasized on September 7 that the United States took "a most serious view" of this action. Accusing the U.S.S.R. of "aggravating an already serious situation which finds Africans killing other Africans," the President solemnly appealed to the Kremlin "to desist from its unilateral activities and to lend its support instead to the practice of collective effort through the United Nations." [44]

It was in the midst of this rapidly deteriorating situation that President Kasavubu suddenly reasserted himself and on September 5 took the drastic step of dismissing Premier Lumumba and naming Joseph Ileo, a moderate by Congolese standards, to succeed him as Premier. Although it lacked the sanction of the Congolese parliament, this unexpected move might under other circumstances have initiated a process of over-all improvement in the internal political situation. Messrs. Kasavubu and Ileo not only indicated their intention of cooperating with the United Nations, but shortly entered into negotiations with M. Tshombe and M. Kalonji with a view to solving the constitutional problem on the basis of a Congolese confederation. This would clearly be a more viable arrangement than the rigid centralization M. Lumumba had tried to enforce.

There was, however, a serious obstacle to these plans in the person of M. Lumumba himself. That notable flatly refused to accept his dismissal. President Kasavubu's action, he claimed, had been invalid under the Congolese constitution; in fact, he said, it had left him, M. Lumumba, with no other choice than to deprive M. Kasavubu of the presidential office and to assume sole control of Congolese affairs. Not surprisingly, M. Lumumba's refusal to consider himself dismissed was fully supported by the U.S.S.R. It was also supported by Ghana, Guinea, the United Arab Republic, and many other Asian, African, and neutral governments which had doubts about the legality of M. Kasavubu's action and still regarded M. Lumumba as the legitimate embodiment of Congolese nationalism. Thus the result of M. Kasavubu's coup was not the political extinction of M. Lumumba but the establishment of two rival Congolese governments, each with its train of domestic and foreign supporters.

Although the United Nations authorities in Leopoldville officially took no stand on this intricate constitutional question, their practical actions in defense of law and order had the effect of laying them open to the charge of supporting Kasavubu against Lumumba. Faced with an imminent threat of civil bloodshed on a scale that might easily become too large for ONUC to handle, United Nations representatives took the precautionary step of closing down the Leopoldville radio on September 6 and also ordered the Congolese airports closed for all non-United Nations operations. These facilities were thus denied to M. Lumumba's supporters. Mr. Hammarskjold, in a report to the Security Council made public early on September 8, drew urgent attention to the increasing gravity of the situation from both a financial and a political point of view, laid heavy stress on the importance of avoiding any kind of outside intervention in the Congo, and dropped a hint that the United Nations might find it necessary to disarm some Congolese military units temporarily to prevent massacres of innocent civilians.[45]

In the eyes of M. Lumumba and his followers, the United Nations by these actions was in effect dropping all pretense of impartiality and coming out openly on the side of the "colonialists." Mr. Hammarskjold's eloquent defense of his subordinates and his renewed warnings before the Security Council on September 9 [46] failed to still the criticism, which continued even after the radio and airports were reopened for civilian purposes on September 13. Ghana and the United Arab Republic threatened to withdraw their units from the United Nations force; the U.S.S.R. accused the United Nations command and Mr. Hammarskjold personally of violating the Security Council's resolutions; [47] M. Lumumba reiterated his threat to turn "elsewhere" for assistance unless the United Nations immediately furnished him with twenty aircraft and crews together with other military items to combat the designs of his enemies.[48]

Convening on September 14 to continue its study of this tense situation, the Security Council found itself faced with a new complication in the presence of two rival delegations from the Congo, one representing M. Lumumba and the other M. Kasavubu, and both claiming the right to speak for the Congo. In view of the uncertainty of the Congolese internal situation, neither was seated. On that very day a third "government" had entered the scene as the Congolese Chief of Staff, Colonel Joseph D. Mobutu, announced that the army was assuming direct control for the balance of the year. Colonel Mobutu was generally thought to be a Kasavubu supporter. At any rate, M. Kasavubu remained unmolested in the following days. On the other hand, the restrictions on M. Lumumba were gradually tightened, and there was also a strong reaction against the U.S.S.R. and Czechoslovakia, the spearheads of Communist infiltration in the country. On September 16 the diplomatic missions of those two countries were actually ordered out of the Congo. Accompanied by their technicians, they departed on the following day—with a promise to return soon.

This turn of events could only accentuate the fury with which V. A. Zorin, the Soviet representative in the Security Council, had been attacking the Secretary-General and the whole conduct of the United Nations operation. Among the demands embodied in Moscow's latest draft resolution were the return of the airfields and radio to the "central government" (obviously meaning Lumumba) and the removal of General von Horn as United Nations commander.[49] The United States, now represented by Ambassador Wadsworth, was supporting the United Nations with equal vigor and advocating a resolution which called for voluntary financial contributions to support the United Nations effort, urged a speedy settlement of the Congo's internal conflicts, and reaffirmed the importance of nonintervention by outside states, especially in the military field.[50] As this latest Security Council debate neared its end on the night of September 16-17, the United States abandoned its own resolution and swung its support to a milder draft submitted by Ceylon and Tunisia which covered essentially the same ground but gave greater emphasis to the role of the Congolese central government—again apparently meaning Lumumba, although this point was not made explicit.[51] Eight countries voted in favor of the Ceylonese-Tunisian text in the early hours of September 17, and France abstained. But this time the U.S.S.R. and Poland voted negatively. The Soviet Union thus cast its ninetieth veto in the history of the Security Council and its first in the Congo crisis.

The usefulness of this move from the Soviet point of view was at least questionable. Resorting to the now familiar "uniting for peace" procedure, the United States immediately sought and obtained a special meeting of the General Assembly, which met in its Fourth Emergency Special Session that very afternoon. The Assembly had no executive powers and was unlikely to turn up any fundamentally new ideas on the Congo situation; but it afforded an admirable means of showing that the world's non-Communist governments had no desire to repudiate the United Nations and its Secretary-General, however they might feel about the Lumumba-Kasavubu contest. So confident was the United States on this point that it took the risk of proposing the immediate admission to the United Nations of fifteen new governments, fourteen of them African, whose applications had already been approved by the Security Council but which had not yet been voted into membership by the Assembly.

Action on this matter was held over to the Assembly's regular session starting on September 20. The existing eighty-two members proved quite enough to provide the vote of confidence in Mr. Hammarskjold and his handling of the Congo situation that the United States had desired. This endorsement took the form of a resolution, introduced by seventeen African and Asian states, which was patterned on the defeated Security Council draft but added the further suggestion that internal conciliation in the Congo might be facilitated by Asian and African representatives appointed by the Secretary-General's new advisory committee.[52] Fully supported by the United States, this draft was adopted early on September 20 by the overwhelming vote of 70 to 0. Since the Soviet bloc, France, and South Africa abstained rather than voting negatively, the endorsement of the main lines of Mr. Hammarskjold's approach was technically unanimous.

30. AFRICA AT THE UNITED NATIONS

(1) *The New Members*

The debate at this emergency session provided a foretaste of the intense preoccupation with African matters that was to characterize the entire course of the regular session of the General Assembly that began on September 20. Had not the name of "African session" already been informally conferred on the Assembly's Thirteenth Regular Session in 1958-59, this title would undoubtedly have been awarded the Fifteenth Session in 1960-61 in view of the great number of African questions which came up for discussion and, in some instances, achieved settlement during its deliberations. Among the most important actions taken by the Fifteenth Assembly during 1960 was the admission to United Nations membership of a total of sixteen new African states and the consequent increase in the organization's over-all membership (with the admission of Cyprus) from eighty-two to ninety-nine. But for a Soviet veto in the Security Council, the admission of a seventeenth African state, Mauritania, would have brought the number to an even hundred. The representation of African members in the United Nations, if South Africa and the United Arab Republic were included, was raised to twenty-six, or over one-fourth of the whole membership. Admittedly some of these new African states fell somewhat below the United Nations average in terms of population, wealth, and experience, but their numbers alone would enable them to exert real influence on the voting of the General Assembly.

The initial group of thirteen African countries admitted on September 20, the opening day of the Assembly's Fifteenth Session, included the three former trust territories of Cameroun, Togo, and Somalia; the Republic of the Congo, whose seat in the Assembly chamber remained temporarily unoccupied pending a clarification of the Kasavubu-Lumumba relationship; and nine members of the French Community which had recently achieved a status which was technically known as "sovereignty," though scarcely distinguishable from "independence," through negotiations with France. The first members of this group to enter the United Nations were the Malagasy Republic on the island of Madagascar (not always listed as an African state); the four Republics of Dahomey, Ivory Coast, Niger, and Upper Volta in former French West Africa, which had recently joined to form a rather shadowy union known as the Council of the Entente; and the Central African Republic and the Republics of Chad, Congo, and Gabon in former French Equatorial Africa.[53] This second Republic of the Congo, with its capital at Brazzaville, boasted the same name but was politically quite distinct from the ex-Belgian Congo. It frequently provided a haven for refugees from Leopoldville on the other side of the Congo River.

Two more states associated with the French Community, the West African republics of Senegal and Mali, were separately admitted to the United Nations on September 28.[54] These two former French colonies, which had previously been known as Senegal and Soudan, had until recently been linked in the so-called Mali Federation established early in 1959. But the Mali Federation had broken apart in August 1960 as the result of internal political rivalries, and its two components had gone separate ways. Senegal, under its French-educated President, Léopold Senghor, maintained an outspokenly pro-French line, whereas Soudan, under its new name of Mali and under the vigorous leadership of President Modibo Keita, embarked on a strongly leftist and neutralist course that seemed quite likely to involve an early withdrawal from the Community itself. But M. Keita, like other African leaders, disclaimed any partiality for Communism, and both France and the United States avoided the mistakes they had made when Guinea had become independent two years earlier. France continued its economic aid to the Mali government, and the United States was quick to accord it diplomatic recognition.

Mauritania, the last of the West African members of the French Community, did not achieve sovereignty until November 28. By that time its chances of admission to the world organization had been severely prejudiced by the opposition of neighboring Morocco, which claimed the new state's entire territory as its own. This claim failed to win wide support in the Assembly, where even Tunisia withheld its backing in spite of its normally close relations with the Moroccan Government. But the U.S.S.R., which had apparently singled out Morocco as another country that presented opportunities for quick political gains, was not so squeamish. When the question of Mauritania's admissibility to the world organization came before the Security Council on December 3-4, its hope of United Nations membership was blasted by another Soviet veto—the ninety-first. The only condition on which the U.S.S.R. would agree to Mauritania's admission was the simultaneous admission of its own client state, the "Mongolian People's Republic," which was as unacceptable to the West as it had been in the past.[55]

In the meantime the much more important and influential Federation of Nigeria had been unanimously admitted to United Nations membership on October 7, a week after its attainment of independence within the British Commonwealth.[56] Nigeria was the most populous sovereign state in Africa and seemed destined to exert a proportionate influence on the international scene. The moderate tone of its leaders' declarations continued to contrast with that of Ghana, hitherto the only Commonwealth representative among the new African states.

This vast increase in African representation at the United Nations inspired some of the most important passages in the address which President Eisenhower delivered to the Assembly on September 22.[57] Perhaps recalling the six-point program for the Middle East which he had laid before the Assembly in 1958,[58] Mr. Eisenhower took this occasion to suggest a five-point program for Africa which amounted to the first authoritative statement of a broad United States policy applicable to the whole of that continent. These were the five ingredients of the Eisenhower formula, the details of which were reserved for later discussion: "[1] Noninterference in the African countries' internal affairs; [2] Help in assuring their security without wasteful and dangerous competition in armaments; [3] Emergency aid to the Congo; [4] International assistance in shaping long-term African development programs; [5] United Nations aid for education."

As in the Middle East, the proclaimed objective of these American recommendations was to protect the newly emerging nations of Africa "from outside pressures that threaten their independence and their sovereign rights." But Mr. Eisenhower's prescription for Africa envisaged no attempt to create a Western-supported security structure like CENTO, or even an anti-Communist political alignment along the lines of the so-called Eisenhower Doctrine. In keeping with the line already adopted by the United States in relation to the Congo crisis, the new American policy pronouncement assigned to the United Nations the main responsibility for protecting African independence and for providing necessary assistance both in the security field and in the economic and technical realm. There was no suggestion in Mr. Eisenhower's speech that the new African states should align themselves with the West politically. "We do not urge—indeed we do not desire—that you should belong to one camp or to the other," Mr. Eisenhower assured a group of African representatives at a White House reception some days later. ". . . The only thing we ask is that, through your own love of freedom and the determination of your people to live their own lives as they choose, you will resist others who have military, economic, or political intent to dominate you." [59]

Obviously the United States was by this time fully aware that participation in any Western-sponsored political alignment was repugnant to virtually all of the new African governments, and that the wisest course was to support their own declared preference for neutrality and noninvolvement. It is true that certain of the African states entertained a concept of neutrality that could arouse little enthusiasm in Washington. In Ghana and Guinea, a status of neutrality had not prevented the acceptance of far-reaching support from the Communist powers and close alignment with the Communist bloc on international questions. President Sékou Touré of Guinea had lately paid his second visit to the U.S.S.R. within less than a year, and had gone on from there to Communist China. In Peking he had been jubilantly welcomed as the first visiting African chief of state and had signed a friendship treaty and a series of economic and technical agreements involving a loan of 100 million rubles.[60] More recently,

M. Touré's government had signed a technical and economic assistance agreement with the United States but had requested that the matter be given no publicity.[61]

President Kwame Nkrumah of Ghana, who had joined with M. Touré in 1959 in sponsoring what it was hoped would become a union of independent African states, was not to be outdone in the matter of political initiatives. Ghana under his leadership had recently become a republic within the Commonwealth, recognized Communist China, and obtained a credit of 160 million rubles from the U.S.S.R.[62] Mr. Nkrumah himself had just made a highly militant statement of the African position before the General Assembly [63] and was playing a prominent role in the activities of the neutral leaders in New York. Rather to the surprise of the Ghanaian President, these activities were interpreted by Secretary Herter as going beyond a mere "bid for the leadership of what you would call a left-wing group of African states." Mr. Nkrumah, the Secretary of State suggested on September 23, had actually "marked himself as very definitely leaning toward the Soviet bloc." [64] But President Nkrumah flatly rejected this interpretation. "Ghana faces neither East nor West, but forward," he insisted.[65]

With the possible exception of Mali, none of the other African states had appeared desirous of leaning as far to the left as Guinea and Ghana were doing. Premier Abubukar Tafawa Balewa of Nigeria, who came to New York for his country's admission to the United Nations and also conferred with President Eisenhower in Washington, had espoused a concept of independence in foreign policy which impressed the United States as much less one-sided than Ghana's. The leaders of most of the new French Community states also seemed to incline toward a rather pro-French or pro-Western type of independence, although the Algerian question was expected to test this attitude severely when it came up for discussion later in the session.

It was largely the numerous abstentions among the new African states that ensured the passage on October 8, though by a slightly diminished majority as compared with the previous year, of the important United States resolution postponing debate on the perennial question of the representation of Communist China. This was an issue on which the African states now held the balance of power in the Assembly. Although none of the newly admitted African members actually supported the United States position —the only African states to do so were Liberia and South Africa—only three of them (Nigeria, Senegal, and Mali) voted against it. Since Ethiopia, Ghana, Guinea, Morocco, the Sudan, and the United Arab Republic also voted against the United States on this question, the record for Africa as a whole amounted to two in favor, nine opposed, and fourteen abstentions.[66]

(2) *The Congo*

A roughly similar division among the African states was evident in the continuing battle over the Congo that ran through the Assembly session and for a time removed the center of the Congo crisis from Leopoldville to New York. Ghana, Guinea, and the United Arab Republic remained identified heart and soul with the cause of the deposed Premier Lumumba. In common with the U.S.S.R., the Soviet bloc states, and such neutrals as Yugoslavia and India, they continued to insist that the dismissal of the Prime Minister by President Kasavubu had been illegal and that M. Lumumba alone represented legitimate executive authority in the Congo. But some of the other African states, including most members of the French Community, inclined to reserve judgment or even to support the position of President Kasavubu and Colonel Mobutu. It was the latter, rather than M. Kasavubu or Premier-designate Ileo, who now seemed to wield practical authority in the Congo. Colonel Mobutu's influence was exerted partly through the army and partly through a so-called "High Commission" of young intellectuals which he had set up in late September to direct the administration.

This change in the local political situation in the Congo had been accompanied by an apparent shift in the position of the local United Nations representatives, whose attempts to maintain an impartial position amid the swirling tides of Congolese politics won little appreciation in any quarter. The attitude adopted by the United Nations in September had undoubtedly been of assistance to President Kasavubu in his successful attempt to exclude M. Lumumba from office. Now, however, the Kasavubu-Mobutu combination began in its turn to feel the weight of United Nations disapproval. While Mr. Hammarskjold in New York was defending past United Nations actions and boldly defying Khrushchev's demands that he resign,[67] his new personal representative in the Congo, Mr. Dayal, was observing developments on the spot with growing dissatisfaction. Ghanaian troops of the United Nations force were still protecting M. Lumumba from arrest, and other United Nations troops were endeavoring to limit the bloodshed in Katanga and other provincial areas. But what particularly impressed Mr. Dayal was the number of Belgians (possibly 2,000 or 2,100) who were now returning to the Congo and taking up important positions under the central and Katanga governments, where they were not subject to United Nations control. In an official report dated November 2, Mr. Dayal gave the impression that he regarded this movement as nothing less than an organized Belgian attempt to recolonize the Congo with the connivance of the *de facto* Congolese authorities.[68]

Although the State Department immediately voiced its confidence in Belgium's "good faith" and "desire to be of assistance in the Congo," [69] the Dayal report gave a powerful weapon to M. Lumumba's backers in New York and increased the pressure for action on his behalf. This pressure was exerted in two main directions. There was a strong demand that M. Lumumba's delegation be seated without further delay as the authorized representative of the Congo in the General Assembly. It was also proposed that a so-called conciliation or good offices group, made up of African and Asian representatives, be sent to the Congo on behalf of the United Nations to assist in ironing out the constitutional and political tangle. This latter move had originated in Secretary-General Hammarskjold's advisory committee on the Congo, which now included representatives of fifteen African and Asian states plus Ireland, Canada, and Sweden. In theory the conciliation group would not favor any particular Congolese leader or faction. In practice, however, the project looked very much like a device for restoring M. Lumumba to power. Its membership was to be limited to African and Asian members of the advisory committee; and the more active pro-Lumumba elements in this group spoke openly of their hope of reconvening what remained of the scattered Congolese parliament and getting it to reconfirm M. Lumumba in office.

This plan was cut short by the sudden decision of President Kasavubu to fly to New York and personally claim a seat in the Assembly as head of the Congolese delegation. Some said that the United States itself had had a hand in this decision; at any rate, the United States no longer attempted to conceal the fact that it greatly preferred M. Kasavubu to M. Lumumba. For a fortnight it was nip and tuck in the Assembly and its Credentials Committee as the pro-Lumumba group struggled to defer a decision on M. Kasavubu's claim until the conciliation committee could depart for the Congo. But on November 22 the Kasavubu delegation was officially seated by a vote of 53 to 24, with 19 abstentions—another Western success for which much of the credit went to the new French African states.[70] The departure of the conciliation group was accordingly postponed until it could be ascertained whether or not M. Kasavubu would permit it to visit the Congo at all. Guinea and Mali resigned from the group in protest, though Ghana remained for the time being.

The Assembly's acceptance of M. Kasavubu as the authorized representative of the Congo seemed likely to strengthen his position at home and thus lessen the danger that Soviet or other unhealthy influences would regain a foothold. There was, however, another possible doorway to outside influence in the Congo, one to which Mr. Hammarskjold had just drawn attention in an ominous statement to the Assembly's budgetary committee. This was the financial doorway. Unless a way was quickly found to meet the heavy expenses of the United Nations operation in the Congo, the Secretary-General declared, it would soon be necessary to start withdrawing the United Nations troops. And, he added, if the United Nations ceased to fill the Congolese vacuum, "it will inexorably be filled in other ways." [71] Statements from the U.S.S.R. and Ghana, among others, indicated that those countries would not be at all averse to seeking "other ways" of filling the vacuum. To the United States, on the other hand, the collapse of the United Nations effort would mean the collapse of its entire policy of relying on the world organization to protect the Congo against the intrusion of undesirable influences.

The financial problem of the United Nations in the Congo had two main aspects. First was the cost of the United Nations military force, by this time numbering some 19,443 men from twenty-eight countries. Estimated at $10 million a month, the bill was expected to come to some $60 million for 1960 and possibly twice that amount for 1961. Like the costs of the United Nations Emergency Force in the Middle East, these sums would presumably be assessed against the members of the United Nations in proportion to their assessments for the regular United Nations budget. But the difficulty experienced in financing the Middle Eastern force, to which the Soviet bloc states had never contributed a cent, was not an encouraging augury for the collection of the much larger sums that were now required for the Congo. In addition, Mr. Hammarskjold had also appealed weeks earlier for a special voluntary fund of $100 million for the restoration of Congolese economic life and public services.[72] The United States had already contributed $5 million for this purpose, in addition to an earlier grant of $5 million in support of current United Nations efforts. Great Britain and Canada had also promised $3 million and $1 million respectively, but the U.S.S.R. had contributed nothing and there was no current indication that other contributions would be forthcoming in anything like the desired amount.

"Why should I pay you to keep me from stirring him up?"

Bastian in the *San Francisco Chronicle*

The most pressing need at the moment was for cash to keep the military operation afloat until the end of the year, and this at least the United States determined to provide. While the Soviet representative in the Assembly's budgetary committee found fault with the world organization's financial management and suggested that the United Nations troops had really better be withdrawn, the United States announced on November 29 that it would bear substantially half the cost of the 1960 operation. In addition to its normal assessment of $16,225,000, it promised a voluntary contribution of $3,500,000 to $4,000,000 and also undertook to write off $10,317,621 of the estimated $14,000,000 owed to it by the United Nations on account of the summer's airlift.[73] In the next few days, Great Britain, Canada, and the U.S.S.R. waived a further $2,471,750 in airlift costs. These moves would ensure the maintenance of the United Nations force for the balance of 1960, and the Assembly later passed a formal resolution asking United Nations members to supply the remaining $48.5 million on the basis of their regular assessments.[74] The question of financing the continuance of the operation in 1961 was left for later discussion.

While these matters were under debate, the fortunes of M. Lumumba and his supporters had undergone a further setback. Having got rid of the Russians and Czechs, Colonel Mobutu had proceeded to go after the Ghanaians. The position assumed by President Nkrumah as M. Lumumba's special patron and counselor—he had sent him letters of political advice addressed to "Dear Patrice"—was gravely weakened on November 22 when Colonel Mobutu expelled the Ghanaian President's personal representative, accusing him of political intrigue with the deposed Prime Minister. An attempt by Tunisian United Nations troops to prevent the execution of the expulsion order brought about a first important clash between Congolese and United Nations forces.

Worse things were in store for M. Lumumba himself. While confined to his residence, the ex-Premier had remained in close touch with loyal Congolese elements, many of whom had recently been congregating in Stanleyville, the capital of Oriental Province. On November 28, M. Lumumba suddenly disappeared from view. Four days later, on December 2, he reappeared—not, however, as a free man but as a prisoner of the Congolese army. According to his captors, he had been run to earth while trying to get to Stanleyville to head a new insurrection. Deprived of the protection hitherto accorded by the United Nations, M.

Lumumba plainly was in for a disagreeable experience. It could make little difference to him that Mr. Hammarskjold was sending urgent cables to President Kasavubu, admonishing the latter to abide by legal processes and bear in mind the anxiety of the Asian-African states. Nor did the similar representations made by the United States have any visible effect.[75]

But events were soon to prove that M. Lumumba as a captive was even more dangerous than M. Lumumba as a mere politician out of office. Conceivably his speedy execution might have deprived his Congolese and international partisans of a rallying cry and thus enabled the Kasavubu-Mobutu government to take a firmer hold in cooperation with the United Nations. But the fact that M. Lumumba was still alive, though somewhat the worse for his treatment, stirred the emotions of his supporters to a point where the whole United Nations operation was placed in greater jeopardy than ever before. Once more the air was filled with menace. In Stanleyville, the pro-Lumumba Congolese proclaimed a "legal" government under Antoine Gizenga, M. Lumumba's leftist-minded associate, seized hostages among the local European population, and set up lines of communication to the United Arab Republic and other sympathetic outside powers. The United Nations force was suddenly confronted with a threat of major defections as Morocco, Guinea, Yugoslavia, Indonesia, the U.A.R., and Ceylon announced that they were withdrawing their contingents in protest against the United Nations' failure to protect the "legitimate government."

Thanks largely to Mr. Hammarskjold's vigorous intercession, none of these threatened withdrawals had actually taken place up to the end of the year. But by that time the political position of the United Nations in the Congo had been further impaired by the inability of either the Security Council or the General Assembly to agree on what was to be done next. The U.S.S.R. had been quick to seize the initiative by demanding a new meeting of the

Security Council and, when that body met on December 7, submitting a typically drastic resolution which called on the United Nations to secure Lumumba's release, restore him to power, and disarm the Mobutu forces.[76] But such a program, as Mr. Hammarskjold pointed out, would go far beyond the terms of the United Nations Charter even if it was capable of being physically carried out. The United States, Great Britain, Argentina, and Italy countered with an alternative resolution which called for fair treatment of arrested persons and asked the Secretary-General to continue his efforts,[77] while Ceylon attempted once again to bridge the two positions by a compromise text. The result of several days' hot debate, lasting into the early hours of December 14, was the defeat of the Western resolution by the ninety-second Soviet veto (the vote was 7 to 3, with one abstention) and the concurrent defeat of the Soviet plan by a vote of 8 to 2, Ceylon abstaining. It was noted that neither Ceylon nor Tunisia supported the Western plan, though only Ceylon actually voted against it with Poland and the U.S.S.R.[78]

The perilous deadlock was then moved back to the General Assembly. There the essence of the pro-Lumumba position was embodied in a fresh resolution which was sponsored by Yugoslavia, India, and other Asian and African states.[79] The United States and Britain again undertook to support the Secretary-General with an alternative text that asked him to continue his efforts to exclude foreign influence from the Congo and expressed hope that the internal conflict would be peacefully resolved through the conciliation commission or by a round-table conference that President Kasavubu had talked of convening.[80] This Western text failed by only one vote to gain the needed two-thirds majority when the Assembly took its final actions of the year at the meeting which began on December 20. Forty-three countries voted in favor, with 22 against and 32 abstentions. The rival, pro-Lumumba proposal was voted down by the more decisive majority of 42 against to 28 in favor, with 27 abstentions.

Most of the French Community members abstained on both resolutions.[81] Mr. Hammarskjold, who had been earnestly warning of the dangers of tribal conflict and even a "Spanish war situation" in the Congo, was thus left to carry on as best he might under the previous decisions of the Security Council.

A new round in the Congo struggle would soon be opening as the pro-Lumumba forces consolidated their position in Stanleyville, extended their influence into adjoining provinces, and prepared to face a threatened offensive by Colonel Mobutu's forces. Meanwhile the ailing General von Horn was preparing to hand over the command of the United Nations force to Major General Sean McKeown of Ireland, who would face a doubly difficult assignment if the disaffected governments carried out their threat to withdraw their contingents. Mr. Hammarskjold himself would be visiting the Congo at the beginning of the New Year on his way to consult with the South African Government under the Security Council resolution of April 1. A somewhat depleted Conciliation Commission was also preparing to travel to Leopoldville and hoping to be received by President Kasavubu, although the latter was still shy of accepting outside mediation and still intended to carry out his own plan to convoke a round-table conference of Congolese political leaders. The essential question remained: Would the Congo be able to pull itself together in 1961 and consolidate its position as an independent entity, or was it doomed to remain a battleground of powerful outside forces?

(3) Algeria, Colonialism, and the United States

The essentially negative result of the Assembly's debates on the Congo showed that the balance of forces in that body had not yet tipped decisively in favor of the extreme "anticolonial" position. A similar distribution of voting power determined the outcome of the annual debate on Algeria, made doubly crucial this year by the rapidity with which the de Gaulle government had been moving in recent months toward a final effort to impose its own solution of this six-year-old conflict. In a speech of November 4 in which he again expressed his preference for an "Algerian Algeria" associated with France, M. de Gaulle had firmly committed himself to abide by the results of the self-determination process and had even gone so far as to predict the emergence of an "Algerian Republic." [82] Sensing the threat of still a third insurrection by French settler groups and their military sympathizers, the Paris government had subsequently announced plans for a nationwide referendum in the hope that metropolitan France, at least, would firmly endorse the de Gaulle program and thus convince the extremists in Algeria that there was no possibility of successful resistance. In this vote, which would take place in metropolitan France on January 8 and in Algeria on January 6-8, 1961, the entire population of France and Algeria would be asked to indicate whether or not it approved of (1) self-determination for Algeria as soon as internal security was reestablished, and (2) the setting up of an autonomous Algerian regime to function until self-determination was exercised.[83]

In view of this prospect it seemed reasonable to the United States and to many other Western-minded governments that the General Assembly should avoid any action that could interfere with M. de Gaulle's plans. The F.L.N., however, would not admit the possibility of an impartial French referendum and continued to insist on its own proposal for an Algerian referendum to be conducted under United Nations auspices. Its numerous supporters in the Assembly fully endorsed this stand, and refused to allow the matter to be postponed as the United States and others suggested. Matters came to a head in the second week of December while President de Gaulle was visiting Algeria to explain his intentions. The riots and demonstrations that occurred on this occasion caused at least 124 deaths, 116 of them Muslims. They also indicated more clearly than before the hold which the F.L.N. had come to exercise over the Muslim Algerians, especially in the large cities.

These events imparted a sense of urgency to the debate in the First (Political) Committee of the General Assembly, which hinged on a resolution submitted by twenty-four Asian and African states that explicitly recognized "the right of the Algerian people to self-determination and independence" and called for a United Nations referendum to settle the destiny of the "entire country." [84] This language, which faithfully reflected the F.L.N. point of view, amounted to a protest in advance against any partition of Algeria such as the French were believed to contemplate. On December 15 the Committee approved the resolution by a vote of 47 to 20 with 28 abstentions, among them all of the French Community states except Mali. But the key paragraph calling for a United Nations referendum failed to gain a two-thirds majority—the vote was 38-33-23—and thus seemed likely to fall short of final adoption.

There followed the usual attempts to modify the terms or at least the language of the resolution in such a way as to ensure passage by the plenary session. A proposal by some of the French-speaking African states to take the place of the United Nations in supervising the proposed referendum came to nothing, and the paragraph about a United Nations referendum was still in the text when the resolution came before the plenary session on December 19. But here the crucial paragraph fell far short of a two-thirds vote, being defeated by a 40-40 tie. Ten of the eleven French Community states once again took the side of France and voted against approval. The remainder of the resolution, shorn of its most important provision, was then endorsed by a vote of 63 to 8, with 27 abstentions.[85]

Throughout this process the United States, together with Great Britain and the other colonial powers (except France, which did not participate), consistently refused to vote against General de Gaulle's program. Recorded as voting "No" on the committee resolution, both powers shifted to abstention once the key paragraph had been excised. Since the resolution as adopted still recognized the Algerians' "right to self-determination *and independence,*" the Anglo-American stand was hardly calculated to please the French, even though it incurred the denunciation of the F.L.N. delegation and many in the Asian-African group.

Everything would now depend on the outcome of the French-controlled referendum, which was, in any case, going to be held in Algeria in less than three weeks' time. While the F.L.N. called on all Muslims to boycott the vote, the French Army received orders to ensure as large a turn-out as possible. A favorable vote would not in itself solve the problem, but it would at least put M. de Gaulle in a more advantageous position for renewing contact with the F.L.N. if that was his intention.

There were other African matters on which the United States found it necessary to oppose the desires of the anticolonial states during these climactic days of the Assembly's African debate. An important resolution calling for the speedy end of colonialism—a watered-down version of a plan originally put forward by Khrushchev—found the United States abstaining in company with its "colonial" allies.[86] Portugal, a country whose policy in its overseas territories had incurred the rising detestation of the anticolonial bloc, was strongly but unsuccessfully supported by the United States for a two-year term on the Security Council which was ultimately split between Ireland and Liberia—the first African country south of the Sahara to win that distinction.[87] The United States also abstained on a much-discussed resolution admonishing Portugal to report to the United Nations on conditions in its overseas territories in Africa and elsewhere.[88]

On the question of South African policies in the territory of South West Africa, the United States again found itself unable to support the principal initiative of the anticolonial bloc. This was a resolution deprecating the application of the *apartheid* policy to South West Africa and calling for the dispatch of a United Nations committee to the scene. This feature was felt by the United States to infringe the jurisdiction of the International Court of Justice, which was already seized of the problem on African initiative.[89] Finally, the United States was unable to support the Assembly's principal resolution relating to the Belgian-administered trust territory of Ruanda-Urundi, were Belgium had planned to hold elections in January 1961 but where the Assembly recommended—on Asian-African initiative—that the elections should be postponed until a United Nations commission had tried to straighten out a complex tangle of local tribal and political rivalries.[90]

These actions gave the impression that there remained a wide gulf between African political aspirations and the position of the United States, notwithstanding the sympathetic words pronounced by President Eisenhower at the opening of the Assembly and the accompanying five-point program for Africa which was still awaiting Assembly consideration at the end of the year.[91] African attitudes, it seemed, were evolving at a much faster rate than United States policy had succeeded in doing, and sometimes in directions which the United States was unable to approve.

The rapidity of political evolution in Africa could be illustrated by other developments which had been taking place on that continent while the Assembly was in session. The extreme neutralist and leftward-inclining bloc of African states, already swelled by the accession of Mali, had won a new recruit during the autumn as Morocco, which had at length won France's promise to withdraw its forces and had gained further encouragement from a promise of Soviet jet aircraft, leaned more and more to a radically anticolonial and even pro-Soviet position. Some close observers believed, however, that this was no more than a temporary aberration on Morocco's part.

Ghana and Guinea, hitherto the leading exponents of an extremist tendency in African affairs, had also not confined their activity to New York and Leopoldville. President Nkrumah, continually striving to expand his country's influence as the nucleus of an African or West African bloc, had startled the world on November 27 by proposing the formation of a nine-nation African army and announcing a parliamentary union between Ghana and Mali. Four weeks later, on December 23-24, the leaders of Ghana, Mali, and Guinea met in Conakry to proclaim a union of all three countries and to announce plans for a common economic and monetary policy and a common diplomatic service.[92] The leaders of all three states planned to meet with the heads of others of the more radically minded African governments at an African "summit conference" which was to be held in Casablanca early in 1961 and was expected to formulate a new course of action on the Congo and Algeria.

Even the ancient empire of Ethiopia was not immune to the new tendencies that were sweeping the African scene. The Emperor Haile Selassie very nearly lost his throne in mid-December when a section of his Imperial Guard, apparently backed by a number of younger, foreign-educated Ethiopians, took advantage of the sovereign's temporary absence from the country to proclaim his dethronement and the accession of his son. The Emperor's quick action enabled him to defeat the insurgents, though not without bloodshed, and his references to "foreign influence" (the U.A.R.?) remained unproved. Nevertheless, the demand for a type of progress attuned to contemporary African ideas seemed certain to play an increasing role in Ethiopian affairs in the future.

Events were also moving rapidly in the British territories of the Central African Federation, where a constitutional conference—the sequel to a somewhat inconclusive report by the Monckton Commission—met in London on December 5 but achieved no immediate result except to reveal the growing impatience of the Federation's African nationalist leaders. Kenya, meanwhile, was preparing for new elections which would inaugurate a phase of broadened African participation in government. In Tanganyika, Mr. Nyerere had become Chief Minister and was calling for independence by 1962 at latest. Uganda was also looking forward to elections in the spring, despite an awkward threat of secession by the province of Buganda. In the Union of South Africa, a troubled white population had staked its country's fate upon a republican form of government in a referendum held on October 5. South Africa's future relationship to the Commonwealth, together with that of newly independent Nigeria, would be coming up for discussion at a conference of Commonwealth Prime Ministers in March 1961.

That the growing pace of African developments entailed a special challenge to American foreign policy had been repeatedly emphasized by Senator Kennedy during the election campaign, and one of his first appointments as President-elect was that of Governor G. Mennen Williams as Assistant Secretary of State for African Affairs. Just how the new American administration would undertake to meet the African challenge while maintaining America's ties in Europe would be for 1961 and subsequent years to reveal. The events of 1960, the "year of Africa," had opened up a set of problems and a field for creative action in relation to that continent such as few world powers had previously confronted.

CHAPTER FIVE

THE MIDDLE EAST AND SOUTHERN ASIA

THE INCLUSION within a single chapter of such widely diverse regions as those of the Middle East and Southern Asia is dictated more by practical convenience than by the requirements of the subject matter. Under the conditions of the second postward decade, the countries allocated to the State Department's Bureau of Near Eastern and South Asian Affairs represented a kind of "bridge" or middle ground in both a geographic and a political sense. Turkey, the westernmost land among those normally classified as belonging to the Near or Middle East, looked almost as much to Europe as to Asia. It participated both in NATO and in CENTO, the "Central Treaty Organization" established in 1955 and previously known as the Baghdad Pact. Pakistan, at CENTO's eastward extremity, was also a key member of the Southeast Asia Treaty Organization or SEATO, whose sphere of responsibility extended for hundreds of miles into the Far East and the Pacific. India, too, though not a member of any regional security arrangement, had interests extending in both directions and shared a number of problems with its western as well as its eastern and northeastern neighbors. Ceylon, though likewise classified as a South Asian country, could equally well be compared with the Southeast Asian republics of Burma and Indonesia, both in its economic and social arrangements and in its political attitude.

Yet the countries to be considered in this chapter had much more in common than mere geographical propinquity. From Turkey and the Arab states to India, Pakistan, and Ceylon, nearly all of them were listed among the "underdeveloped" or "developing" countries. Israel, thanks to a rate of internal development that none of the others could match, was perhaps the one clear exception. A majority of the Middle Eastern and South Asian countries, moreover, had been independent for only a few years. Practically all of them had come to independence by a struggle against the Western powers and still maintained, in greater or less degree, an antipathy to anything that looked like Western imperialism. Finally, most of these countries lay close enough to the Communist bloc to be aware that the "cold war," however much they might disapprove of it on principle, was bound to influence their own destinies to an appreciable degree. A few of them had perceived in the methods of Soviet and Chinese Communist imperialism a sufficient threat to their own interests to justify a policy of alliance with the Western powers. Others had taken the view that the best way of safeguarding their independence was to refuse to be drawn into the quarrels of the great powers and to stick to a policy of "noninvolvement" or "positive neutrality."

31. BETWEEN EAST AND WEST

These differing reactions to the Communist threat were partially responsible for the variegated political pattern that had developed in this region in the fifteen years since World War II. At the close of that conflict in 1945, almost the entire Middle East as well as the whole of Southern Asia had been either under Western (principally British) control or at least nominally identified with Western policies. The U.S.S.R., apart from a temporary lodgment in northern Iran which was eliminated in 1946, had possessed no military or political foothold below its southern frontier. Its attempt to secure a stranglehold on Turkey through territorial annexations in northeastern Anatolia and a modification in the regime of the Straits had been decisively repelled, thanks in large part to the moral and material support extended by the United States under the so-called Truman Doctrine. Moscow, during the later 1940's, had seemed to have little chance of realizing the ambitions for southward expansion which it had incautiously disclosed during the period of its wartime association with Nazi Germany. Tibet, farther to the east, had threatened no one. China, though convulsed by civil conflict, had still ranked as a member of the free world.

How different was the situation fifteen years after the war! Except for China and Tibet, no country in this part of the world had actually fallen under Soviet or Communist control; but few of them had maintained their former identification with the West, and still fewer could be considered wholly immune to Communist intrigue or pressure. Of the dozen or so major countries that lay within striking distance of one or other of the Communist powers, only three—Turkey, Iran, and Pakistan—were definitely aligned with the West as members of CENTO. That alliance undoubtedly possessed a certain symbolic value, despite the refusal of the United States to become a full member; but it was nowhere regarded as a particularly effective deterrent to the expansion of Soviet power. The internal stability of its regional members, especially Iran, was by no means thoroughly established.

This "northern tier," as Secretary of State John Foster Dulles had called it, had been further weakened by the attitude of some of the countries that geographically might have seemed destined to form a part of it. Iraq, one of the original members, had dropped out completely as the result of a revolution in July 1958 that had eliminated its pro-Western government and opened the door to Communist infiltration on a broad scale. Afghanistan, never a member of the Baghdad Pact, had professed neutrality between East and West and, though it sought to cultivate an advantageous relationship with the United States, had year by year expanded its military, economic, and cultural ties with the Communist world. Uncommitted India had persisted in its disapproval of all military alliances even after its own security had been called into question by Communist China's occupation of Tibet in 1959 and its subsequent seizure of extensive Indian border territories.

Whatever the value of the Baghdad Pact, or CENTO, as a protection to the countries of the "northern tier," it had been wholly unable to bar the advance of Communist influence in the Arab lands to the south. The Arab world, by and large, had been too intent on completing its emancipation from the West, too obsessed by its quarrel with Israel, and too preoccupied by the struggle for power among its own leaders to reflect with any seriousness on the possibility that its newly won independence might some day be threatened by the U.S.S.R. Aided by this attitude, the Soviet Union since the mid-1950's had been gradually implanting its influence in the Arab countries through much the same combination of political chicanery and economic and military benefits that it had more recently begun to employ in Africa. In Iraq, the chaos that followed the 1958 revolution, plus the tolerance of the new regime, had actually enabled the local Communists and their associates to reach a position in which they might have made a successful bid for power had not Moscow apparently decided at the last moment in favor of caution.

Discouraging as these tendencies had seemed at times, neither the growth of Communist influence and pressure nor the continuing antagonism that prevailed among some of its indigenous peoples would have justified "writing off" the Middle East as lost to the non-Communist world. Some of the Arab leaders, like King Hussein of Jordan, had not disdained Western help when independence was menaced, whether by Communism or by the pan-Arab nationalist forces that looked to President Abdel Nasser of the United Arab Republic as their chief inspiration. The experience in Iraq had even precipitated something of an anti-Communist reaction within that country and in the Arab world generally. President Abdel Nasser, though accepting Soviet aid on a large scale and displaying marked intolerance toward King Hussein, Premier Abdel Karim Kassim of Iraq, and any other Arab leader who refused to recognize the ascendancy of the U.A.R., had nevertheless evinced a certain mistrust of Khrushchev's intentions during 1959 and had gone to some pains to cultivate a better relationship with Great Britain and the United States.

Both in the Middle East and in Southern Asia, the situation thus retained a certain fluidity as 1960 began. The old idea of organizing a broad regional coalition to resist Communist aggression or infiltration no longer possessed much validity as a guide to Western policy. Nevertheless there might still be opportunities for purposeful and imaginative action, both diplomatic and economic, aimed at alleviating local conflicts and helping the countries of the area into a better position to defend their independence from whatever direction it might be threatened.

32. THE POLITICS OF THE ARAB WORLD

The United States did not attempt any major new initiative in policy toward the Arab world in 1960. Its attitude toward Arab problems continued to reflect the principles of the so-called Middle East Resolution or "Eisenhower Doctrine" adopted early in 1957.[1] That document had declared the preservation of the independence and integrity of the Middle Eastern nations to be "vital to the national interest and world peace," had authorized a program of economic and military assistance to countries threatened by international Communism, and had thus provided the rationale of such later American actions as the furnishing of special assistance to Jordan and the temporary dispatch of armed forces to Lebanon after the Iraqi revolution in 1958. Although the Eisenhower Doctrine had been anything but popular with most of the Arab countries, the United States could claim that the actions it had undertaken within its terms had played a big part in preserving the independence of the Middle Eastern nations during that critical year.

In August 1958, while this crisis was still in a fairly acute phase, President Eisenhower had gone before the United Nations General Assembly to propose a new Middle Eastern program of international scope involving, among other things, the establishment of a United Nations "peace force" and a "regional Arab development institution." [2] But this program, which might have represented at least a partial substitute for the Eisenhower Doctrine, had never advanced beyond the blueprint stage. In its absence, the underlying principle of the Eisenhower Doctrine—the American interest in the independence and integrity of the Middle Eastern nations—remained an active and vital component of United States policy, even though the Middle East Resolution itself was seldom mentioned except in the periodic reports which the President was required to send to Congress. That there had been a considerable abatement of tension and growth of stability in the area since the 1958 crisis was duly noted in one such report which was transmitted to Congress on February 15, 1960.[3]

This trend toward greater stability—always a very relative term in the Middle East—continued through most of 1960 in almost every aspect of Arab affairs except for the quarrel with Israel, which will be examined in the next section. Especially gratifying to Western observers was the comparative quiet that now prevailed in Iraq, after many tense months in which revolutionary uprisings had succeeded one another at frequent intervals and a "Nasserist" or Communist takeover had several times appeared imminent. Premier Kassim, seriously wounded by a would-be assassin in October 1959, was still in the saddle and still insisting on his neutrality both in the East-West conflict and in Iraq's three-cornered internal struggle among Communists, Kurds, and pan-Arab nationalists. Actually, the Iraqi leader seemed not unwilling to lend a hand in reducing the Communists' influence, a process that was materially aided by divisions within the local Communist party. In February 1960, the "regular," pro-Moscow Communist party was actually excluded from the permission to resume political activity which was accorded to certain other specified parties. That privilege was reserved to a dissident Communist group with more nationalist leanings. In a parallel move, Premier Kassim got rid of the principal pro-Communist figure in his cabinet, Dr. Ibrahim Kubba.

In foreign policy, the Iraqi Government continued to maintain its position of independence both toward the great powers and toward the other Arab states. Its feud with the United Arab Republic had abated somewhat in recent months, although no real reconciliation between Premier Kassim and President Abdel Nasser was to be expected so long as the former continued to assert that Iraq was the real leader of Arab nationalism and that it would presently undertake to "liberate" Abdel Nasser's compatriots in the Syrian region of the U.A.R. Iraq was absent when the Arab League Council met in February to discuss the Palestine problem and other issues. That it was not moving closer to the Soviet bloc, despite its acceptance of substantial military and economic aid from the U.S.S.R. and the satellite countries, was made very evident by the cool reception accorded Soviet First Deputy Premier A. I. Mikoyan when the latter visited Baghdad in April in order to open a Soviet industrial exhibition and try to straighten out the difficulties among the local Communists.

Paradoxically, it was the government of President Abdel Nasser, which in 1959 had appeared to be trying to reduce its dependence on the U.S.S.R., that now seemed most willing to extend its ties with the Communist world. The policy of the U.A.R. had long been subordinated in large degree to the need for outside assistance in connection with the High Dam which Abdel Nasser was determined to construct at Aswan on the Nile as the showpiece of his country's development program. The U.S.S.R. had already undertaken to finance the first stage of this mammoth enterprise with a credit of some $100 million, made available under circumstances which had been widely lamented in the West as one of the more regrettable results of misdirected Western diplomacy in the area. But construction of the first stage of the dam was only beginning in January 1960, and it had been understood that Western enterprise would still have the opportunity to participate in the second of the project's three stages, which would begin in 1964. Negotiations to this end were already going forward with certain West German interests when Khrushchev apparently perceived another opportunity to steal a march on his Western competitors. On January 18, 1960, Cairo announced that the U.S.S.R. had agreed to finance the second stage as well. A subsequent agreement providing for a Soviet loan of 900 million rubles ($225 million at the exaggerated official exchange rate) assured the U.S.S.R. of a central if not a dominant role in U.A.R. financial and economic affairs for at least a decade to come.[4]

President Abdel Nasser did not disdain the smaller loans and other forms of economic assistance made available by the United States, and did not allow his political outlook to be swayed by economic benefits from either side. If his general political attitude seemed more often to coincide with that of the U.S.S.R. than with that of the United States, this was mainly because the United States was closely identified with Israel and the "colonial" powers, whereas the U.S.S.R. had made it its business to support and encourage the neutralist, anticolonial tendencies of which the U.A.R. leader was a typical representative. Abdel Nasser's horizons and influence as a neutral leader were by no means limited to the Arab world. His determination to play a role on the larger world stage was attested once again in the course of an early spring visit to India and Pakistan which did much to enhance his standing as an Afro-Asian statesman and a leading exponent of the nonalignment principle. There were even signs that he aspired to exercise an influence in Latin American affairs and sought an opportunity for collaboration with Premier Castro and the other discontented Latin American elements that were carrying on a fight against "Yankee imperialism."

Although observers in the United States found a good deal to criticize in Abdel Nasser's attitude, they could at least take satisfied note of the temporary abatement of his feud with King Hussein of Jordan and of the radio and propaganda warfare that had raged so violently between Cairo and Amman in recent years. Jordan, backed by American moral support and budgetary and technical assistance at a rate that now exceeded $50 million a year, appeared to have ridden out the most serious threats to its independence and to have a better prospect of survival than at any time in the past half-dozen years. Even the assassination of Premier Hazza Majali on August 29 in a bomb explosion—attributed by King Hussein to Jordanian exiles in Syria—caused no major political upset, although it did revive the tension between Jordan and the U.A.R. on the eve of the General Assembly session in New York. (See below.) It was King Hussein's contention that Abdel Nasser had once again resorted to clandestine attacks on Jordan in order to distract attention from the U.A.R.'s internal troubles, especially in the Syrian region. This, however, was an allegation that few outsiders had the means of verifying.

Developments in the other Arab states attracted little notice in Washington during these months, although there was disturbing evidence of a growth of Communist activity in distant Yemen as that country gradually emerged from its hermit-like seclusion. President Eisenhower summarized the available intelligence in August in another of the semi-annual reports submitted under the Middle East Resolution: "An extensive effort is being carried forward by the Sino-Soviet bloc in Yemen where port facilities constructed by the Soviets are nearing completion, as is a road from the country's principal port to its largest inland city. For construction of the latter, Communist China has sent to Yemen over 800 engineers and skilled workmen." [5] Other official sources in Washington reported several additional projects being carried out in Yemen with Communist funds and personnel.[6]

These activities were linked in the President's report with Iraq's acceptance of "indiscriminate offers of assistance" from the Soviet bloc and with the arrangement for Soviet financing of the Aswan Dam. The latter project, the report conceded, was clearly intended "to become a symbol of Soviet interest in the economic growth of countries in the Middle East and Africa." Nevertheless it remained the view in Washington that these efforts had "not so far enabled the forces of international communism to threaten seriously the independence and integrity of any countries of the region." Consequently, there had been no occasion for the employment of American armed forces under the terms of the Middle East Resolution. That possibility, the report suggested, could still be regarded as "a safeguard in reserve," available to any Middle Eastern country desiring outside assistance against an external Communist threat.[7]

33. ARABS, ISRAELIS, AND AMERICANS

The Eisenhower Doctrine, being directed essentially against the Communist threat to the Middle East, could have only limited application to the situation of hostility that had prevailed between Israel and the states of the Arab world throughout the dozen years since Israel's first appearance on the Middle Eastern map. The Middle East Resolution did, indeed, provide for continued United States support of the United Nations Emergency Force, established in the Suez crisis of 1956 and still deployed along the armistice demarcation line between Israel and the Egyptian part of the United Arab Republic. But although UNEF had done invaluable service in preventing raids or military attacks by either side in this sensitive area, it could do little if anything to mitigate the basic animosities which had made a mockery of the word "peace" as applied to this part of the world.

The United States had long recognized that the Arab-

Israeli antagonism represented a critical weakness for the entire Middle East, a potential source of wider international complications of the kind that had so alarmed the world in 1956. Yet its well-meant attempts to encourage a permanent peace settlement between Israel and the Arab states had encountered so many rebuffs and disappointments that Washington now seemed disinclined to undertake new initiatives in this direction and gave the impression of preferring to try to live with the existing situation, unsatisfactory though it was.

Israel had insisted for many years that it was ready to conclude peace with the Arab states immediately, but only on the understanding that it would give up no territory and would take back none—or at most only a small part—of the million Arab refugees from its soil who were currently being supported by the United Nations in the surrounding Arab-ruled areas. The Arab governments were somewhat divided in their own approach, because Hussein of Jordan insisted that his country must keep the territory it had annexed on the west bank of the Jordan, whereas other Arab states declined to support this ambition. Premier Kassim had even gone so far as to call for the inclusion of the territory in question in a new, Arab-ruled "Palestine entity." But all Arabs agreed that so far as they were concerned, peace with Israel would be out of the question unless that country would at least agree to permit the refugees to return to their former homes and accept the narrow frontiers originally assigned to it by the United Nations in 1947. "Palestine must be liberated," Abdel Nasser declared once again in a speech to his Syrian constituents on February 20, 1960. He and all his ministers, the U.A.R. President added, were ready to shed their blood to help recover "the stolen parts of the Arab nation." [8]

Under these conditions of unconcealed antagonism, sniping and small-scale military encounters were a regular occurrence along those sections of the Israeli frontier that did not have the benefit of UNEF's protection. The

United Nations Truce Supervision Organization, which was responsible for general surveillance of the armistice lines, could seldom prevent such skirmishes, although it often intervened to good effect to stop the fighting before it could spread. A pair of unusually severe clashes which took place in the neighborhood of the Israeli-Syrian border in February 1960, shortly before Abdel Nasser's speech, raised a prospect that the situation might engage the attention of the United Nations Security Council as it had frequently done in past years. The Western powers, however, were normally reluctant to discuss the Palestine problem in the Security Council because of the uncertain attitude of the U.S.S.R., and the Council refrained from meeting on this occasion in spite of a formal complaint from Israel, dated February 25, about the "warlike threats" and "extensive military preparations" which it claimed were going forward in the United Arab Republic.[9]

One factor in the "atmosphere of general distrust" [10] that had become particularly noticeable at this period was the competition in armaments between the Arab states and Israel that had been going on ever since Abdel Nasser had turned to the Soviet bloc for military assistance back in 1955. Premier David Ben-Gurion of Israel, noting that Soviet arms were still flowing to Iraq as well as to the U.A.R., had been insisting with even more than his usual vigor that it would be only fair for Israel to receive equivalent assistance from the West in order to prevent a relative deterioration in its security position. So far as Washington was concerned, however, President Eisenhower adhered to the established view that there was no reason for the United States to become a "major supplier" of arms to Israel or any other country in the area. Israel, the President pointed out on February 17, had long been getting arms from Great Britain and France. "I think we're sending arms to enough nations, really," he said. "I think let somebody else carry a little responsibility."[11]

Nevertheless the Israeli Premier did not abandon his hope of enlisting American support for some move to strengthen Israel's over-all position, and he undoubtedly canvassed the possibilities with President Eisenhower when he called at the White House on March 10 in the course of a private visit to the United States. There was some thought in Mr. Ben-Gurion's mind that the Arab-Israeli problem might be a fitting subject for discussion at the forthcoming summit conference. It seemed to him that the Big Four might even be persuaded to issue some kind of joint declaration guaranteeing the *status quo* in the area, as the United States, Britain, and France had tried to do in the now outmoded Tripartite Declaration of 1950.[12] Although Khrushchev subsequently evaded a request for a personal meeting with the Israel leader, the idea that Russia might now be ready to join the West in trying to impose a peace settlement caused some alarm in Arab political quarters, and the breakdown of the summit conference in May was greeted in this part of the world with more relief than disappointment.

In the meantime the United States had been exposed to considerable embarrassment as a result of Abdel Nasser's policy of refusing transit through the Suez Canal to Israeli vessels and to foreign vessels carrying cargoes to or from Israel. The legality of this procedure had been frequently called in question, but since the U.A.R. had physical control of the Canal it was difficult to prevent it from regulating the traffic in accordance with its own interpretation of international law. Two non-Israeli vessels which had run afoul of the U.A.R.'s views, the Danish *Inge Toft* and the Greek *Astypalea,* were obliged to unload their cargoes and depart during the early part of 1960 after vainly waiting for months for permission to pass through the Canal. Although the United States had strongly supported the principle of freedom of passage through the Canal,[13] it preferred to take no initiative at this time and left it to Mr. Hammarskjold to try to straighten out the matter with Abdel Nasser.[14] "I don't know what you can do unless you want to resort to force in such affairs," said

President Eisenhower, "and I'm certain that we're not trying to settle international problems with force." [15]

There was, however, considerable demand within the United States for a more energetic stand, both on the Suez question and on certain kindred matters on which the Arab states had taken positions that were felt to conflict with American rights and principles. In addition to the criticism occasioned by Saudi Arabia's long-standing policy of excluding American personnel of Jewish faith, a good deal of resentment had been stirred up in recent weeks in connection with the practice of the U.A.R. and other Arab states of blacklisting American vessels that traded with Israel as part of their attempt to isolate Israel economically. In April, New York longshoremen spontaneously instituted a retaliatory boycott of the Egyptian vessel *Cleopatra,* an action which led to counter-boycotts of American vessels by the Arab states and eventually compelled an alarmed White House and State Department to intercede directly with the chiefs of the American labor movement.[16]

Concurrently, certain amendments were attached to the pending Mutual Security legislation with the general objective of denying American assistance to nations engaging in practices of this kind. These initiatives, too, encountered strong resistance from the State Department, which professed to fear "the deep resentment or hostility not only of the ten Arab nations but of their natural friends, the states of Africa and Asia." Despite these warnings, the Mutual Security Act as passed in May included a special pronouncement in favor of freedom of navigation and international economic cooperation, a condemnation of "economic warfare . . . boycotts, blockades, and the restriction of the use of international waterways," and a statement that American aid should be administered "to give effect to these principles." [17]

Some prominent Americans, including Chairman Fulbright of the Senate Foreign Relations Committee, deplored the intrusion of "irresponsible pressure groups" into such delicate areas of foreign policy. Nevertheless, the sympathy for Israel prevailing in important segments of American opinion would undoubtedly continue to influence the actions of the United States Government in relation to the Middle East, despite the evident risk of adding to the discontent of the Arab governments with American policy. This basic sympathy with the Israeli position was evidenced in a different context a few weeks later when the Security Council was called on to adjust a quarrel between Argentina and Israel over the kidnaping on Argentine soil of Adolf Eichmann, one-time Nazi secret police official, and his removal to Israel for trial on charges of mass extermination of Jews during World War II.[18] The net effect of the Security Council's action was to make possible a restoration of Argentine-Israeli diplomatic relations, which Argentina had broken off.

Concern for Israel's interests was even more evident in the declarations of the two American presidential candidates, each of whom promised that if elected he would lose no time in making a renewed effort to bring about an Arab-Israeli peace settlement. Senator Kennedy proposed to convoke a conference of Israeli and Arab leaders for this purpose; Vice-President Nixon said he would give the matter highest priority and assign responsibility for directing negotiations to his own running mate, Ambassador Lodge.[19] There were, perhaps, some differences of emphasis on this issue as between the two American parties. In the Middle East, at any rate, there was a tendency to regard the party of former President Truman as more pro-Israeli and less pro-Arab than the party of the late Secretary of State Dulles. Yet both parties undoubtedly shared a basic commitment in Israel's favor—a commitment which, though thoroughly understandable in American terms, represented an undeniable handicap in relations with Arab countries. When Abdel Nasser called upon the President in New York a few weeks later, he apparently told him plainly that "to our great regret Israel would always remain a barrier to any rapprochement between us." [20] Although experience in 1956-57 had shown that American partiality for Israel had definite limits, it was one of the numerous important foreign policy matters on which there appeared to be no essential disagreement between America's two major parties.

34. ALONG THE NORTHERN TIER

The countries of the "northern tier," to use Mr. Dulles' name for the row of states extending eastward from Turkey to Pakistan, were comparatively unaffected by the Arab-Israeli quarrel. They had their own problems arising out of conflicting national and ethnic claims, some of them made doubly acute by proximity to the U.S.S.R. and resultant exposure to Soviet intrigue and subversion. For obvious reasons, the Soviet Government was wholly unsympathetic to the alliance which Turkey, Iran, and Pakistan had maintained along its southern frontier since 1955, in full association with Great Britain and with the strong support of the United States. Although Moscow had avoided military action against any of the alliance partners, it had conducted and was still conducting an unremitting diplomatic and psychological offensive against the three Asian members in the obvious hope of weakening and eventually destroying their fidelity to the West.

Moscow's "hostile propaganda campaigns" and its practice of exploiting local conflicts "as a means of interfering in the internal affairs of other countries and increasing international tension and subversion" came in for renewed criticism at the Eighth Session of the CENTO ministerial Council, held in Tehran on April 28-30, 1960. The presence of Secretary of State Herter as head of the American delegation to this meeting testified to the undiminished importance which Washington attached to CENTO, despite its unwillingness to contemplate full membership in the alliance—and despite its hope, still not quite extinguished at that time, of a basic improvement in East-West relations. Secretary Herter and Foreign Secretary Lloyd, who led the British delegation at Tehran, were going to Istanbul for the spring session of the NATO Council and thereafter would be attending the summit meeting in Paris. Much of the discussion at Tehran accordingly revolved around the prospects for an East-West *détente,* the importance of continued strength and solidarity in the free world, and the necessity that Soviet efforts to ease tension "should be genuine and should be expressed not only in words but also in deeds." In the course of their three-day meeting the ministers also reviewed the progress of the alliance in the fields of technical assistance and defense coordination, examined the plans that were being drawn up for a CENTO military command structure, and agreed that the next meeting should take place in Ankara in February 1961.[21]

Prime Minister Menderes of Turkey was unable to attend the Tehran session. A political crisis which had suddenly developed in his country in the last days of April had led to serious riots and the imposition of martial law in Istanbul and Ankara on the very day the CENTO meeting began. These violent manifestations, doubly shocking in view of Turkey's past record of political stability, apparently owed nothing to Communist inspiration but were directly traceable to the authoritarian methods of the Menderes government and the increasingly repressive measures that the Prime Minister and his Democratic party supporters had employed against the opposition Republican People's party.

In the following weeks, continued large-scale rioting, in which students played a conspicuous part, was met by new repression and the closing of the universities. On May 27, a military committee led by Lieutenant General Cemal Gursel suddenly took action to depose the entire government from President Celal Bayar downward. The provisional regime headed by General Gursel then proceeded to initiate a vast purge of Turkish political life—the necessary preliminary, it was asserted, to drawing up a new constitution and holding "free and just elections" untainted by the influence of "politicians blinded by ambition."

The implacable spirit in which the Gursel government proceeded against the representatives and supporters of the old regime during the next months could not fail to arouse some misgivings abroad about the ultimate direction of the movement. General Gursel insisted, however, that the military dictatorship he had established was purely temporary; and he emphasized repeatedly that although he hoped for good relations with the U.S.S.R., there would be no change in Turkey's foreign policy of complete loyalty to the collective security arrangements entered into by the previous government. An opportunity to reaffirm this latter point was shortly provided by the U.S.S.R. itself, which had addressed a sharp protest to the Menderes government in connection with the U-2 incident but now undertook an important diplomatic probe that was obviously intended to test the attitude of the new regime. A personal letter from Khrushchev to General Gursel, dispatched on June 28, invited the new Turkish leader to make an immediate start on restoring Turkish-Soviet friendship and suggested that the best way to do so would be for Turkey to "take the path of neutrality." General Gursel politely replied that while he was all in favor of normalizing Turkish-Soviet relations, Turkish policy would continue to be based on existing international commitments, particularly NATO and CENTO.[22] Moscow nevertheless gave evidence by its subsequent actions that it had not abandoned hope of eventually swinging Turkey away from its allies.

In its relations with Iran, the U.S.S.R. in recent months had employed a much less friendly tone. Iran's international ties, Moscow evidently calculated, would be more likely to yield to fear than to enticement. The mass of internal and external problems besetting the government of Muhammad Reza Shah and Premier Manouchehr Eghbal undoubtedly justified the prevalent opinion that Iran was one of the most vulnerable links in the chain of

Western defense. Its inequitable and increasingly detested social pattern was a source of chronic instability. In addition to the constant pressure of the U.S.S.R., there had been difficulties with neighboring Middle Eastern states, including a sharp frontier dispute with Iraq in the Shatt-al-Arab River. In the summer of 1960, Iran encountered the unbridled wrath of the Arab states and a rupture of diplomatic relations by the U.A.R. as a result of its acknowledged policy of *de facto* recognition of Israel.

Possibly more serious in its implications for Iran's national future was the dismal outcome of the parliamentary elections that were held in August 1960, supposedly as a step toward realizing the Shah's long-held ambition to organize a modern two-party political system. Charges of widespread electoral fraud were followed by the resignation of Premier Eghbal at the end of August, his replacement by Jaffar Sharif-Imami, and the opening of a new Soviet political offensive. In a characteristic reversal of method, Moscow sent its long-absent ambassador back to Tehran in September with new offers of economic and technical aid to be had for the asking—though only on the condition that Iran would loosen its ties with the United States. Iran's leaders would need strong nerves if they were to stand up indefinitely under this constant alternation of Soviet "hard" and "soft" tactics.

In neutral Afghanistan, the U.S.S.R. had no need to agitate against Western political or military ties, because the government of Muhammad Zahir Shah and his Prime Minister, Prince Muhammad Daud, had voluntarily avoided them. Afghanistan was a classic example of a politically uncommitted country which was open to "peaceful competition" by East and West on equal terms—and in which the East appeared to many observers to be making the more solid progress. One of the earliest beneficiaries of Khrushchev's "trade and aid" policy, Afghanistan by 1960 had become a favorite showcase for the results of Soviet assistance, which had been provided with a liberality, a flexibility, and, above all, a showmanship that the

United States had quite failed to match. By early 1960 the total value of Soviet economic and technical assistance (exclusive of military aid) was reckoned by some observers at as much as $250 million, compared to perhaps $144 million in grants and loans from the United States. In terms of political and psychological effects, there was reason to believe that the disproportion was considerably greater.[23]

The U.S.S.R. had also been much more successful than the United States in associating itself with Afghanistan's political outlook. President Eisenhower had received a most friendly welcome during a brief stopover in Kabul in December 1959; but Khrushchev, who paid his second visit to Afghanistan in early March 1960, achieved a far greater political effect by the simple expedient of endorsing the Afghan demand for a new political status for the Pathan or Pushtu tribesmen in neighboring Pakistan. Since the U.S.S.R. had no obligations toward Pakistan, it was an easy matter for Khrushchev to join the Afghans in calling for self-determination for Pakistan's Pathan population. Undeterred by the inconsistency of this stand with the notorious denial of political rights in Soviet-controlled areas, Khrushchev declared on his return to Moscow that the people of "Pushtunistan," as the Afghans like to call the territory, should have the right to choose their future allegiance in a plebiscite.[24]

Afghanistan had been somewhat resentful at the failure of the United States to take an equally pro-Afghan position on this delicate issue, and its leaders experienced a further disillusionment about American policy on learning of the subsequent flight of the U-2 across its territory. The Communist powers gave them no such grounds for complaint. Afghanistan's association with the East was carried another step forward in August when Foreign Minister Chen Yi of Communist China visited Kabul for the signature of a Sino-Afghan treaty of friendship and non-aggression.[25] Basically, however, the Afghan Government still seemed to most observers to be clinging to its traditional policy of playing off one camp against the other rather than committing itself definitely to either.

The government of Pakistan, where President Muhammad Ayub Khan had taken office as the result of a military coup in 1958 and was confirmed in his position by a special referendum in February 1960, had been understandably incensed by Khrushchev's interference in the Pathan question. At the Tehran meeting of the CENTO Council, Pakistan had secured a special denunciation of the action by all of the governments associated with CENTO. But Pakistan, too, was severely shaken by the subsequent U-2 incident and the resultant Soviet protests; and it, too, expressed dissatisfaction with what it considered a lack of United States support on the "Pushtunistan" issue, just as it had long resented Washington's refusal to endorse its position on the Kashmir conflict with India. With its second five-year plan about to begin on July 1, Pakistan also evinced some dissatisfaction with the level of economic aid from the United States, and gave some indications that it was willing to consider assistance from the U.S.S.R. if it could be provided on satisfactory terms. But although some observers detected signs of a neutralist drift in Pakistani policy, the country's association with the West underwent no obvious impairment during these months. The settlement during the spring of 1960 of one very important problem in its relations with India enabled the United States to hope that the relationship between Pakistan and India, perhaps the outstanding political issue in this sector of the non-Communist world, was moving gradually toward adjustment.

35. PAKISTAN, INDIA, NEPAL, AND CEYLON

The widely ramifying conflict which had divided India and Pakistan since their foundation in 1947 had long been recognized as one of the most tragic weaknesses of the non-Communist world, not only because of the size and importance of the two countries but also because of the key position both occupied in the global political and military balance. It was with corresponding relief and gratification that the United States was able to welcome on February 29, 1960, the long-awaited solution of at least one of the major points at issue between them: the division of the waters of the Indus River and its tributaries, part of which flowed through India on the way to Pakistan and the sea. The basis of the settlement, worked out over a period of years by W. A. B. Iliff and other representatives of the International Bank, was a plan for the construction of certain engineering works to assure Pakistan of its fair share of precious irrigation water after the division went into effect. Of the total cost of some $1 billion, the United States undertook to contribute $280 million in dollar grants and loans, which would be freed from some of the customary restrictions imposed by the Mutual Security Act, as well as another $235 million in local currency. Smaller amounts would be contributed by Australia, Canada, Germany, New Zealand, the United Kingdom, the International Bank, and India and Pakistan themselves.[26]

The formal treaty between India, Pakistan, and the International Bank which was necessary to put the scheme into effect was duly signed on September 19, culminating a six-year process that had in some ways presented a model of constructive international cooperation. President Eisenhower was not alone in feeling that the solution of this intricate problem augured well for the eventual settlement of other India-Pakistan issues and might even have a beneficial effect on the "very touchy question" of Kashmir.[27] Although Prime Minister Nehru during his visit to Karachi to sign the treaty showed no sign of yielding to Pakistani views on the Kashmir issue, he did launch a fervent appeal for unity and cooperation between the two sister countries in the interests of world peace. In a world of such tremendous scientific advances, the Indian leader told the two peoples, "our problems are small." [28]

Mr. Nehru's changing perspective on Indian-Pakistani relations was undoubtedly influenced in part by the gathering troubles that confronted his own vast country as it struggled to remain at peace and solve the problems of economic development within a democratic framework. In addition to the internal hazards imposed by massive poverty and rapid population growth, India had become aware within the previous twelve months of a serious external challenge, the direct result of Communist China's absorption of neighboring Tibet and its claim to some 40,000 square miles of what Indian considered its own territory in the Northeast Frontier Agency and the Ladakh Province of Kashmir.[29] These Chinese claims, supported by military occupation of a part of the disputed areas, were revised and expanded at the beginning of 1960 to a total of 51,000 square miles. The United States, while condemning the violent manner in which the Peking government had asserted its claims, had taken no position on the merits of the issue, which was also of great interest to the allied government of Nationalist China.[30] Unofficially, Washington found much to reflect upon in the predicament of a Prime Minister whose policy of friendship for Communist China had borne such indigestible fruit and who was now under sharp attack within India for his attempts to keep the dispute on an equable level.

In April 1960, Premier Chou En-lai of Communist China came to New Delhi at Mr. Nehru's invitation to discuss the frontier dispute in person. No agreement was reached except to refer the matter to a commission of experts, who seemed quite unlikely to be able to reconcile the widely divergent positions of their governments. Meanwhile the issue continued to weigh heavily on Indian opinion, already somewhat oppressed by the numerous shortcomings of Indian political life and the slow pace of economic progress. Scarce resources had now to be diverted from internal construction to meet the defense requirements of the northern frontiers, and the possibility of more trouble with China had to be taken into account in every important decision on domestic or foreign policy.

Even the U.S.S.R. had appeared not to approve Peking's

abrupt manner of raising the frontier question. The news that Premier Khrushchev intended to visit India "unofficially" in mid-February in the course of his proposed Asian tour had encouraged a hope in India that the Soviet leader might be persuaded to intercede with his Chinese colleagues and get them to moderate their demands. But nothing came of these expectations, and Khrushchev's public reception during his five-day stay in India was noticeably cooler than the one he had encountered on his previous visit in 1955, not to mention the ecstatic welcome accorded President Eisenhower in December 1959. Prime Minister Nehru nevertheless found words of praise for Khrushchev's labors in the cause of "peace," and a number of agreements were concluded regarding the use of Soviet credits, expansion of the Soviet-constructed Bhilai steel mill, and cooperation in the cultural, scientific, educational, and technological fields.[31]

Only five months before this time, in September 1959, the U.S.S.R. had granted India a development credit in the unusually large amount of 1.5 billion rubles, ostensibly equivalent to $375 million. In August 1960 this commitment was supplemented by a new credit of 500 million rubles, bringing the total economic assistance received from or promised by the U.S.S.R. to the substantial figure of $804.3 million at the unrealistic official exchange rate.[32] The United States, whose own economic aid to India in various forms since 1947 could be reckoned at some $3.6 billion or over four times the maximum Soviet figure, had never disputed India's right to accept assistance from Eastern as well as Western sources. The needs of India's 425 million people were too clamorous to admit of any unnecessary political hurdles, and Washington had more confidence in India's ability to avoid undue dependence on the Communist bloc than it had in the case of some of the smaller developing countries. The extent of India's continuing need for foreign assistance over the next decade or more was sufficiently evident in the outlines of its third five-year plan, scheduled to begin on April 1, 1961, which envisaged a total investment of nearly $21 billion of which some $4.6 billion would have to come from foreign sources.

President Eisenhower had already promised that the United States would provide what help it could in this effort, and on May 4, 1960 the two countries concluded a four-year "food-for-peace" agreement which would go far to secure India's food position in the plan period by enabling it to purchase 16 million tons of wheat and 1 million tons of rice for $1,276 million in its own currency. Most of these funds would be returned to India as grants or loans for economic development projects.[33] In the meantime the second five-year plan for 1956-61 had had to be heavily cut back because of a lack of adequate financing, but sufficient foreign exchange to carry it through the last few months was scraped together as the result of a September meeting in Paris of the informal "aid-to-India club," which included representatives of the United States and five other non-Communist industrial countries.[34]

India was not the only country whose future had been clouded by the Chinese Communist absorption of Tibet. A comparable uneasiness had developed in Nepal, whose position as an independent buffer state between the Communist and free worlds had made it increasingly a battleground of competing Chinese, Indian, Soviet, and American influences. Premier B. P. Koirala, who had his own worries about Chinese frontier claims, journeyed to Peking in March 1960 and there obtained considerable relief in the form of a comprehensive agreement to entrust the demarcation of the frontier to a joint commission, establish diplomatic negotiations at the embassy level, negotiate a treaty of peace and friendship, and accept a Chinese Communist grant of 100 million rupees or $21 million.[35] For a moment it seemed that any threat to Nepal's frontiers had been eliminated; but by the time Premier Chou En-lai arrived in Katmandu to sign the treaty at the end of April,[36] the situation had been complicated afresh by indications that Communist China intended to lay claim to Nepal's best-known geographic feature, Mount Everest. In the meantime Nepal's ruler, King Mahendra Bir Bikram Shah Deva, was paying a ceremonial visit to the United States. While in Washington he explained his country's independent policy to Congress and held a discussion with President Eisenhower, which, however, apparently did not go beyond the generalities that were customary on such occasions.[37]

Premier Koirala's year-old government gave outsiders the possibly deceptive impression of being reasonably well established and genuinely alert to maintain the country's independence against any threat. In the island state of Ceylon, which was less subject to direct Communist pressure and where the sentimental ties of membership in the Commonwealth had weakened somewhat of late years, a more openly unstable situation prevailed. Ceylon, too, was officially neutral, but the quality of its neutrality was subject to the play of unpredictable internal forces. Of the two parliamentary elections held in Ceylon in 1960, the first, on March 19, brought in a relatively pro-Western government under D. S. Senanayake which lost the confidence of parliament within a month. The second, on July 20, reversed the political scales as the result of an electoral alliance between the neutralist Sri Lanka (Freedom) party and a congeries of Trotskyist and Communist groups. Mrs. Sirimavo Bandaranaike, the candidate of the Sri Lanka and widow of the neutralist Prime Minister assassinated in 1959, succeeded to the premiership and managed to form a cabinet without the help of her leftist allies. Governments throughout the world prepared to observe the effects of feminine direction of Ceylonese policy, both at home and at the United Nations, where Ceylon's representative on the Security Council had been playing a noticeably constructive role in relation to the Congo crisis. Some months would evidently have to elapse before the political tendencies of Mrs. Bandaranaike's government became entirely clear.

36. OIL AND ECONOMICS

The comparative lull in Middle Eastern and South Asian affairs that followed the May revolution in Turkey persisted through the autumn of 1960. Despite innumerable inner tensions, the area stood out as an island of relative quiet compared to the turmoil in the Congo, in parts of Southeast Asia and the Caribbean, and at the United Nations. The region's two most prominent international statesmen, President Abdel Nasser and Prime Minister Nehru, were among those who traveled to New York for a portion of the General Assembly session, and both took a leading part while there in the unsuccessful effort to bring about a meeting between President Eisenhower and Premier Khrushchev.[38] Both also had brief personal meetings with Mr. Eisenhower as well as longer sessions with the Soviet Premier, Prime Minister Macmillan, and other world leaders. Possibly the most significant aspect of their activities in New York lay in their collaboration with President Tito, President Sukarno of Indonesia, and President Nkrumah in what was beginning to emerge as a kind of neutral "steering committee." Prime Minister Nehru, though he disclaimed any special preference as between the United States and the U.S.S.R., had never favored the establishment of a neutral bloc and entered into these activities with rather less zest than some of his younger colleagues.

President Abdel Nasser's first visit to New York was marred by none of the hostile demonstrations that greeted Khrushchev and other Communist leaders, yet it did not lack reminders of the embattled position of the U.A.R. in world affairs. In his formal address to the Assembly on September 27,[39] the U.A.R. President took a very militant anti-Western line on the questions of the Congo, Algeria, and China. He also reaffirmed strongly the Arab thesis that the only solution for the Palestine problem was a "return to the condition prevailing before the error was committed"—meaning, apparently, before the creation of

Israel. But Mr. Nasser's own government was not exempt from criticism in the Assembly. That of Foreign Minister Golda Meir of Israel had been expected; [40] that of King Hussein of Jordan was more of a surprise. Addressing the Assembly on October 3, the Jordanian ruler breached Arab tradition and caused serious offense in Cairo by reviewing at length his country's troubles with the U.A.R., recalling the recent assassination of Premier Majali, and strongly implying that the attacks to which Jordan had been subjected were directly related to the world-wide Communist offensive. [41]

While the "general debate" dragged on in New York, the Arab states and various other countries in the region had been trying to assess the implications of a new development outside the political field which might conceivably herald another phase in the Communist offensive, this time on the economic front. The development in question was a change in the world petroleum situation which had resulted from the opening up of new sources of supply and a consequent weakening in the position of traditional oil suppliers in the Middle East and the Western Hemisphere. The international oil industry and the petroleum producing countries had already perceived a need for some adjustment in view of the development of new fields in North Africa. There were now indications that they also faced a potential threat from the U.S.S.R., which had greatly expanded its petroleum exports within the past year or two and gave evidence that it planned to expand them still further in the future.

Outsiders were not yet certain whether the U.S.S.R. was contemplating a deliberate attempt to disrupt the international oil market, as it could easily do by unloading its supplies at artificially low prices or by making special deals with some of the less developed countries that had hitherto depended on the Western oil companies for their petroleum supplies. Such tactics, if carelessly pursued, might easily result in antagonizing established oil producing countries like Iraq whose friendship the Soviet

Union had hitherto sought to cultivate. What was certain, however, was that the new supply situation had already adversely affected the price structure in the industry as a whole, compelled the Western oil companies to reduce their own prices in certain instances, and threatened the major oil producing countries outside the Soviet bloc with a reduction of the earnings on which they depended to balance their budgets and to pay for necessary imports.

The threat to established price levels had led in recent weeks to the convening of a special conference in Baghdad which was attended by Venezuela and by four of the leading producing countries of the Middle East, Iraq, Iran, Kuwait, and Saudi Arabia. These countries had agreed on September 14 to form a kind of cartel, the so-called Organization of Petroleum Exporting Countries, with the stated objective of arriving at a unified oil policy and, in particular, of resisting any price-cutting tendencies on the part of the oil companies that operated in their territories.[42] This move was followed on October 17-22 by an Arab petroleum congress, held in Beirut under Arab League auspices, which likewise called for coordination of policy among the producing countries and urged the oil companies to consult them before making any further price changes.[43] The immediate objective in both cases was to persuade the oil companies to maintain their established prices while the governments of the producing countries continued to draw their stipulated share of the profits, amounting in most instances to 50 per cent.

The difficulty with this approach was that both the oil companies and the producing countries stood to lose if Soviet oil was to be sold on the world market at a price below that charged for non-Soviet oil. In such an event, the non-Soviet suppliers could hardly fail to lose a part of their traditional markets. Already there had been difficulties of this kind in several parts of the world. Cuba was now getting its petroleum supplies from the U.S.S.R. at reduced rates and snapping its fingers at the oil companies whose local holdings it had expropriated. India, too, had been offered Soviet crude oil at reduced prices and had declined only because the Western companies who controlled India's refinery capacity had given notice that they would refuse to refine it. India had, however, obtained one reduction in the price charged it for Western oil, and was pressing for another. Pakistan, where the U.S.S.R. had just promised to lend assistance in the search for new oil deposits, was asking for similar concessions and preparing to seek a Soviet loan for petroleum and mineral development at home. Ceylon, unable to obtain price reductions from the Western companies, was talking of shifting as far as possible to Soviet sources of supply. In October it broke an Anglo-American monopoly by agreeing to purchase a quantity of Soviet refined petroleum products at a 25 per cent saving. It also made plans to establish a state-owned petroleum refinery with Soviet support.[44]

Of even greater economic importance was the future of the huge Western European market, where oil consumption was growing rapidly and where many industrial firms were only too eager to sell their products to the Soviet Union if the latter could offer something tangible in return. A pipeline system linking the Soviet Union to Eastern Europe, and capable of extension to Western Europe, was already under construction. Early in November it was revealed that Italy was entering into a long-term agreement with the U.S.S.R. to supply pipeline material in exchange for Soviet oil, which would be furnished at approximately half the Middle Eastern price.[45] Italy, some observers thought, might have been selected as the spearhead of a coming Soviet oil drive throughout Western Europe.

If these prospects were confirmed, there would be serious effects on the fiscal position and development prospects of several Middle Eastern countries; nor could the West take any satisfaction in the thought that a country like India might ultimately become dependent on the U.S.S.R. for a part of its growing petroleum requirements.

Thus far, however, there had been no overt sign in Washington of governmental concern over these possibilities. In most parts of the Middle East and Southern Asia, the United States and its partners already confronted other economic problems of a more pressing character.

The United Arab Republic, for example, though now bound over to the U.S.S.R. so far as the vital Aswan Dam project was concerned, was receiving a steady flow of American economic aid through the Development Loan Fund, the Export-Import Bank, and the agricultural surplus program. Jordan, too, continued to depend on the United States for substantial budgetary aid as well as emergency grain shipments.[46] Lebanon was another country which had recently experienced a drought and grain shortage and had reason to look forward to a promised shipment of 15,000 tons of American wheat.[47]

Turkey, which had received $359 million in special stabilization aid from American and international sources in 1958, had recently entered into negotiations aimed at securing another $250 million from the International Monetary Fund, the Organization for European Economic Cooperation, and the United States to stabilize its economy in 1961 and 1962. A preliminary understanding along these lines was disclosed at the end of the year.[48] According to General Gursel, Turkey had also received an offer of assistance from the Soviet Union, but did not intend to let such offers affect its Western political commitments.[49]

Iran, too, sent its Deputy Prime Minister to Washington during this period with a successful request for additional credits from the Development Loan Fund and the Export-Import Bank.[50] Afghanistan, which proposed to begin a $700 million five-year plan in 1961, was understood to be planning to ask the United States for a substantial contribution, if only to relieve it of the necessity of accepting everything from the U.S.S.R.[51] India, which obtained $114 million in new credits from the Development Loan Fund at the beginning of December,[52] was still worried about the financing of its own third five-year plan; but there was hope in New Delhi that the chances of large-scale American assistance would be improved by the prospective advent of a Democratic administration in Washington. Indians surely had no reason to regret the designation of former Ambassador Chester Bowles as the new American Under-Secretary of State.

The development problems of India, Pakistan, and the smaller Southeast Asian countries underwent their customary review and appraisal at the annual meeting of the twenty-two-nation Colombo Plan organization, held in Tokyo on November 14-17 with Theodore C. Achilles of the State Department heading the American delegation. As had increasingly been the case in recent years, attention in the Colombo Plan Consultative Committee was divided between the need for more outside capital throughout the region and the parallel issue of rapid population growth, with its constant tendency to nullify any increase in per capita income.[53] This was a matter of special poignancy to overcrowded India, one of the few countries that had adopted an official policy of trying to limit population increase. But nothing that might be accomplished along this line in the coming years seemed likely to lessen the need for continuing and even increased assistance from the United States as well as from the other non-Communist countries that were now in a position to provide it.

37. LANDS IN FERMENT

It would be tempting to stress the dramatic or sensational aspect of events in these countries during late 1960 —the slow and unrelenting progress of the trial of ex-Premier Menderes and his associates in Turkey; the long-awaited birth of a male heir to the throne of Iran; the storms and tidal waves that took the lives of thousands in East Pakistan. The status and prospects of Premier Kassim's Iraqi government, now largely freed from domestic Communist influence but still closely involved in assistance schemes with the U.S.S.R. and other Communist countries, offered another subject for anxious contemplation as popular disillusionment with the fruits of the 1958 revolution increased. Would the Kassim regime be threatened with renewed attacks from the pan-Arab nationalist wing that still drew its inspiration from Abdel Nasser? Or would Iraq's Kurdish population, which had originally welcomed the revolution but was now tending toward open hostility, become a vehicle for renewed Soviet manipulation and pressure?

These were questions that might again fix international attention in months to come, but which seemed to present no acute problem during what remained of 1960. International concern with the Middle East at this period was mainly limited to the three questions that had found their way onto the agenda of the United Nations Assembly. Two of these, the problems of the Palestine refugees and of the United Nations Emergency Force, were already familiar. The third, which had not previously confronted the Assembly, concerned the British-supported Sultanate of Muscat and Oman at the southeast corner of the Arabian peninsula. For several years the ruler of this territory and his British allies had been intermittently contending against a tribal "independence movement" in the interior which was headed by another local potentate, the Imam of Oman, with the backing of the United Arab Republic, Saudi Arabia, the Arab League, and the U.S.S.R. An attempt by the Imam's supporters to bring the matter before the Security Council in 1957 had failed,[54] and the question had since been more or less forgotten by the outside world. In the summer of 1960, however, the Arab countries had determined to seek a hearing by the General Assembly. Although the British delegate flatly denied their charges of "aggression" against the people of Oman and insisted that the area had been at peace for many months, the matter was duly placed on the Assembly's agenda [55] and would presumably be debated during the second half of the session in 1961.

The questions of the United Nations Emergency Force

and of the Palestine refugees were of more obvious international import. The first directly affected the maintenance of the peace between Israel and the U.A.R.; the second involved the life and health of a million human beings who would, perhaps, be left to perish unless the United Nations continued to care for them.

No new questions of principle were raised at the 1960 session concerning the deployment of the 5,300-man Emergency Force along the Israeli-U.A.R. demarcation line and in the Gulf of Aqaba. The only problem—serious enough in view of the parlous state of United Nations finances, plagued by unpaid assessments and now burdened by the costly operation in the Congo—was that of meeting UNEF's estimated expenses of some $19 million for 1961. While the U.S.S.R. reiterated its determination to pay nothing toward this venture, which was already about $24 million in arrears, the United States as usual announced that it would make a voluntary contribution over and above its regular assessment of some $6.4 million. "If peace and security are not worth sacrificing for, then nothing else is," remarked Senator George D. Aiken of the American delegation as he announced the allocation of an extra $1.8 million to reduce the assessments of other member countries.[56]

The United States had contributed much larger sums to the ten-year-old program of the United Nations Relief and Works Agency for Palestine Refugees in the Near East (UNRWA). One American estimate set the ten-year total at $222 million, out of a global figure of $319 million.[57] To meet the most elementary needs for relief and vocational training of a refugee group which was now officially numbered at 1,047,437, UNRWA had proposed a budget of $40.6 million for 1961. Though this amounted to little more than $40 per person, it substantially exceeded the total of $29.5 million which was pledged for the purpose at a special United Nations conference on October 20.[58] As its own contribution the United States announced an allocation of $23 million for the fiscal year 1961, on the usual condition that it would not pay more than 70 per cent of the combined total subscribed by all governments.[59]

Partly because of the large financial outlays involved and partly because of its central relationship to any Arab-Israeli peace settlement, the United States had long been urging the need to prepare the ground for an orderly liquidation of the whole refugee operation. Though it had not directly threatened to withhold financial support from UNRWA, it had indicated rather clearly that it could not go on subsidizing it indefinitely. UNRWA's current mandate was due to expire in 1963, and the responsibility of Israel and the Arab states to assist in working toward a fundamental solution of the refugee problem was emphasized once again by the United States at the Assembly's 1960 session.[60]

But Israel's only constructive proposal, apart from an expression of general readiness to enter into peace negotiations, was the repetition of a previous offer to compensate the refugees for their abandoned properties on condition that the refugees themselves were "integrated" into the Arab world.[61] The Arabs, on their side, had no idea of "integrating" the refugees. They could suggest nothing better than the placing of the refugee properties under UNRWA administration and the addition of new members to the Palestine Conciliation Commission. This tripartite body, composed of France, Turkey, and the United States, had long been charged with seeking a solution of the whole Palestine problem and had been instructed in 1959 to make further efforts to bring about the repatriation or compensation of the refugees in accordance with earlier United Nations resolutions.[62] Action on the Arab proposals, which were not at all favored by Israel, was put over until the second half of the session, by which time there might be some indication as to whether the new American administration had succeeded in devising any fresh approach to the problem.

With neither side in the Palestine controversy showing any real disposition for compromise, peace in the Near

East continued for the present to hinge very largely on the maintenance of a rough military balance between Israel and the Arab states. A sudden increase in the military strength of either side might present an overwhelming temptation to reopen hostilities. This latent possibility helps to explain the unconcealed alarm with which official Washington reacted early in December to a report that Israel was constructing a hitherto unreported nuclear reactor in the Negev and might be on the way to acquiring a strategic nuclear capability, presumably with French assistance.[63] Belated assurances from Israel apparently set these apprehensions at rest, though not before a world-wide sensation had been stirred up. Abdel Nasser warned on December 23 that if Israel tried to make an atomic bomb it would mean war. In such an event, he added, the U.A.R. would see to obtaining a supply of nuclear weapons of its own.

The U.A.R. President, whose government had just been elected to a two-year term on the United Nations Security Council in spite of its defiance of that body's rulings about freedom of navigation in the Suez Canal, had been very active politically since his return to Cairo, and had assumed a foremost place among the supporters of ex-Prime Minister Lumumba of the Congo. In his speech of December 23 he took occasion to attack a number of other political targets, among them NATO, the French, and his old enemy the King of Jordan. "We shall not rest until we destroy Hussein, the agent of colonialism," he threatened.[64]

In his uncomfortable position as the object of recurrent attacks by the head of a sister Arab government, King Hussein had formerly been able to count on a measure of sympathy and support from King Saud of Saudi Arabia, one of the few Arab leaders who had refused to incline before the wind from Cairo. But King Saud had retired from the active direction of Saudi affairs in March 1958, and under the leadership of his half-brother, Crown Prince Faisal, his kingdom had ceased to represent an important counterweight to Nasserist influences. The new Saudi Premier had, indeed, accomplished wonders in curbing extravagance and setting the national finances in order, but he had not satisfied his royal brother. It was just at this time, on December 21, 1960, that King Saud undertook to reassert himself by removing Faisal from his top positions and resuming personal direction. "Absolute neutrality" was the program he announced, and no one could tell immediately how far if at all this concept might include an intention to dispute President Abdel Nasser's leadership of the Arab world. American authorities feared that the change of regime might portend no more than a renewed deterioration in the Saudi finances. But the announcement of plans to draft a constitution suggested that the King was not unaware of the growing demand for political progress on the part of some of his own subjects.

Another royal coup took place during December in far-away Nepal, where King Mahendra on December 15 suddenly dismissed the government of Premier Koirala, dissolved the parliament, and cast the ex-Prime Minister and a number of other political leaders into prison. The alleged offenses of Nepal's late government fell under the general heading of antinational activities, apparently a euphemism for what the King had considered an unduly compliant attitude toward the Chinese People's Republic and other Communist powers. Although the new government, which King Mahendra himself proposed to head, promised strict neutrality and good relations with friendly countries, its early days were marked by an extraordinary secretiveness that made it impossible to forecast its future tendency with any accuracy. Conceivably Mr. Koirala's deposition had really been necessary in order to check some Communist design of which the outer world had been unaware. Others speculated that the coup had been directed mainly against corruption at home. In any case, it afforded one more illustration of the difficulty with which democratic governments took root in those Asian countries that had hitherto lacked a democratic tradition.

CHAPTER SIX

COMMUNIST CHINA AND ITS NEIGHBORS

IN EACH of the regions examined so far, the policy of the United States could be viewed as a system of military, economic, and political or psychological mechanisms whose overriding purpose was to curb the expansionist proclivities of Soviet Communism. American policy in the Far East, though similar in aim, was primarily directed against a different opponent and in some respects took a rather different form. In this part of the world the major threat to international peace and the security of peoples came not so much from the U.S.S.R. as from the Chinese People's Republic, a Marxist and revolutionary power like the Soviet Union, but one whose central geographic position, Oriental heritage, and growing material strength assured it of an influence in Far Eastern affairs which in some respects transcended that of the U.S.S.R. itself.

38. THE GIANT OF EAST ASIA

At no time since the establishment of the Chinese Communist regime in the fall of 1949 had Americans possessed any certain knowledge as to how far these two giants of international Communism should be regarded as partners pursuing a common revolutionary aim and how far, if at all, they might be viewed as rivals competing for power and influence behind a façade of Communist unity. At times Peking and Moscow had seemed to be executing a well-coordinated military and political strategy aimed at promoting the general interests of the "camp of Socialism" and creating maximum difficulty for the Western powers by compelling the latter to divide their forces and attention between two or more widely separated theaters. At other times there had been indications that the two Communist powers' professions of "indestructible friendship" cloaked a ruthless struggle for advantage of the kind that might some day even explode in open conflict. Though the U.S.S.R. had been and would remain for some time the stronger power from an industrial and military point of view, there could be little doubt that China with its tremendous manpower and wealth of undeveloped resources was capable of narrowing the gap and, perhaps, eventually moving into first place. By the later 1950's a good many Europeans and some Americans had begun to suspect that the U.S.S.R. might already be casting about for ways of protecting its interests when the balance within the Moscow-Peking axis began to shift to it disadvantage.

Partly because of domestic political considerations which limited its freedom of maneuver with respect to the "China problem," the United States had made no attempt to encourage a rift between the U.S.S.R. and Communist China. On the whole it had tended to discount the likelihood of such a rift occurring. At the basis of the official American attitude toward Communist China was the view that the Peking government had no legitimate right to exercise authority in China and, in the words of Secretary of State John Foster Dulles, that Communist rule of the China mainland was "a passing and not a perpetual phase." [1] For practical purposes, however, the American Government had taken full account of the tremendous and growing power of the Chinese People's Republic and had shaped its policies accordingly. Without attempting in any serious way to upset Communist control on the mainland, it had set itself to oppose the ambitions of the Peking authorities by every other means within its power—by withholding diplomatic recognition of their government, by insisting on the exclusion of their representatives from international bodies, by embargoing United States trade with mainland China and other Communist-controlled areas in the Far East, and, most important, by lending diplomatic support and military protection to the "legitimate," non-Communist government of the Republic of China under President Chiang Kai-shek, which still maintained its seat on the island of Formosa (Taiwan) and still spoke for China in the Security Council and the other organs of the United Nations.

In addition to fighting the Communists to a standstill in Korea under the United Nations flag in 1950-53 and exerting itself to limit Communist gains in Indochina in 1954, the United States under Mr. Dulles' leadership had taken the initiative in negotiating a network of defensive treaties which still formed the legal basis of the American and allied position throughout the Far East. Concluded under a variety of conditions between 1951 and 1954, all of these arrangements, from the ANZUS pact with Australia and New Zealand to the Southeast Asia Treaty Organization (SEATO) and the bilateral mutual defense treaties with the Republic of China, Japan, and the Republic of Korea, had come to be regarded by the United States as parts of a single system whose main object was to meet the need for mutual protection against a possible military aggression by Communist China.

As with some other mutual defense arrangements in other parts of the non-Communist world, these treaties and the military dispositions that rested upon them could be awarded much of the credit for the fact that no full-scale military aggression had occurred in the Far East since their conclusion. It could be argued that they contributed to the security even of those countries that disapproved them. They had not, however, proved especially well adapted for countering the nonviolent forms of expansionism on which Communist China, like the U.S.S.R., had tended to place its main reliance since the conclusion of the war in Indochina in 1954. As an Asian power and a bitter foe of Western "imperialism," Communist China had been able to count on a certain amount of sympathy in some non-Communist Asian states. The magnitude of its achievements in the field of industrialization inspired respect even among those Asians who were appalled by the ruthless exploitation on which they depended. So prominent a free Asian leader as President Sukarno of Indonesia could find elements in the Chinese experience that seemed capable of imitation in his own country. Indonesia and Cambodia, like Ceylon and Nepal in Southern Asia, were the beneficiaries of small but significant Chinese Communist grants or loans for economic development. In countries with strongly anti-Communist governments, like Thailand and the Philippines, these Chinese tactics initially made little headway; but even they were impressed by the rising power of the Chinese colossus. By the later 1950's there were indications that Peking was gradually achieving a kind of psychological ascendancy, compounded of admiration and fear, in large parts of Southeast Asia. This phenomenon was especially evident in such neutral countries as Indonesia and Cambodia, and, to a somewhat lesser extent, in Burma and Laos.

But the Peking government had been unwilling or unable to pursue this "soft" policy consistently or carry it to its logical conclusions. In its professed determination to oust the United States and the Chiang Kai-shek government from Formosa, it had several times resorted to military actions in the Taiwan Strait, directed in the first instance against the Nationalist-held islands of the Quemoy and Matsu groups, which had sent shivers of apprehension throughout Southeast Asia. The almost superhuman requirements of Communist China's successive five-year plans, the second of which had begun with the ill-fated "great leap forward" of 1958, apparently compelled the Communist leaders to maintain a degree of external tension as a means of wringing the necessary exertions from the Chinese people. The introduction of the much-hated system of rural "communes" in the summer of 1958 had coincided with a major crisis over the offshore islands.

In 1959, the absorption of Tibet and the ruthless crushing
of Tibetan nationalist resistance had been followed by
frontier incidents with India, an outbreak of Communist-
fomented internal disturbances in Laos, and a bitter quarrel with Indonesia over the status of Chinese residents in
that country. Burma, too, had been given some cause for
anxiety about its unsettled frontier with China. Throughout Southeast Asia, Peking's surliness during these months
had resulted in a noticeable cooling-off in official and
popular sentiment toward Communist China and some
signs of increased appreciation of the role being played by
the United States and its associates in the checking of
Chinese Communist expansionism.

The misgivings aroused by this shift in Chinese Communist tactics had not been confined to Southeast Asia
or to the non-Communist world. Premier Khrushchev,
whose meeting with President Eisenhower at Camp David
in September 1959 had enabled him to achieve one of the
main goals of his "peaceful coexistence" policy, the sched-
uling of a summit conference for the spring of 1960, had
apparently sensed in the Chinese attitude a definite challenge to his own plans for promoting Communist interests
through a "relaxation of international tensions." On a visit
to Peking immediately following his return from the
United States, he had openly cautioned the Chinese
Communist leaders against "predatory wars" and attempts
to "test the stability of the capitalist system by force." [2]
The coolness wih which these admonitions were received
in Communist China had accentuated the suspicion of a
difference on tactics, if not on basic policy, between Peking
and Moscow. Reports that Communist China might soon
be in a position to develop a supply of atomic weapons—
some said as early as 1962 or 1963—added to the feeling
in the West that Soviet-Chinese relations might be approaching a critical turning point.

These diverse trends were presumably taken into account in Washington in connection with President Eisenhower's decision to visit the Far East in the late spring

of 1960 as a sequel to his tour of certain Middle Eastern, South Asian, and African countries in December 1959. Although the President's proposed itinerary included only the Philippines, Taiwan, Japan, and Korea, it was expected to serve as a symbol of American interest in all the free lands of the Far East and to point a contrast between the idealistic aims of American policy and the expansionist motivations of the Communist powers. The impending conclusion of a new Japanese-American treaty of mutual cooperation and security, which was expected to enter into force by the time the President arrived in Tokyo, was cited in Washington as additional proof of American readiness to cooperate with the free Asian countries on a basis of equality and mutuality. Very few people could have foreseen as 1960 began how seriously the events of the next few months would challenge the American position in Japan and, indirectly, throughout the Far East.

39. SOUTHEAST ASIAN SURVEY

The circumstances of the President's earlier tour had encouraged the expectation of a livelier display of American interest in the Southeast Asian countries, and this expectation was kept alive by the emphasis on economic development problems that characterized the President's January messages. As so often happened, however, any action that might be contemplated by the United States in relation to Southeast Asia was robbed of at least a part of its effect by the prior actions of Khrushchev. Perhaps annoyed by the President's success in India, the latter had lost no time in announcing plans for an Asian visit of his own which would include not only India and Afghanistan but also Burma and Indonesia, two countries that President Eisenhower had not included in either of his Asian itineraries. Some observers suspected that the Soviet leader's decision to renew his contacts in non-Communist Asia at this particular moment was not inspired solely by the spirit of competition with the United States but might be con-

"—and Eastern?"

(Reproduced by permission of the Register and Tribune Syndicate)
Low in *The Manchester Guardian*

nected in some way with the political differences between Moscow and Peking. In any event, it was a foregone conclusion that Khrushchev would do his best to persuade those Asians with whom he came in contact that their best friends were to be found in the "Socialist" camp and not in any "imperialist" country.

But Khrushchev's stop in India, as we have seen, got the visit off to a relatively undistinguished start, and his stay in neutral Burma on February 16-18 likewise failed to produce the expected sensation. The Burmese at the moment were concerned with two matters of even greater importance to them than a visit from the Soviet Premier: a settlement of Burma's frontier problems with Communist China, and a return to parliamentary government after nearly eighteen months of military rule. Premier Ne

Win, the army leader who had assumed control of Burmese affairs in October 1958, was just back from a visit to Peking, where he had joined with Premier Chou En-lai on January 28 in signing a treaty of friendship and non-aggression plus a border agreement that promised to settle once for all the disputed frontier claims that had recurrently agitated Burmese opinion for a number of years.[3] Under this arrangement, Burma gave up several disputed areas along its eastern frontier but obtained in return the firm recognition of the rest of its boundary with China. Chou En-lai, when he visited Burma in April on his way to New Delhi to discuss the Sino-Indian frontier problem, could point to the frontier settlement as one of the factors that made relations between Burma and the Chinese People's Republic a model of "peaceful coexistence." [4]

General Ne Win's initiative had appeared to enjoy the full approval of former Premier U Nu, who had surrendered the reins of authority to his military colleague in 1958 but was now preparing to resume the premiership in view of the army's announcement that it had completed its task of cleaning up political life and halting a drift toward Communism. Some improvements in internal administration had undoubtedly been effected under Ne Win's premiership, and most of the remaining sparks of Communist rebellion in the country had been stamped out. Although U Nu's renewed bid for office had been backed by the fellow-traveling National United Front, he had repudiated Communist support and gained a clear non-Communist majority in the election that preceded his redesignation as Premier. The head of the restored civilian government, which formally took office on April 5, was known as a firm believer in neutrality and friendship with the Communist powers, but this attitude had not in the past been found incompatible with warm relations with the United States.

In Indonesia, where Khrushchev spent the twelve days from February 18 to March 1, the Soviet leader found a climate more receptive to Soviet attentions. One reason was the current strain in Chinese-Indonesian relations; another was the accumulation of economic troubles confronting this rapidly growing nation of nearly 100 million inhabitants. Khrushchev's visit might have been a still greater success had he managed to restrain the snappish ill temper that broke through more than once in the course of his barnstorming tour of the country with President Sukarno. The Soviet leader did, however, pile an unusually large credit of $250 million on top of the estimated $118 million already made available to Indonesia from Soviet sources. Though the Indonesians evaded his request for a formal promise to stay out of the Western defense alliance, such a pledge would have been highly superfluous in view of their well-known commitment to neutrality or "noninvolvement" and their readiness to endorse the main outlines of Soviet policy on current international questions.[5]

President Sukarno, who had on occasion accepted American as well as Soviet aid, was less concerned with foreign policy during these months than he was with the implementation of his theories of "guided democracy," a homegrown alternative to the Western-type democracy which he considered unsuited to Indonesian conditions. The spring and summer of 1960 were to witness a series of drastic constitutional and political readjustments in Indonesia. Their net effect, in the eyes of outside observers, was to eliminate any parliamentary check on the authority of the executive and to provide a greatly enlarged field of action to Indonesia's Communist party through the creation of new governmental organs in which the Communists were awarded a prominent place. If there was to be any move to curb the expanding Communist influence in Indonesian affairs, it seemed likely to originate in the army rather than in political circles. The army had intervened for this purpose on at least one occasion in the past, but for the moment it displayed an unexpected passivity.

Army intervention in Southeast Asian politics had become a rather frequent occurrence in recent years, especially in cases where it could be claimed that Communist influence was threatening to get out of hand. A very recent instance had occurred in Laos as a sequel to the renewal of guerrilla activity by the Communist-led Pathet Lao movement in that country in the summer of 1959. In this case, however, the establishment of direct military control proved to be even more transitory than had been true in Burma. A parliamentary election held on April 24, 1960 was conducted in such a manner as to produce a strong conservative majority, and on May 31 an anti-Communist, pro-Western government was installed under Tiao Somsanith, with the anti-Communist General Phoumi Nosavan as Minister of Defense. To the United States, which was subsidizing the Laotian Government to the extent of some $40 million a year, this was a highly welcome (though unexpectedly short-lived) arrangement.

The neighboring Republic of South Vietnam had meanwhile remained under the firmly anti-Communist if authoritarian rule of President Ngo Dinh Diem, who likewise relied on the United States for political, economic, and military support in the continuing struggle to make head against subversive efforts fomented by the neighboring Communist state of North Vietnam. To the west, Cambodia responded to the more mercurial guidance of the neutralist-minded Prince Norodom Sihanouk. When Chou En-lai visited Cambodia on his way back from India on May 5-9, there was talk of closer Cambodian economic and cultural ties with the Chinese People's Republic, but no public reference to new economic aid agreements.[6]

Western observers could take more thorough satisfaction in the current state of affairs in Malaya, another neutral though Western-orientated state which was enjoying an unwonted prosperity and getting ready to end the twelve-year state of emergency necessitated by a Communist rebellion that had broken out in 1948. Its government's friendly feelings toward the United States were to be reaffirmed when Prime Minister Tunku Abdul Rahman visited Washington later in the year.[7] The separate state of Singapore, still subject to a measure of British guidance, was having hard times economically but gave no special evidence of political instability at this period in spite of the uncertain loyalties of its overwhelmingly Chinese population.

Only two of the principal Southeast Asian states, the Philippines and Thailand, had definitely thrown in their lot with the West through membership in the Southeast Asia Treaty Organization. These two countries thus shared with Pakistan the burden of representing the Asian viewpoint when the SEATO Council of Ministers assembled in Washington for its sixth annual meeting, the first to be held outside the SEATO treaty area, which was held on May 31-June 2. Secretary of State Herter served as chairman of this gathering, but the ministers were also entertained at luncheon by the President and heard a speech by Vice-President Nixon explaining American views on the recent failure of the summit conference and stressing the need to provide an economic and ideological as well as a military answer to Communism.[8]

These sentiments were reechoed in the formal communiqué of the SEATO Council, which noted with evident regret that the meeting had not taken place "in that improved international climate that had been hoped for." The Chinese Communists, it was pointed out, "continued their uncompromising attitude," and the ministers drew attention to an "intensification during the past year of Communist subversion, insurgency and terrorism in several countries in the Treaty Area." Nevertheless the Council expressed confidence that SEATO, thanks to the work of its Military Advisers, would "be able successfully to resist aggression" and was making good progress in its efforts in the countersubversion, economic, and cultural fields. Pote Sarasin of Thailand, Secretary-General of the organization since 1957, accepted the Council's invitation to continue in office until 1963.[9]

The reference to "subversion, insurgency and terrorism" presumably related primarily to Laos and South Vietnam, both of which had been included in the SEATO treaty area by a special protocol, and both of which had been the object of a certain amount of terrorist activity inspired from Communist North Vietnam. Thailand and the Philippines, in contrast, had been reasonably free of such disturbances in recent years. Each of these countries was now enjoying what could be safely described as normal conditions, Thailand under the authoritarian rule of Field Marshal Sarit Thanarat and the Philippines under the American-type congressional regime currently headed by President Carlos P. García. While Thailand prepared to send its King and Queen on a ceremonial visit to the United States at the end of June,[10] the Philippines expectantly awaited the arrival of President Eisenhower on the first stop of his Far Eastern tour.

The jubilant "welcome home" accorded the President on his arrival in Manila on June 14 attested once again the underlying strength of the Philippine-American tie, whatever the resentment aroused from time to time by the American stand on specific economic and defense questions.[11] If a cloud had descended on the Philippine visit before the President's departure on June 16, the fault did not lie in any way with his Filipino hosts. Rather it was the work of the riotous Japanese mobs which had compelled their government to cancel Mr. Eisenhower's visit to Tokyo just three days before its scheduled commencement.

40. TAIWAN AND KOREA

The first sign that something might be going wrong with American policy relationships in the Far East had come not from Japan but from the Republic of Korea, where the increasingly unpopular regime of President Syngman Rhee had been overthrown at the end of April after harrowing days of mob action and police slaughter. The Korean experience was the more disconcerting because, to those who looked beneath the surface of events, it appeared not to be an isolated development but the result of factors which operated in varying degrees in several other countries allied with the United States. Among such countries were Japan, the Republic of China on Taiwan, and, as we have already observed, Turkey.

Known for their strong antipathy to Communism, the governments in authority in these countries had usually been counted among the most reliable allies of the United States. This impression had not been diminished by the tendency of such leaders as President Chiang Kai-shek and President Rhee to try to commit the American Government to a more bellicose policy than Washington could countenance. In none of these countries, however, had the attitude of the government been entirely representative of political and popular opinion. In Taiwan and Korea, as in Turkey, the forms of parliamentary democracy had cloaked a rather severely authoritarian one-party rule. Although the Liberal-Democratic regime of Japanese Premier Nobusuke Kishi had not been open to any serious reproach of this nature, its pro-Western and anti-Communist policies had been violently objectionable to an active and influential, if numerically restricted, section of the Japanese public. In Japan, as in Taiwan and Korea, the government supported the United States but there was room for uncertainty as to just how far the nation supported the government.

A hint of the dangers to which such a situation could lead had been afforded three years earlier by the anti-American riots that had suddenly broken out in Taiwan on May 24, 1957, to the chagrin and dismay of American authorities on the spot and in Washington.[12] The effect of this episode had been comparatively short-lived, however, and while Washington had strongly discouraged Chiang Kai-shek from trying to realize his ambition of reconquering mainland China, it had not been able to persuade him to modify his methods of government or place his regime on a broader popular basis. Political control in Taiwan was still concentrated in the hands of mainland Chinese associated with the Generalissimo's Kuomintang organization, while the local Taiwanese population and the few outspoken critics of the Kuomintang remained in outer darkness. The end of Chiang Kai-shek's second six-year term as President in the spring of 1960 brought no essential change in this situation. Although the Chinese constitution limited the President to two successive terms, it was arranged that this provision should remain in abeyance until such time as Nationalist rule of the mainland was restored. In the meantime the National Assembly on March 21 obediently elected the Generalissimo to a third term commencing some two months later.

The presidential election which took place in the Republic of Korea on March 15 would probably have produced a similar result but for the excessive eagerness of some elements associated with President Rhee's own Liberal party. The eighty-five-year-old Dr. Rhee, who had held the presidency ever since the Republic of Korea was established in 1948, was unopposed for reelection, his opponent having died a month before the poll. Interest thus centered on the vice-presidential contest between the incumbent Dr. John M. Chang, who belonged to the opposition Democratic party, and the Republican party challenger, Lee Ki Poong. Mr. Lee, who had lost to Dr. Chang in 1956, did better in 1960: he was elected by a majority of some four to one. But this result was clearly due less to any personal merit than to widespread fraud, terrorization and violence which caused the death of at least ten persons and were sufficiently glaring to draw critical expressions from Secretary Herter and President Eisenhower [13] as well as from many Koreans in all walks of life.

In the following days there were growing protest demonstrations by opposition politicians in the Korean capital of Seoul and by street crowds, often led by students, in Pusan, Masan, and other centers. Though President Rhee attributed these outbreaks to Communist inspiration,

American observers found no basis for his theory. What they saw was a spontaneous revulsion against the methods of the Rhee regime and particularly the brutality of the police. On April 18-19 matters reached a climax as the police fired on a protest demonstration in Seoul and killed at least eighty persons. The country-wide death toll of 115 or more exceeded even the fatalities in the recent South African riots. Apart from the bad name being given to Korean democracy, the situation had an element of real danger because troops were being withdrawn from the armistice line to help in enforcing martial law. There was no assurance that the Communists in the north might not attack if order was not promptly restored.

Partly, no doubt, for this reason, the United States made no pretense of treating the crisis as a matter that concerned only the Koreans. Secretary Herter called in the Korean Ambassador on April 19 and told him plainly that in view of its close association with Korea in the eyes of the world, the United States had been "obliged to take cognizance" of a state of affairs which he described without mincing words as "unsuited to a free democracy." [14] President Eisenhower later explained that while the United States had not in any way interfered in Korean affairs, he himself had sent word to President Rhee, as "a friendly gesture for a man I know and respect and admire," "that trouble could come out of such irregularities and [he] hoped that they could be stopped." [15] This message was conveyed to Dr. Rhee through various channels and with growing urgency in the next few days as the demonstrations continued and the aged Korean President fought to save what he could from Dr. Chang and his increasingly exigent supporters. Finally, on April 27, the dam broke and Dr. Rhee submitted his resignation, leaving Foreign Minister Huh Chung to pick up what remained of the country's executive authority.

Happily for the United States and the free world, the forces which had toppled the Grand Old Man of Korean nationalism were not only opposed to Communism but were most favorably inclined toward the United States as the result of the forthright stand it had adopted. There might be room for misgivings about the frenzied character of the opposition and the immaturity of some of its leaders, but the sensible attitude displayed by Mr. Huh's provisional regime encouraged the hope that Korean policy might develop in future along somewhat more realistic lines than had been possible under Dr. Rhee's headstrong leadership. Apart from the pressure for democratic constitutional reforms, there was an evident need for modifications in the arrangements governing United States aid. A new attempt to improve relations between Korea and Japan was also long overdue; and it was hoped in Washington that a new Korean regime might take a more objective view of the problems of Korean unification and abandon Dr. Rhee's impractical idea of liberating Communist-held North Korea by a "march north." That Korean affairs were in fact moving in this salutary direction was fairly clear by the time President Eisenhower began his Far Eastern trip.

The enforced omission of Japan from the presidential itinerary did not diminish and may even have accentuated the warmth with which Mr. Eisenhower was received on the later stages of his journey. His reception in Taipei, the Nationalist capital, on June 18 was made the more tumultuous by the fact that the Chinese Communists had chosen to demonstrate their own "contempt and scorn" for the occasion by subjecting Quemoy to its heaviest bombardment since 1958. The President's talks with Chiang Kai-shek did not bear heavily on Taiwanese political problems, and Mr. Eisenhower said nothing of liberating the mainland; but he pledged America's "steadfast solidarity" with the free Chinese government, assured his host that there had been no change in American policy regarding the defense of the offshore islands, and promised that the United States would continue to assist free China's economic expansion.[16] The attitude of the crowds made it plain that at this moment pro-Americanism was a highly popular sentiment.

If the President's mood was momentarily darkened by the hostile demonstrations he encountered on the American-administered island of Okinawa, the one spot of technically Japanese territory on which he was able to set foot, his spirits must have been revived by the tremendous outpouring of popular enthusiasm that marked his arrival in Seoul on June 19. "We regard the United States," Premier Huh told him, "as our closest friend, our most powerful ally, and our greatest benefactor among the nations of the world." Addressing the Korean National Assembly next day, Mr. Eisenhower complimented Korea's citizens on their recently demonstrated awareness of "the rights and obligations of a free people." "We will be watching your progress with ever-growing concern," he declared. "You can always count on our friendship as long as we endure." [17] In his conversations with Huh Chung the President once again affirmed the American commitment to Korean independence and agreed with the interim Korean leader that "every effort must be continued to bring a peaceful end" to the country's tragic division between the Communist and free worlds.[18] The likelihood that Communist North Korea and its backers in Peking and Moscow would agree to the unification of Korea on any but Communist terms might be no greater than in the past. But for the moment it was sufficiently gratifying that South Korea itself had come through its crisis with no weakening of its allegiance to the free world.

41. JAPAN: A NARROW ESCAPE

How did it happen that a President who could be so deliriously welcomed in Manila, Taipei, and Seoul had to be kept away from Tokyo lest he suffer bodily harm at the hands of an uncontrollable mob? It was not because the United States and Japan had been enemies in World War II. There was no hostility in Japan to Mr. Eisenhower personally, and comparatively little to the country he represented. There was, however, very definite hostility to the policy of close association with the United States which had been maintained by successive Japanese governments over the past decade and which had led to the inclusion of Japan within the American defense system, the reestablishment of a modest Japanese defense force, and the presence in Japan, even after the removal of American ground combat troops, of some 65,000 officers and men of the American armed forces.

Most of the thousands of Japanese who opposed the President's visit did so because, apart from any dissatisfaction they may have felt with their own government on other grounds, they wanted at all costs to avoid involvement in a third world war and had become convinced that the way to do so was to break their country's ties with the United States and substitute a policy of neutrality. Among their leaders, some were undoubted Communists or fellow travelers who knew perfectly well that this was the very objective toward which the two big Communist powers had been working for many years. Their efforts would not have come so near success, however, had they not had behind them a popular movement of very considerable scope and depth.

Ironically, the President's long-planned visit to Japan had in no sense been intended as a demonstration of American domination over Japanese policy. On the the contrary, its purpose had been to celebrate the emergence of postwar Japan into a position of full and equal partnership with the United States. The completion of Japan's economic recovery, attested by dramatic production and trade figures and an unmistakable increase in popular well-being, had paved the way for full Japanese participation in the collective efforts now being contemplated by the industrialized nations to raise the standard of living in less developed countries. On the political side, an equally fundamental transformation was about to be registered in the new United States-Japanese Treaty of Mutual Cooperation and Security which Ambassador Douglas MacArthur, II, had negotiated with the Japanese Foreign Office as a substitute for the original United States-Japanese Security Treaty of 1951.

The keynote of the earlier security treaty,[19] negotiated as an integral part of the Japanese peace settlement, had been the right granted by Japan to the United States to dispose land, air, and sea forces in and about Japan which could be utilized, without any interference on the part of the Japanese, for the purpose of contributing to the maintenance of peace and security in the Far East and the defense of Japan itself. The basic principle of the new treaty was to be the replacement of these unilateral American rights by new arrangements which would give Japan an influential if not a decisive voice in any military activities undertaken by the United States on its territory.

A clearer understanding of this changed relationship might have done much to weaken the popular hostility to the new treaty which had become apparent in Japan even before its formal conclusion. But although the terms of the new arrangement were inherently much more favorable to Japan than those of the old treaty, this fact was effectually hidden amid the confusing sequence of treaty articles, supplementary agreements, clarifying notes, and interpretive statements that were to form the basis of the new relationship.

Of the two key articles of the new treaty,[20] Article V committed both countries to take action of an unspecified nature in case either one was attacked in territories under Japanese administration—a formula that made Japan responsible for resisting any attack on American forces in the Japanese home islands, but implicitly relieved it of any obligation to react against an attack on American-administered Okinawa. Article VI confirmed the grant to the United States of facilities and areas in Japan for use by American land, air, and naval forces; but it said nothing of the important restrictions to which this privilege (no longer called a "right") would henceforth be subjected. Some of these restrictions were spelled out in a detailed technical agreement that accompanied the treaty.[21] The most important one, however, was reserved for a special exchange of notes between Prime Minister Kishi and Secretary Herter. These documents stipulated that major changes in the deployment of American forces into Japan, major changes in their equipment, and the use of Japanese facilities and areas as bases for combat operations (except for operations under Article V) should be the subjects of "prior consultation" with Japan.[22]

This meant that Japan would have to be consulted before the United States undertook, for example, to introduce atomic weapons into the country or to make use of Japanese bases in repelling an attack on Formosa. But it still did not expressly state how far the United States would be obliged to abide by Japan's opinion once the consultation had taken place. Would Japan have a "veto" on United States actions, or would it not? This crucial point was not included in the formal documentation at all, but was at least partially resolved in the official communiqué that was issued when Premier Kishi and Foreign Minister Fujiyama came to Washington to sign the treaty and accompanying documents on January 19, 1960. According to this authoritative statement,[23] President Eisenhower "assured [Mr. Kishi] that the United States Government has no intention of acting in a manner contrary to the wishes of the Japanese Government with respect to the matters involving prior consultation under the treaty." Premier Kishi, who agreed that "common interest, mutual trust, and the principles of cooperation" were the basis of the "new era" in American-Japanese relations, interpreted this language as in effect giving Japan the last word. There might, he had said, be cases in which Japan would actually have to say "No" to the United States, although he also expressed his confidence that the United States would make only "reasonable" requests on matters covered by the consultation clause.[24]

That the new treaty should be immediately denounced by the U.S.S.R. and Communist China caused no particular surprise, although the Japanese were somewhat taken aback by Moscow's threat to annex the small, Soviet-occupied Japanese islands of the Habomai group and Shikotan unless the arrangement was repudiated.[25] More disconcerting was the evident hostility to the treaty of a wide section of Japanese leftist and neutralist opinion, including the Socialist party opposition in the Diet, a variety of leftist or fellow-traveling labor and student organizations, and the bulk of the Japanese press. Even before the treaty was made public, leftist mobs had almost prevented Premier Kishi from departing for the United States for the signing ceremonies. The subsequent political overturns in Korea and Turkey, and particularly the U-2 incident with its suggestion of the kind of activities that could conceivably be engaged in by American aircraft based in Japan, helped to inspire an ever-widening mass protest. Questions were soon being raised as to whether the treaty could be ratified by the Japanese Diet in time for President Eisenhower's scheduled arrival on June 19.

The lower house of the Diet did in fact approve the treaty in a tumultuous session on May 20, although the absence of the Socialist opposition cast some doubt on the regularity of the procedure. As the upper house prepared to debate the treaty and the demonstrations in Tokyo continued to increase, the suggestion was heard in Washington that the plans for the President's impending visit might have to be reconsidered. White House sources nevertheless insisted that the trip would take place as planned. To cancel it at this late date, it was argued, might bring down the Kishi government and the treaty along with it. Yet the disorders grew and grew. On June 11, White House press secretary James C. Hagerty and Ambassador MacArthur had to be rescued by helicopter from a surging mob which had surrounded their automobile at the Tokyo airport. Though it was evident by this time that the Communists were committed to an all-out effort to block the Eisenhower visit as well as the treaty, there was still no word of hesitation as President Eisenhower and his party proceeded with the earlier stages of their itinerary. It was Premier Kishi who announced on

June 16, shortly after 20,000 leftists had occupied a part of the Diet building, that he was reluctantly asking the President to postpone his visit.[26]

It was also Mr. Kishi who managed to preserve the substance of the Japanese-American relationship by refusing to resign and by insisting that ratification of the treaty must be completed. Amid continuing demonstrations and renewed threats from the U.S.S.R., the Diet was obstinately held in session for the period required to make ratification effective even without a vote in the House of Councillors. This moment was reached at midnight on June 18-19. Three days later, on June 22, the United States Senate overcame its own uneasiness and gave its advice and consent to ratification by a vote of 90 to 2. Instruments of ratification were promptly exchanged in Tokyo, and the treaty formally went into effect on June 23, Japanese time.

Only when this process had been safely completed did Mr. Kishi confirm the report that he would resign and allow a successor to begin the heavy task of rebuilding Japanese-American friendship and preparing for the parliamentary elections to be held in the autumn. Prospects for restoring the former cordiality with the United States were enhanced by the understanding attitude adopted by the American Government, as well as by the evident determination of many Japanese who had been shocked by recent events to try to correct the weaknesses and errors that had made them possible. Hayato Ikeda, who succeeded Mr. Kishi as Premier on July 18, was known as a firm adherent of a pro-American policy, although he shared his predecessor's frequently expressed view that collaboration with the free world did not necessarily imply hostility to the Communist powers.

42. PEKING, MOSCOW, WASHINGTON

In the Far East as elsewhere, the climactic events of May and June were followed by a period of some uncertainty as the nations of the area digested the experience of recent months and waited to see how the new, post-summit phase of the "cold war" was going to develop. International attention during this period was largely monopolized by developments in Africa, in Latin America, and at the United Nations. In the Far East the principal subject of interest, once President Eisenhower had returned to the United States and the Japanese treaty was safely in effect,[27] was the manner in which Communist China intended to exploit its position as the second most powerful member of the Communist bloc. A highly noteworthy development in this connection was the growing clarity and vigor with which the Peking regime was now beginning to insist on its disagreement with the Khrushchev doctrine of "peaceful coexistence."

It might have been supposed that Communist China's internal problems would have given Chairman Mao Tsetung and his associates enough grounds for anxiety without taking on a major ideological quarrel with the leading power in the "camp of socialism." Since the drastic cutbacks in Communist China's Second Five-Year Plan which had been announced in the summer of 1959, it had been obvious that the pace of agricultural and industrial development originally decreed by the Peking rulers had been more strenuous than the Chinese masses were able to sustain. The economic plans for 1960, though they envisaged a "continued leap forward," had been considerably more modest than those of the preceding year;[28] and the attainment of even these more moderate goals was later to be called in question by a series of agricultural failures which were attributed in Peking to the worst floods, droughts, and other natural calamities in the history of the "People's Republic."[29] (Some outside observers were more inclined to ascribe the troubles to maladministration and to excessive demands on China's highly regimented peasant population.)

Such setbacks, however awkward, did not negate the belief in the West that Communist China was rapidly thrusting its way into the front rank of industrial nations.

Peking itself was to assert at the year's end that industrial production had increased substantially despite the admitted difficulties in agriculture.[30] Steel production, for example, was claimed to have achieved a level of 18,450,000 tons and to have exceeded that of France. There could, however, be no doubt that China's emergence as a modern industrial power was occurring somewhat more slowly and a good deal more painfully than had originally been anticipated. The stream of refugees that continued to flow into overcrowded Hong Kong and into Portuguese Macao testified to the persistence of substantial, if politically ineffectual, discontent among the Chinese people. In areas of predominantly non-Chinese population, there was reason to believe that conditions were worse. This was plainly the case in Tibet, where the patriotic revolt of 1959 had been mercilessly put down but where sizable guerrilla resistance to the Chinese occupying forces was still reported at frequent intervals.

If the U.S.S.R. had been more generous in its assistance to Chinese industrial and technical development, the acuteness of some of these internal problems might have been lessened and the Peking rulers might have been more ready to support the Soviet approach to international policy. As things stood, the Chinese Communists apparently saw no reason to conceal their fundamental disagreement with Khrushchev's way of doing things. Even before the summit conference, their publications had openly questioned Khrushchev's theories about the usefulness of a "relaxation of international tensions" and about the possibility of avoiding war with the capitalist world. To some observers it had seemed that the Peking leaders were worried lest Khrushchev make a "deal" with the capitalist world at their expense. After the U-2 incident and the failure at the summit, the Chinese authorities displayed enough sense of Communist solidarity to endorse the declaration on "peaceful coexistence" adopted at the June meeting of Communist representatives in Bucharest.[31] In their own party and theoretical journals, how-

ever, they continued to repudiate Khrushchev's outlook
with unmistakable clarity.

The main theoretical differences, as developed in a
series of authoritative articles in Peking and Moscow,
appeared to be these. In Khrushchev's view, which remained the official view of the U.S.S.R. and most of the
European Communist parties, the balance of forces in the
world had changed to such an extent that there was now
a prospect of avoiding war with the "imperialist camp"
and achieving a decisive Communist victory in the international arena by the methods of "peaceful coexistence."
Similarly, in the Soviet view, the Communists in individual "capitalist" countries now had a prospect of coming
to power by nonviolent, parliamentary means; and, in
the meantime, it was expedient to support the national
movements in colonial countries in their battle against
"imperialism" even when these forces were not themselves
Communist. Peking, on the contrary, tended to take the
position that Communist victory without war was incon-
ceivable; that class struggle and violent revolution were
the only road to power for Communist parties; and that
only the avowed Communist movements in colonial countries had a valid claim to external Communist support.[32]

As with the conflict between the U.S.S.R. and Yugoslavia in the later 1940's, it was generally assumed that
these theoretical differences were related to important
conflicts of practical policy and interest. Among the effects
envisaged by the latest Soviet disarmament plan,[33] it was
noted, would be the denial of nuclear weapons to Communist China—another among the numerous indications that
Moscow was not at all happy about the prospect that
Peking might soon force its way into the "nuclear club."
It was also widely suspected, though without definite confirmation, that the two powers were involved in a competition for influence in Communist Outer Mongolia. In
May, Communist China had promised the "Mongolian
People's Republic" a development credit of 200 million
rubles; in September, the U.S.S.R. undertook to support

the Mongolian five-year plan to the extent of 615 million rubles or over three times as much.[34]

As the ideological debate waxed hotter, there were also signs of growing frigidity in day-to-day Sino-Soviet relations. Chinese scholars failed to make an appearance at a much-heralded world conference of orientalists in Moscow. In mid-August it became known that the U.S.S.R. was in the process of withdrawing hundreds of Soviet technical experts assigned to work in China. At the same time Moscow was known to be mobilizing support for its position not only among the Communist-dominated European countries but also in North Korea and North Vietnam.

Peking's harping on the inevitability of war with the "imperialist" powers did not make any pleasanter reading in the West than it presumably did in Moscow. The Chinese Communists, it was suggested, might be proceeding on the dubious assumption that China could survive an atomic war more easily than highly industrialized powers like the United States or the U.S.S.R. If so, they might be tempted to take risks of a kind that the other great powers had found it better to avoid. But despite the bellicosity of its theoretical utterances, it was noticeable that Communist China seemed in no hurry to force a showdown with its non-Communist adversaries. While insisting on its determination to "liberate" Taiwan, it undertook no aggressive moves in that direction and showed no haste to renew its attack on the offshore islands in any serious way.

All this might change when and if Communist China got possession of even a few atomic weapons. In the meantime its practical approach to Far Eastern affairs, as contrasted with its theoretical pronouncements, suggested if anything a renewed emphasis on the methods of "peaceful coexistence" which it was questioning so scornfully in the intraparty controversy with Moscow. Not only did it settle the frontier problem with Burma, conclude a friendship treaty with Nepal, and make some attempt to ameliorate relations with Indonesia. As a long-term solution for Far

Eastern problems it continued to advance the recommendation, reiterated in a speech by Chou En-lai on August 1 and subsequently quoted with approval by Khrushchev himself, "that the countries in Asia and around the Pacific, including the United States, conclude a peace pact of mutual non-aggression and make the whole region a nuclear weapon free area." [35]

The American Government, which promptly dismissed this specious proposal as "another meaningless propaganda gesture," had thus far shown no interest in reconsidering its own policy with respect to Chinese matters despite the accumulating evidence of dissension between Peking and Moscow. President Eisenhower and Secretary Herter had noted more than once that Communist China would eventually have to be brought into any disarmament agreement that might be reached with the U.S.S.R. At the moment, however, such an agreement still seemed distressingly remote. In the meantime United States policy toward Communist China was mainly concerned with such detailed matters as the fate of the five Americans being held in Chinese Communist jails [36] and the arrangements, if any, whereby American journalists might be admitted to report on Chinese internal conditions.[37] On neither of these points could any satisfaction be obtained in the occasional meetings between American and Chinese Communist ambassadorial representatives in Warsaw, the utility of which was beginning to be questioned on both sides.[38]

In view of the lack of any essential change in Chinese Communist policy—the reported promise of aid to the Algerian insurgents in September [39] represented, if anything, a change for the worse from the American viewpoint —authorities in Washington could see no reason to alter the traditional American policy of resisting the annual attempt to secure a voice for Communist China in the United Nations General Assembly. When the Assembly began its Fifteenth Session on September 20, Ambassador Wadsworth introduced the customary resolution designed to exclude debate on the question at the Assembly's current session, and made the customary speeches setting forth the considerations which seemed to the United States to disqualify the Peking regime for any role in the United Nations.[40]

Khrushchev himself led a vigorous fight for Communist China's admission to the Assembly on this occasion, taking over a responsibility which had normally been exercised by India in past years. As we have already observed, however, most of the new African states declined to follow the lead of the Asian-African bloc and preferred to abstain from voting. In consequence, the American resolution was adopted on October 8 by a vote of 42 to 34, with 22 abstentions—not a wide margin, but not much less than the vote of 44-29-9 registered in 1959.[41] Many Americans nevertheless wondered whether Khrushchev and Peking might not be right when they asserted that this slender American majority was doomed to disappear within the near future.

43. THE TROUBLE IN LAOS

In cataloging the misdeeds which were felt by the United States to render Communist China unfit for representation in the United Nations, Ambassador Wadsworth made no mention of the confused situation that had developed in Laos over the past several weeks and raised a renewed threat to the independence of that small Southeast Asian country. Though recent events in Laos had unquestionably reopened the possibility of serious Communist gains in Southeast Asia, it was impossible to prove that they resulted from any direct initiative by Communist China, the U.S.S.R., North Vietnam, or even the local Communist elements in Laos itself. The man who had touched off the Laotian crisis on August 9 by overthrowing the rightist-oriented Tiao Somsanith government was an obscure paratroop captain, Kong Le by name, who convincingly disclaimed any Communist affiliations and

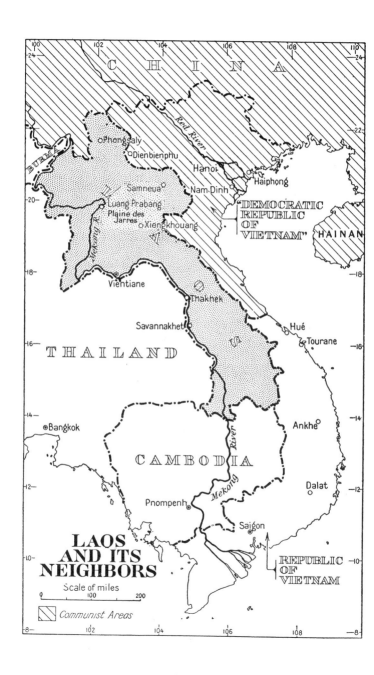

LAOS
AND ITS
NEIGHBORS

Scale of miles
0   100   200

Communist Areas

insisted that the only motive of his action was his disapproval of what he considered the pro-Western and unneutral policy of the ousted regime. Like much else in the Laotian situation, the genuineness of Kong Le's story was to prove exceedingly difficult either to confirm or to refute.

The immediate result of Kong Le's coup was the return to the Prime Minister's office of Prince Souvanna Phouma, the well-known neutralist politician who had relinquished the government in 1958 after the abysmal failure of his attempt to "reintegrate" the Communists into the national life and govern the country with their cooperation. Since that time, the Communist Pathet Lao army and its political arm, the Neo Lao Hak Xat, had been excluded from any regular voice in the government, although they had continued to exert a highly disturbing influence in Laotian affairs. We have already referred to the renewal of Pathet Lao guerrilla activity, supported from Communist North Vietnam, which engaged the attention of the United Nations in 1959. Souvanna had not been back in office long before it became evident that he meant to reverse the existing political situation and renew the attempt to work with the Communists instead of ostracizing them. Such a policy, assuming that the Communists were willing to cooperate, would almost automatically imply a reinterpretation of Laos' neutrality, a reduced reliance on the United States and the West, and the formation of closer ties with the Communist powers. Such a program seemed thoroughly in line with what was already known of Souvanna Phouma's general outlook.

If this prospect was distasteful to the United States, which had by this time invested some $300 million in the attempt to keep Laos on the side of the West, it was equally so to quite a number of Laotians. Most especially was it distasteful to General Phoumi Nosavan, the Minister of Defense in the preceding government and *de facto* commander of those sections of the armed forces that had not been affected by Kong Le's coup. General Phoumi did not in any way accept the new turn of events. Instead he undertook to resist and, if possible, reverse the tide from his headquarters at Savannakhet on the Mekong River. The struggle that would determine the future of Laos was thus converted into a three-cornered contest whose main protagonists were Premier Souvanna Phouma at the administrative capital of Vientiane, General Phoumi Nosavan and an associate, Prince Boun Oum, at Savannakhet, and the Pathet Lao in and around its traditional base of operations in the northeastern provinces of Phongsaly and Samneua.

The international ramifications of this situation were complex and delicate, particularly for the interested non-Communist countries. Little as they might relish the "deal" that was presumably going to be made between Souvanna Phouma and the Pathet Lao, they found it difficult to agree on suitable means of opposing it. Thailand, as the country that would be most directly affected if Laos were to go Communist, favored strong measures: a blockade of Laos and direct support of a counterrevolutionary movement under General Phoumi Nosavan. The United States, however, was most reluctant to take any action that might have the effect of precipitating civil war in Laos. Once begun, there was no telling where such a process might end. Great Britain and France, which were directly interested through their membership in SEATO, were even more reluctant to countenance any use of force. Both countries had entertained serious doubts about the wisdom of the United States in relying so heavily on the right wing in Laotian politics. It was their view that Souvanna Phouma, who repeatedly disclaimed any special partiality for Communism, should at least be given the chance to see what terms he could make with the Pathet Lao.

The course of action adopted by the United States in these circumstances was bound to appear somewhat ambiguous to the parties involved, however clear and consistent may have been its intentions.[42] Having assumed the obligation of maintaining the Laotian army and paying its troops under the military assistance program, Washington did not let itself be influenced by the fact that the army was now split into government and antigovernment factions. Apart from a few administrative delays, it continued to provide support to both groups, although Souvanna Phouma complained that his opponents were getting the lion's share of the weapons the United States was handing out. But if its aid to General Phoumi Nosavan's forces appeared to place it in the position of subsidizing a rebellion against the legal government, the United States took no responsibility for the General's military moves, which by late September had led to scattered fighting with both loyalist and Pathet Lao forces. Instead it attempted by diplomatic means to ward off a showdown between Vientiane and Savannakhet, to dissuade Premier Souvanna Phouma from making unwise concessions to the Communists, and to encourage all non-Communist groups to rally around King Savang Vathana, who had carefully avoided direct involvement in the crisis.

This diplomatic effort reached its climax in a mission to Laos which was undertaken by J. Graham Parsons, Assistant Secretary of State for Far Eastern Affairs, in the second week of October. The results were inconclusive at best. Prince Souvanna Phouma, who had already arranged for diplomatic relations with the U.S.S.R. and was relying on Soviet assistance to overcome the effects of Thailand's blockade, again disclaimed any intention of allowing the Communists to come to power; but he also refused to deviate from his plan of bringing the Pathet Lao into the government. His bargaining position in negotiations with the Pathet Lao had admittedly been weakened by the necessity of keeping one eye on General Phoumi's movement—while Kong Le, in turn, continued to keep a vigilant eye on him. Nevertheless Souvanna Phouma remained confident that a satisfactory adjustment could be made—especially, he intimated, if the United States would refrain from making things more difficult by giving aid and comfort to his adversaries.

Despite this rebuff, the United States continued to avoid either repudiation of or outright identification with the Phoumi Nosavan forces. The latter had experienced a major setback at the end of September in the loss of the northeastern town of Samneua; but this loss was more than compensated on November 11 when the garrison at the royal capital of Luang Prabang went over to the anti-Communist side, together with various important political figures. Premier Souvanna Phouma had by this time signified his readiness to accept the Soviet aid which had been eagerly proffered by a new Soviet ambassador, and had come close to agreement with the Pathet Lao on a program which involved the latter's participation in a "national unity" government, the establishment of "good neighborly" relations with Communist China, and the dispatch of friendship missions to that country and to North Vietnam. The defection of Luang Prabang would seem to have hastened the conclusion of these negotiations, the obvious aim of which, so far as the Communists were concerned, was to obtain a position within the government and swing Laos toward the Communist camp.

Yet Souvanna Phouma continued to deny that he was selling out to the Communists. "I am the only one who reasons with both sides," he asserted; [43] and he pointed out that he wanted the Savannakhet people, as well as the Communists, to participate in the proposed government of national unity. That Savannakhet would be willing to do so seemed more than doubtful, however, even though the United States for a time halted military assistance to the Phoumi Nosavan forces at Souvanna Phouma's request. A more likely prospect as the forces in Laos began to polarize was a military showdown which might well have the effect of driving Souvanna Phouma even more decisively into the arms of the Communists. By the end of November, military encounters were again occurring even while the Prime Minister continued his efforts to persuade the rightist forces to join the coalition.

Apart from Soviet and Chinese Communist declarations

supporting Souvanna Phouma and denouncing the role of the United States, the Laotian crisis thus far had nominally retained the character of an internal rather than an international conflict. This fiction was not to be preserved much longer, because the anti-Communist forces were beginning to threaten Vientiane and the U.S.S.R. was moving toward open intervention on the other side. Captain Kong Le, who now appeared to be working hand in glove with the advancing Pathet Lao contingents, carried out a second coup in Vientiane on December 8. Premier Souvanna Phouma, his efforts at conciliation frustrated once again, fled to Cambodia and from there sent in his resignation. A new, "legal" government was established at Savannakhet under the leadership of Prince Boun Oun and later validated by a royal ordinance.

The U.S.S.R. had already begun an airlift of gasoline and other supplies to Vientiane. It now began to step up its assistance by airlifting heavy weapons and other military material to the remnants of the Souvanna Phouma regime. Apparently based in North Vietnam, some of the aircraft had been previously identified in the Congo. At the same time the United States swung its own full support to the anti-Communist forces, which by December 16 had fought their way into Vientiane and begun to clear the capital of Kong Le and Pathet Lao fighters. A Soviet protest against American "interference" in Laotian internal affairs was promptly rejected in Washington with the retort that it was the U.S.S.R. that had been guilty of interference by its deliveries of military equipment to the "rebels." [44]

But the capture of Vientiane was only the beginning of what might still become the protracted civil war the United States had so much feared. While the U.S.S.R. continued its arms drops to the retreating Pathet Lao, the world-wide Communist propaganda orchestra began to sound the theme of United States "intervention." A Soviet commentator suggested that unless the "intervention" ceased, Laos might become "a second Korea." [45] Ostensibly to avert such a catastrophe, Moscow now began to agitate for the convening of an international conference of the powers that had been involved in the Geneva armistice arrangements of 1954. Such a gathering would presumably include the Big Four, Communist China, and perhaps Laos, Cambodia, and the two Vietnamese states. But this expedient was hardly calculated to appeal to the United States, which had no desire to see the problem inflated and would have been quite satisfied if the U.S.S.R. had simply desisted from aiding the pro-Communist forces.

Nor could much enthusiasm be mustered in Washington for an alternative plan, advocated principally by India but favored also by Great Britain, which called for the reestablishment of the tripartite International Commission for Supervision and Control in Laos which had been set up by the Geneva armistice. That body, which had consisted of representatives of India as chairman together with Canada and Poland, had been regarded by the United States as far too favorable to the Pathet Lao. Having greatly welcomed its suspension in 1958, Washington could not feel that its reestablishment in 1960 would contribute to a favorable development of the Laotian situation. On the other hand, there were indications that opinion in London, Paris, and elsewhere would strongly favor such a move if it appeared to be the only alternative to an exhausting civil conflict sustained by rival great powers. A third possibility, assuming that matters did not quiet down promptly, was a referral of the case to the United Nations as had been done in 1959. But this procedure, too, involved considerable risks from the American standpoint in view of the growth of neutralist sentiment in the world organization and the uncertain attitude of even Great Britain and France.

The situation was further complicated by a lack of reliable intelligence about the military situation, especially about the rumored involvement of North Vietnamese military units on the side of the Pathet Lao. On December 30 the Laotian government asserted that several battalions of North Vietnamese troops had actually crossed the frontier, and the Laotian representative in New York immediately called on Secretary-General Hammarskjold to request United Nations support. There was, however, no independent evidence of the alleged invasion, which eventually turned out to have been either a figment of the imagination or a feint to assist the Pathet Lao forces in seizing the strategic Plaine des Jarres area and the key town of Xiengkhouang.[46] Nevertheless the situation was felt in Washington to be sufficiently serious to call for a special White House conference on December 31 and an announcement that the United States was consulting with allied governments, was mindful of its obligations under the SEATO treaty, and "would take the most serious view of any intervention in Laos by the Chinese Communists or Viet Minh [North Vietnam] armed forces or others in support of the Communist Pathet Lao, who are in rebellion against the Royal Laotian Government." [47]

44. FAR EASTERN PERSPECTIVE

Any further deterioration in the situation in Laos would obviously have an unfavorable influence on the fate of neighboring states and might even threaten to renew the "falling domino" process in Southeast Asia that the United States had halted with such difficulty in 1954. Already the events in Laos had caused considerable uneasiness not only in Thailand but also in the neighboring republics of Vietnam and Cambodia. For several months President Ngo Dinh Diem's government in South Vietnam had been contending against a rising wave of Communist terrorism which, in this instance, was clearly inspired and supported from Communist North Vietnam. It is true that there was also significant anti-Communist opposition to President Ngo, whose highly personal methods of government had occasioned somewhat the same kind of resentment that had recently led to the overthrow of President Syngman Rhee in Korea. On November 11-12, the Vietnamese President narrowly escaped removal from office by dissatisfied military elements—advocates, in this case, of a "more effective" anti-Communist policy—who were frustrated only by the personal courage and cool thinking of the chief executive. For the moment, President Ngo's position seemed not to have been impaired; some even thought it had been strengthened. But if Laos were to lose its independence, Vietnam's chances of survival would undoubtedly be greatly reduced.

That the threat from North Vietnam had more than local significance was emphasized once again on December 23, at the height of the Laotian crisis, when the U.S.S.R. concluded a long-term economic agreement with the North Vietnam regime providing, among other things, for a development loan of 43 million "new" rubles or $47,770,-000.[48] Outsiders could not be sure just how this gesture related to the current situation in Laos and South Vietnam, nor could they judge to what extent, if at all, it might reflect a sharpening rivalry between the U.S.S.R. and Communist China for influence in Southeast Asia. It did seem, however, that the U.S.S.R. was asserting its interest in this part of the world more actively than in the past. Cambodia, too, had lately received a promise of Soviet aid in hydroelectric construction and resource surveys on the occasion of a visit to Moscow by Prince Norodom Sihanouk.[49]

Communist China had also proffered both hospitality and promises of assistance to the Cambodian leader in recent weeks,[50] and it was noticeable that Peking, too, was making an effort to improve its relations with more than one Southeast Asian state. The last details of the Burma frontier question had been settled when Premier Nu visited Peking at the beginning of October; plans were now being made for increased trade between Burma and China over the old Burma Road, and Chou En-lai was expected shortly in Rangoon for ratification of the frontier treaty.[51] An agreement clarifying the status of Indonesia's Chinese residents was also put into effect late in December. Indonesia, less preoccupied with the Laotian problem than the continental countries, was preparing at this moment to send a high-level mission to the U.S.S.R. in search of military equipment with which to counter an alleged buildup of Dutch forces in Western New Guinea. Indonesians had few political qualms where their claim to "West Irian" was concerned, although they had not ventured to submit the matter to the United Nations in recent years in view of the difficulty they had encountered in securing effective backing from the Assembly.[52]

It was not only in Southeast Asia that the U.S.S.R. and Communist China displayed unusual activity during this closing period of 1960. Communist North Korea, traditionally regarded as a Soviet area of influence, was also benefiting from Chinese as well as Soviet attentions. In October, Communist China had undertaken to lend the North Koreans the unprecedented sum of 420 million rubles (nominally $105 million) and assist them in building various industrial plants.[53] Such munificence was more than the Soviet Union apparently cared to match; but a Soviet-North Korean agreement signed in Moscow on December 24 provided for Soviet assistance in the construction of several industrial enterprises and power stations, as well as an 80 per cent increase in commercial exchanges during the next five years.[54] In addition, the U.S.S.R. continued its support of the political initiatives undertaken by the North Korean regime with the obvious purpose of trying to disrupt the democratic progress of South Korea and prepare the way for Communist domination of the whole country.

Since President Eisenhower's June visit to Seoul, conditions in the Republic of Korea had stabilized to a gratifying degree. Elections held on July 29 had produced Democratic party majorities in both houses and permitted the installation of former Vice-President Chang as Premier on August 19. By abandoning the Rhee project of a "march north," the new government had for the first time brought itself fully into harmony with the official United

Nations doctrine that Korea should be unified through nationwide free elections under United Nations supervision.[55]

But such a plan remained wholly unacceptable to the North Korean Communists, who had proposed any number of alternative procedures more favorable to their own interests. On November 11 the Pyongyang regime came forward with a new plan of the same general type, this one involving a "confederation" of North and South Korea together with interim measures to promote economic and cultural relations and a mutual reduction of military forces. This proposal was strongly supported by the U.S.S.R. and officially commended by it to the attention of the United Nations Assembly.[56] Its fundamental incompatibility with United Nations objectives would undoubtedly be pointed out by the United States when the Assembly came to debate the Korean question in the spring of 1961. That debate might also reveal to what extent the Assembly's attitude on the Korean question, which had shown a tendency to waver in recent years, had been affected by the recent increase in the neutralist bloc.

The latent Soviet-Chinese Communist rivalry which some observers professed to detect in current Far Eastern politics came to public attention at another level in connection with the Moscow meeting of Communist parties that followed the Bolshevik anniversary celebration on November 7. The result of those deliberations, embodied in the eighty-one party declaration of December 6,[57] has already been described: a verbal compromise between the Soviet and Chinese viewpoints which appeared to place few if any practical restraints on Peking's pursuit of a militant policy at home and abroad. But while insisting on the legitimacy of promoting Communism by military action, the Chinese Communists still refrained from renewing their attack on the Nationalist-held offshore islands. Perhaps they were deterred by the food shortages and supply difficulties which had followed the summer's agricultural catastrophe. Perhaps they were waiting to test the intentions of the new American administration, since Senator Kennedy had indicated during the campaign that although he supported President Eisenhower's policy in regard to the Formosa Strait, he did not regard Quemoy and Matsu as the most advantageous positions on which to base the defense of the free world.[58] Or perhaps the Chinese Communists were waiting for the atomic weapons which nearly all authorities expected them to possess within the next few years.

That the Peking regime still looked upon the United States and "American imperialism" as its fundamental enemy was evident in every phase of its varied international activity, no longer confined to the Far East as in the past but increasingly conspicuous in Africa and Latin America as well. In the Latin American countries, Chinese political, psychological, and economic efforts had achieved a scope that rivaled those of the U.S.S.R. The United States might possess in Chiang Kai-shek an ally on Communist China's doorstep; but the Chinese Communists were now acquiring in Fidel Castro at least a potential ally on the doorstep of the United States. Cuba, to which the Peking government granted a 240 million ruble ($60 million) loan on November 30,[59] lay at approximately the same distance from the United States that Formosa did from the Chinese mainland. Would Communist China some day be giving military as well as economic aid to Cuba, as the Soviet bloc countries were already doing?

If there was still one major Far Eastern country whose situation could be viewed from the United States with comparative optimism, that country was Japan. The determination of the Japanese and American governments to repair the political damage caused by the June riots had produced excellent results at the official level,[60] and the Japanese people had given renewed evidence of a fundamental moderation that contrasted sharply with the hysteria of recent months. In the crucial parliamentary elections held throughout Japan on November 20, the ruling Liberal Democrats won 57.6 per cent of the popular vote and 296 out of 467 seats in the lower house—enough to exercise effective parliamentary control of that body, though still short of the two-thirds majority needed for constitutional changes. This result, which conformed fairly closely to the pattern of previous Japanese elections, was interpreted by Premier Ikeda as a popular endorsement of the policy in international affairs that he himself was pledged to carry forward. Independent observers were more inclined to discount the foreign policy aspect of the vote and to credit the popular appeal of the government's plan to double the national income in ten years.

It was also noted that the Japanese Socialists, the most powerful opponents of the security treaty, had themselves captured 27.4 per cent of the popular vote, to 8.9 per cent for the more moderate Democratic Socialists, 2.9 per cent for the Communists, and 3.2 per cent for miscellaneous candidates.[61] These figures justified a note of caution and led some observers to prophesy a continuing agitation for revision of the security treaty and the removal of American bases. In any case, the new government which Mr. Ikeda formed early in December would plainly be far more solidly based than had seemed likely a few months earlier. Japan's economy, moreover, had been flourishing to such a degree that even the prospective curtailment of overseas purchasing by the United States seemed unlikely to interfere substantially with the government's plans for economic growth. Hard work and good fortune had placed Japan in a position where it could, if it chose, begin to make a real contribution to the development of less favorably situated countries. If it did so, as the government apparently intended, the efforts made by the United States to ensure Japan's own rehabilitation over the past fifteen years could be regarded as amply justified.

CHAPTER SEVEN

THE INTER-AMERICAN SYSTEM

THE PLACE of the twenty Latin American republics in
United States foreign policy is a subject of permanent debate among the peoples of the Western Hemisphere. The
precise terms of the argument naturally undergo considerable change as conditions alter from decade to decade.
Through most of the fifteen years that followed World War
II, the generalizations most current among Latin Americans (and many North Americans) concerned the United
States' alleged neglect of its American neighbors while it
concentrated on meeting the threat of international Communism in more distant areas. True, the validity of this
criticism was never admitted by the United States Government, whose spokesmen frequently pointed out that the
United States was actually expending large sums in aid
of Latin American economic development and had followed the trend of political affairs below the Rio Grande
with unflagging attention and sympathetic interest. These
protestations had carried little weight with the critics of
United States policy in Latin America. The financial outlays in question, the latter insisted, had been of minor
importance compared with those in Europe and Asia.
Washington, in their view, had failed even to under-
stand, much less confront, the full challenge of Latin
America's evolution during these years.

By 1960 the charge of neglect and inattention was beginning to lose its point. A series of unpleasant surprises
that had begun with mob attacks on Vice-President Nixon

during a visit to South America in 1958 had convinced
authorities in Washington that whatever might have been
true in the past, conditions in Latin America were now
really threatening to develop in a direction unfavorable to
United States interests. There was unmistakable evidence
of hostility to the United States among the masses and
even among the ruling élite in many Latin American
countries. The latent threat of large-scale Communist
operations in the Americas, momentarily checked by the
overthrow of a leftist-oriented regime in Guatemala in
1954, had begun to revive as the U.S.S.R. and Communist
China developed the strategy of cultural, economic, and
political penetration they had already employed with such
effect in Asia and the Far East.[1] The revolutionary government established by Fidel Castro in Cuba at the beginning
of 1959 had early revealed signs of Communist infiltration
as well as virulent animosity toward the United States. In
the course of 1960, the attempt of the Soviet Government
to take the Cuban revolution under its direct protection
was to bring the "cold war" for the first time into the
heart of the Americas and establish a Communist bridge-
head ninety miles from the United States. This development ensured that there would be no further "neglect" of
Latin America in Washington, whatever might be the
ultimate judgment on past United States policy in the
hemisphere.

45. A CONTINENT IN TRAVAIL

The disconcerting feature of the Cuban experience was
the fact that it appeared not to be an isolated development
but, rather, the product of conditions that were widespread in Latin America and could conceivably produce
similar results in other countries. What the Communists
liked to call a "revolutionary situation" actually prevailed
in large parts of Latin America. Traditionally regarded
in Washington as a bulwark of the free world and a model
of institutionalized international cooperation through the

Organization of American States, Latin America at the beginning of the 1960's had become a victim of chronic economic instability and a tinderbox of social and political discontent. Material development was unquestionably going forward at a rapid rate—the over-all increase in gross product was estimated at some 5 per cent a year—but the benefits to the average Latin American were imperceptible. A great part of the increase was eaten up by rapid population growth; more of it flowed into the pockets of an already wealthy ruling class; continued inflation in many countries made even the bare necessities of life increasingly inaccessible. Many Latin Americans had been reduced to a state of near desperation in which they were only too ready to blame the United States for their difficulties and to applaud the radical economic and social policies that were now being implemented in Cuba with the direct encouragement of the Communist powers.

To say these things is not to imply that the peoples and governments of Latin America were incapable of taking an objective view of their situation and initiating corrective action along orderly and democratic lines. Much had in fact been accomplished in this respect in recent years. On the political side, one serious impediment to modernization and progress had been substantially eliminated with the disappearance of most of the old-fashioned military dictatorships that had flourished in the Caribbean area and in South America during the earlier postwar period. By 1960 the only surviving examples of this once familiar type were the government headed by General Alfredo Stroessner in Paraguay and the widely detested regime of Generalissimo Rafael L. Trujillo in the Dominican Republic. While there might be room for differences of opinion about the democratic qualities of some other governments in Central America and the Caribbean, every Latin American administration except that of Premier Castro in Cuba was at least nominally committed to the ethical and political principles of the inter-American system. Most of them appeared genuinely concerned, even though in somewhat varying degrees, with the extension of democracy and popular well-being.

The leaders of the recent Cuban revolution offered a glaring exception to this pattern. Not only did they expressly repudiate the traditional concept of representative democracy; they showed less interest in reforming the existing political and economic system than in promoting a thoroughgoing social revolution—a revolution which, moreover, was not to be confined to Cuba but, in their view, was ultimately destined to be extended to the rest of Latin America. Already their support of revolutionary movements directed against other Latin American governments of more conservative stripe had required emergency action by the Organization of American States, including a special meeting of American Foreign Ministers at Santiago, Chile in August 1959. The Latin American reaction to Cuba's activities had not, however, been by any means uniform. The governments against which Cuba had thus far directed its fire, especially the Trujillo regime in the Dominican Republic, were widely regarded as an affront to democratic sentiment. There was at least some feeling in Latin America that Cuba was performing a meritorious service in attacking them. On the other hand, most Latin American governments were no more eager than the United States to see Trujillo's regime succeeded, as could conceivably happen, by another revolutionary government on the Castro model. Still less could they regard with equanimity the possibility that Cuba might one day turn its attention to stirring up the discontented masses in their own countries.

Though accompanied by a certain amount of cooperation between like-minded elements in different Latin American countries, the modernization of Latin American political structures which had taken place in recent years had gone forward essentially within a national rather than an international framework. The United States, in keeping with the accepted principle of nonintervention in the internal affairs of other American states, had scrupulously held aloof from the entire process, although its attitude had earned it scant credit from the more progressive elements in Latin America. But if the problem of political institutions was at least officially regarded as one that each Latin American country must solve by itself, the problems of economic and social advance were universally regarded as a proper subject for cooperative endeavor, both through bilateral channels and through such instrumentalities as the Inter-American Economic and Social Council and the United Nations Economic Commission for Latin America.

Here, too, the basic responsibility for progress indisputably rested with the peoples of the individual Latin American countries. As United States spokesmen from President Eisenhower down had never tired of pointing out, only the Latin American peoples themselves could produce the bulk of the savings required for new capital investment in productive enterprise. They alone could ensure the maintenance of a "climate" which would attract private investment from abroad. But Washington had never denied that the need to promote economic growth, diversify production, and raise living standards in Latin America required important supplementary action on the international plane, nor did it overlook the fact that this requirement placed exceptional demands on the resources and imagination of the United States. Within the past year or two it had shown a markedly increased readiness to lend assistance for these purposes, although its plans still fell far short of what most interested Latin Americans felt necessary.

Technical cooperation between the United States and its American neighbors in such fields as agriculture, health, and education had long been a valued feature of the inter-American relationship. The present need, however, in the opinion of such Latin Americans as President Juscelino Kubitschek of Brazil, the author of the imposing blueprint known as "Operation Pan-America," was to supplement these endeavors by large-scale action in two other directions which to Latin Americans seemed even more important:

(1) by making available increased amounts of capital for economic development, particularly for roads, dams, and similar projects for which private financing was not available; and (2) by developing measures to stabilize the prices of Latin American agricultural and mineral exports, thus enabling the Latin American countries to secure the foreign exchange to pay for necessary imports of machinery and other capital goods and consumer items.

Although the United States still shied away from any comprehensive program of this nature, it had agreed in 1958 to the establishment within the Organization of American States of a special committee of presidential representatives, the so-called Committee of Twenty-One, which had already held two fruitful meetings devoted to exploring the whole range of inter-American economic problems. It had further agreed to join in establishing an Inter-American Development Bank with a capital of $1 billion—45 per cent of which would ultimately come from the United States—which was expected to begin operations in the course of 1960. In addition, Washington had offered to participate in discussion of Latin American commodity problems, and had supported efforts by the Latin American countries to improve their trading position by arrangements among themselves. It had expressed approval of the preparations being made by seven South American states and Mexico to set up a free trade area similar to the European Free Trade Association; and it had actively promoted the conclusion in the fall of 1959 of an International Coffee Agreement designed to stabilize prices for that key Latin American commodity through the withholding of excess supplies from the market. These measures were regarded throughout the Americas as steps in the right direction, though few persons below the Rio Grande would have considered them a sufficient answer to the needs they were intended to meet.

46. "OUR HEART IS IN THE RIGHT PLACE"

A more vivid mark of United States interest was the announcement early in 1960 that President Eisenhower was contemplating a personal visit to South America to round out the series of good-will tours that had already taken him to parts of Europe, Asia, and Africa and was expected to culminate later in the year in his projected trip to the U.S.S.R. and the Far East. Although the President could find time to visit only four of the twenty Latin American republics, it was made clear from the first that he regarded the venture as a manifestation of United States friendship for all of Latin America and that he relied on Brazil, Argentina, Chile, and Uruguay, the four countries in which he would be stopping, to communicate the spark to the others. The mass of Latin Americans were obviously appreciative of this effort by a statesman who retained great personal popularity in Latin America despite the discontent aroused by some phases of his government's policy. The big question in their minds was whether the visit would be confined to the utterance of noble sentiments or presaged a further shift in the United States attitude on practical problems.

The address which President Eisenhower delivered to a national audience in the United States before beginning his southward flight on February 22 [2] did not suggest that he was contemplating any major change in policy, nor did it suggest that existing United States policy could be in any way at fault. Our policies, the President said, had been widely misrepresented and misunderstood in Latin America. "Wherever I go," he promised, "I shall state again and again the basic principles and attitudes that govern our country's relationships in this hemisphere." Among these principles, he recalled, were nonintervention, mutual respect and juridical equality of states; desire for rapid economic progress and for cooperation in sound development schemes; commitment to help maintain the security of the Americas in conformity with the Rio treaty of 1947; faith in the rule of law; determination to foster the triumph of human liberty throughout the hemisphere. "It is my profound hope," Mr. Eisenhower said, "that upon my return I shall be able to report to you that the historic friendship and trust among the nations of this hemisphere has been strengthened and that our common cause—justice and peace in freedom—has been reaffirmed and given new life."

This idealistic emphasis was to be apparent at every stage of the President's two-week mission, which included five days in Puerto Rico as well as nine in South America. In itself such a journey could obviously resolve none of the pressing problems of the hemisphere, least of all the Cuban problem, which had been growing more acute from day to day and figured extensively in the private discussions held by Mr. Eisenhower and Secretary Herter with their various South American counterparts. What the visit did accomplish was to dispel, at least temporarily, a good deal of the suspicion and uncertainty that had surrounded United States objectives and thus reestablish an atmosphere more conducive to effective inter-American cooperation in the months ahead. As he had promised, President Eisenhower lost no opportunity to explain the United States viewpoint on both Latin American and world affairs. Repeatedly he disavowed the prevalent notion that the United States supported dictators or was interested only in helping the rich people of Latin America. "We are not saints," he told a Chilean-United States audience in Santiago. "We know we make mistakes, but our heart is in the right place, and we believe that aid given by the United States to the people who want to work, who welcome some help, who are energetically working for themselves to raise their standards of living, . . . those are the people . . . which we get great satisfaction in helping." [3]

In Brasília, Rio de Janeiro, and São Paulo in Brazil, in Buenos Aires and Mar del Plata in Argentina, and in the Chilean capital of Santiago, the President's reception by the crowds along his route left little to be desired in the way of warmth and cordiality. True, there were occasional hostile shouts; but only in Montevideo was an otherwise very friendly reception marred by an unruly student demonstration which obliged the President's automobile to pass through a cloud of tear gas. Mr. Eisenhower's personal coolness in this emergency evoked the same admiring comments as did his urbane reception in Santiago of a critique of United States policy presented in the name of the students of Chile—to whose spokesmen he not only promised a full reply but offered the good-humored suggestion that their first obligation was to make sure of their facts.[4]

As was to have been expected, the visit produced a veritable flood of official rhetoric in the form of welcoming speeches and acknowledgments, addresses to legislative bodies, toasts, and overflowing communiqués.[5] In three of the four countries visited, Mr. Eisenhower joined his fellow chief executives in solemn declarations of American principles—the Declaration of Brasília, the Declaration of San Carlos de Bariloche (Argentina), the Declaration of Montevideo. A joint statement issued with President Jorge Alessandri of Chile served a similar purpose. (There was already a Declaration of Santiago de Chile, promulgated by the American Foreign Ministers the summer before.) The declaration of Brasília, the most specific of these documents, reflected President Kubitschek's acute concern with inter-American economic problems and included a polite though noncommittal reference to Operation Pan-America. It also expressed the confidence of the two Presidents "that the hemispheric crusade for economic development will lead toward greater prosperity and harmony for all."

In contrast to Premier Khrushchev's technique on similar missions, the President scattered no largesse along his route in the form of grants or loans for economic development. Undoubtedly he lent an attentive ear to the reports of President Kubitschek, President Alessandri, and President Arturo Frondizi of Argentina on the anti-inflationary fights their governments were waging with the support of the United States and, in the case of Argentina and Chile, with that of the International Monetary Fund.

During and after his visit to Chile Mr. Eisenhower also showed special interest in a plan developed by President Alessandri for regional disarmament measures aimed at averting local arms races, relieving inflationary pressures, and releasing more resources for economic development. This concept might have seemed to conflict in some measure with the traditional notion of hemisphere defense requirements which had guided the United States in supplying arms to a considerable number of Latin American countries under the military assistance program. In Argentina, whose coastal waters had recently been invaded by a pair of unidentified submarines, there was some feeling that the need of the moment was for more military equipment rather than less. But few military experts considered the armed forces of the Latin American countries to be of any great importance in relation to an outside threat against the hemisphere; and President Eisenhower was sympathetic to the argument that they ought not to be needed within the hemisphere, either. The proven worth of the inter-American mutual security system, he suggested on his return home, "should now enable some of the American Republics to reduce expenditures for armaments and thus make funds available for constructive purposes." [6]

It was also in Chile that Mr. Eisenhower enjoyed the sight of a group of prospective homeowners at work on a low-cost housing project for which the government had provided land and utilities while they themselves furnished the labor during time spared from their regular jobs. "Personal accomplishments brought pride to their eyes, self-reliance to their bearing," the President reported. "Their new houses are modest in size and character, but I cannot possibly describe the intense satisfaction they take in the knowledge that they themselves have brought about this great forward step in their living conditions." [7] If there was one significant new idea that emerged from the President's journey, it had to do with the value of this kind of achievement and the need for greater stress on development efforts that really touched the lives of the people. Considerably more was to be heard of this concept before the year was over.

In other respects the President and his party were obviously well satisfied with the results of their expedition. They had found "a vast reservoir of respect, admiration, and affection for the United States," as well as some "serious misunderstandings" of the kind the President had done his best to dissipate. All in all, Mr. Eisenhower reported in his homecoming broadcast on March 8, "our relationships with our sister Republics have, with notable —but very few—exceptions, reached an alltime high. Leaders and populations alike attested to this truth. But an even firmer partnership must be our goal." [8]

The President did not, indeed, suggest any specific steps to this end, other than the cultivation of mutual understanding through language study and similar means. He had already repudiated "any thought of the United States alone developing a so-called master plan for the raising of living standards throughout the hemisphere." [9] Secretary Herter nevertheless suggested that he thought there would inevitably be a "followup" to the visit. The United States, he emphasized, was "very much aware of the desirability of moving as fast as it is possible in assisting the nations of Latin America to develop themselves." What was involved, in Mr. Herter's opinion, was not a fundamental change of policy but rather a judgment as to degrees and priorities in the allocation of resources. The net result of the trip, he implied, was a fuller appreciation of the urgency of Latin American needs in relation to those of other areas.[10]

47. CUBA FACES EAST

The urgency of Latin American needs was not to be forgotten in Washington in the months that followed, but it was already evident that a constructive approach to hemispheric·problems was being made increasingly difficult by the behavior of the Castro regime in Cuba. Throughout their South American journey, Secretary Herter noted, the President's party had encountered "real anxiety" about the trend of Cuban affairs. They had also found appreciation of the "patience" the United States had shown toward Cuba thus far, together with a strong belief that the principle of nonintervention must continue to be observed in future dealing with that country.[11] It was clear that Latin Americans, despite the intemperate actions of the Cuban regime, continued to attach great importance to the national and social objectives for which Premier Castro and his associates professed to be fighting. The Cuban leaders' announced objectives of liberating Cuba from foreign "exploitation" and providing a square deal for the Cuban masses was one with which a great many Latin Americans were bound to sympathize, whatever they might think of the methods employed.

There was every indication, moreover, that even after a year and more of revolution the Castro government retained the support of the great bulk of Cuba's working population. This mass support seemed to be relatively little affected by the prevalent shortages of provisions and consumers' goods, the growing disillusionment of upper- and middle-class Cubans, the defection of numerous political and military leaders in protest against Communist influence in the regime, or even the armed military resistance that was reported from time to time from the Cuban countryside.

The United States itself had repeatedly made clear that it had nothing but good will for the Cuban people and fully recognized their right to undertake such social, economic, and political reforms as they thought desirable, subject only to the fulfillment of their country's normal obligations under international law.[12] What had disturbed the United States from a very early period was the fact that Cuba's revolutionary government appeared to go out of its way to trample on the legitimate interests of the United States and its citizens and to insult and vilify this country before the Cuban people and before the world. It would take many pages to itemize the successive acts of expropriation, aggregating over a billion dollars, the arrests and expulsions, and the propaganda attacks against which Washington felt it necessary to file formal protests in the course of 1959 and 1960.[13] Their net effect—aggravated, it is true, by some admittedly very serious anti-Castro activities carried on by Cuban exiles in the United States—was to reduce Cuban-United States relations to a condition perceptibly worse than those prevailing between the United States and the U.S.S.R. There are two sides to every story, and the Cuban leaders plainly felt that Cuba was the aggrieved party throughout this distressing period. By any normal standards, however, the self-restraint displayed by the United States through many months of Cuban harassment would have been remarkable even had the Cuban situation seemed unrelated to the global offensive of international Communism.

In actual fact, the counterpart of Cuba's progressive alienation from the United States was a growing ascendancy of Communist influences within Cuba and an increasing gravitation toward the Communist bloc in matters of international policy. Outside observers had long been uneasy about the prominence among Dr. Castro's lieutenants of such apparent Communist sympathizers as Major Ernesto (Che) Guevara, who had early achieved a dominant position in the organization and direction of the Cuban economy. A much more definite cause for anxiety was afforded by Soviet First Deputy Premier A. I. Mikoyan when he visited Cuba in February 1960 and signed two agreements with the Cuban Government whereby the U.S.S.R. undertook to extend a credit of $100 million to Cuba, provide technical assistance in the construction of industrial facilities, and purchase 5 million tons of Cuban sugar over a five-year period.[14] From the point of view of the United States, such Soviet trade-and-aid deals,

"I know who my real friends are"

Ed Valtman in *The Hartford Times*

with their implication of permanent Soviet influence, were even less welcome in the Western Hemisphere than they were in Asia and Africa. This was the more true because the Cuban-Soviet deal had features that directly affected important United States interests in Cuba. As part of the sugar agreement, Cuba was promised substantial quantities of Soviet crude oil, and in May the three foreign-controlled oil companies operating in the country were informed that they would be expected to process it. On their refusal to do so, they were summarily seized.

During this same period there were many reports that Cuba was obtaining planes and other military equipment from Czechoslovak or other Communist sources, ostensibly to protect itself against "aggression" from the United States. It was quite openly receiving trade missions, making trade agreements, and generally multiplying its ties with East Germany, Poland, and other "iron curtain" countries; it was attempting—with relatively little success—to form an anti-United States alignment in Latin America; and it was also cultivating such support as it could find among neutral and less developed nations such as the United Arab Republic. In May it announced that it was resuming diplomatic relations with the U.S.S.R. after an eight-year interval. It was easy to picture the Communist network that could develop throughout the Americas around the nucleus of a Soviet embassy in Havana, headed, as matters turned out, by one of the leading espionage experts among Soviet diplomats.

Throughout these months the United States had refrained from using what some observers had considered its most potent instrument for keeping Cuba in line. This was its power to modify or eliminate the preferential quota arrangement whereby Cuba was enabled to sell the United States the largest part of its annual sugar crop at a figure substantially above the world market price. The United States Sugar Act was up for renewal in 1960, and some congressmen had long been urging that the time had come to bring Cuba to heel by reducing or eliminating its quota and awarding the extra tonnage to more deserving suppliers. The Cubans themselves had been decidedly apprehensive on this score. In February they had gone so far as to offer to negotiate their differences with the United States on condition that the latter would take no unilateral action in the matter. Although the United States had declined to give such a commitment,[15] it had hesitated nevertheless to invoke a measure that could hardly fail to work severe hardship on the Cuban people.

By late spring, however, the cumulative effect of Cuban provocations and pro-Soviet gestures (including a post-summit invitation to Khrushchev to visit Havana) had begun to bring the administration around to a harder position. What remained of the United States economic aid program in Cuba was terminated late in May.[16] In June, Congress was urged to amend the Sugar Act in such a way as to give the President discretionary authority to alter the import quota of any nation. Congress, instead, authorized a reduction of the Cuban quota but established a rigid formula for the allocation of the unused tonnage to other countries. This done, Mr. Eisenhower announced on July 6 that in view of the Cuban Government's "deliberate policy of hostility toward the United States" he was regretfully reducing Cuba's quota for the balance of 1960 from 739,752 to 39,752 short tons.[17]

Taken at this late stage, such action was perhaps bound to accentuate the adverse trend of United States-Cuban relations. "Economic aggression!" cried Premier Castro and his lieutenants as they accelerated their plans to nationalize the remaining United States enterprises in Cuba and prepared to step up their intermittent war of nerves against the United States-leased naval base at Guantánamo Bay. On July 11 they took the further grave step of appealing to the United Nations Security Council for protection against what were described in an official United Nations document as "the repeated threats, harassments, intrigues, reprisals and aggressive acts" perpetrated against Cuba by the United States Government.[18] Such action was in itself a challenge to normal inter-American procedure, which called for the submission of disputes among the American republics to the Organization of American States rather than to the world organization. Like Guatemala in 1954, Cuba obviously hoped to enlist the support of the U.S.S.R. and other extra-hemispheric countries against the United States and felt that the best way of doing so was to carry its case before a global rather than an inter-American forum.

A still more disconcerting consequence of the President's move was the reaction of the U.S.S.R., which chose this moment to shed its last remaining inhibitions about claiming a direct role in Western Hemisphere affairs. With the Congo crisis already boiling furiously, Khrushchev in a speech of July 9 planted both feet in the Cuban situation by promising the Cuban people full support in defeating the United States "economic blockade" and, in addition, offering them Soviet military protection in case of a United States attack. "It should be borne in mind," said the Soviet Premier, "that the United States is now not at such an unattainable distance from the Soviet Union as formerly. Figuratively speaking, if need be, Soviet artillerymen can support the Cuban people with their rocket fire, should the aggressive forces in the Pentagon dare to start intervention against Cuba." [19]

But the United States had had no idea of "starting intervention against Cuba," and President Eisenhower's reply from the summer White House at Newport was prompt and resolute. "The statement of the Soviet Premier," it said, "reflects the effort of an outside nation and of international communism to intervene in the affairs of the Western Hemisphere. . . . I affirm in the most emphatic terms that the United States will not be deterred from its responsibilities [to oppose such interference] by the threats Mr. Khrushchev is making. Nor will the United States, in conformity with its treaty obligations, permit the establishment of a regime dominated by international communism in the Western Hemisphere." [20]

This pledge went beyond anything that Mr. Khrushchev had threatened. The Soviet leader had not spoken of establishing a Communist-dominated regime in the Western Hemisphere, any more than the United States had spoken of intervening in Cuba. But Khrushchev was not to be overawed. At a news conference on July 12 he mockingly thanked the President for making statements which, he said, actually helped to "popularize" Communism. Disclaiming any selfish designs on Cuba, he went on to castigate all aspects of United States policy in the hemisphere and declared that even the Monroe Doctrine had "outlived its time" and "should best be buried as every dead body is." [21]

It was easy for the United States to issue another statement affirming in strong terms the continued validity of the Monroe Doctrine, both for the United States and for the American community as a whole.[22] But how was it to deal with the dangers to its peace and safety inherent in what had become, in spite of Khrushchev's disclaimers, a fairly obvious attempt by an alien power to introduce its system to the Western Hemisphere?

48. CONFERENCES AT SAN JOSÉ

In later discussions, President Eisenhower implied that while the Monroe Doctrine had undergone an important extension in recent years through the Rio treaty and other inter-American instruments, this fact could not inhibit the United States from acting unilaterally to protect its interests in the hemisphere in case of necessity. Such a development as the emergence of a Communist "satellite" in the Americas, the President said, would "call for very definite action," although he could not specify in advance what the action would be. But Mr. Eisenhower also made it clear that so far as possible the United States would greatly prefer to avoid unilateral action, to continue working through the Organization of American States, and to encourage that body "to use its collective influence, its moral and political influence, in straightening out these things." [23]

Working through the O.A.S. was a much more complicated matter than the old-time procedure of dispatching the Marines to occupy some recalcitrant Caribbean country. The Guatemalan experience in 1954 had shown that the other American states would not automatically use their influence in accordance with United States views, even if they shared Washington's anxiety about Communist penetration in the hemisphere—as many of them had done in 1954 and as many of them clearly did again in 1960. Khrushchev, indeed, had hardly uttered his missile threat before Peru came forward with a suggestion that the situation that had developed in reference to Cuba demanded a special meeting of the American Foreign Ministers. This view was strongly supported by the United States before the O.A.S. Council, which agreed on July 18 to convoke a Foreign Ministers' meeting on the subject on a similar pattern to the one that had been held in Santiago in August 1959. The subject matter of the new meeting was somewhat vaguely defined as "exigencies of continental solidarity, and defense of the regional system and of American democratic principles in the face of threats that might affect them." [24]

But action along several other lines would clearly be necessary if the proposed Foreign Ministers' consultation was to lead to useful results. The first requirement was to get Cuba's complaint against the United States out of the United Nations and back into the O.A.S. where it belonged. This was accomplished without much difficulty on July 19 by a vote of the Security Council itself, with the U.S.S.R. and Poland abstaining but no one voting in opposition.[25] Another useful step, the timing of which did not appear entirely fortuitous, was President Eisenhower's request to Congress to authorize a new $600 million aid program for Latin America. (See below.) Finally, it could be foreseen that favorable O.A.S. action in the Cuban matter would presuppose a satisfactory resolution of another important issue already before the O.A.S., one on which some Latin American governments felt even more strongly than they did about Cuba. This was the issue raised by the Trujillo government and the alleged activities of the Dominican Republic against the peace and security of its American neighbors.

That the Trujillo regime represented both a mockery of democratic ideals and a potential threat to the peace of the Americas had been generally recognized even before the Santiago conference of Foreign Ministers, which had been as much concerned with its activities as with those of Cuba.[26] More recently, in February 1960, the Dominican Government had been formally indicted before the O.A.S. by Venezuela on charges of mass arrests and "flagrant violations of human rights" in connection with the suppression of an alleged revolutionary plot. In June, these charges were largely confirmed by the five-nation Inter-American Peace Committee, the O.A.S. organ which had been commissioned to investigate them on behalf of the O.A.S. Council. Chaired by Ambassador John C. Dreier of the United States, the committee concluded that tensions in the Caribbean would continue to increase as long as the "flagrant violations" in question persisted.[27]

Sixteen days later, on June 24, President Rómulo Betancourt of Venezuela narrowly escaped death in Caracas when a bomb exploded in his immediate neighborhood, killing two persons and injuring sixteen. Señor Betancourt immediately charged that Trujillo had had a "bloody hand" in the assassination attempt, and demanded that Dominican "aggression and intervention" against Venezuela be given priority consideration by the O.A.S. On July 8, ten days before its action on Cuba, the O.A.S. Council agreed to convoke a meeting of Foreign Ministers on this subject and appointed a preliminary fact-finding committee to investigate the Venezuelan charges.[28] This committee, on which the United States was again represented, reported on August 14 that there was definite evidence of Dominican complicity in what had clearly been a widespread plot against Venezuela's government.[29] In the meantime Trujillo had shaken up his regime and installed a new president to initiate what was officially described as a program of "progressive democratization," though it was generally looked upon by outside observers as a last-minute attempt to avoid retribution when the Foreign Ministers met.

With both the Dominican Republic and Cuba requiring attention at the Foreign Ministers' level, it was decided to consider the two questions at two successive Meetings of Consultation, both of which would be held at San José, Costa Rica starting on August 16. Though formally distinct, the two problems were politically linked in such a way that what was done about the Dominican Republic would largely determine what could be done about Cuba. The United States was thus caught in a characteristic difficulty. On the one hand, Washington hoped to obtain a very strong expression of American opinion on the Cuban problem; on the other, it did not want to go nearly as far against the Dominican Republic as did Venezuela and some of the other American states. With no special tenderness for the Trujillo regime, the United States had important interests to protect in the Dominican Republic and was inclined to prefer the existing government to the Castro-type regime that might well emerge if Trujillo was driven from power.

Even before he arrived in San José, Secretary Herter was thus doomed to the position of trying to hold back his Latin American colleagues on the Dominican Republic while they in turn tried to hold him back on Cuba. Naturally, there were differences in the positions of the individual Latin American states on both issues. If none of them fully accepted the United States approach, several of them worked hard for compromise and thus helped to ensure a positive outcome, even though it was one that fell substantially short of United States objectives.

The debate on the Dominican Republic, the subject of the Sixth Meeting of Consultation of American Foreign

Ministers, began on August 16 and required five days. To Venezuela's demand for far-reaching sanctions against the Dominican Republic under the Rio treaty, the United States opposed the concept of a "constructive" approach involving the establishment of a special inter-American committee or "watchdog group" to supervise the holding of free elections and a return to democratic processes in the country. But most of the other Foreign Ministers inclined to side with Venezuela. The upshot of the meeting was the adoption on August 20, by a vote of 19 to 0 (the Dominican Republic and Venezuela abstaining), of a resolution which emphatically condemned the Dominican actions against Venezuela and called on all of the other American states (1) to break diplomatic relations with the Dominican Republic, and (2) to impose a partial interruption of economic relations with that country, beginning with an immediate suspension of the trade in arms while the O.A.S. Council studied the extension of the embargo to other articles.[30]

This resolution was not at all what the United States had sought. Nevertheless Washington severed diplomatic relations with the Dominican Republic within a week. It also began to lay the groundwork for a future modification of the Dominican sugar quota, although the possibility of action along these lines was severely limited by the failure of Congress to enact the requisite legislation.[31]

The Dominican Government, which showed no appreciation of the United States' moderate stand, made an unsuccessful attempt to deny the validity of the actions taken at San José on the ground that they lacked the approval of the United Nations Security Council. In this position it was supported, somewhat paradoxically, by the U.S.S.R., which likewise maintained that the United Nations Charter forbade "enforcement action" by regional agencies without Security Council authorization. At two meetings of the Security Council on September 8 and 9, several other delegates appeared to feel that the Soviet argument might not be entirely without merit. On the other hand, they could not overlook the fact that the underlying objective of the Soviet move was to develop a new method of interfering in inter-American affairs—or, in the words of Ambassador Wadsworth, to obtain "a veto over the operation of the inter-American system." The issue was closed, for the time being at any rate, by the adoption of a resolution which merely took note of the San José action without expressing an opinion on it.[32]

With the Dominican issue temporarily disposed of, the Foreign Ministers at San José had turned on August 22 to the question of Cuba and its relations with the Soviet bloc. The matters to be dealt with at this Seventh Meeting of Consultation were incomparably more difficult and delicate than those before the meeting just concluded. Indifferent as most of the Foreign Ministers had shown themselves to the fate of the Dominican regime, none of them wanted to take action against Cuba that would antagonize public opinion in their own countries, drive Cuba further into the arms of the U.S.S.R., or provoke it into renewed attempts to stir revolution in the Americas. Even the four-point agenda of the conference, in which the name of Cuba was nowhere mentioned, had been framed by the O.A.S. with a careful avoidance of specifics and a great deal of vague phraseology about such matters as "strengthening of continental solidarity and the inter-American system especially in the face of threats of extracontinental intervention that might affect them." [33]

That the United States intended to seek a strong condemnation of Cuba's attitude had nevertheless been evident from the mass of critical material about that country which it had already submitted to the O.A.S.[34] Cuba, which had recently supplemented its Soviet ties by a five-year trade and credit agreement with Communist China, had made it equally clear that it had no intention of taking up a defensive position but would vigorously attack the United States. "We did not come to be accused but to accuse," Foreign Minister Raúl Roa announced on his arrival in San José. "There is no such thing as extracontinental aggression, but there is intracontinental aggression." [35]

In spite of these unfavorable auguries, hope had persisted among some of the Latin American delegations that a head-on clash could be avoided and that Cuba could be quietly persuaded to renounce the protection of the U.S.S.R.—which, after all, was quite unnecessary, since no country planned to attack it—and to work out its difficulties with the United States with the aid of an inter-American conciliation group. Such hopes were now blasted by Premier Castro himself. While Secretary Herter in San José was citing the "urgent challenge" of Sino-Soviet imperialism and charting what he described as Cuba's movement toward full Communist control, Premier Castro in a Havana speech of August 24 was publicly ridiculing the O.A.S. and boasting of his government's friendship with the Communist powers.[36] Next day, August 25, Foreign Minister Roa formally announced that in view of the danger of United States "aggression," Cuba would not renounce Soviet protection. Mr. Herter responded that Cuba's government was "walking hand in hand with the Sino-Soviet bloc" and apparently was "willing to assist the Soviet Union in spreading communism in the rest of the hemisphere." [37]

Neither the Cuban charges of "aggression" nor the United States charges of Communist influence were entirely convincing to some of the other Foreign Ministers. But they could have little hope of conciliating such utterly opposed viewpoints. Eventually, on August 28, all of them—except the Cuban representative, who had walked out, and the Dominican representative, who was not present—agreed on a document known as the "Declaration of San José" which embodied at least a part of what the United States had hoped to secure. It did not, indeed, mention Cuba, but it condemned "energetically" any intervention or threat thereof by an extracontinental power. It also rejected "the attempt of the Sino-Soviet powers to make use of the political, economic, or social situation of any American state" and reaffirmed various inter-American principles regarding nonintervention, rejection of totalitarianism, and the obligations of the American system.[38] Before completing their work on August 29, the ministers also created a six-nation *Ad Hoc* Good Offices Committee to help settle controversies between American governments; rejected a Cuban resolution on United States "aggression"; commended Chile's initiative in the arms limitation field; and adopted several resolutions on economic matters.[39]

Although Secretary Herter professed to read the Declaration of San José as a "clear indictment" of the Castro government and characterized the two conferences as an unquestioned success,[40] other judgments were more reserved. The Mexican delegation denied that any condemnation or threat toward Cuba was intended in the San José Declaration; the Foreign Ministers of Peru and Venezuela (both of whom subsequently resigned) refused to sign the document at all, leaving that ungrateful task to their deputies.[41] If the United States could regard the San José meetings as a vindication of the inter-American system, some observers felt that their most significant result had been a revelation of the extent of popular sympathy for Cuba throughout Latin America. It was clear, in any event, that the deeper problems of the Americas were not going to be resolved by political declarations, however ingeniously worded. Momentarily diverted by the San José meetings, attention in the continent was already shifting back to the economic field as the time approached for a long-awaited meeting of the Committee of Twenty-One in Bogotá, Colombia.

49. ECONOMIC MEETING AT BOGOTÁ

A number of important developments had occurred in the field of inter-American economic relations during these months, though none of them seemed likely to reverse the generally unfavorable trend of Latin American economic affairs at any early date. That matters were in a bad way was emphasized by most recent statistics. Although the balance-of-payments difficulties that beset almost all Latin American countries had been less acute in 1959 than in 1958, largely because of drastic reductions in imports, the terms of trade had become increasingly unfavorable to Latin America. The flow of new private capital from the United States had fallen off in 1959 from the extraordinary heights recorded the year before, and continued to drop in 1960. A sharp decline in Export-Import Bank loans reduced economic assistance from the United States Government to all of Latin America in the year ending June 30, 1960 to a mere $240 million, less than half the amount made available in the preceding fiscal year.[42]

While population continued to rise, gains in productivity had slowed virtually to a halt. Inflation, checked here and there with the aid of the stabilization programs supported by the United States and the International Monetary Fund, remained a permanent hazard and a potential threat to political stability, especially in such important South American countries as Argentina, Brazil, and Bolivia. In Chile, a series of disastrous earthquakes and tidal waves in the latter part of May 1960 had taken up to 10,000 lives, caused untold property damage, and imposed a gigantic relief and rehabilitation problem on an economy which was just beginning to achieve a measure of stability after a long and peculiarly painful inflationary siege.

It was against such a background that the new Inter-American Development Bank, the fruit of decades of Latin American hopes and plans, had been formally established at an inaugural meeting held in San Salvador in February. Secretary of the Treasury Anderson and the other United States delegates to this meeting were greatly encouraged by the businesslike attitude of their Latin American colleagues, including Dr. Felipe Herrera of Chile, the new institution's president-elect. With an eventual lending capacity of $850 million for regular loans and another $150 million for special "soft" loans, the Bank would clearly represent a valuable adjunct to other sources of development capital, especially if it could stimulate the investment of additional private funds in worthwhile enterprises. But these amounts were small in relation to Latin America's unsatisfied capital requirements, and all agreed that the Bank would have to start slowly and exercise great caution in the projects selected for support. Despite the failure of Cuba to ratify the Bank's charter, operations were actually begun in Washington on October 1 with an initial capital of roughly $114 million in dollars and $34 million in other currencies.[43]

Another event of considerable import was the conclusion at Montevideo on February 18 of the seven-nation treaty establishing a Latin American Free Trade Area and Free Trade Association. Argentina, Brazil, Chile, Mexico, Paraguay, Peru, and Uruguay were the initial signatories of this arrangement, which aimed at the eventual establishment of a Latin American common market and envisaged a gradual elimination of internal customs duties and the like over a twelve-year period which might begin as early as 1961.[44] Colombia later joined the group, with indications that Venezuela and Ecuador might soon follow. President Eisenhower indicated during his visit to Chile that the United States, as the largest common market in the world, "could not but look with favor" on such efforts, provided they served not only to increase intraregional trade but to raise the level of world trade generally.[45]

This comment was clearly directed not only to the Montevideo enterprise but also to the parallel effort in Central America that had already produced the five-nation Tegucigalpa treaty of 1958 and had led to the conclusion on February 6, 1960 of a further "economic association treaty" among Guatemala, Honduras, and El Salvador.[46] The main problem in this area was to adjust the pace of economic integration in such a way as to avoid a split between Guatemala, Honduras, and El Salvador on the one hand and Nicaragua and Costa Rica, the other signatories of the Tegucigalpa pact, on the other. (See below.)

Much as it welcomed these efforts by Latin Americans to help themselves, the United States did not lose sight of the fact that any basic, long-term improvement in economic conditions would continue to depend very largely on action in Washington. Some further action by the United States had in fact been under consideration ever since the President's return from his Latin American tour; but it was not until July 11, when the Cuban crisis was already at its height, that the administration was ready to make a public announcement on the subject.

Drawn up in consultation with the National Advisory Committee on Inter-American Affairs, this latest United States initiative differed considerably from its predecessors. It was larger in scale, and it placed a sharper emphasis on meeting the human needs of "the bulk of the population" in Latin America through such measures as land reform and resettlement and the promotion of individual home ownership. No large sums of money were involved in the new program, Mr. Eisenhower emphasized at the Newport news conference at which its outlines were first disclosed. He was not thinking of a "Marshall Plan" type of operation.[47] The real objective, as the President put it again a few weeks later, was "to begin to give more hope directly to people throughout this hemisphere." [48]

An example of the sort of thing the United States had in mind was provided by a $53.2 million credit extended to Peru at the end of July for a program of land improvement and low-cost housing.[49] The prospective cost of the program, by no means modest by previous hemispheric standards, was indicated for the first time in the special message of August 8 in which Mr. Eisenhower asked Congress to authorize an additional expenditure of $600 million for Latin America over and above the current Mutual Security estimates.[50] One-sixth of this amount, Secretary Herter explained, was intended for earthquake rehabilitation in Chile; the balance of $500 million would be for "projects designed to contribute to opportunities for a better way of life for the individual citizens of the countries of Latin America." [51]

Neither the Senate Foreign Relations Committee nor Congress as a whole could muster any enthusiasm for a program of this magnitude, presented late in the session and with the specific request that it be approved before the Committee of Twenty-One began its meeting at Bogotá on September 5. Yet a refusal to approve it would have placed the United States in a peculiarly awkward position at a time when it was so anxious to rally the other American republics against the threat of "extracontinental intervention." There would be an opportunity for further consideration when the time came for actually appropriating the funds requested. Meanwhile, action on an authorization bill carrying the full $600 million was completed four days before the President's deadline.[52]

There had been some doubt in Bogotá as to whether even this comparatively large gesture would create a wholly satisfactory impression on the delegates of the other American governments when they assembled for the third meeting of the Committee of Twenty-One, officially known as the "Special Committee of the Council of the O.A.S. to Study the Formulation of New Measures for Economic Cooperation." But President Alberto Lleras Camargo of Colombia, the host, tempered his warnings about the depth of Latin America's crisis with words of praise for the United States initiative; and Under-Secretary Dillon, who headed the United States delegation, made an excellent impression when he explained that the plan was not intended as a substitute for economic development aid but rather as a "first step" in adding "the new and broad dimension of social development." The United States, Mr. Dillon added, would expect to continue its support of the program with additional funds as progress was made through joint and cooperative efforts.[53]

Although the derisive attitude of the Cuban delegation struck a jarring note and the Dominican Republic was not represented at all, the general atmosphere of the confer ence thus remained highly favorable. There was much the United States could approve, and little to which it could object, in the restatement of inter-American social and economic objectives that was adopted by the conference (over Cuba's dissenting vote) on September 13 and received the formal designation of the "Act of Bogotá." [54] Particularly welcome to the United States was the inclusion of detailed recommendations for action by individual Latin American countries in such comparatively neglected areas as land improvement, tax reform, housing, education, and public health.

In November the United States announced a further initiative, albeit on a much smaller scale, by declaring its support for a new Central American Bank for Economic Integration whose aim would be to strengthen and consolidate the developing Central American common market. Nicaragua had now rejoined Guatemala, El Salvador, and Honduras in promoting this enterprise, and the United States, in proof of its belief that Central American integration could significantly contribute to economic development and popular welfare, promised early financial assistance in the amount of $10 million and held out the possibility of additional help in the future. Membership in the Bank was left open to Costa Rica and other countries provided they were willing to participate substantially in the economic integration effort.[55] Meanwhile the other four Central American republics proceeded to negotiate a new economic integration treaty, signed at Managua on December 13, which envisaged the establishment of a common market within five years.[56]

In still another field of economic cooperation of interest to several Latin American countries, the United States had played an important part in broadening the scope of the International Coffee Agreement concluded in 1959. Encouraged by the inclusion of three British African territories and eight African members of the French Community, the parties to this agreement were continuing the endeavor to combat the chronic oversupply in the coffee market and maintain a reasonable price level by setting agreed export quotas. Plans were also on foot for an attempt to stabilize the coffee market on a world-wide basis by agreement among both producing and consuming countries, although there was no decisive step in this direction during 1960.[57]

50. AMERICAN MISCELLANY

Preoccupation with the questions raised by the Cuban revolution and the hemispheric drive toward economic betterment should not blind us to other Latin American developments that claimed their share of official attention on the part of the United States. Some of these developments were more encouraging than others from the standpoint of United States interests in the hemisphere. The comparatively uneventful character of the presidential elections that occurred in Latin America during 1960 could presumably be welcomed as a sign of growing democratic vitality and increasing readiness to permit the settlement of political issues by way of the ballot box. This trend had already been evidenced in Colombia by the fragile but still viable political truce that underlay the two-year-old administration of President Alberto Lleras, one of Washington's most distinguished official visitors of 1960.[58] Panama, Bolivia, Ecuador, and Brazil all elected new chief executives during the year, with a decorum that contrasted favorably with the violence that had marred some earlier elections in those countries and elsewhere in Latin America. The successful candidates —Dr. Roberto F. Chiari in Panama, Víctor Paz Estenssoro in Bolivia, José María Velasco Ibarra in Ecuador, and Jánio Quadros in Brazil—could be broadly characterized as combining a somewhat nationalistic outlook with a firm regard for the inter-American tradition. Two of them, Paz Estenssoro and Velasco Ibarra, had already had experience as chief executives of their respective countries. The Brazilian election on October 3 was perhaps of special interest to the United States, not only because of the important role that would surely fall to President Kubitschek's successor but also because of the fact that the losing candidate, Marshal Henrique Teixeira Lott, had been the choice of Brazil's more stridently anti-Yankee elements, including the Communists. Although Senhor Quadros professed a determination to cherish and develop Brazil's already excellent relations with the United States, the significance of his victory was qualified in some measure by ignorance of his exact intentions as well as by the concurrent reelection of Vice-President João Goulart, a more radically inclined leader who commanded wide backing among the Brazilian masses and had never boasted any friendly feelings for the United States. Brazil's new chief executive, who would be inaugurated January 31, 1961, would undoubtedly need to employ all his talents in the unremitting battle against inflation and the various political pressures that went with it. This point was emphasized during the autumn by indications that Brazil was heading into a very serious financial crisis, aggravated in some degree by complete uncertainty as to what Senhor Quadros intended to do about it.

The return of Señor Velasco Ibarra to the presidency of Ecuador on September 1 had one unexpected consequence in the sudden reopening of Ecuador's long-standing territorial claim against Peru, a matter involving 77,000 square miles of territory which had supposedly been settled by a treaty concluded under inter-American auspices in 1942. The settlement of 1942, of which the United States was one of the guarantors, had awarded the territory in question to Peru without reservation. Ecuador, however, now claimed that its acquiescence in this arrangement had been obtained under duress. Unless steps were taken to redraw the map in its favor, it intimated, it would bring the matter before the Eleventh Inter-American Conference. This authoritative gathering, representing the institutional pinnacle, so to speak, of the inter-American system, had already been postponed once at Ecuador's request and was now scheduled to be held in Quito in March 1961.[59]

This abrupt revival of a long dormant territorial claim, of which more was to be heard in the ensuing weeks, ran counter to a recent trend to deemphasize such boundary controversies within the Americas and permit them to be quietly settled by international adjudication. The United States had particularly welcomed a recent decision by Argentina and Chile to submit a pair of long-standing boundary disputes to arbitration by the International Court of Justice.[60] A similar controversy between Nicaragua and Honduras had been referred to the same tribunal with O.A.S. encouragement in 1957, although Nicaragua displayed a certain hesitancy about accepting the Court's judgment when that body ruled in favor of Honduras in November 1960.[61]

The United States itself was involved in a minor territorial dispute with Honduras concerning the sovereignty over the Swan Islands, three specks of land in the Caribbean some 110 miles from the Honduran coast. Inhabited mainly by United States citizens, the islands provided the site of governmental weather and air navigation centers as well as a private radio station that was currently being used for anti-Castro broadcasts. This issue, however, had not reached an acute stage and perhaps would not do so.[62] Of much greater current importance to the United States were the security and legal status of a number of its military bases and installations in the Caribbean area, particularly the facilities of the Panama Canal Zone, the Guantánamo naval base in Cuba, and the Chaguaramas naval base in the West Indian island of Trinidad. In all three of these areas the rights exercised by the United States under past international agreements had become in some degree offensive to local nationalist feeling, and there had been growing pressure for their surrender or, at least, for substantial revision of the contractual arrangements under which they were held.

So far as Guantánamo was concerned, there was no disposition in Washington to abridge the treaty rights of the United States simply because they happened to be displeasing to the Castro regime. If Cuba wanted to raise the issue in a formal manner instead of confining itself to threats and innuendoes, the United States indicated that it was prepared to defend its position either on the legal and diplomatic plane or if need be by force—a possibility that the Cubans, on their side, indignantly dismissed.[63] In the Panama Canal Zone, on the other hand, the United States found it desirable to make certain concessions to Panamanian feeling in the hope of avoiding a recurrence of the ugly riots that had taken place there in the fall of 1959. The principal concession, resolved upon after many months of interagency discussion in Washington, involved a limited display of the Panamanian flag within the zone [64] —a measure that did not go far toward solving this fundamental problem of Panama-United States relations, but at least proved good enough for 1960. As regards Chaguaramas, obtained from Great Britain under a ninety-nine-year lease in 1941 but more recently envisaged as the capital of the new West Indies Federation, the United States was able to secure its position until at least 1977 as a result of discussions with the British and West Indian governments. In the course of these talks, which were crowned by a preliminary agreement in December 1960, the United States agreed to relinquish numerous other areas which had lost their military value, and also promised economic assistance to the new Federation.[65]

Because of the presence of several British, French, and Dutch dependencies in the Caribbean, United States interests in that area involved contact with three European governments as well as a number of the American republics. International cooperation in the economic and social development of the Caribbean territories, including Puerto Rico and the Virgin Islands, had been carried on since 1946 under a special four-power international organization known as the Caribbean Commission. In June 1960 the four governments concluded a new agreement providing for the continuation of this work through a new Caribbean Organization, centered in Puerto Rico, which was designed to reflect recent constitutional and economic changes in the area by giving the territories themselves a stronger voice in policy making.[66]

The United States also continued to develop the close ties with Mexico that resulted from the two countries' geographical contiguity even more than from their common concern in the affairs of the hemisphere. One reflection of this increasing intimacy was the conclusion of a new aviation agreement providing for an expansion of air services between the two countries; [67] another was the plan to establish a United States-Mexican interparliamentary group similar to the one which already linked the United States and Canada. President Eisenhower, who had met twice with Mexican President Adolfo López Mateos in 1959, took time from the 1960 political campaign for a third and final meeting which occurred on October 24 at a bridge on the Rio Grande and in the adjacent Mexican town of Ciudad Acuña. The most important matter of bilateral interest touched upon by the two chief executives was the prospective commencement of work on the nearby international project which had once been known as the Diablo Dam but had lately been given the more symbolic name of Amistad (Friendship) Dam.[68]

51. THE CARIBBEAN TURMOIL

Significantly, the Cuban problem was not included among the subjects chosen for discussion by the United States and Mexican Presidents.[69] Mexico was one of the countries where sympathy for the Castro experiment had been particularly noticeable. In this, however, it was not alone. Two months after the meetings at San José, there still remained a noticeable divergence between the United States and its American neighbors with regard to the critical issues discussed by the Foreign Ministers. The failure of the United States to rescind the sugar quota of the

326 THE UNITED STATES IN WORLD AFFAIRS

Dominican Republic had been particularly regretted in the Americas, and had elicited a formal complaint from Venezuela.[70] The United States, on its side, had not yet succeeded in bringing about the establishment of the O.A.S. Good Offices Committee envisaged at San José as a possible means of dealing with the Cuban situation.[71]

The recent activities of the Cuban government had given no indication that the "clear indictment" registered at San José was having any chastening effect on Dr. Castro and his lieutenants. On the contrary, from Washington's point of view Cuban behavior had grown steadily worse. In September, Premier Castro had devoted a ten-day visit at the United Nations to an extraordinary display of anti-United States histrionics,[72] interspersed with demonstrative manifestations of affection for Khrushchev and assorted neutralist leaders. Among other recent Cuban actions were the recognition of Communist China (the first such recognition in the Americas), the execution of three United States citizens convicted of counterrevolutionary activities,[73] the expropriation of the remaining United States business properties in the country,[74] an intensification of the threats to Guantánamo, the mounting of an intensive propaganda campaign on the theme of an allegedly imminent "invasion" by the United States, and a demand for prompt consideration of these charges by the United Nations Assembly.[75] While Senator Kennedy and Vice-President Nixon debated the methods by which the United States might help to bring about a change of regime in Cuba—an objective on which both seemed to agree[76]—the United States Government had reacted to these offenses on Cuba's part by advising its citizens to avoid the country, by declaring an embargo on all United States shipments to Cuba except for foodstuffs, medicines, and medical supplies,[77] and by recalling Ambassador Philip W. Bonsal for "an extended period of consultations."[78]

Especially disturbing to the United States had been a recent accumulation of evidence which seemed to indicate that Cuba might be reverting to its former tactic of supporting armed revolts against some of its Caribbean neighbors. Washington was aware that Cuba had been receiving very substantial quantities of Soviet bloc arms, at least a part of which were presumably destined for export to supporters abroad.[79] It was difficult to be sure that Cuba had not been involved in the military coup in El Salvador which unseated the conservative regime of President José María Lemus on October 26 and was immediately followed by the establishment of a mixed military-civilian junta that was regarded in Washington, and in some Latin American countries, as a potential channel for infiltration by Castro sympathizers.[80] The resultant delay in United States recognition of the new regime, which was not accorded until December 3, produced no solid evidence of Cuban involvement but prolonged the uncertainty in El Salvador and caused some uneasiness to its new authorities as they prepared for what was presumably intended to be a gradual return to constitutional government.

A potentially more serious situation developed in Nicaragua in the second week of November with the outbreak of another in the long series of revolutionary attempts against the government of President Luis Somoza Debayle. Some of the forces involved in this affair were based in nearby Costa Rica, whose government did what it could to restrain them; others were active near the Nicaraguan capital itself. According to the Nicaraguan Government, most of the rebels were acting under Cuban influence. By November 13 the immediate threat to Nicaragua had been warded off; but on that day Guatemala in its turn reported a military revolt, allegedly supported by Communist and leftist elements, against the regime of President Miguel Ydígoras Fuentes. This revolt, too, was short-lived; the first announcement of its "liquidation" was issued the very next day. But Guatemala, too, now asserted that Cuba had been behind the movement, and forecast a joint Guatemalan-Nicaraguan complaint to the O.A.S. It was further disclosed that the United States had been asked by Guatemala to patrol its Caribbean coastline in order to deter (or at least give notice of) any invasion attempt from Cuba.[81]

The United States had no direct knowledge of any Cuban involvement in the Nicaraguan and Guatemalan troubles. The immediate crisis appeared to be over, in any event. Nevertheless the White House dramatically announced on November 17 that in response to written requests from Guatemala and Nicaragua, surface and air units of the United States Navy had been placed in a position to help those countries "seek [out] and prevent intervention on the part of Communist-directed elements in [their] internal affairs . . . through the landing of armed forces and supplies from abroad." [82] This unusual action, decided upon without preliminary consultation with the O.A.S., aroused little enthusiasm elsewhere in Latin America, where the general tendency was to regard the two governments to which the United States was extending its protection as semi-dictatorships. Cuba, for its part, lost no time in denouncing the move as a disguised preparation for a United States attack on its territory. But President Ydígoras showed great appreciation of President Eisenhower's action, and the patrol was continued until December 7 when all immediate danger was clearly past.[83]

In the meantime two new crises had developed—a minor one in Haiti, where President François Duvalier was trying to break a student strike that he insisted was Communist-inspired, and a much more serious one in Venezuela. There, the twenty-one-month-old government of President Betancourt had faced its severest test to date as leftist mobs in Caracas rioted for three days (November 25-27) in what Señor Betancourt himself described as a Communist-encouraged attempt to set up a government on the Cuban model. Already a victim of clandestine attack from the Dominican Republic, the Venezuelan regime now faced a perhaps more serious menace from the opposite quarter. Instead of seeking outside support against Cuba, however,

Señor Betancourt announced on November 30 that Venezuela was still threatened from the Right as well as the Left and that he was asking the O.A.S. to investigate the aid allegedly being given by the Dominican Republic to certain exiled Venezuelan military men. He also intimated that if the United States was as interested in supporting his regime as it claimed to be, its most useful contribution would be a substantial credit to assist Venezuela's straightened finances in what was beginning to look like a serious economic depression.[84]

Venezuela's continuing preoccupation with the Dominican problem and its hesitancy about provoking a showdown with Cuba suggested the kind of obstacles the United States would have faced had it sought further action against Cuba by the O.A.S. at this period. In Washington's view, the time was fast approaching when it might be desirable to supplement the Declaration of San José with some of the more concrete measures which were available under the Rio Pact and had already been invoked against the Dominican Republic—severance of diplomatic relations, for example, and perhaps multilateral economic sanctions of the kind that the United States was already applying against Cuba unilaterally. But diplomatic conversations with other American governments indicated that there was still a pronounced reluctance to deal with Cuba in any decisive way. Cuba, most of the other governments seemed to feel, would find it only too easy to strike back by promoting more revolutionary disturbances by "Fidelista" sympathizers in their own countries. Venezuela in particular took the view that it was essential to clear up the Dominican situation before anything further was done about Cuba.[85]

By late November, some observers even professed to detect a kind of softening in Cuba's recent attitude. Talk of an imminent United States invasion had subsided for the moment, and Cuba's delegation at the United Nations had agreed to a postponement in the discussion of its charges. There were reports that the U.S.S.R. had quietly advised the Cubans to stop boasting about Khrushchev's pledge to defend Cuba with Soviet rockets: Khrushchev himself had told a recent Cuban visitor that this promise was intended to be "really symbolic." [86] Some saw a link between this air of relative moderation and Khrushchev's apparent desire to slow down the "cold war" until he could test the intentions of the incoming Kennedy regime. Even Premier Castro suggested on one occasion that Senator Kennedy might eventually "come to his senses," despite his pre-election advocacy of direct support for the democratic anti-Castro elements.[87]

But if Cuba was really moderating its attitude in response to Soviet suggestions, it seemed to the United States that this merely demonstrated the close link between Cuban and Soviet policy. There were disturbing indications, moreover, that in working to strengthen its ties with Communist China as well as the Soviet Union, Cuba was even tending to side with Peking in its ideological differences with Moscow. Major Guevara was obviously echoing Communist China's militant revolutionary line on a current tour of the Communist countries. While in Peking the Major also opened a new door to Chinese Communist influence in the Americas by signing on November 30 an economic cooperation agreement under which Cuba was to receive a five-year, interest-free Chinese loan in the amount of 240 million rubles or $60 million and would benefit by Chinese assistance in the construction of twenty-four factories.[88]

So far as official United States views were concerned, the question of whether Cuba had fallen under Communist domination was no longer a subject for useful argument. In allocating $1 million from his contingency fund for the relief of the 30,000 or more Cuban refugees who had fled to the United States in recent months, President Eisenhower on December 2 availed himself of a section of the Mutual Security legislation which authorized the use of such funds "to encourage the hopes and aspirations of peoples who have been enslaved by communism." [89] In the eyes of the United States, the situation in Cuba was apparently reaching the stage at which President Eisenhower had previously said that "very definite action" would be required. What action might be taken or contemplated, however, was still far from clear as the Eisenhower administration entered its last weeks in office.

52. "FIDELISMO" ON THE MARCH

In the years preceding the overthrow of the Perón dictatorship in Argentina, much of Latin America had been troubled by the occurrence of sympathetic manifestations in other countries which had been more or less openly supported from Buenos Aires and apparently aimed at the establishment of similar regimes in neighboring states. But the dangers of "Peronismo," as this movement had been called, seemed pale beside the new, Cuban- and Communist-inspired threat of "Fidelismo," with its seat in Havana and its outposts in virtually every country of the hemisphere. It had been Fidel Castro's boast that his government would turn the Andes Mountains into the same kind of revolutionary center that Cuba's own Sierra Maestra had been in the days of his war against Batista. Unlike Perón, moreover, Dr. Castro could count on the support of at least one and probably two great powers, the U.S.S.R. and Communist China, in the pursuit of his self-imposed mission of spreading revolution in the Americas. This association, substantiated afresh by the sheaf of new economic agreements brought home by Major Guevara from his visits to Moscow, Peking, and other Communist capitals,[90] would henceforth provide a threatening undertone to all developments in Latin America.

The United States made no further direct moves toward countering this threat during the balance of 1960, although the President on December 16 extended through March 31, 1961 the suspension of the Cuban sugar import quota, redistributing the extra tonnage among other supplying countries in accordance with existing law.[91] This

action drew a threat from Dr. Castro to wreck the world
sugar market by dumping that part of the Cuban produc
that was not bought by the U.S.S.R. It also elicited sharp
complaints from Brazil at being passed over in the redis
tribution of quotas, especially when the Dominican Re
public had been awarded a large additional quota as the
result of the failure of Congress to change the law as the
President had requested.[92]

The question of further economic sanctions against the
Dominican Republic under the San José decisions had
meanwhile been held in abeyance pending a study by a
seven-nation committee of the O.A.S., which recommended on December 19 the imposition by the other
American states of a selective ban on exports to that country covering petroleum, petroleum products, trucks, and
spare parts. The United States was understood to support
this recommendation; but Brazil and several other South
American countries showed marked reluctance to undertake further action against the Trujillo regime immediately, and the O.A.S. Council decided on December 21 to
let the matter rest until the new year.[93]

But while the United States and the O.A.S. marked time
on the central issues of the Caribbean, events were occurring in South America which testified to a rapid growth of
Soviet, Communist, and Fidelista influences. In Bolivia,
where a series of anti-United States demonstrations had
shown that someone—presumably the Communists—knew
how to exploit the prevalent social discontent for political ends, the United States also found itself engaged in a
direct economic competition with the U.S.S.R. Bolivia's
nationalized tin industry had long been handicapped by
the lack of a smelting plant, and Khrushchev and Gromyko
had suggested to Bolivian representatives at the United
Nations that the U.S.S.R. would be glad to provide this
or other equipment, to a value estimated by the Bolivians
at $10 million. The offer proved highly popular in Bolivia,
and an exploratory mission was just about to leave for
Moscow when the United States on November 28 an-

nounced that it would grant $10 million to the Bolivian mines corporation for similar purposes.[94]

But Moscow was evidently playing for high stakes in Bolivia. In December a special Soviet delegation was sent to La Paz with instructions to offer Bolivia an unconditional loan of $150 million to help develop the mining and petroleum industries and the transportation network. This was definitely not the kind of offer the United States was in the habit of matching, whatever the dangers of allowing the U.S.S.R. to get a foothold in the heart of South America. But Washington had already been in touch with Western Germany in the hope of interesting it in investing in Bolivia, and there were indications that some kind of counterproposal would be made in which Great Britain and the Inter-American Bank as well as the Federal Republic would probably have a part.[95]

If direct Soviet intrusion was the most obvious danger in Bolivia, the immediate threat in Peru and Ecuador stemmed rather from Cuba and from Communist-supported "Fidelismo." Peru's government alleged that Cuba had been using its diplomatic and press channels to give aid and comfort to Peruvian Communists.[96] In Ecuador, Fidelista elements were noticeably prominent among those who had continued to agitate throughout the autumn for a revision of the Peruvian boundary. This territorial dispute had developed in recent weeks into a serious crisis. Ecuador had declared the 1942 protocol null and void; but the four "guarantor" powers, of which the United States was one, had met on Peru's request and ruled on December 8 that the treaty could not be abrogated by one party. In the following days there were anti-United States and pro-Cuban demonstrations in Ecuadorian cities. In Washington, a State Department spokesman publicly cautioned against any resort to force in the dispute. Latin American diplomats, noting the Communist tinge of the demonstrations, began to refer to Ecuador as the hemisphere's most threatening trouble spot.[97]

By Christmas, the situation had quieted somewhat as the

result of the dismissal of the most vehement Castro supporter from the Ecuadorian cabinet. Foreign Minister José Chiriboga, a believer in cooperation with the United States who was just about to proceed to Washington for a discussion of economic development problems,[98] insisted that Ecuador still wanted the Eleventh Inter-American Conference to be held in Quito in March 1961 despite the fact that the local Communists were agitating against it. He also made it clear that Ecuador would insist on a full hearing of its territorial claims if the conference met. Peru, however, intimated that it would not attend the conference under such circumstances; and some of the other American governments, recalling the disorders that had marred the Ninth Inter-American Conference in Bogotá in 1948, inclined to the view that it would be just as well to postpone the meeting if only because of the fireworks that would be certain to occur if Premier Castro attended.[99]

Another delay in the holding of this long-awaited conference would be all the more disappointing because many Latin Americans had been hoping that the new administration in the United States would bring to Quito some substantial remedies for the current distress of the Americas. News of Senator Kennedy's election had sent a wave of optimism across Latin America, based less on anything he had said during the campaign than on the unreflecting assumption that any change in Washington was bound to represent an improvement. In the nature of things, many of these hopes were certain to be disappointed; but there was no doubt that conditions in the hemisphere, from Havana downward, merited the best and most perceptive attention that the new leaders in Washington might be capable of giving them.

Three weeks before President-elect Kennedy's inauguration, events in Latin America were still moving so rapidly that it was impossible to foresee just what kind of situation the new administration would confront when it took office on January 20, 1961. A new and possibly climactic

hapter in the Cuban story opened on December 30, 1960
vhen Peru severed its diplomatic relations with the Castro
overnment, following an example already set by the Do-
ninican Republic and Guatemala and one that now
eemed likely to be imitated by Uruguay and perhaps
ther South American countries. The latest indications of
Cuban interference in other countries' internal affairs had
lone more than all the exhortations of the United States
o persuade Latin American governments that the time
or action was approaching.

Perhaps anticipating a general movement to isolate
Cuba diplomatically, the Castro government reacted
promptly. On December 31 it resorted once again to the
amiliar device of declaring a United States invasion im-
ninent "within a few hours" and demanded an immediate
neeting of the United Nations Security Council.[100] Ob-
ervers of this now hackneyed procedure found themselves
vondering how much longer Dr. Castro and his associates
vould be in a position to abuse the processes of the United
Nations as they had done so frequently in 1960.

CHAPTER EIGHT

THE WORLD SOCIETY

FEW EVENTS in the eight-year history of the Eisenhower administration will perhaps leave a more lasting memory than the addresses delivered by President Eisenhower to the General Assembly of the United Nations in 1953, in 1958, and in 1960. The historical importance of these pronouncements transcends the specific proposals they put forward, only a part of which turned out to be acceptable to the United Nations membership. Together these addresses constitute a record of America's renewed acceptance of the United Nations as an institution which, lamentably though it might fall short of the expectations originally entertained for it, was nevertheless an essential and on the whole a meritorious feature of the international scene.

In his first appearance in the Assembly, on December 8, 1953,[1] Mr. Eisenhower had proposed the international "atoms-for-peace" program which had subsequently given rise to the seventy-nation International Atomic Energy Agency. In the second, on August 13, 1958,[2] he had sought to apply the principle of action through the United Nations to the critical circumstances then prevailing in the Middle East. His third address, delivered to the Assembly's Fifteenth Regular Session on September 22, 1960,[3] went beyond these more limited preoccupations to advance the concept of "a true world community" as the necessary goal of all evolution in the domain of international affairs. "The United Nations," Mr. Eisenhower declared on this occasion, "is available to mankind to help it create just such a community. It has accomplished what no nation singly, or any limited group of nations, could have accomplished. It has become the forum of all peoples and the structure about which they can center their joint endeavors to create a better future for our world."

The significance of this far-reaching endorsement was not underrated by those who recalled the skepticism and even hostility on the part of some sections of the public which had affected American participation in the United Nations during the period of the Korean war and the changeover from the Truman to the Eisenhower administration. The mere fact that the Assembly now ventured to hold its annual session in New York in the midst of an American election campaign could be viewed as a sign of how greatly popular resistance to the United Nations within the United States had declined. The change was even more remarkable if it was remembered that the increased representation of the Communist and uncommitted countries had made the Assembly a good deal less responsive to American views than had been true six or eight years earlier. Most Americans now seemed reconciled to the idea that the United Nations would not only pursue a fully autonomous existence within the United States but would on occasion take actions of which the American government and public might not entirely approve. The precise limits of this tolerance, assuming that it still had limits, would be for the future to determine.

53. "THE ASSEMBLY OF HUMANITY"

The importance of an improved relationship between the United Nations and the host country was underlined by the mounting difficulties and pressures to which the world organization had lately found itself exposed from other directions. "Our human commonwealth," President Eisenhower observed in his address to the Assembly, "is once again in a state of anxiety and turmoil." There were those, the President implied, who would "attempt to hinder or stultify the United Nations or to deprecate its importance"—although, he said, to do so was "to contribute to world unrest and, indeed, to incite the crises that from time to time so disturb all men."

It was certainly true that the favorable estimate of United Nations endeavors that was currently held by the United States was by no means universally shared even by America's close allies. President de Gaulle of France, who particularly resented the Assembly's annual expressions of interest in the Algerian problem, had made a number of caustic comments about that body's "strange, impassioned and tumultuous proceedings." [4] Belgium had been deeply mortified of late by the Security Council's repeated admonitions to get out of the Congo. The Soviet Union had been at least equally critical of United Nations actions in the Congo, and had indicated that it would continue to press its views in this regard despite the overwhelming endorsement of Secretary-General Hammarskjold's conduct of the Congo operation at the Assembly's emergency session on September 17-20.[5]

The development of the Congo situation had typified the difficulties that the United Nations was bound to confront in trying to act as the organ of an international community which, in reality, was not so much a community as a meeting point of conflicting national interests and ambitions. The initial decision to saddle the United Nations with the responsibility for restoring order in the Congo—a decision which the U.S.S.R. had approved, although it could have used its veto—might be regarded either as a mark of confidence in Mr. Hammarskjold and his associates, as a regrettable abdication of responsibility on the part of the member states, or as an implied acknowledgment by the two major powers that United Nations responsibility was greatly to be preferred to the possibility of open competition between them in this sensitive area. But once the decision had been made and the dimensions of the Congo problem had become clear, it would have been most unrealistic to expect the performance to turn out in a manner that could satisfy all of the interested parties.

The technical and financial difficulties of the Congo assignment were only a part of the problem, although they far exceeded anything the United Nations had thus far confronted. The root of the world organization's embarrassment lay in the fact that it had been put in the position of trying to carry out a consistent action on behalf of eighty-two governments whose aims were in no wise consistent and, in some instances at least, were basically incompatible. To the extent that the actions of Mr. Hammarskjold and his subordinates might have furthered the realization of Communist objectives in the Congo, they would clearly have violated the spirit of the Security Council resolutions as these were interpreted by the United States and the other anti-Communist powers. To the extent that United Nations actions tended in the opposite direction, however, they were foredoomed to incur the wrath of the Communist world and of the numerous uncommitted governments which felt that the Soviet line coincided with the interests of true "nationalism" in the Congo.

Moscow's unconcealed dissatisfaction with the Congo operation, reflected in its branding of the Secretary-General as a tool of "colonialism," was among the factors that promised to make the Assembly's Fifteenth Regular Session one of the most critical in United Nations history. The decision of Premier Khrushchev to attend the session in person, accompanied by the ranking Communist representatives from the Eastern European states, gave the occasion a dramatic quality which was enhanced by the parallel action of numerous chiefs of state and government from outside the Communist bloc. Among the other momentous developments in prospect as the session began was the expected admission to United Nations membership of eighteen new countries—seventeen African states and Cyprus—and the consequent increase in the organization's total strength from eighty-two to one hundred. Probably no one could have foreseen at that time the Soviet veto which was to keep Mauritania outside the United Nations and limit the total membership to ninety-nine.

Various other items among the eighty-seven on the Assembly's preliminary agenda [6] could be identified in advance as likely to produce intense debate and, possibly, historic decisions. Among the most prominent were the questions of Algeria, disarmament, and the representation of China. The course of debate on some of these matters has, of course, already been reviewed in earlier chapters and will be only briefly alluded to here. Certain other international questions which will be touched upon in this chapter did not come up directly in the Assembly's 1960 deliberations because they were the responsibility of other United Nations organs or outside international groupings. Despite these limitations on its own field of action, however, the General Assembly stood out unmistakably as the central feature of the international landscape and the chief repository of man's hopes for the emergence of a more authentic international community than had yet proved possible. The Assembly itself, as Frederick H. Boland of Ireland observed in acknowledging his election as President of the Fifteenth Regular Session on September 20, was gradually coming closer to the ideal concept of a body "fully representative of the entire human race." If this accession of numerical strength could be matched by "a corresponding sense of community, as dwellers on this small and threatened planet," Mr. Boland suggested, "then indeed this Assembly may deserve a noble title—the assembly of humanity." [7]

54. "THE UNITED NATIONS IS IN A CRISIS"

The history of the Fifteenth Assembly during 1960 falls into two distinct phases: an initial period of three weeks or more during which the presence in New York of a couple of dozen heads of state and government gave it almost the character of a "summit" conference; and a more normal, "working" phase which began with Khrushchev's departure on October 13 and continued until the session was interrupted for the year-end holidays. Because of the loss of time occasioned by Khrushchev's antics and by the great number of speakers to be heard in the general debate, the work of the session could not be completed during 1960 and a third phase had to be scheduled for the spring of 1961 to deal with unfinished business.

It has already been suggested that the initial, "summit" phase of the Assembly was dominated by two main subjects, one of which, the question of a meeting between President Eisenhower and Premier Khrushchev, has been dealt with in an earlier chapter.[8] The second main theme, which continued to be heard at frequent intervals throughout the session, was the demand for modifications in the United Nations' structure and methods of doing business that would make them more responsive to the views of countries which felt that they had reason to be dissatisfied with present arrangements.

That there would eventually be a need to overhaul the machinery and procedures of the United Nations had been fully anticipated when the Charter was drafted in 1945, and the problem had been discussed more than once in the intervening years. But since there had never been any real prospect that the major powers could agree among themselves as to the kind of changes that were desirable, there had thus far been a general disinclination to attack the problem in any fundamental way, and the Charter review conference originally expected to be held in 1955 had not taken place. Various improvements had, however, been suggested and in some cases carried out within the terms of the existing Charter. President Eisenhower, expanding on a suggestion advanced by Secretary-General Hammarskjold, proposed still another one in his address of September 22—the earmarking of national military contingents to be available to the Secretary-General on a standby basis for use in any future emergency like the one that had occurred in the Congo.[9] But when Khrushchev arose to deliver his own major address on September 23 it became apparent that Soviet thinking had advanced much further. Stung by its frustrations in the Congo, the U.S.S.R. now appeared ready to jettison basic elements in the structure of the United Nations as it had existed up to that time, and to substitute something that would be both fundamentally new and much more amenable to Soviet influence.

The radical nature of Khrushchev's assault on the existing United Nations concept—Secretary Herter called it "an all-out attack, a real declaration of war"—can be appreciated only from the full text of his 19,000-word speech.[10] The scathing critique of Western policy, the submission of a new Soviet disarmament plan, the demand for complete and final elimination of the "colonial regime," the renewed insistence on the right of Communist China to United Nations representation, even the proposal to remove the United Nations from the United States to some more sympathetic environment—all these were overshadowed by Khrushchev's direct and unqualified attack on the office of the Secretary-General, identified by the Charter as one of the "principal organs" of the United Nations, and on the way in which Mr. Hammarskjold had filled (or "abused") it. The time had come, Khrushchev asserted, to abolish the post of Secretary-General altogether and to substitute a new type of executive body that would directly reflect the existing political divisions in the world. What he proposed, in brief, was to substitute for the existing individual executive a "collective," three-man executive body whose members would be drawn respectively from the "Western," "socialist," and "neutralist" countries. In later statements, Khrushchev confirmed the suspicion that each of the three executive heads would be expected to possess a veto over the actions of the other two.

Few of the delegates who listened to Khrushchev's tirade could fail to perceive that such a plan would cripple the operation of an organ which, under its existing leadership, had developed far beyond the restricted role originally envisaged for it, displaying a capacity for effective action that went far to compensate for the deficiencies of the Security Council and the General Assembly. To destroy the office of the Secretary-General, as Ambassador Wadsworth immediately pointed out, would amount in effect to destroying the United Nations itself. "The United Nations is in a crisis," Mr. Wadsworth declared. ". . . The United Nations . . . must face this crisis head on. If it does not, it will fail." [11]

The extent of the crisis was to become more evident in the following days as the Soviet Premier, in addition to his almost daily interventions in the debate, developed his tactics of interrupting and heckling other speakers, pounding his desk, waving his shoe, and generally infringing the dignity of the Assembly. Faithfully imitated by the other Soviet bloc delegations, this form of behavior evoked no particular enthusiasm on the part of the Asian and African representatives who now made up nearly half the Assembly, and whom the Soviet leader was obviously trying hard to impress. The latter might or might not be aware that what they were witnessing was a time-honored Communist technique for disrupting and eventually immobilizing a democratic parliamentary body. But most of them had a strong respect for the United Nations and a genuine admiration for Mr. Hammarskjold, dating from his role in the Suez crisis in 1956. They had just given him a strong vote of confidence at the special session on the Congo, and they had no desire to see his position undermined or his usefulness destroyed. Few if any non-Communist delegates could be found willing to give the Khrushchev plan a direct endorsement.

At the same time, there was a widespread feeling in the Assembly that the existing organization of the United Nations was not entirely satisfactory from the standpoint of the smaller and newer countries, and that some more limited movement in the direction of Khrushchev's pro-

"WHICH DID YOU SAY ARE THE NEW NATIONS?"

Herblock in *The Washington Post*

posals might actually be desirable. The existing setup, as President Sukarno of Indonesia observed a few days later, reflected "the economic and military and power map of the world of 1945," a period before "the rise of the Socialist countries" and before "the rocketing of Asian and African independence." It might be advisable, Mr. Sukarno thought, to revise the various United Nations organs, including the Secretariat, in a way that would "reflect the true position of our present world"; and while he carefully avoided criticism of the United States, he also expressed sympathy for the suggestion that the United Nations might function better if removed from "the atmosphere of the cold war." [12]

Various concrete suggestions were put forward with a view to modifying the internal arrangements of the Secretariat in a manner that would fall short of Khrushchev's drastic proposal. President Nkrumah of Ghana felt that Mr. Hammarskjold might be retained at the head of the structure but might properly be assisted by three deputy Secretaries-General representing the three political groups into which Khrushchev had divided the world.[13] Prime Minister Nehru suggested that the Secretary-General might surround himself with a group of senior political advisers from different geographic areas.[14] The obvious merit of such proposals lay in their attempt to find a formula that would preserve the integrity of the Secretariat while affording some satisfaction to the claims of those countries that felt themselves discriminated against under existing arrangements. Their potential danger lay in the possibility that any tampering with the existing structure might tend either to reduce the effectiveness of the Secretariat or to give it a political bias of the kind that Mr. Hammarskjold had tried to avoid—successfully, in the eyes of most of the Western powers, although Khrushchev and some of the neutral states obviously felt differently.

Intertwined with this discussion of the Secretariat as an institution was an intense debate about Mr. Hammarskjold's personal future. The painful experiences of

Trygve Lie, Mr. Hammarskjold's predecessor, had made it sufficiently clear that no Secretary-General could work effectively if the U.S.S.R. withheld its support in the way that Khrushchev seemed to be threatening. But Mr. Hammarskjold, in an eloquent defense of his policy in the Congo, had promptly assured the Assembly that he had no intention of departing from the principles that had hitherto guided him: "I would rather see [the] office break on strict adherence to the principle of independence, impartiality and objectivity than drift on the basis of compromise." [15] Khrushchev, however, professed to find none of these qualities in the Secretary-General's record to date. "Mr. Hammarskjold has always been biased with regard to the Socialist countries," he told the Assembly on October 3. "He has always upheld the interests of the United States and other countries of monopoly capital. . . . To avoid misinterpretation, I want to reaffirm that we do not trust Mr. Hammarskjold and cannot trust [him]. If he himself does not muster up enough courage to resign, so to say, in a chivalrous manner, then we shall draw the necessary conclusions. . . ." [16]

Mr. Hammarskjold's reply bespoke a different kind of courage. "It is very easy to bow to the wish of a big power," he reminded the Assembly. "It is another matter to resist." The U.S.S.R., the Secretary-General pointed out, had made it clear that if he did resign, it would insist that the Secretariat be reorganized along the lines of Khrushchev's proposal before any successor was elected. This, he insisted, would have the effect of incapacitating the United Nations and making an effective executive impossible. "The man does not count, the institution does," Mr. Hammarskjold emphasized. ". . . By resigning, I would . . . at the present difficult and dangerous juncture throw the organization to the winds." Such a step, Mr. Hammarskjold suggested, would be a violation of his special responsibility to those smaller countries to which the United Nations was of decisive importance. In an obvious bid for the support of this group, he promised that he would remain at his post in their interest as long as they desired him to do so.[17]

The ovation with which the Assembly received this pledge dispelled any doubt as to the Secretary-General's current popularity. It put an end for the time being to the personal attacks on Mr. Hammarskjold by the U.S.S.R. and its satellites. But it did not quiet the demand for some rearrangement of the United Nations machinery, even though the U.S.S.R. presently agreed to let the matter ride until 1961.[18] Nor did it take the sting out of Khrushchev's threat that the "socialist and neutralist" states would henceforth refuse to recognize United Nations decisions taken to their "detriment." The U.S.S.R., Khrushchev had said, was "persistently sowing the seeds of peace," and though he knew that some of them would fall on stony ground, he was equally sure that some of them would strike root and grow.[19]

55. MOVE OVER, PLEASE!

It is uncertain whether Khrushchev's long-range objective in regard to the United Nations was to discredit and destroy the organization or merely to convert it to Soviet uses with the aid of those non-Communist countries that had shown themselves responsive to Soviet influence. Whatever his ultimate intention, the immediate tactic of the Soviet dictator plainly consisted in attacking the established organization and procedures of the United Nations from as many directions as possible. Aside from the campaign against the Secretary-General and the undermining of Assembly decorum by noisy personal demonstrations—a form of political activity that shortly began to make its appearance in other international organizations in which the Soviet Union was represented—there was also an attack on the financial front through the withholding of funds due for the support of the United Nations forces in the Congo as well as the Middle East. As already pointed out, the attitude of the Communist states on this issue had helped to plunge the world organization's finances into a state of crisis from which they were only temporarily rescued by emergency action on the part of the United States and other Western powers.[20]

Before leaving New York, Khrushchev launched still a further attack on established custom by insisting that the three principal questions submitted to the Assembly by the U.S.S.R. should be considered in plenary session instead of going through the normal preliminary examination by one of the Assembly's committees. On two of these issues, disarmament and the question of American air incursions, the Soviet initiative was disallowed by heavy adverse votes, though upward of thirty nations abstained on each. But on the third issue, the question of immediate abolition of the colonial system, Khrushchev's demand enjoyed such wide support among the Asian and African states that the West gave in without a fight and allowed the matter to be taken up directly by the full Assembly. (See below.) This, too, was a precedent which might tend to militate against orderly procedure in future years.[21]

Even without Khrushchev's attack on the Secretariat, the 1960 Assembly would have faced proposals for various organizational readjustments designed to keep the United Nations in tune with changing world conditions, especially the progress of the independence movement in Africa and elsewhere. As already noted, the total membership of the world organization was expanded during this session from eighty-two to ninety-nine through the admission of seventeen new states, the eighteenth candidate, Mauritania, being kept out by a Soviet veto in the Security Council.[22] The United States, on its side, succeeded once again in forestalling debate on the annual proposal to seat Communist China in the Assembly in place of Nationalist China.[23] But although the United States continued to regard the Chinese Communist regime as inherently unqualified to fill a place in the world organization, it could not overlook the fact that world support for its views in

this respect had been dwindling for several years. Whatever Communist China's merits or demerits, there was a
widespread feeling at the United Nations that its exclusion
represented an anomaly that would have to be corrected
before very long. On this issue, "America is not winning,
but losing," said Khrushchev,[24] who had vigorously advocated Communist China's admission to the Assembly in
spite of his own ideological differences with the Peking
regime.

To expedite what was evidently regarded in Soviet
quarters as an inevitable American defeat on this issue,
the Soviet delegation presently brought into play an in-
genious device which had already been hinted at in past
years but now promised to be even more effective. This
was the establishment of a link between the question of
Chinese representation and the increasingly topical question of an expansion or readjustment in the membership
of the Security Council and other United Nations organs.

The growth in United Nations membership in recent
years had already led to a demand on the part of African
and Asian states for an expansion in the membership of
such influential bodies as the eleven-nation Security Council and the eighteen-nation Economic and Social Council,
both of which still retained the form and make-up they
had acquired when the United Nations machinery was
first set up in 1945-46. The argument for such an expansion
was greatly strengthened by the further increase in United
Nations membership in 1960, which raised the strength
of the so-called Afro-Asian bloc in the United Nations to
forty-five out of a total of ninety-nine—whereas Afro-Asian
representation on the Security Council, for example,
amounted to at most two out of eleven (or three if Nationalist China was counted). This under-representation
of Asia and Africa was all the more keenly felt because
the Security Council, after a period of relative disuse, had
recently taken on a new lease of life and had held some
seventy meetings up to December 1960 on everything from
the U-2 and RB-47 incidents to the Congo and the Adolf

Eichmann case. Not surprisingly, most African and Asian states felt strongly that something should be done to give them a larger voice in this important phase of United Nations work.

It was the prevalence of this feeling that had enabled Khrushchev (who could dismiss the existing Security Council as a "spittoon" or, worse still, a "cuspidor") [25] to proceed with some confidence in putting forward his own proposals for a radical reform of the United Nations structure. This reform, according to Khrushchev's plans, was not to be limited to the Secretariat. What the Soviet leader advocated, in effect, was the introduction of a tripartite principle of organization which would give equal representation to the three political blocs—the East, the West, and the neutrals—in the Secretariat and in the Security Council as well. Express provision for such a reorganization, already hinted at in Khrushchev's opening address to the Assembly, was subsequently included in the U.S.S.R.'s omnibus disarmament resolution. [26]

Although the Asian and African states might not be ready to go all the way with Khrushchev's proposals, they heartily agreed on the necessity for some measure to increase their general influence within the United Nations mechanism. Their own preference, as embodied in a pair of resolutions which were presently placed before the Assembly, lay in the direction of a moderate expansion, rather than a re-structuring, of the existing organs—specifically, an enlargement of the Security Council from eleven seats to thirteen and of the Economic and Social Council from eighteen to twenty-four. The United States, while it had welcomed the admission of the new African states to the United Nations, [27] may have felt some misgivings as to the way in which an increase in African and Asian representation would affect the work of established United Nations organs. But the very least that could be said for the Afro-Asian plan was that it involved no dangers at all comparable to those of the Soviet proposal. Accordingly, it was warmly supported by the American delegation. [28]

To put the Afro-Asian plan into effect, however, would require an amendment of the Charter. This could be accomplished only with the cooperation of the U.S.S.R. And the U.S.S.R. now repeated what it had said in past years—namely, that it would not agree to any enlargement of the two Councils unless Communist China was first brought into the United Nations. The obvious purpose of this stand was to increase the pressure of the Asian and African states on behalf of Communist China, whose claims many of them already favored on other grounds. The full effect of Moscow's attitude would probably not be felt before 1961, when the China question was next brought up for debate. In the meantime, Afro-Asian attention was forced to shift from the idea of an expansion of the two Councils to that of a redistribution of the existing seats in a way that would give a larger voice to the Afro-Asian group. But at this point strong resistance was encountered from the Latin American countries, which were by no means anxious to give up their own relatively favored position in order to make room for the newcomers. The result, so far as 1960 was concerned, was the defeat of the entire project after a confused debate in the Assembly's Special Political Committee.[29]

The Assembly also encountered some difficulty in carrying out its routine task of electing three nonpermanent members of the Security Council for 1961-62. Chile and the United Arab Republic were elected without incident on December 9, despite some criticism in the United States of the American delegation's vote in favor of Abdel Nasser's government. Turkey was also elected to a one-year term as successor to Poland, in accordance with a special arrangement made the previous year.[30] But Portugal, put forward by the Western powers for the seat normally assigned to a Western European country, encountered strong opposition on the part of the "anti-colonial" bloc because of its attitude and record as the most immovably "colonialist" of all the Western countries. Liberia, brought into the race as an alternative candidate, immediately gained a sufficient lead to ruin Portugal's chances, though not enough to assure the two-thirds majority needed for election. The matter was resolved on the last day of the session by electing Liberia to a one-year term with the understanding that Ireland would take over the seat at the beginning of 1962.

A similar conflict developed in the voting for new members of the Economic and Social Council. Here there was another deadlock between a "colonial" and an "anticolonial" power—in this case Belgium and India.[31] A settlement of this issue was deferred until spring. These were but two more indications of the growing weight of the African and Asian element, which had already shifted the center of gravity in the United Nations and would surely force a modification in its formal structure before much more time had passed.

56. AWAY WITH COLONIALISM!

If Khrushchev's attack on Secretary-General Hammarskjold had evoked little enthusiasm among non-Communist delegations, his other political initiatives were much more closely attuned to the thinking of the Asian, African, and neutral states that now made up approximately half the Assembly. The continuing popularity of the Soviet concept of "general and complete disarmament" was amply demonstrated during the autumn in the course of a protracted debate in the Assembly's First (Political) Committee.[32] The overwhelming desire for a relaxation of East-West tensions found renewed expression in a twenty-eight-power resolution, introduced by V. K. Krishna Menon of India, which cited the existing "grave risk to world peace and cooperation" and urged "immediate and constructive steps" to improve matters. This eloquent if not very definite text was approved by unanimous vote of the entire Assembly on October 17, four days after Khrushchev's departure.[33]

But it was Khrushchev's summons to "mount the final

offensive against colonialism," his demand for the "complete and final elimination of the colonial regime in all its forms and manifestations," that most closely touched the emotions of the African and Asian states. Here was a sweeping proposition on a question that deeply concerned them, one on which most of them felt as strongly as they did about world peace itself. Familiar as they themselves had been with the frustrations and indignities of a dependent status, most Asian and African governments were already determined to bring about the eradication of this monstrous evil, as they considered it, in Algeria, in Portuguese Africa, in Netherlands New Guinea, and wherever else it might still exist. They might not agree with every line of Khrushchev's highly inflammatory declaration on the subject,[34] which demanded "immediate" independence for all types of dependent territories and, characteristically, made a special point of calling for the elimination of leased areas like the Panama Canal Zone which were strategically important to the Western powers. But the general principle was one with which they could not fail to agree.

To Western observers it might seem that Khrushchev's all-out attack on colonialism had come a little late in the day. Now that France had granted sovereignty to most of its African possessions, the liquidation of the "colonial regime" could surely be considered as already in full swing. National colonies in the old sense were no longer very numerous, and the scope of the United Nations trusteeship system was also being greatly reduced by the accession of one trust territory after another to independence. British and French Togoland, French Cameroons, and Somalia had already become independent or merged with independent states; British Cameroons, Ruanda-Urundi, and Tanganyika were expected to follow before long. New Zealand's trust territory of Western Samoa was definitely scheduled to become independent in 1962 if the inhabitants so decided in a plebiscite which, as the Assembly presently determined, would be held under United Nations supervision in May 1961.[35] That would leave only the three trust territories of Nauru, Australian-administered New Guinea, and the American-administered strategic trust territory of the Pacific Islands.

Many of the non-self-governing territories outside the trusteeship system were also advancing toward self-government, if not necessarily toward outright independence. The United States felt able to claim special credit in this connection for the constitutional progress being made by its three remaining non-self-governing territories of Guam, American Samoa, and the Virgin Islands.[36] Great Britain could make similar claims. But there were other governments in the Western world which took a wholly different attitude toward their overseas territories. Spain and particularly Portugal held large tracts overseas to which they had not the least intention of granting self-government. On the contrary, they took the same juridical position with regard to these territories that the French had done in Algeria—namely, that they were not colonies or non-self-governing territories at all, but integral parts (or "overseas provinces") of the respective home countries.

These claims, which had no validity whatever in the eyes of the "anticolonial" countries, gave rise to a sharp skirmish in the Assembly's Fourth (Trusteeship) Committee while the delegates prepared for the main fight on liquidation of the colonial system. The specific point at issue concerned the alleged obligation of Spain and Portugal to submit information on their overseas territories to the United Nations in the same way as was done by other countries administering non-self-governing territories. Portugal stoutly maintained that it was under no such obligation; Spain made a show of resistance but presently agreed to meet the committee's wishes. After several days of excited debate, a resolution calling on Portugal to report on nine overseas territories "without further delay" was passed by the committee and subsequently adopted in plenary session.[37] Although the United States abstained from voting, at least partly in deference to the sensibilities of its Portuguese ally, the principal effect of the resolution was to irritate Portuguese opinion against the United Nations and also against the United States and certain other allied governments which either abstained or voted affirmatively.

In the meantime, the Asian and African states had been considering what to do about Khrushchev's proposed anti-colonial declaration. Decidedly it was not the kind of document that could be expected to pass the Assembly in its original and highly provocative form. As a possible alternative to the Soviet demand for "immediate" liquidation of the colonial system, Guinea suggested that a deadline might be set at the end of 1961. But even this was felt to be unrealistic by some of the other Asian and African states. Eventually it was decided to sponsor an alternative text, drafted largely by India and sponsored by forty-three Afro-Asian nations, which set no definite time limit but declared the process of liberation to be "irresistible and irreversible," proclaimed "the necessity of bringing to a speedy and unconditional end colonialism in all its forms and manifestations," and called for "immediate steps . . . to transfer all powers" to the peoples of all dependent territories "without any conditions or reservations." In what seemed to Western eyes an almost wilful disregard of recent events in the Congo, the authors of the resolution included a stipulation that "Inadequacy of political, economic, social or educational preparedness should never serve as a pretext for delaying independence."

This might seem strong doctrine to the West, but it was still too mild for the Soviet Union. The Soviet delegation continued to urge that the colonial system be liquidated either "forthwith" or at latest by the end of 1961. As Khrushchev had insisted, the entire debate took place in plenary session rather than in committee, and various Western speakers took advantage of the opportunity to defend the record of the West in colonial matters and to denounce the far greater evils of Communist "colonialism" in Hungary and Tibet. Behind the scenes, an effort was made to persuade the Asians and Africans to moderate their draft in such a way that at least some of the Western powers would be able to vote for it. These efforts were only partially successful. When the issue reached its climax on December 14, various Soviet proposals were voted down by adequate majorities, and the Asian-African resolution was approved by a technically unanimous vote of 89-0.[38] Even the Communist countries were recorded in the affirmative; but nine non-Communist countries abstained. Among them were not only the leading "colonial" powers but the United States as well.

The American delegation in New York was well aware that its abstention on this issue, reportedly under instructions from the White House itself, would not endear the United States to the nations of the anticolonial group. The latter were in no mood to sympathize with Ambassador Wadsworth's references to difficulties of "language and thought" in the resolution.[39] Their disillusionment over the American attitude was to be redoubled in the next few days by the refusal of the United States to support their position on Algeria or their demands for the liberation of M. Lumumba in the Congo.[40] Yet the United States could not have embraced the standard anticolonial position on any of these issues without antagonizing its allies at a critical point in NATO's evolution and, in addition, endorsing principles and courses of action concerning which it had genuine reservations. Abstention, if not the most popular course that might have been taken, was perhaps the most honest one under the circumstances.

The passage of the anticolonial resolution completed the major political business at this part of the session, except for the questions of Algeria and the Congo. Most of the remaining political issues before the Assembly—general disarmament, the U-2 and RB-47 cases, Hungary, Tibet, Korea, Cuba, etc.—were left to be taken up at the second part of the session beginning March 7, 1961. By this time no one was any longer referring to the 1960 Assembly as the "Assembly of Humanity." In the corridors and in the Secretariat building, there were caustic refer-

ences to "the do-nothing Assembly." Although the U.S.S.R.
had pressed for a resumption of work immediately after
the holidays, most delegates preferred to leave time for
the new American administration to find its bearings before attacking the balance of the agenda.

When the Assembly reconvened in eleven weeks' time,
Ambassador Wadsworth's position as chief of the United
States delegation would be filled by Adlai E. Stevenson,
the nominee of President-elect Kennedy. The popularity
of this choice in United Nations circles did not lessen the
force of Mr. Stevenson's initial understatement concerning
his new responsibilities. "Due to the admission of so many
new countries," he observed on learning of his nomination,
"the United States and the Western countries no longer
control the United Nations. Our position is much more
difficult and it will be my task to help maintain our position
in these changing circumstances." [41]

57. DEVELOPING WORLD LAW

We must now widen our field of vision to embrace that
extensive area of international legal, economic, social, and
scientific interests in which the Assembly and the United
Nations shared responsibility with a wide variety of other
international organs, some of them only remotely con-
nected with the world organization. Extremely diverse in
detail, all of these activities had certain essential features
in common. They had to do with questions that could be
satisfactorily resolved only through cooperation by the
various interested governments; they were related at least
indirectly, and often directly, to the central objective of
establishing a more peaceful and prosperous world order;
and they were strongly affected by the same interplay of
national, regional, and ideological interests that was so
conspicuous in the political arena.

The endeavor to develop a more effective international
legal framework which would mitigate the effect of national rivalries was a particularly vital concern of mid-

century international society, and one that had long held a high priority in American foreign policy. In addition to its support of the work of codification and expansion of international law that was going forward in the International Law Commission of the United Nations, the United States had been a leader in the efforts undertaken in recent years to clarify or develop the legal principles that would be needed to govern prospective activity in such areas as the high seas, the Antarctic, and the newly opening realm of outer space. Important initiatives in each of these fields had been undertaken in 1958 and 1959 and called for further action in 1960.

The most successful effort along these lines in recent years had been the one that led up to the conclusion of the twelve-nation Antarctic Treaty, signed in Washington on December 1, 1959 with the declared purpose of ensuring "in the interest of all mankind that Antarctica shall continue forever to be used exclusively for peaceful purposes and shall not become the scene or object of international discord." [42] The salient features of the Antarctic treaty, apart from its emphasis on the promotion of international scientific cooperation in the southernmost continent, were a moratorium on the assertion of new territorial claims and an outright prohibition on any form of military activity in the Antarctic—a prohibition backed up by extensive rights of inspection which were regarded in Washington as sufficient to ensure that any attempted violation of its terms would be promptly detected. Though opposed by some in the United States as an unnecessary surrender of American rights, the treaty was strongly endorsed by the administration and was approved by the Senate on August 10, 1960 by a vote of 66 to 21. Its subsequent ratification by the Soviet Government [43] considerably strengthened the prospect that at least one part of man's world might be lastingly protected from the intrusion of the "cold war."

One reason for the relative ease with which Soviet and Western interests had been harmonized in this case was the fact that Antarctica had no obvious military value and no more than a potential economic importance. That such adjustments were much more difficult to make when identifiable strategic or economic interests were involved had been shown by the recurrent attempts in recent years to define the rights of nations over the waters of the sea adjacent to their coastlines. Many of the Asian, African, and Latin American countries, together with some others like Iceland which depended heavily on coastal fisheries, had refused to be bound by the historic three-mile limit for territorial waters and claimed sovereignty over the adjacent seas for distances of anywhere from twelve to two hundred miles. Generally supported by the Soviet Union, which itself claimed a twelve-mile limit, such claims were strongly opposed by the principal Western powers and particularly by the United States. An important factor in the American attitude was the belief of the Joint Chiefs of Staff that any limit greater than six miles might inhibit operations by the United States Navy in the vicinity of neutral states, thus giving a military advantage to the Soviet Union with its large submarine fleet.[44]

A special United Nations Conference on the Law of the Sea which was held at Geneva in 1958 had found itself unable to resolve this problem, although it did succeed in drawing up four important conventions concerned with other aspects of the law of the sea which were approved by the United States Senate on May 26, 1960.[45] A second United Nations Conference on the Law of the Sea, devoted exclusively to the problem of defining the breadth of the territorial sea and the related issue of national fishing zones, was held in Geneva in March and April 1960, with eighty-eight nations participating and with Arthur H. Dean once again heading the United States delegation. It was scarcely more successful than the first in finding an acceptable middle ground between the advocates of a wide and a narrow territorial sea. The former group, which again included most of the less developed countries as well as the U.S.S.R., held out unsuccessfully for a straight twelve-mile zone and ultimately lost by a committee vote of 36 in favor, 39 against, and 13 abstentions. Among the various alternatives suggested, the nearest approach to a solution was a compromise plan submitted by the United States and Canada which provided for (1) a six-mile territorial sea, and (2) an adjacent six-mile fishing zone in which the coastal state would enjoy exclusive fishing rights after a ten-year transitional period. In the final voting on April 26, this plan won 54 affirmative votes to 28 negative.[46] But since this total was one vote short of the necessary two-thirds majority, the question was doomed to remain unsettled—except for a widespread feeling that the three-mile limit, still officially upheld by the United States and the other Western maritime powers, was now outmoded.

Even this baffling problem was simple compared with the task of defining the rights of nations, and of the international community, in the new realm of outer space. Here there were virtually no reliable guidelines available, apart from a 1944 convention which stated in general terms that national sovereignty extended to the upper limits of the atmosphere. This concept was much too vague to meet the requirements of the new space age. The dimensions of the problem were now being constantly extended by the development of new types of rockets and satellites, and a host of questions were being raised about such matters as traffic control, damage liability, and the legitimacy of satellite overflights and possible photographic or radar observation of another country's territory. Thus far there had been no comprehensive attempt to deal with these problems at the international level, apart from the inclusion of certain provisions relating to outer space in the various disarmament plans. For practical purposes, the American space program appeared to rest on the assumption that the use of outer space—for peaceful purposes, at least—was not subject to limitation by the countries underneath. The U.S.S.R., by its failure to protest the passage of American satellites across its territory (a marked contrast to its reaction to the U-2 flights), had thus far appeared to take a similar view, although it gave indications of shifting its ground late in 1960 when it published a warning that it intended to deal with "espionage" satellites just as it had done with aircraft that intruded into its airspace.[47]

In preparation for the day when such problems would reach the international agenda, the United States had endeavored to encourage the study through the United Nations of both the legal and the scientific aspects of international cooperation in outer space. A special United Nations Committee on the Peaceful Uses of Outer Space had been established for this purpose by the General Assembly in 1959, following an informal American-Soviet agreement which had been designed to ensure Soviet participation by granting strong representation to Communist and neutral states.[48] But disagreements about the chairmanship of a proposed scientific conference on outer space, which it had been hoped to hold under United Nations auspices in 1960 or 1961, prevented the committee from getting to work during the early months of 1960. Thereafter the prospects for worthwhile accomplishment were seriously impaired by the deterioration of East-West relations that followed the U-2 incident and the failure at the summit. Although President Eisenhower in his September 22 address to the Assembly offered a number of suggestions for applying the Antarctic principle and declaring outer space "off limits" to military preparations,[49] Khrushchev and his government showed no immediate interest in taking up the challenge.

In its concern to extend the influence of law in world affairs, the American Government had not forgotten that its own sincerity was being questioned in some quarters —not only because of the U-2 flights but also because of the restrictions imposed on its acceptance of the compulsory jurisdiction of the International Court of Justice. These restrictions, embodied in the so-called Connally Amendment of 1946, enabled the United States to determine on its own responsibility whether or not a given matter was within its domestic jurisdiction and, hence, not subject to adjudication by the Court. Repeal of this "self-judging" proviso had been strongly urged by administration spokesmen in the past, and was again recommended by the President in his 1960 State of the Union message.[50]

But even in 1960 there was sufficient isolationist feeling in America to make such a venture hazardous from a domestic point of view. Impressed by the opposition to repeal, and reluctant to embark on a major legislative battle without the assurance of full administration support, the Senate Foreign Relations Committee decided on March 29, by a vote of 9 to 8, to postpone indefinitely a matter which one of its members described as "just too hot to handle" in the existing legislative climate.[51] Although the President and Secretary Herter continued to call attention to the prejudicial effect of this restriction on wider American interests,[52] Vice-President Nixon during the campaign receded somewhat from his former advocacy of outright repeal.[53] Any action toward correcting what Secretary Herter had called "an exceedingly poor example" on the part of a leading world power [54] would clearly have to await a new administration and a new Congress.

In the meantime the Security Council and General Assembly joined forces during the autumn to fill a vacancy on the International Court and elect five new justices to nine-year terms. Although the fifteen members of the Court were elected without regard to nationality, one of them would continue to be an American. In the past, Judge Green H. Hackworth had held this distinction; after February 5, 1961, it would be held by Dr. Philip C. Jessup.[55] While the United States retained its influence in the voting of the Security Council and the Assembly, it could be assumed that the membership of the Court would continue to reflect the strength of the Western legal tradition.

58. AIDING ECONOMIC GROWTH

The interest of the United States in promoting economic and social advance throughout the free world had long been recognized as one of the mainsprings of American foreign policy, one that fully coincided with the objectives of the international community. The nature of this interest, together with some of the factors that influenced United States participation in international efforts directed toward a similar end, was outlined once again by President Eisenhower in an unusually frank address to the Automobile Manufacturers Association in Detroit on October 17, 1960.[56] In a world situation marked by gross disparities in income and living standards, by a rising clamor from "the poverty-stricken masses of a score of nations," and by the growing competition of an alien political and economic philosophy, the President found it inescapable that the United States should "boldly . . . strike out for the preservation of our cherished values of freedom, by striving to see that others may, with us, possess and enjoy them."

At the same time, the action that the United States might take to this end was qualified, in the President's eyes, by considerations of great importance: by commitment to the free enterprise system, whose "socially conscious" American form, Mr. Eisenhower acknowledged, was little understood or appreciated abroad; and also by a realization that American resources were far from inexhaustible, especially at a time of heavy armament expenditures and growing balance-of-payments difficulties. A further consideration, not mentioned by the President on this occasion but perhaps almost equally deep-rooted, was a preference for bilateral as opposed to multilateral arrangements in allocating the bulk of such aid as the United States felt able to make available for purposes of economic improvement abroad.

However natural in American eyes, these peculiarities in the American position helped to account for certain chronic differences which existed in the United Nations and elsewhere between the United States (frequently in association with Great Britain and other major industrial powers) and the poorer or less developed countries which stood most in need of help. The predisposition in favor of private enterprise and the free market economy not only influenced the United States in the administration of its foreign aid programs, but made it rather unsympathetic to the demand of less developed countries for international machinery designed to regulate the prices of primary commodities and thus, it was hoped, alleviate the disadvantages from which they suffered in international markets as compared with the industrialized countries. The same factor, combined with the already overloaded condition of the national budget, explained the American preference for private investment, as distinguished from public loans or grants, as the principal mechanism for assuring a flow of development capital to less developed areas. This preference was too strongly rooted in official quarters to be much influenced by evidence that private investment, even when acceptable to the less developed countries, did not always find its way to those areas and projects where it was most urgently needed.

Finally, the preference for bilateral rather than multi-lateral aid arrangements tended both to reduce the scale of the United States' own contribution and, indirectly, to limit the whole international effort in the economic field, to which the United States, in spite of these limitations, had always been the principal contributor. It also raised an important political issue with a large number of countries that were reluctant to accept aid "with strings attached" and thus preferred to deal with an international organization rather than a national government. The Soviet Union, it is true, went even farther than the United States in its preference for bilateral over multilateral aid, and contributed little except oratory to the United Nations economic programs. On the other hand, Moscow went out of its way to differentiate its aid procedures from those of the United States by creating the not wholly justified impression that its own bilateral assistance was provided without "strings." Within the United Nations, moreover, the U.S.S.R. generally associated itself with the complaints of other countries against the American attitude. There thus tended to appear in the international economic area the same alignment of forces that prevailed on many political questions—on one side, the United States and the other principal Western powers; on the other, a coalition of Asian, African, Latin American, and Communist countries.

Comparatively the least subject to such controversy among the United Nations programs in the economic field was the Expanded Program of Technical Assistance, which had performed outstanding services over the past decade and had been buttressed within the last couple of years by the creation of a Special Fund, devoted to preinvestment studies and the like, under the direction of Paul G. Hoffman. Although the two institutions had aimed at a combined budget of $100 million a year, to which the United States had offered to contribute 40 per cent, the amounts actually available to them thus far had fallen substantially short of that amount. In the meantime, the growing needs of African countries had pointed up the desirability of a substantial increase in the technical assistance effort, with particular reference to the so-called OPEX program for training operational, executive, and administrative personnel. President Eisenhower in his September 22 address to the Assembly supported an expansion to the $100 million target figure for 1961 as part of his five-point program for Africa,[57] and the Assembly later decided to raise the budgetary goal to $150 million to cover operations in 119 countries and territories.[58] But since the voluntary pledges toward the program amounted initially to less than $89 million, including the maximum United States contribution of $40 million,[59] this was an expression of hope rather than probability. Mr. Hoffman warned that the Special Fund would probably be compelled to reduce its already modest level of activity unless more funds were forthcoming.[60]

The sympathy with which the United States regarded the United Nations technical assistance program did not extend to another project long favored by the under-developed countries, the establishment of a United Nations capital development fund to make long-term loans for economic development projects. It had been hoped in Washington that the recent establishment of the Special Fund and the new billion-dollar International Develop-ment Association (see below) would serve to quiet the demand for this project, popularly known as SUNFED (Special United Nations Fund for Economic Development). But the hunger for development capital was as great as ever, the voice of the underdeveloped countries had been further strengthened by the recent increase in United Nations membership, and the proposal was brought for-ward once again at the 1960 Assembly in spite of warnings from the American delegation that there was no indication where the necessary money was to come from.

No fewer than forty-five countries lent their support to the resolution in question, which termed the existing flow of capital "wholly inadequate in nature and scope" and called for the establishment of a preparatory group to lay the groundwork for a United Nations fund. "Futile and wasteful" was the description of this project attributed to an American delegate. An Indian representative, on the other hand, insisted that "A United Nations fund is the only authority we can see where we, the underdeveloped countries, would have an effective voice in the use of the funds." [61] When the matter was voted on in committee on December 6, the United States was one of four nations that voted against the project, the others being Great Britain, Australia, and South Africa. Sixty-eight nations voted for the resolution, while eight Western countries abstained. In plenary session the vote was 71-4, with ten abstentions. [62]

It was seldom that the United States found itself so conspicuously in the minority on a question to which many non-Communist countries attached such obvious impor-tance. Nor was the United States position normally as negative as it was on this particular issue. The United

States did not, for instance, refuse its favorable vote on a closely related resolution which asked in effect that the economically advanced countries step up the flow of international assistance and capital until it equaled 1 per cent of their combined national incomes.[63] The United States, whose 1959 national income was estimated at $400 billion, could claim that private investment plus overseas economic aid already approximated such a figure.

The United States itself undertook one initiative of some importance at the 1960 General Assembly in connection with President Eisenhower's "food-for-peace" program. "We must never forget," the President told the Assembly on September 22, "that there are hundreds of millions of people, particularly in the less developed parts of the world, suffering from hunger and malnutrition, even though a number of countries, my own included, are producing food in surplus. This paradox should not be allowed to continue." [64] As one means of bridging the gap, the United States took the lead in proposing a plan whereby the United Nations would align itself with a "Freedom from Hunger" campaign already initiated by the Food and Agriculture Organization. This latter agency, under the American proposal, would be asked to develop a program designed to facilitate the transfer of the largest practicable quantities of surplus foods from surplus to deficit countries. Quick action by the Assembly was specially recommended to meet the timetable of the F.A.O., whose own Assembly was scheduled to meet in January 1961.

Some of the underdeveloped countries pointed out in their comments on the American proposal that the distribution of surplus foods was no substitute for economic development, and representatives of food exporting nations expressed some anxiety lest the program interfere with normal commercial operations. Nevertheless the plan was generally well received, and even the Soviet Union voted in favor of a revised text which was unanimously adopted by the Assembly on October 27.[65] After study by the F.A.O. and the Secretary-General, it was expected that the problem would be referred back to the Economic and Social Council with recommendations by mid-1961. From the point of view of the United States, which had been engaged in bilateral transfers of excess foodstuffs since 1954 and claimed to have made available over $9 billions worth of agricultural commodities to needy countries on "special terms" during the past six years, the program represented a second major step in the constructive international use of its embarrassing farm surplus.

59. SOCIAL AND HUMANITARIAN ENDEAVORS

Improved machinery for getting surplus food to the world's hungry was all the more desirable because there were more mouths to feed each year—some 48 million of them, if the estimates of the United Nations *Demographic Yearbook* were to be believed.[66] Taken as a whole, world food production was probably increasing at a slightly faster rate than world population. But the greatest increases in the food supply were occurring in already well-fed countries like the United States. In densely populated and rapidly growing countries like India, and to an even greater extent in Chile, Pakistan, and certain other Far Eastern and Latin American countries, food resources were not increasing fast enough to overcome the prevailing dietary deficiencies unless substantial additional help could be provided from outside.[67]

The general question raised by the rapid growth of world population during these years was one that increasingly preoccupied the West, the underdeveloped countries, and, it was suspected, the major Communist governments as well. Thanks largely to the success of national and international health programs and the resultant sharp decline in death rates, the number of living human beings had swelled by 1959-60 to an estimated 2.9 billion—roughly sixteen times the 1960 United States population of some 180 million. Continuation of present trends would mean a further doubling of the world population to about 6 billion by the end of the century. The question of how this additional 3 billion or more people could be fed, clothed, housed, and otherwise accommodated had become a matter of anxious debate throughout much of the world. Some maintained that a rational development of resources on a world-wide scale would suffice to meet the problem, though such a solution seemed to presuppose a much more effective international effort than had yet been attempted in the United Nations or elsewhere. Others insisted that there was no alternative to drastic limitation of births, particularly in the poorer countries where the great bulk of the increase was concentrated. Neither the United States nor the United Nations had yet taken a definite position on this highly controversial issue. Already, however, it represented a factor that had to be taken account in all decisions in the economic and social fields.

The phenomenon of population increase was not confined to people with a home and a settled manner of life in town or country. It also affected the various refugee groups whose plight stood out as one of the great failures of postwar international society. Some 15 million human beings were currently counted among the world's exiled and homeless, the largest groups being the million Arab refugees in the Near East, a million or more Chinese refugees in Hong Kong and Macao, at least 250,000 Algerian refugees in Tunisia and Morocco, perhaps 40,000 Tibetan refugees in India and Nepal, and smaller groups in various countries of Europe and Asia—not excluding a steadily increasing number of Cuban refugees in the United States. Many of these people had been uprooted within the past two or three years, a fact which suggested that the dimensions of the refugee problem were not decreasing despite the efforts made by many nations to help in bringing it under control.

The United States had opened its doors to something like 750,000 refugees during the fifteen postwar years, as well as helping to keep the Palestine refugee community alive by contributing 70 per cent of the funds made available to the United Nations Relief and Works Agency (UNRWA).[68] Through its participation in the twenty-nine-nation Intergovernmental Committee for European Migration, it had also helped to find new homes overseas for over a million refugees and other migrants from Europe since the agency was established in 1951.[69] In addition, the American Government had promised its full backing of the World Refugee Year which had been proclaimed by the United Nations for 1959-60 as a means of mobilizing support for a concentrated attack on the refugee problem. Up to June 1960 the United States had contributed slightly over $5 million to World Refugee Year projects, bringing its total expenditure for refugees during the preceding twelve months, exclusive of private contributions, to over $70 million.[70] As part of the same effort, Congress enacted a new refugee law in 1960 to permit the acceptance of a limited number of additional European refugees, amounting broadly to 25 per cent of the number accepted by all other countries during the World Refugee Year.[71]

Though there were differences of opinion about the adequacy of these efforts, they played a part in what Mr. Hammarskjold was able to characterize on its conclusion as a highly successful international enterprise. World Refugee Year activity in one form or another had engaged the participation of ninety-seven governments and territories, produced over $80 million in governmental and private contributions, and made possible the complete solution of some long-standing refugee problems and the alleviation of others. Particularly gratifying was the prospect for reasonably prompt resettlement of all of the 32,000 refugees still living in camps in Europe under the mandate of the United Nations High Commissioner for Refugees, Dr. Auguste R. Lindt.[72] With the focus of the refugee problem shifting increasingly from Europe to Africa and Asia, Dr. Lindt was now preparing to relinquish his responsibilities to a fellow Swiss, Ambassador Felix Schnyder, whose choice as High Commissioner was unanimously approved by the General Assembly on December 5.

Among the many other United Nations activities in the social and humanitarian field, some continued along established lines in 1960 without raising any important new issues of international policy. An example was the United Nations Children's Fund (UNICEF), whose modest resources of around $25 million a year were supplemented by local funds and benefiting an estimated 55 million mothers and children in over 100 countries and territories.[73]

At the United Nations, the attention of the Economic and Social Council and of the Assembly's Third (Social) Committee continued to be much occupied by the related questions of human rights and freedom of information, both of which had figured extensively in United Nations debates for many years. Violations of human rights and limitations on freedom of information were perhaps no less prevalent than they had been before the world organization was established; but the effort to define and clarify the principles involved and, if possible, reduce them to binding legal form went forward with extraordinary seriousness.

United States participation in these efforts was limited not by any disagreement with their objectives but rather by serious doubts about the efficacy of trying to promote such rights by international legislation. As with the American attitude toward the International Court of Justice, there was also an element of sensitivity about the distinction between international and domestic affairs and the separation between federal and state jurisdiction within the United States. A characteristic reflection of this attitude was the abstention of the United States delegate when the Assembly's Third Committee, continuing its effort to draft a pair of international covenants on human rights, approved an article during the 1960 session which aimed at the protection of privacy, family, home and correspondence. Such matters, the American representative explained, went beyond the United States Constitution and directly affected the rights of the states; therefore the American delegation could not take a position on them.[74] Partly as a result of considerations of this kind, the United States had long since given notice that it did not intend to sign the human rights covenants when completed, although it continued to place its experience at the disposal of those countries that desired to do so.

In the field of freedom of information, the United States had lately suggested a practical alternative to the drafting of a formal covenant, submitting instead a brief declaration of principles that might serve as a guidepost whether or not a full-fledged covenant was ultimately adopted. An amended version of this draft, proclaiming that "the right to know and the right freely to seek the truth are inalienable and fundamental rights of man," was approved in April 1960 by the Economic and Social Council for transmission to the General Assembly. That body's Third Committee, however, was too immersed in its attempts to draft a binding covenant on freedom of information to take up the draft declaration during the 1960 session. One article of the draft convention on freedom of information was approved by the committee, but the draft declaration was held over for consideration at the Sixteenth Session of the Assembly in 1961.[75]

60. OTHER INTERNATIONAL ORGANIZATIONS

Some of the most important business of the world community was carried on by specialized international organizations which were administratively independent of the United Nations, though often closely associated with it. The developments of 1960 tended in some ways to strengthen the association between the United Nations and these peripheral agencies, especially in dealing with emergencies. The breakdown of administration and public services in the Congo necessitated a cooperative effort on an unprecedented scale in that country, in which representatives of various branches of the United Nations worked closely and effectively with those of the World Health Organization, the Food and Agriculture Organization, and several others of the United Nations family.[76]

Some of the political tendencies that operated within the parent body also found an echo in the specialized agencies, several of which, like the United Nations itself, underwent an increase in membership during the latter part of 1960 through the admission of newly independent states. In addition to the familiar problem of Chinese representation (hitherto always resolved in favor of Nationalist China), those agencies in which the Soviet Union participated now had to face the likelihood of a Soviet attempt to introduce the principle of tripartite control which had already been brought forward in the United Nations. Such a proposal was actually introduced at the General Conference of the United Nations Educational, Scientific, and Cultural Organization (UNESCO) in Paris, where Communist delegates also resorted on at least one occasion to the table-thumping tactics that Khrushchev had inaugurated in the General Assembly.

Space permits only the briefest survey of the developments of 1960 among the specialized agencies and other important international organizations of which the United States was an active member. We have already noted the outstanding diplomatic contribution made by the International Bank for Reconstruction and Development, directed by Eugene R. Black of the United States, in the settlement of the Indus Basin dispute.[77] With its financial resources newly increased from $10 billion to $21 billion, the Bank was also able to increase its rate of development lending to some extent. On September 30 it reported that since the beginning of operations in 1946 it had committed a gross total of $5,384.5 million in 271 loans in fifty-four countries and territories.[78] As the result of a recent United States initiative, the International Development Association was formally established on September 24, 1960, as an affiliate of the Bank with authority to make "soft" loans on projects that did not qualify for regular World Bank financing. As of that date, fifteen governments had pledged a total of $686 million toward the I.D.A.'s authorized capital of $1 billion; and eleven others had joined by the end of the year.[79] Meanwhile the International Finance Corporation, established under the wing of the International Bank in 1956, continued its own more modest work of furthering investment in productive private enterprise.[80]

The International Monetary Fund, the twin sister of the Bank in the international financial field, was involved in fewer spectacular new developments during 1960, but used its own newly exanded resources to continue its invaluable assistance to countries in need of outside aid in stabilizing their economies and strengthening their balance of payments. This was an area in which the Fund had played a particularly indispensable role since the post-Suez financial crisis of 1956-57; but Per Jacobsson, its Swedish Managing Director, several times expressed the opinion that this particular phase of its activity was now drawing to a close and that the world financial structure as a whole had been impressively strengthened, notwithstanding the current difficulties being experienced by the United States.

The third main international agency in the economic and financial field, the General Agreement on Tariffs and Trade (GATT), was less closely associated with the United Nations but represented much the same kind of authority in the realm of international trade that the Bank and Fund did in international development and finance. Much of the attention of GATT's thirty-seven contracting parties was occupied with trying to bring the trading practices of the individual member countries (including, in some instances, the United States) into conformity with the multilateral and nondiscriminatory principles that had inspired the General Agreement when it was first drawn up in 1947. A special concern at the two regular sessions held in Geneva in 1960 [81] was to discourage any undue departure from these principles on the part of regional trade groups such as the European Economic Community, the European Free Trade Association, and the Latin American grouping established by the Montevideo treaty.

During GATT's autumn session, Nigeria became the thirty-eighth contracting party under the General Agreement, while Argentina, Ireland, Poland, and Yugoslavia moved closer to that status. Meanwhile, on September 1, there opened at Geneva the major tariff conference which the United States had originally suggested at a meeting of the GATT Contracting Parties some two years earlier. Expected to extend well into 1961, the conference might conceivably represent an important further step in the progressive lowering of barriers to world trade.[82]

Among the important international agencies operating outside the economic area, it was undoubtedly UNESCO, which had been concentrating its efforts especially in the field of education, that was hit hardest by the current Soviet political campaign. It was with a bitter complaint against UNESCO's alleged "unilateral and pro-Western orientation" that the Soviet delegation to the Paris meeting brought forth its formal proposal to replace Director-General Vittorino Veronese with a three-man directorate representing the three political blocs.[83] Although this plan was not adopted, the conference did later follow the example of the United Nations Assembly in adopting a resolution condemning "colonialism" in all its forms and manifestations.[84] In the International Labor Organization, on the other hand, the Governing Body rejected a Soviet demand that the subject of "colonialism" be listed for debate.[85]

Less subject to political pressures, the Food and Agriculture Organization was currently engaged on the five-year "Freedom from Hunger" campaign which had opened on July 1 and aimed at nothing less than the "eradication of hunger in its manifest and hidden forms throughout the world."[86] Still another example of the current vogue for special one-year or five-year campaigns was a pending proposal that an International Health Year be proclaimed under the auspices of the World Health Organization. But this plan, though recommended by the United Nations Assembly and supported by both the United States and the U.S.S.R., was turned down by the World Health Assembly in May 1960 on the ground that the efforts and expenditures involved were likely to outweigh the benefits to the peoples affected.[87]

Another international enterprise from which the peoples of the world had been encouraged to expect perhaps excessive benefits was the atoms-for-peace program which President Eisenhower had proposed to the United Nations in 1953 and which had since been entrusted in part to the seventy-nation International Atomic Energy Agency, set up in 1957 as a rather distant cousin of the United Nations. Many of these benefits had proved unexpectedly slow in materializing. The promise of economically produced nuclear power had receded greatly in the past few years, and the I.A.E.A., under its American Director-General, Sterling Cole, was currently devoting most of its limited funds to training and research programs, technical assistance, and preparation of the legal and administrative groundwork for future endeavors.[88]

An important issue in this connection concerned the safeguards on which the United States had insisted in order to ensure that any nuclear material and technology made available to the atomic agency would in fact be utilized only for peaceful purposes. Countries like India and Yugoslavia were inclined to oppose any close supervision of their atomic work by the agency as an infringement of their sovereignty. This attitude persisted even after the United States undertook to prove the contrary during I.A.E.A.'s Fourth General Conference, held in Vienna in the autumn of 1960, by offering to place four of its own atomic facilities under the safeguards procedure. Objections on the safeguards issue were also raised by former Soviet Foreign Minister V. M. Molotov, who had recently been named as Soviet representative to I.A.E.A. with the apparent assignment of mobilizing the neutrally minded countries against the United States as Khrushchev had tried to do in New York. The principle of safeguards was nevertheless approved by a substantial majority,[89] although some feared that the question was already tending to become academic as more and more countries approached the stage at which they might be able to achieve a military nuclear capability by methods over which the agency would have no control.

Experience with the atom provided a further illustration of the difficulties inherent in the building of a world community. Yet it could not wholly invalidate the ideal conception of an international society which President Eisenhower had held up before the General Assembly in what had been, in effect, his valedictory to the world organization.

"Opposed to the idea of two hostile, embittered worlds in perpetual conflict," Mr. Eisenhower had said on September 22, "we envisage a single world community, as yet unrealized but advancing steadily toward fulfillment through our plans, our efforts, and our collective ideas.

"Thus we see as our goal, not a superstate above nations, but a world community embracing them all, rooted in law and justice and enhancing the potentialities and common purposes of all peoples.

"As we enter the decade of the 1960's, let us launch a renewed effort to strengthen this international community, to forge new bonds between its members in undertaking new ventures on behalf of all mankind." [90]

Distant though it might at times appear, the recollection of this ultimate goal of a nation's effort might still afford the surest guide to American foreign policy in the difficult times that lay ahead.

NOTES

N.B. *"Bulletin"* refers to *Department of State Bulletin* (Washington: Government Printing Office).

"*Documents*" refers to *Documents on American Foreign Relations* (New York: Harper, for the Council on Foreign Relations; volumes previous to 1952 published by Princeton University Press for the World Peace Foundation).

Resolutions of the United Nations General Assembly, here referred to by serial number, are published in a supplement to the *Official Records* of each session.

Introducing 1960

1. Eighty-one party declaration, Moscow, December 6, in *New York Times*, December 7, 1960.

2. Address to members of the South African Parliament, February 3, in *New York Times*, February 4, 1960.

3. Summary of a study on "The Cold War Economic Gap," prepared by the Operations Research Office of the Johns Hopkins University, in *New York Times*, November 6, 1960. For the underlying economic calculations see the statement of Allen W. Dulles, Director, Central Intelligence Agency, November 13, 1959, in *Bulletin*, December 14, 1959, pp. 867-874.

Chapter I. Foreign Policy through American Eyes

1. *Bulletin*, January 25, 1960, pp. 111-119; *Documents, 1960*, no. 1.

2. Budget message, January 18, in *New York Times*, January 19, 1960; excerpts in *Documents, 1960*, no. 2.

3. Message on the Mutual Security Program, February 16, in *Bulletin*, March 7, 1960, pp. 369-375; *Documents, 1960*, no. 3.

4. Report to the 21st Congress of the Soviet Communist Party, January 27, 1959, quoted in *The United States in World Affairs, 1959*, p. 114.

5. *New Times*, no. 4, January 1960, supplement, pp. 12-15.

6. Rockefeller Brothers Fund, *International Security—The Military Aspect:* Report of Panel III of the Special Studies Project (New York: Dou-

bleday, 1958); same, *The Challenge to America—Its Economic and Social Aspects:* Report of Panel IV of the Special Studies Project (Garden City: Doubleday, 1958).

7. *New York Times,* February 4, 1960.

8. *Congressional Record,* Daily edition, March 5, 1960, p. 4221.

9. *New York Times,* February 7, 1960; see further Section 8.

10. For more detailed discussion see the appropriate regional chapters.

11. For documentation on the U-2 incident see especially *Documents, 1960,* nos. 13-18. A detailed review of the published facts in the case is Quincy Wright, "Legal Aspects of the U-2 Incident," *American Journal of International Law,* October 1960, pp. 836-844. An informal account of the U-2 incident and the summit conference appears in Merriman Smith, *A President's Odyssey* (New York: Harper, 1961), pp. 188-208 and 259-262.

12. *Bulletin,* May 23, 1960, pp. 816-817; *Documents, 1960,* no. 15.

13. *Bulletin,* May 30, 1960, pp. 851-852; *Documents, 1960,* no. 17.

14. For documentation on the summit conference see especially *Documents, 1960,* nos. 19-27, and cf. Section 13, below.

15. For details see Section 41.

16. S. Rept. 1761, 86th Cong., 2d sess. (Washington: G.P.O., 1960); excerpts in *New York Times,* June 26, 1960.

17. See Sections 29 and 47.

18. Details in Section 14.

19. Details in Section 14.

20. For documentation on the RB-47 incident see especially *Documents, 1960,* nos. 29-33 and notes to Chapter II, Section 14.

21. *New York Times,* July 13, 1960; see also Senator Kennedy's speech of June 14 in *Documents, 1960,* no. 7.

22. *New York Times,* July 24, 1960. For Mr. Nixon's views see also his speech of July 28 in *Documents, 1960,* no. 8.

23. *New York Times,* April 7, 1960.

24. Same, August 9, 1960; excerpts in *Bulletin,* August 29, 1960, pp. 314-315 and *Documents, 1960,* no. 4. For further details see *Bulletin,* September 5, 1960, pp. 367-373.

25. For details see Sections 48 and 49.

26. For details see Section 5.

27. See further Section 57.

28. "U.S. Government Grants, Credits, Other Assistance Abroad Total $4 Billion," *Foreign Commerce Weekly,* December 26, 1960, pp. 3 and 28. For background information pertinent to this section see especially *Report to Congress on the Mutual Security Program For the Fiscal Year 1960* (Department of State Publication 7099; Washington: G.P.O., 1961).

29. *Economic Assistance as a Cooperative Effort of the Free World* (Washington: Department of State, 1960), p. 25; partial text also in *Bulletin,* August 22, 1960, pp. 289-295. Soviet bloc figures from *Communist Economic Policy in the Less Developed Areas* (Department of State Publication 7020; Washington: G.P.O., 1960), p. 13.

30. *Bulletin,* February 22, 1960, pp. 299-300; see further Section 60.

31. Message of the President, February 18, in *Bulletin,* March 14, 1960, pp. 422-423; Public Law 86-565, approved June 30, 1960; Public Law 86-651, approved July 14, 1960; see also Section 60.

32. Details in Section 49.

33. For details see Sections 19 and 23.

34. *New York Times,* February 19, 1960.

35. Same as note 3.

36. Public Law 86-472, approved May 14, 1960; Public Law 86-704, approved September 2, 1960.

37. Statement by the President, August 26, in *Bulletin,* September 12, 1960, p. 417.

38. Public Law 86-722, approved September 8, 1960.

39. Public Law 86-735, approved September 8, 1960; cf. Section 49.

40. For details of D.L.F. activity see *Bulletin,* September 19, 1960, pp. 444-445.

41. For details see Section 35.

42. For details see Samuel Pizer and Frederick Cutler, "United States Foreign Investments: Measures of Growth and Economic Effects," *Survey of Current Business,* September 1960, pp. 15-24. For a survey of U.S. policies relating to private investment cf. *Bulletin,* December 12, 1960, pp. 890-894.

43. For details see "The Balance of International Payments: Developments in the Fourth Quarter and Year 1959," *Survey of Current Business,* March 1960, pp. 6-11 and 18-20; later figures in same, September 1960, p. 9.

44. Presidential message and related material in *Bulletin,* April 11, 1960, pp. 560-565; message only in *Documents, 1960,* no. 5.

45. For a report of progress in this field see *Bulletin,* May 30, 1960, pp. 870-888.

46. For details see Section 19.

47. Statement by Bradley Fisk, Assistant Secretary of Commerce for International Affairs, September 21, in *Foreign Commerce Weekly,* September 26, 1960, pp. 18-20; see further Section 8.

48. *New York Times,* September 24, 1960.

49. Same, September 24 and 29, 1960; Anderson text in *Bulletin,* October 17, 1960, pp. 611-616.

50. *The United States in World Affairs, 1958,* pp. 114-115, 407; see also Section 60. For important U.S. tariff actions during 1960 see especially *Bulletin,* January 9, 1961, p. 50 and January 16, 1961, pp. 87-90.

51. *New York Times,* February 5, 10, and 12 and April 22, 1960. On other aviation negotiations see *Bulletin,* August 1, 1960, p. 165; September 5, 1960, p. 365; September 12, 1960, pp. 423-427; October 3, 1960, p. 514; October 17, 1960, p. 629.

52. U.S. activities in this field are reviewed by Don Paarlberg, Food-for-Peace Coordinator, in *Bulletin,* August 15, 1960, pp. 248-251; see also the President's speech of September 1 in same, September 19, 1960, pp. 441-443.

53. See Section 35.

54. Cf. *Bulletin,* September 19, 1960, pp. 449-451, and Section 58, below.

55. Cf. *Bulletin,* October 3, 1960, pp. 521-524.

56. Address of September 23, in *New York Times,* September 24, 1960; excerpts in *Documents, 1960,* no. 152.

57. For details see Section 54.

58. Letter of October 2, in *Bulletin*, October 17, 1960, pp. 595-596 and *Documents, 1960*, no. 67; for details see Section 16.

59. Address of September 22, in *Bulletin*, October 10, 1960, pp. 551-557; *Documents, 1960*, no. 151.

60. *Bulletin*, November 7, 1960, pp. 713-715 and December 19, 1960, pp. 922-923.

61. Television debate, October 7, in *New York Times*, October 8, 1960.

62. See especially the reports of the U.S. Information Agency printed in *New York Times*, October 27 and 29 and November 2, 1960.

63. Cf. the record of the television debate of October 21 in *Documents, 1960*, no. 9.

64. *New York Times*, October 8 and 11-14, 1960.

65. Statement of October 20, in same, October 21, 1960; further comments in same, October 19, 22, and 23, 1960.

66. Same, October 13 and 21, 1960; cf. Section 57.

67. See further Section 17.

68. *New York Times*, January 7, 1961.

69. See especially the announcement on the meeting of the President and the President-elect, December 6, in *Bulletin*, December 26, 1960, p. 968 and *Documents, 1960*, no. 10.

70. For details see the appropriate regional chapters.

71. *New York Times*, December 11, 1960; further details in "Expansion of Exports Supports Domestic Business," *Survey of Current Business*, December 1960, pp. 11-20. Full year figures from *Foreign Commerce Weekly*, March 6, 1961, pp. 7-8 and 40.

72. "U.S. Balance-of-Payments Position Worsens in Third Quarter 1960," *Foreign Commerce Weekly*, November 28, 1960, p. 2; "The U.S. Balance of Payments, 1959-60," *Federal Reserve Bulletin*, October 1960, pp. 1095-1101; "The Balance of International Payments Was More Adverse in Third Quarter," *Survey of Current Business*, December 1960, pp. 6-10 and 20.

73. *New York Times*, January 6, 1961.

74. *Bulletin*, December 5, 1960, pp. 861-863; *Documents, 1960*, no. 6.

75. For details see Section 23.

76. See Section 24.

77. Text in *New York Times*, November 28, 1960 and in *Goals for Americans: Programs for Action in the Sixties, comprising the Report of the President's Commission on National Goals and Chapters Submitted for the Consideration of the Commission* (New York: Prentice-Hall, 1960).

Chapter II. The Soviet Bloc and East-West Relations

1. Report to the Supreme Soviet, January 14, in *New Times*, no. 4, January 1960, supplement, p. 18.

2. Same, p. 7.

3. For the documentary background of East-West relations see *Background of Heads of Government Conference, 1960: Principal Documents, 1955-1959 (with Narrative Summary)* (Department of State Publication 6972; Washington: G.P.O., 1960).

4. *The United States in World Affairs, 1959*, pp. 332-333.

5. White House release, December 29, 1959, in *Documents, 1959*, pp. 332-333. For further details on the subject matter of this section see William J. Gehron, "Geneva Conference on the Discontinuance of Nuclear Weapons Tests," *Bulletin*, September 26, 1960, pp. 482-497; also U.S. Senate, Committee on Foreign Relations, 86th Cong., 2d sess., *Conference on the Discontinuance of Nuclear Weapons Tests: Analysis of Progress and Positions of the Participating Parties, October 1958-August 1960* (Committee print, Subcommittee on Disarmament, October 1960; Washington: G.P.O., 1960).

6. *Bulletin*, September 26, 1960, pp. 494-497; *Documents, 1960*, no. 59.

7. White House release, February 11, in *Bulletin*, February 29, 1960, pp. 327-328 and *Documents, 1960*, no. 61. For the Soviet attitude see the excerpt from Khrushchev's address of January 14 in same, no. 60.

8. *New York Times*, March 20, 1960; *Soviet News* (London), March 21, 1960; *Documents, 1960*, no. 62.

9. Joint declaration, March 29, in *Bulletin*, April 18, 1960, pp. 587-588 and *Documents, 1960*, no. 63.

10. *New York Times*, March 18 and 19 and April 20, 22, and 23, 1960.

11. White House statement, May 7, in *Bulletin*, May 23, 1960, p. 819 and *Documents, 1960*, no. 64.

12. News conference, May 11, in *New York Times*, May 12, 1960.

13. *The United States in World Affairs, 1959*, pp. 165-166. For background see Joseph Nogee, "The Diplomacy of Disarmament," *International Conciliation*, no. 526, January 1960, pp. 235-303; *Disarmament—The Intensified Effort, 1955-1958* (Department of State Publication 7070; Washington: G.P.O., 1960); *Documents on Disarmament, 1945-1959* (Department of State Publication 7008; Washington: G.P.O., 1960, 2 v.).

14. *The United States in World Affairs, 1959*, pp. 166-167; *Documents, 1959*, pp. 304-308.

15. General Assembly Resolution 1378 (XIV), November 20, 1959; same, pp. 308-309.

16. *Bulletin*, March 7, 1960, pp. 354-358; *Documents, 1960*, no. 39. For the Soviet disarmament appeal see same, no. 38.

17. *Documents, 1959*, pp. 301-304.

18. *Bulletin*, April 4, 1960, pp. 511-513; *Documents, 1960*, no. 41. For a detailed account of the conference see especially the official report of the U.S. delegation in *Bulletin*, August 22, 1960, pp. 267-274 (released with annexes as Department of State Press Release 430, August 5, 1960; abridged text in *Documents, 1960*, nos. 40 and 46); also *Verbatim Records of the Meetings of the Ten-Power Disarmament Committee held at the Palais des Nations, Geneva, March 15-April 29 and June 7-27, 1960* (Miscellaneous No. 10; Cmnd. 1152; London: H.M.S.O., 1960).

19. News conference, March 30, in *New York Times*, March 31, 1960.

20. Department of State Press Release 430, August 5, 1960; *Documents, 1960*, no. 42; see also the Western document of April 26 in same, no. 43.

21. *Bulletin*, January 19, 1959, pp. 181-189; excerpts in *Documents, 1958*, pp. 220-231.

22. *The United States in World Affairs, 1959*, pp. 149-157; *Documents, 1959*, pp. 257-296.

23. *The United States in World Affairs, 1959,* pp. 163-164; *Documents, 1959,* p. 199.

24. *New Times,* no. 4, January 1960, supplement, p. 17.

25. *New York Times,* February 5, 1960.

26. Joint communiqué, March 15, in *Bulletin,* April 4, 1960, pp. 517-518.

27. *New York Times,* March 1, 1960.

28. Same, April 3, 1960.

29. *Bulletin,* April 25, 1960, p. 638.

30. Same, May 9, 1960, p. 725; *Documents, 1960,* no. 11.

31. *New York Times,* April 26, 1960; *Documents, 1960,* no. 12.

32. For brief narrative see Section 3; for documentation see Chapter I, note 11.

33. See especially the statement of Secretary Herter to the Senate Foreign Relations Committee, May 27, in *Bulletin,* June 13, 1960 and *Documents, 1960,* no. 19. For documentation on the summit conference see *Documents, 1960,* nos. 19-27, and *Meetings: Documents Relating to the Meetings between the President of the French Republic, the President of the United States of America, the Chairman of the Council of Ministers of the Union of Soviet Socialist Republics and the Prime Minister of the United Kingdom, Paris, May 15 to 17, 1960* (Cmnd. 1052; London: H.M.S.O., 1960).

34. *New York Times,* May 17, 1960; *Documents, 1960,* no. 20.

35. *New York Times,* May 17, 1960.

36. Same, May 17 and 19, 1960, and *Documents, 1960,* nos. 20 and 24.

37. *New York Times,* May 21, 1960, and (in part) *Documents, 1960,* no. 34.

38. *Bulletin,* June 6, 1960, pp. 899-903; *Documents, 1960,* no. 26.

39. U.N. Document S/4321, in *Bulletin,* June 13, 1960, p. 961.

40. U.N. Document S/4328, in same; *Documents, 1960,* no. 28. For details see *Bulletin,* June 13, 1960, pp. 955-961; *United Nations Review,* July 1960, pp. 6-9 and 38-50; Quincy Wright, "Legal Aspects of the U-2 Incident," *American Journal of International Law,* October 1960, pp. 836-844.

41. Khrushchev speech in *Current Digest of the Soviet Press,* July 20, 1960, pp. 3-9 and 25. Declaration in same, July 27, 1960, p. 14 and in *Documents, 1960,* no. 70.

42. See further Section 42.

43. *New York Times,* May 31 and June 4, 1960.

44. See Section 4.

45. U.N. Document S/4406, in *Bulletin,* August 15, 1960, p. 244 and *Documents, 1960,* no. 31.

46. U.N. Documents S/4409/Rev. 1 and S/4411, in *Bulletin,* August 15, 1960, p. 244 and *Documents, 1960,* nos. 32 and 33. For background and details see *Bulletin,* August 1, 1960, pp. 163-165; August 8, 1960, pp. 209-212; August 15, 1960, pp. 235-244; August 22, 1960, pp. 274-276; also *United Nations Review,* September 1960, pp. 34-37.

47. *Bulletin,* August 1, 1960, p. 165; same, August 8, 1960, p. 214.

48. Same, August 29, 1960, p. 350; *New York Times,* August 11 and 27, 1960.

49. *Bulletin,* August 8, 1960, pp. 212-214.

50. For the U.S. attitude see *Bulletin*, August 22, 1960, pp. 276-277; August 29, 1960, p. 350; September 5, 1960, p. 361.

51. *New York Times*, September 7, 1960.

52. See Sections 29 and 47.

53. Department of State Press Release 430, August 5, 1960; *Documents, 1960*, no. 47. For Khrushchev's letter of June 2 and U.S. reply of June 7 see *Documents, 1960*, nos. 44 and 45.

54. *Bulletin*, July 18, 1960, pp. 90-92; *Documents, 1960*, no. 48.

55. Report of U.S. Delegation, in *Bulletin*, August 22, 1960, pp. 271-272 and *Documents, 1960*, no. 46; see further *Bulletin*, July 18, 1960, pp. 89-90.

56. Same, pp. 92-93 and *Documents, 1960*, no. 49. See also U.S. note, July 2, in *Bulletin*, July 18, 1960, pp. 88-89 and *Documents, 1960*, no. 50.

57. *Bulletin*, August 15, 1960, p. 253; same, August 22, 1960, p. 274; *Documents, 1960*, no. 51.

58. *Bulletin*, September 5, 1960, pp. 376-382; *Documents, 1960*, nos. 52 and 53.

59. News conference, August 10, in *New York Times*, August 11, 1960.

60. See Section 2.

61. See Sections 34 and 39.

62. Cf. Section 36.

63. *New York Times*, March 5, 1960.

64. *Communist Economic Policy in the Less Developed Areas* (Department of State Publication 7020; Washington: G.P.O., 1960), pp. 20-21.

65. Same, pp. 13-14.

66. For details see the appropriate regional chapters. Further Soviet aid commitments are listed in Section 17.

67. Letter to Disarmament Commission, August 1, in *New York Times*, August 2, 1960.

68. *Bulletin*, September 5, 1960, pp. 362-363; same, September 19, 1960, pp. 439-440; same, September 26, 1960, pp. 473-475; same, November 14, 1960, pp. 748-751; *Documents, 1960*, nos. 35-37.

69. *New York Times*, September 24, 1960, and (in part) *Documents, 1960*, no. 152.

70. U.N. Documents A/4505 and A/C.1/L.249; *Documents, 1960*, nos. 54 and 56.

71. U.N. Document A/4509; *Documents, 1960*, no. 55. For the U.S. attitude see *Bulletin*, October 17, 1960, pp. 620-621.

72. *New Times*, no. 41, October 1960, pp. 33-39; see further Section 56.

73. For details see Section 54.

74. *Bulletin*, October 10, 1960, pp. 554-556; *Documents, 1960*, no. 151; see further Section 57.

75. U.N. Document A/L.317, in *New York Times*, October 1, 1960 and *Documents, 1960*, no. 66.

76. *Bulletin*, October 17, 1960, pp. 595-596; *Documents, 1960*, no. 67.

77. *New York Times*, October 4, 1960; *Documents, 1960*, no. 68.

78. General Assembly Resolution 1495 (XV), October 17, 1960; *Documents, 1960*, no. 154; see also Section 56.

79. *New York Times*, September 30, 1960.

80. News conference, October 7, in same, October 8, 1960.

81. Television debate, October 7, in same.

82. Same, October 10, 1960.

83. For details see Sections 54-56.

84. See further Section 42.

85. *Bulletin*, August 8, 1960, p. 219.

86. Address to the Polish-American Congress, September 30, in *New York Times*, October 1, 1960. See also the address of Under-Secretary Dillon to the same group, October 2, in *Bulletin*, October 17, 1960, pp. 597-602.

87. Kennedy views in *New York Times*, October 2, 1960; Nixon views in same, October 28, 1960.

88. *Bulletin*, August 8, 1960, pp. 226-228; same, August 15, 1960, pp. 259-260.

89. Same, December 5, 1960, pp. 863-864.

90. Same, May 16, 1960, p. 797.

91. For details see same, September 12, 1960, p. 422; same, October 17, 1960, p. 623; same, November 7, 1960, pp. 727-729; also *United Nations Review*, January 1961, pp. 35-36.

92. *Bulletin*, April 25, 1960, pp. 670-673; same, December 26, 1960, pp. 968-972.

93. *New York Times*, December 28, 1960; *Bulletin*, January 16, 1961, p. 85; *United Nations Review*, February 1961, p. 3.

94. *New York Times*, November 10 and 11, 1960; *Documents, 1960*, no. 69.

95. Cf. Section 51.

96. Resolutions 1576 (XV), 1577 (XV), and 1578 (XV), December 20, 1960. For details see *United Nations Review*, December 1960, pp. 6-9 and 82-85; same, January 1961, p. 49; report of the First Committee of the General Assembly, with texts, in U.N. Document A/4680, December 20, 1960; *Bulletin*, January 16, 1961, pp. 94-96. Texts of the principal Soviet and Western draft resolutions appear in *Documents, 1960*, nos. 55-57. The U.S. position was fully outlined by Ambassador Wadsworth in a speech of October 19 in *Bulletin*, November 28, 1960, pp. 760-769 and *Documents, 1960*, no. 58.

97. *New York Times*, October 18, 1960. For an outline of the U.S. position see the statement of Ambassador Wadsworth, November 29, in *Bulletin*, December 19, 1960, pp. 930-935, and (in part) in *Documents, 1960*, no. 65.

98. *New York Times*, October 10 and 14, 1960. For Mr. Nixon's stand see same, October 27, 1960.

99. Text in *New York Times*, December 7, 1960 and *New Times*, no. 50, December 1960, supplement; excerpts in *Documents, 1960*, no. 71.

100. *New Times*, no. 51, December 1960, pp. 34-37; *Documents, 1960*, no. 72.

101. *New York Times*, November 14, 1960 and January 3, 1961; on the dollar problem see Section 8.

102. For details see the appropriate regional chapters.

103. *New York Times*, January 1, 1961.

Chapter III. The Western Community

1. Text in Cmnd. 1026 (London: H.M.S.O., 1960).

2. For documentation see *Bulletin*, February 1, 1960, pp. 139-147; Dillon speech also in *Documents, 1960*, no. 75.

3. *Bulletin*, April 11, 1960, pp. 577-578; July 25, 1960, p. 153; October 24, 1960, pp. 645-646.

4. For details see especially *Relazioni internazionali* (Milan), April 23, 1960, p. 557; June 4, 1960, p. 742; July 30, 1960, p. 1011. See further Section 23.

5. For details see especially "Common Market Speeds Ahead," *Foreign Commerce Weekly*, September 12, 1960, pp. 5-6; also "Completely Free Trade for Members EFTA's Goal by 1970," same, pp. 9 and 24.

6. News conference, February 3, in *New York Times*, February 4, 1960.

7. Same, March 3 and 11, 1960.

8. Same, April 14 and 22, 1960.

9. Cf. Section 2.

10. Cf. Section 57.

11. *New York Times*, February 5, 1960; cf. Section 12.

12. Same, April 22 and 29, 1960.

13. Cf. Sections 9-11.

14. Cf. Section 34.

15. *Bulletin*, May 23, 1960, p. 840, and *Documents*, 1960, no. 73; cf. also *New York Times*, May 4, 1960.

16. *Bulletin*, May 23, 1960, pp. 839-840.

17. *New York Times*, June 1, 1960, and *Documents, 1960*, no. 27. On European reactions to the summit failure see especially the report of the U.S. Information Agency dated June 1960 and printed in *New York Times*, October 27, 1960.

18. Same, July 15, 1960.

19. Same, October 26, 1960.

20. *Bulletin*, November 21, 1960, p. 778; *New York Times*, November 2, 3, 5, and 9, 1960.

21. On U.S.-Canadian relations see especially *Documents, 1960*, nos. 77 and 78. On the Columbia Basin agreement see *Bulletin*, November 28, 1960, pp. 831-832.

22. *Bulletin*, August 29, 1960, pp. 347-349; same, October 31, 1960, pp. 676-677; also *Soviet News* (London), October 11, 1960.

23. See further Section 30 (3).

24. For details see especially de Gaulle's news conference of September 4, in *New York Times*, September 5, 1960.

25. Address of September 8, in *Bulletin*, September 26, 1960, p. 470; news conference, September 14, in same, October 3, 1960, p. 516.

26. Cf. Section 41.

27. *Bulletin*, November 7, 1960, pp. 717-720.

28. Cf. Section 56.

29. Address of July 15 and related material in *Bulletin*, August 8, 1960, pp. 215-219.

30. General Assembly Resolution 1497 (XV), October 31, in *Bulletin*,

December 19, 1960, p. 940. For details see same, pp. 939-940 and *United Nations Review*, December 1960, pp. 47-48.

31. *New York Times*, September 5 and November 25, 1960.

32. Cf. Section 8.

33. *New York Times*, November 24, 1960; statement by the President, November 28, in *Bulletin*, December 19, 1960, pp. 925-926.

34. *Bulletin*, December 12, 1960, p. 895. For other expressions of U.S. views see same, June 13, 1960, pp. 975-976 and September 19, 1960, pp. 453-455.

35. Text of convention and related documents in *Bulletin*, January 2, 1961, pp. 11-15, and *Documents, 1960*, no. 76.

36. *New York Times*, September 24 and 25, 1960.

37. Same, December 22, 1960.

38. Address to NATO parliamentary conference, November 21, 1960; excerpts in *NATO Letter* (Paris), January 1961, pp. 15-17.

39. *New York Times*, December 13, 1960.

40. Same, December 17, 1960.

41. NATO Council communiqué, December 19, 1960, in *Bulletin*, January 9, 1961, pp. 39-40, and *Documents, 1960*, no. 74. Related material in *Bulletin*, January 9, 1961, pp. 39-41.

42. *New York Times*, December 17, 1960.

43. Same as note 41.

Chapter IV. The Year of Africa

1. General Assembly Resolution 289 (IV), November 21, 1949.

2. Useful surveys of the political divisions of Africa appear in *Bulletin*, August 22, 1960, pp. 283-286 and December 26, 1960, pp. 959-967.

3. Details in *United Nations Review*, December 1960, pp. 10-13.

4. For documentation on Congolese events see especially "La Crise congolaise," *Chronique de politique étrangère* (Brussels), July-November 1960, pp. 411-1012.

5. Ambassade de France, Service de Presse et d'Information, New York, *Speeches and Press Conferences*, no. 152, September 5, 1960.

6. Quoted by a Malagasy delegate to the U.N., in *New York Times*, September 22, 1960.

7. *The United States in World Affairs, 1959*, pp. 253-254.

8. *New York Times*, February 22 and 27, 1960.

9. Same, January 20, 1960.

10. Same, February 4, 1960.

11. Statement of March 22, in *Bulletin*, April 11, 1960, p. 551 n.

12. Lodge statement and resolution (U.N. Document S/4300) in *Bulletin*, April 25, 1960, pp. 668-669, and *Documents, 1960*, nos. 79 and 80. For details see *Bulletin*, April 25, 1960, pp. 667-668, and *United Nations Review*, May 1960, pp. 16-19 and 35-40.

13. For surveys of U.S. interests and policies in Africa see especially Joseph C. Satterthwaite, "Our Role in the Quickening Pace toward Independence in Africa," *Bulletin*, May 2, 1960, pp. 686-693; and James K. Penfield, "Africa: A New Situation Requiring New Responses," same, June 6, 1960, pp. 918-923.

14. *The United States in World Affairs, 1957,* p. 180.

15. *New York Times,* February 1, 1960.

16. Address to the Economic Club of New York, in *United Nations Review,* April 1960, p. 11.

17. *New York Times,* February 11, 1960.

18. Mutual Security message, February 16, in *Bulletin,* March 7, 1960, p. 373, and *Documents, 1960,* no. 3; for further details see *Bulletin,* March 21, 1960, pp. 449-451.

19. Penfield (cited note 13), p. 922.

20. Unofficial estimates in *New York Times,* November 1 and December 6, 1960.

21. Same as note 7.

22. *New York Times,* January 30, 1960.

23. Same, March 6, 1960.

24. Same, March 26, 1960.

25. Same, April 13, 1960.

26. News conference, April 27, in *New York Times,* April 28, 1960; for reactions see same, May 5, 1960.

27. See especially same, June 15, 21, and 30 and July 5, 1960.

28. Same, August 23, 1960.

29. Same, September 6, 1960.

30. Same, September 24, October 3, 4, 24, 28, and 30, and November 3, 1960.

31. Statement by Premier Gaston Eyskens, August 18, reported in *New York Times,* August 19, 1960.

32. U.N. Document S/4382, in *New York Times,* July 14, 1960. For the detailed history of the Congo crisis see note 4.

33. U.N. Document S/4387, in *Bulletin,* August 1, 1960, p. 161, and *Documents, 1960,* no. 82. For details see *Bulletin,* August 1, 1960, pp. 159-161; *Documents, 1960,* nos. 81 and 83; and *United Nations Review,* August 1960, pp. 6-7 and 45-50.

34. Details in *Bulletin,* September 5, 1960, p. 385.

35. For details on U.N. civilian operations see especially *United Nations Review,* November 1960, pp. 15-25 and January 1961, pp. 26-28.

36. *Bulletin,* August 8, 1960, p. 223; *Documents, 1960,* no. 84.

37. *Bulletin,* August 8, 1960, pp. 205-206; *Documents, 1960,* no. 85.

38. U.N. Document S/4405, in *Bulletin,* August 8, 1960, p. 223, and *Documents, 1960,* no. 86. For details see *Bulletin,* August 8, 1960, pp. 221-223; *United Nations Review,* August 1960, pp. 8-12 and 50; same, September 1960, pp. 52-60.

39. *Bulletin,* August 15, 1960, pp. 245-246.

40. U.N. Document S/4426, in *Bulletin,* September 5, 1960, pp. 385-386, and *Documents, 1960,* no. 88. For details see *Bulletin,* September 5, 1960, pp. 384-385; *Documents, 1960,* no. 87; *United Nations Review,* September 1960, pp. 12-21, 47-51, and 61-62.

41. Same as note 35.

42. *Bulletin,* September 12, 1960, pp. 421-422; *Documents, 1960,* no. 89. Fuller details in *United Nations Review,* October 1960, pp. 33-44.

43. For a chronology of Congolese events from September 1 onward see

United Nations Review, December 1960, pp. 36-42; January 1961, pp. 31 and 34-35; February 1961, pp. 37-39 and 49; March 1961, pp. 41-43.

44. *Bulletin,* September 26, 1960, p. 473; *Documents, 1960,* no. 90.

45. Fourth report of the Secretary-General (U.N. Document S/4482), in *United Nations Review,* October 1960, pp. 57-59.

46. Same, pp. 46-47 and 59-60; further details in same, pp. 44-45.

47. U.N. Document S/4506, in *New York Times,* September 14, 1960.

48. *New York Times,* September 14, 1960.

49. U.N. Document S/4519, in same, September 16, 1960.

50. U.N. Document S/4516, in *Bulletin,* October 3, 1960, p. 531, and *Documents, 1960,* no. 91.

51. U.N. Document S/4523, in *Bulletin,* October 3, 1960, p. 532, and *Documents, 1960,* no. 92. For details see *Bulletin,* October 3, 1960, pp. 527-531, and *United Nations Review,* October 1960, pp. 48-54.

52. General Assembly Resolution 1474 (ES-IV), September 20, in *Bulletin,* October 10, 1960, pp. 588-589, and *Documents, 1960,* no. 94. For details see *Bulletin,* October 10, 1960, pp. 583-588; *Documents, 1960,* no. 93; *United Nations Review,* October 1960, pp. 8-19 and 28-29.

53. Details in *Bulletin,* July 25, 1960, pp. 149-153; September 19, 1960, pp. 456-457; October 10, 1960, p. 589. On the Council of the Entente cf. same, January 2, 1961, p. 19.

54. Cf. same, October 17, 1960, pp. 618-619.

55. Same, December 4, 1960, pp. 976-977; *United Nations Review,* January 1961, pp. 25 and 62.

56. *Bulletin,* October 24, 1960, pp. 659-660.

57. Same, October 10, 1960, pp. 551-557; *Documents, 1960,* no. 151.

58. Address of August 13, 1958, in *Documents, 1958,* pp. 350-360.

59. *Bulletin,* November 7, 1960, p. 714.

60. *New York Times,* September 14, 1960.

61. Same, October 31, 1960; *Bulletin,* November 7, 1960, p. 734. On U.S.-Guinean relations cf. also same, December 19, 1960, p. 922.

62. *New York Times,* August 29, 1960; *Current Digest of the Soviet Press,* September 28, 1960, p. 21.

63. *New York Times,* September 24, 1960.

64. News conference, September 23, with Nkrumah comment, in same, September 24, 1960. Other material on U.S.-Ghanaian relations in *Bulletin,* August 22, 1960, p. 287, and September 5, 1960, pp. 364-365.

65. *New York Times,* November 21, 1960.

66. Same, October 9, 1960; see further Section 42.

67. Statement of October 17, in *United Nations Review,* November 1960, pp. 13-14; see further Section 54.

68. Text in *United Nations Review,* December 1960, pp. 24-36 and 81.

69. Statement of November 4, in *New York Times,* November 5, 1960.

70. Same, November 23, 1960; details in *Bulletin,* December 12, 1960, pp. 904-909.

71. *New York Times,* November 22, 1960.

72. Report of September 7, 1960, cited in note 45. U. S. contributions noted in *Bulletin,* October 3, 1960, p. 530, and October 10, 1960, p. 588.

73. *New York Times,* November 30, 1960; *Bulletin,* December 26, 1960, pp. 975-976.

74. Resolution 1583 (XV), December 20, 1960; for details see U.N. Document A/4676, December 19, 1960, and *United Nations Review*, January 1961, pp. 34-35.

75. Same, pp. 28-31; *Bulletin*, January 9, 1961, p. 53.

76. U.N. Document S/4579.

77. U.N. Document S/4578/Rev. 1, in *Bulletin*, January 9, 1961, p. 56, and *Documents, 1960*, no. 96.

78. *New York Times*, December 15, 1960. For details see *Bulletin*, January 9, 1961, pp. 51-56; *Documents, 1960*, no. 95; *United Nations Review*, January 1961, pp. 10-15 and 40-49.

79. U.N. Document A/L.331/Rev. 1, in *Bulletin*, January 9, 1961, pp. 60-61.

80. U.N. Document A/L.332, in same, pp. 61-62, and *Documents, 1960*, no. 98.

81. *New York Times*, December 21, 1960. For details see *Bulletin*, January 9, 1961, pp. 56-60; *Documents, 1960*, no. 97; *United Nations Review*, February 1961, pp. 5-8.

82. *New York Times*, November 5, 1960.

83. For details see Ambassade de France, Service de Presse et d'Information, New York, "The Referendum of January 8, 1961," *French Affairs*, no. 109, January 3, 1961.

84. Text and details of committee debate in U.N. Document A/4660, December 16, 1960.

85. Resolution 1573 (XV), December 19, 1960, in *Bulletin*, January 9, 1961, p. 64, and *Documents, 1960*, no. 100. For details see *Bulletin*, January 9, 1961, pp. 62-64; *Documents, 1960*, no. 99; *United Nations Review*, February 1961, pp. 39-45.

86. Resolution 1514 (XV), December 14, 1960, in *Documents, 1960*, no. 156. For details see Section 56.

87. See Section 55.

88. See Section 56.

89. Resolution 1568 (XV), December 18, 1960. For details see U.N. Document A/4643, December 13, 1960; also *New York Times*, November 5, December 19, and December 20, 1960, and *United Nations Review*, January 1961, pp. 16-20.

90. Resolutions 1579 (XV) and 1580 (XV), December 20, 1960. For details see U.N. Document A/4672, December 19, 1960; *New York Times*, December 21, 1960; *United Nations Review*, January 1961, p. 3.

91. Cf. *Bulletin*, October 24, 1960, pp. 657-659.

92. *New York Times*, December 25, 1960.

Chapter V. The Middle East and Southern Asia

1. Public Law 85-7, approved March 9, 1957; *Documents, 1957*, pp. 206-207.

2. Address of August 13, 1958, in *Documents, 1958*, pp. 350-360.

3. *Bulletin*, March 14, 1960, pp. 424-426.

4. *New York Times*, January 19 and August 28, 1960.

5. *Bulletin*, September 19, 1960, pp. 448-449; *Documents, 1960*, no. 101.

6. *Communist Economic Policy in the Less Developed Areas* (Department of State Publication 7020; Washington: G.P.O., 1960), p. 27.

7. Same as note 5.

8. *New York Times*, February 21, 1960.

9. Same, February 26, 1960.

10. Comment by Mr. Hammarskjold, quoted in same, February 19, 1960.

11. News conference, February 17, in same, February 18, 1960.

12. *Documents, 1950*, pp. 658-659.

13. Address by the President, February 20, 1957, in *Documents, 1957*, p. 269; address by Secretary Herter to the U.N. General Assembly, September 17, 1959, in *Documents, 1959*, p. 37; further details in *The United States in World Affairs, 1959*, pp. 239-240.

14. News conference statements by Secretary Herter, February 8 and March 25, in *Bulletin*, February 29, 1960, p. 321 and April 11, 1960, p. 551.

15. News conference, April 27, in *New York Times*, April 28, 1960.

16. Cf. *Bulletin*, May 23, 1960, pp. 834-835, and *Documents, 1960*, no. 103.

17. Section 2, Public Law 86-472, approved May 14, 1960; for details see *Bulletin*, May 23, 1960, pp. 832-834.

18. Same, July 18, 1960, pp. 115-117; see further *United Nations Review*, August 1960, pp. 14-15.

19. *New York Times*, August 26 and 28, 1960.

20. Same, October 13, 1960.

21. Final communiqué in *Bulletin*, May 16, 1960, pp. 802-803, and *Documents, 1960*, no. 102.

22. *Current Digest of the Soviet Press*, September 28, 1960, pp. 16-18.

23. For a balanced account see Henry A. Byroade, "The Changing Position of Afghanistan in Asia," *Bulletin*, January 23, 1961, pp. 125-134.

24. *Current Digest of the Soviet Press*, April 6, 1960, pp. 6-9.

25. *Peking Review*, August 30, 1960, pp. 6-7. On U.S.-Afghan relations cf. *Bulletin*, April 18, 1960, p. 615; May 23, 1960, pp. 831-832; December 5, 1960, p. 872.

26. Announcement of February 29, in *Bulletin*, March 21, 1960, pp. 441-443, and *Documents, 1960*, no. 105. For further details see *Bulletin*, May 9, 1960, pp. 740-743, and October 10, 1960, pp. 577-578; Public Law 86-472 (Mutual Security Act of 1960), approved May 14, 1960, sec. 204 (e); Eugene R. Black, "The Indus: A Moral for Nations," *New York Times Magazine*, December 11, 1960, pp. 24 ff.

27. News conference, September 7, in *New York Times*, September 8, 1960.

28. Same, September 23, 1960.

29. See map in *The United States in World Affairs, 1959*, p. 286.

30. News conference statement by Secretary Herter, November 12, 1959, in *Documents, 1959*, pp. 459-461.

31. *New York Times*, February 13 and 17, 1960; *Current Digest of the Soviet Press*, March 16, 1960, pp. 7-8.

32. *New York Times*, August 31, 1960; *Current Digest of the Soviet Press*, September 28, 1960, p. 15.

33. *Bulletin*, May 30, 1960, pp. 889-892; *Documents, 1960*, no. 106. See also Section 6.

34. *New York Times,* September 16, 1960.

35. Same, March 25, 1960; *Peking Review,* March 29, 1960, pp. 7-10.

36. *New York Times,* April 30, 1960; *Peking Review,* May 3, 1960, pp. 6-14.

37. *Bulletin,* May 23, 1960, pp. 827-831. On U.S.-Nepal relations see also *Bulletin,* August 15, 1960, p. 248.

38. For details see Section 16.

39. *New York Times,* September 28, 1960.

40. Address of October 10, in same, October 11, 1960.

41. Same, October 4, 1960.

42. Same, September 25, 1960; *Middle Eastern Affairs,* November 1960, pp. 321-322.

43. *New York Times,* October 18-22 and 30, 1960.

44. Same, November 1 and December 8, 13, and 14, 1960.

45. Same, November 11, 1960.

46. U.S. aid to Jordan is conveniently summarized in same, January 8, 1961.

47. *Bulletin,* January 9, 1961, p. 50.

48. *New York Times,* November 27 and December 30, 1960; see also *Bulletin,* December 12, 1960, p. 901; same, February 6, 1961, pp. 197-198; *United Nations Review,* February 1961, p. 3.

49. *New York Times,* October 30, 1960.

50. *Bulletin,* January 9, 1961, pp. 49-50.

51. *New York Times,* December 4, 1960.

52. Same, December 6, 1960.

53. For details see same, November 1 and 18, 1960; also *Bulletin,* November 7, 1960, p. 733, and January 2, 1961, pp. 31-34.

54. *The United States in World Affairs, 1957,* p. 187.

55. *New York Times,* November 1, 1960; U.N. Document A/4521.

56. *New York Times,* December 17, 1960.

57. Statement by Assistant Secretary of State Francis O. Wilcox, November 16, in *Bulletin,* January 2, 1961, pp. 28-31, and *Documents, 1960,* no. 104.

58. *United Nations Review,* November 1960, pp. 6-8 and 89.

59. *Bulletin,* November 21, 1960, pp. 803-804.

60. Same as note 57. For details of the debate see *United Nations Review,* February 1961, pp. 32-36.

61. *New York Times,* November 29, 1960; *Israel Digest,* December 9, 1960.

62. *New York Times,* November 30, 1960; cf. General Assembly Resolution 1456 (XIV), December 9, 1959, in *Documents, 1959,* pp. 403-404.

63. *New York Times,* December 18-23, 1960; *Bulletin,* January 9, 1961, p. 45.

64. *New York Times,* December 24, 1960.

Chapter VI. Communist China and Its Neighbors

1. Address of June 28, 1957, in *Documents, 1957,* p. 343.

2. Address of September 30, 1959, quoted in *The United States in World Affairs, 1959,* p. 332.

3. *Peking Review,* February 2, 1960, pp. 12-15.

4. Speech of April 16, in *Peking Review,* April 19, 1960, pp. 15-17; also *New York Times,* April 17, 18, and 20, 1960.

5. See especially *New York Times,* February 29, 1960, and *Current Digest of the Soviet Press,* March 30, 1960, pp. 7-8.

6. *Peking Review,* May 10, 1960, pp. 9-10, and May 17, 1960, p. 30; also *New York Times,* May 9 and 10, 1960.

7. *Bulletin,* November 21, 1960, pp. 782-785.

8. Same, June 20, 1960, pp. 983-985.

9. Same, pp. 986-988, and *Documents, 1960,* no. 114.

10. *Bulletin,* July 25, 1960, pp. 143-147. For the President's departure statement of June 12 see same, July 4, 1960, pp. 7-8, and *Documents, 1960,* no. 115. For an informal account of the President's Far Eastern tour see Merriman Smith, *A President's Odyssey* (New York: Harper, 1961), pp. 212-237.

11. *Bulletin,* July 25, 1960, pp. 127-133. On U.S.-Philippine relations see also same, December 5, 1960, pp. 850-851.

12. *The United States in World Affairs, 1957,* p. 225.

13. *New York Times,* March 17, 1960.

14. Same, April 20, 1960; *Documents, 1960,* no. 113.

15. News conference, April 27, in *New York Times,* April 28, 1960.

16. Communiqué, June 19, in *Bulletin,* July 25, 1960, p. 136; see also same, pp. 133-135, and *New York Times,* June 18-20, 1960.

17. *Bulletin,* July 25, 1960, pp. 136-138; *New York Times,* June 20, 1960.

18. Communiqué, June 20, in *Bulletin,* July 25, 1960, pp. 138-139.

19. *Documents, 1951,* pp. 266-267.

20. Treaty and agreed minute in *Bulletin,* February 8, 1960, pp. 184-185, and *Documents, 1960,* nos. 109-110. See also Secretary Herter's analysis of June 7 in *Bulletin,* June 27, 1960, pp. 1029-1032, and *Documents, 1960,* no. 107.

21. *Bulletin,* February 8, 1960, pp. 185-198.

22. Same, pp. 198-199, and *Documents, 1960,* no. 111.

23. *Bulletin,* February 8, 1960, pp. 179-181, and *Documents, 1960,* no. 108.

24. *New York Times,* January 15 and 25, 1960.

25. Note of January 27, in *Current Digest of the Soviet Press,* February 24, 1960, pp. 19-20. For background cf. *The United States in World Affairs, 1956,* pp. 147-148.

26. *New York Times,* June 17, 1960; *Bulletin,* July 25, 1960, p. 131.

27. For the President's reflections on his Far Eastern tour see his address of June 27 in *Bulletin,* July 25, 1960, pp. 123-127, and *Documents, 1960,* no. 116.

28. Details of 1959 production in *Peking Review,* January 26, 1960, pp. 9-13; 1960 plan in same, April 5, 1960, pp. 5-21.

29. *New York Times,* December 30, 1960.

30. Same, December 31, 1960.

31. Cf. Chapter II, note 41.

32. A typical expression of the Soviet view is the article in *Current Digest of the Soviet Press,* September 28, 1960, pp. 8-10. The Chinese attitude is reflected in *Peking Review,* July 5, 1960, pp. 6-9. A fuller ré-

sumé of the Chinese arguments appears in *Relazioni internazionali* (Milan), September 24, 1960, pp. 1230-1232.

33. Cf. Chapter II, note 53.

34. *New York Times*, June 1 and September 10, 1960; *Current Digest of the Soviet Press*, October 12, 1960, p. 23.

35. *Peking Review*, August 9, 1960, p. 14; Khrushchev's reference in *New York Times*, October 2, 1960.

36. For details see *Bulletin*, April 11, 1960, p. 556, and September 26, 1960, p. 497.

37. Details in same, May 16, 1960, pp. 789-790, and September 26, 1960, pp. 497-499.

38. Cf. the Chinese Communist statement of September 13, as reported in *New York Times*, September 14, 1960.

39. Cf. Section 28.

40. *Bulletin*, October 31, 1960, pp. 678-689; *Documents, 1960*, no. 117.

41. General Assembly Resolution 1493 (XV), October 8, 1960; details in *United Nations Review*, November 1960, pp. 9-12; see also Section 30 (1), above.

42. For an official statement of U.S. policy, dated September 10, see *Bulletin*, September 26, 1960, p. 499, and *Documents, 1960*, no. 118.

43. *New York Times*, November 22, 1960.

44. Soviet note, December 13, and U.S. reply, December 17, in *Bulletin*, January 2, 1961, pp. 15-17; *Documents, 1960*, nos. 119-120. For the U.S. version of these events see also *Bulletin*, January 23, 1961, pp. 114-117.

45. *New York Times*, December 23, 1960. See also the Soviet note to the U.K., December 22, in *Soviet News* (London), December 30, 1960.

46. *New York Times*, December 31, 1960, and January 1, 6, and 27, 1961.

47. *Bulletin*, January 16, 1961, p. 76; *Documents, 1960*, no. 121.

48. *New York Times*, December 24, 1960; *Soviet News*, December 31, 1960; *Current Digest of the Soviet Press*, January 25, 1961, pp. 27-28.

49. *New York Times*, December 4, 1960; *Soviet News*, December 6, 1960.

50. *New York Times*, December 26 and 27, 1960.

51. Same, October 2 and 3 and December 25, 1960.

52. Same, December 23, 25, and 29, 1960; for background see *The United States in World Affairs, 1957*, pp. 342-343.

53. *New York Times*, October 14, 1960.

54. Same, December 25, 1960; *Soviet News*, December 31, 1960.

55. For background see *The Record on Korean Unification, 1943-1960* (Department of State Publication 7084; Washington: G.P.O., 1960).

56. U.N. Documents A/C.1/830, November 25, and A/C.1/832, December 8, 1960.

57. Chapter II, note 99; for details see Section 17.

58. For the campaign debate on Quemoy and Matsu see Chapter I, note 64.

59. *New York Times*, December 1, 1960; see further Section 51.

60. See especially *Bulletin*, October 10, 1960, pp. 561-562, and October 24, 1960, pp. 642-643.

61. *New York Times*, November 22, 1960; U.S. reaction in *Bulletin*, December 19, 1960, p. 923.

Chapter VII. The Inter-American System

1. On Soviet economic penetration cf. especially Clifford Frank Owen, "U.S. and Soviet Relations with Underdeveloped Countries: Latin America—A Case Study," *Inter-American Economic Affairs*, Winter 1960, pp. 85-116.

2. Broadcast address, February 21, in *Bulletin*, March 7, 1960, pp. 351-353, and *Documents, 1960*, no. 122. For an informal account of the President's tour see Merriman Smith, *A President's Odyssey* (New York: Harper, 1961), pp. 143-187; for full documentation, see *Strengthening Friendship and Trust Among the American Republics: President Eisenhower's Visit to Brazil, Argentina, Chile, and Uruguay, February-March 1960* (Department of State Publication 6974; Washington: G.P.O., 1960).

3. *New York Times*, March 2, 1960.

4. Same; see further *Bulletin*, April 25, 1960, pp. 648-658.

5. Same, March 28, 1960, pp. 474-486; Declaration of Brasília also in *Documents, 1960*, no. 123.

6. Broadcast address, March 8, in *Bulletin*, March 28, 1960, p. 472, and *Documents, 1960*, no. 124.

7. Same; see also address to the Caribbean Assembly, March 4, in *New York Times*, March 5, 1960.

8. *Bulletin*, March 28, 1960, p. 473; *Documents, 1960*, no. 124.

9. Address of March 4, in *New York Times*, March 5, 1960.

10. News conference, March 9, in *Bulletin*, March 28, 1960, pp. 487 and 492.

11. Same, pp. 491-492.

12. See especially the President's policy statement of January 26, in *Bulletin*, February 15, 1960, pp. 237-238, and *Documents, 1960*, no. 125.

13. For details see *Bulletin, passim*.

14. *New York Times*, February 14, 1960.

15. Cuban note, February 22, and U.S. reply, February 29, in *Bulletin*, March 21, 1960, pp. 440-441; *Documents, 1960*, no. 126.

16. *Bulletin*, June 13, 1960, p. 692.

17. Same, July 25, 1960, pp. 140-141; *Documents, 1960*, no. 127. For background cf. *Bulletin*, July 11, 1960, pp. 58-59.

18. U.N. Document S/4378, July 11, 1960.

19. *New York Times*, July 10, 1960.

20. *Bulletin*, July 25, 1960, pp. 139-140; *Documents, 1960*, no. 128.

21. *New York Times*, July 13, 1960.

22. State Department statement, July 14, in *Bulletin*, August 1, 1960, pp. 170-171; *Documents, 1960*, no. 129.

23. News conferences, August 10 and 24, in *New York Times*, August 11 and 25, 1960.

24. *Bulletin*, August 8, 1960, p. 225. For details on the subject matter of this section, see J. Fred Rippy and Alfred Tischendorf, "The San José Conference of American Foreign Ministers," *Inter-American Economic Affairs*, Winter 1960, pp. 59-72.

25. U.N. Document S/4395, in *Bulletin*, August 8, 1960, pp. 204-205, and *Documents, 1960*, no. 131. For details see *Bulletin*, August 8, 1960, pp.

199-204; *Documents, 1960,* no. 130; *United Nations Review,* September 1960, pp. 32-33 and 37.

26. *The United States in World Affairs, 1959,* pp. 355-357.

27. *New York Times,* June 9, 1960.

28. *Bulletin,* August 8, 1960, pp. 224-225.

29. *New York Times,* August 12 and 15, 1960.

30. *Bulletin,* September 5, 1960, p. 358; *Documents, 1960,* no. 133. For details see *Bulletin,* September 5, 1960, pp. 355-360; *Documents, 1960,* nos. 132 and 134; and U.N. Document S/4476, September 1, 1960.

31. Presidential message, August 23, in *Bulletin,* September 12, 1960, pp. 412-413, and *Documents, 1960,* no. 138. See further *Bulletin,* September 12, 1960, pp. 413-414; same, November 7, 1960, pp. 716-717; *Documents, 1960,* nos. 139 and 141.

32. U.N. Document S/4491, in *Bulletin,* October 3, 1960, p. 543, and *Documents, 1960,* no. 140. For details see *Bulletin,* October 3, 1960, pp. 542-544, and *United Nations Review,* October 1960, pp. 68-69 and 88.

33. U.N. Document S/4471, August 26, 1960.

34. Memoranda to the Inter-American Peace Committee, June 27 and August 2, and supplement, August 22, in *Bulletin,* July 18, 1960, pp. 79-87; August 29, 1960, pp. 317-346; September 12, 1960, pp. 409-412.

35. *New York Times,* August 15, 1960.

36. Same, August 25, 1960; Herter speech, August 24, in *Bulletin,* September 12, 1960, pp. 395-400, and *Documents, 1960,* no. 135.

37. *New York Times,* August 26, 1960; Herter statement in *Bulletin,* September 12, 1960, pp. 400-401. See further the Herter speech of August 26 in same, pp. 401-407, and in *Documents, 1960,* no. 136.

38. *Bulletin,* September 12, 1960, pp. 407-408; *Documents, 1960,* no. 137.

39. Final Act of the meeting, in O.A.S. Document OEA/Ser. C/II.7 and U.N. Document S/4480, September 7, 1960; resolution on Good Offices Committee also in *Documents, 1960,* no. 137.

40. Statements of August 29, in *Bulletin,* September 12, 1960, pp. 408-409.

41. *New York Times,* August 30, 1960; U.N. Document S/4480, p. 21.

42. *New York Times,* July 5, September 19, and October 3, 1960, and January 11, 1961; *Foreign Commerce Weekly,* October 17, 1960, pp. 3 ff., and December 26, 1960, p. 3.

43. For details see *Bulletin,* February 15, 1960, pp. 263-264; same, February 29, 1960, pp. 344-346; same, March 14, 1960, pp. 427-428; *New York Times,* February 8, 1960; Robert Cutler, "New Inter-American Bank Fosters Progress of Latin America," *Foreign Commerce Weekly,* November 14, 1960, pp. S5-S7.

44. "Treaty of Montevideo Provides Eventual Free-Trade Area, Association," *Foreign Commerce Weekly,* April 11, 1960, p. 5. Treaty text in U.N. *Economic Bulletin for Latin America,* March 1960, pp. 7-20.

45. Address to the Chilean Congress, March 1, in *New York Times,* March 2, 1960.

46. "Guatemala, Honduras, El Salvador Sign Economic Association Treaty," *Foreign Commerce Weekly,* March 14, 1960, p. 5; U.S. comment in *Bulletin,* February 29, 1960, p. 344.

47. Presidential statement and news conference, July 11, in *Bulletin*, August 1, 1960, pp. 166-170, and (in part) in *Documents, 1960*, no. 146.

48. News conference, August 10, in *New York Times*, August 11, 1960.

49. *Bulletin*, August 29, 1960, pp. 346-347.

50. Same, p. 315; *Documents, 1960*, no. 4.

51. *Bulletin*, August 29, 1960, p. 316.

52. Public Law 86-735, approved September 8, 1960.

53. *New York Times*, September 6 and 7, 1960; Dillon text in *Bulletin*, October 3, 1960, pp. 533-537, and in *Documents, 1960*, no. 147.

54. *Bulletin*, October 3, 1960, pp. 537-540; *Documents, 1960*, no. 148.

55. Joint statement, November 3, in *Bulletin*, November 21, 1960, pp. 782-783; also *New York Times*, November 4, 1960.

56. *New York Times*, October 30 and December 14, 1960, and January 11, 1961.

57. *Foreign Commerce Weekly*, November 7, 1960, p. 7; Chase Manhattan Bank, *Latin-American Business Highlights*, Fourth Quarter 1960, pp. 1-6.

58. *Bulletin*, May 2, 1960, pp. 699-705.

59. *New York Times*, September 2, 28, and 29 and October 3, 9, and 17, 1960. For background see same, December 19, 1960. Cf. further Section 52.

60. *New York Times*, March 23 and 30, 1960.

61. Same, November 19 and 27, 1960.

62. Same, April 20, May 14, September 9, October 28, and November 27 and 30, 1960.

63. Cf. the statement of President Eisenhower, November 1, in *Bulletin*, November 21, 1960, p. 780, and *Documents, 1960*, no. 144; also the comment of Cuban President Osvaldo Dorticós in *New York Times*, November 3, 1960.

64. Same, September 18, 1960; *Bulletin*, October 10, 1960, p. 559. See also *Bulletin*, May 16, 1960, pp. 798-799.

65. *Bulletin*, November 28, 1960, p. 822; December 12, 1960, p. 889; January 9, 1961, pp. 42-45; more briefly, *Documents, 1960*, no. 150.

66. Agreement of June 21, in *Bulletin*, July 11, 1960, pp. 68-72, and (in part) in *Documents, 1960*, no. 149.

67. *Bulletin*, September 12, 1960, pp. 423-427.

68. Same, November 14, 1960, pp. 742-743, and December 5, 1960, p. 851.

69. *New York Times*, October 17, 1960.

70. *Bulletin*, October 24, 1960, pp. 640-641; see also same, November 7, 1960, pp. 716-717.

71. U.S. note to O.A.S., October 28, in *Bulletin*, November 14, 1960, pp. 747-748, and *Documents, 1960*, no. 143.

72. See especially the excerpts from the Castro speech of September 26 in *New York Times*, September 27, 1960; also the formal U.S. reply of October 12 in *Bulletin*, October 31, 1960, pp. 690-701.

73. Same, November 28, 1960, pp. 814-815; see also same, December 19, 1960, pp. 924-925.

74. *New York Times*, October 15 and 26, 1960.

75. Same, October 19 and 20, 1960. On the preliminary debate see *Bulletin*, November 21, 1960, pp. 787-792.

76. Cf. Chapter I, note 65.

77. State Department statement, October 19, in *Bulletin*, November 7, 1960, pp. 715-716; *Documents, 1960*, no. 142.

78. *New York Times*, October 21, 1960.

79. State Department release, November 18, in *Bulletin*, December 5, 1960, pp. 852-853.

80. See especially *New York Times*, November 5, 1960.

81. Same, November 15, 19, and 20, 1960.

82. *Bulletin*, December 12, 1960, p. 888.

83. Same, December 26, 1960, p. 958; see also same, December 19, 1960, p. 924.

84. *New York Times*, December 1, 1960.

85. Same, December 4 and 7, 1960.

86. Same, October 29 and 30 and November 19, 1960.

87. Same, November 29, 1960.

88. Same, December 1 and 3, 1960.

89. Same, December 3, 1960. For material on the refugee problem see *Bulletin*, December 12, 1960, pp. 888-889, and January 9, 1961, pp. 45-48.

90. *New York Times*, December 16-20 and 27, 1960, and January 14, 1961; *Current Digest of the Soviet Press*, January 18, 1961, pp. 21-23.

91. *Bulletin*, January 2, 1961, pp. 18-19; *Documents, 1960*, no. 145.

92. *New York Times*, December 21, 24, and 25, 1960.

93. Same, December 21 and 22, 1960; *Bulletin*, February 20, 1961, pp. 274-276.

94. *New York Times*, November 2, 24, and 30, 1960.

95. Same, December 21, 22, and 24, 1960.

96. Same, December 22 and 28, 1960.

97. Same, December 10-15 and 19, 1960.

98. Cf. *Bulletin*, January 16, 1961, pp. 83-84.

99. *New York Times*, December 18, 21, and 25, 1960.

100. Same, January 1 and 2, 1961; U.N. Document S/4605.

Chapter VIII. The World Society

1. *Documents, 1953*, pp. 45-52.

2. *Documents, 1958*, pp. 350-360.

3. *Bulletin*, October 10, 1960, pp. 551-557, and *Documents, 1960*, no. 151. For other Eisenhower statements supporting the U.N. cf. *Bulletin*, October 17, 1960, pp. 624-628, and *New York Times*, October 19, 1960.

4. Letter from de Gaulle to Khrushchev, quoted in same, August 24, 1960.

5. Cf. Section 29 (3).

6. An annotated list of agenda items appears in *New York Times*, September 19, 1960. For additional background, see "Issues Before the Fifteenth General Assembly," *International Conciliation*, no. 529, September 1960, pp. 1-173.

7. *New York Times*, September 21, 1960.

8. Cf. Section 16.

9. *Bulletin*, October 10, 1960, p. 554; *Documents, 1960*, no. 151.

10. Unofficial translation in *New York Times,* September 24, 1960; excerpts in *Documents, 1960,* no. 152. Herter comment in *New York Times,* September 24, 1960. For a sampling of other reactions see *A United Nations or a Disunited Nations? Opinions in the General Assembly on the Khrushchev Proposal* (Washington: Department of State, n.d.).

11. *Bulletin,* October 17, 1960, pp. 619-620; *Documents, 1960,* no. 153.

12. *New York Times,* October 1, 1960.

13. Same.

14. Same, October 11, 1960.

15. Same, September 27, 1960.

16. Same, October 4, 1960.

17. Same.

18. Same, November 5, 1960.

19. Same, October 4, 1960.

20. Cf. Section 30 (2).

21. *New York Times,* October 12 and 14, 1960; further details in *Bulletin,* November 7, 1960, pp. 723-727.

22. For details see Section 30 (1).

23. Resolution 1493 (XV), October 8, 1960; for details see Sections 30 (1) and 42.

24. *New York Times,* October 9, 1960.

25. Same, October 14, 1960.

26. U.N. Document A/C.1/L.249, in *Documents, 1960,* no. 56.

27. Herter statement, September 20, in *Bulletin,* October 10, 1960, p. 589.

28. Statement by Francis O. Wilcox, November 3, in same, December 5, 1960, pp. 874-876.

29. *New York Times,* November 1 and 3 and December 6 and 7, 1960; *United Nations Review,* January 1961, p. 54.

30. *The United States in World Affairs, 1959,* p. 390.

31. *New York Times,* December 10 and 21, 1960.

32. Chapter II, note 96.

33. Resolution 1495 (XV), October 17, 1960, in *Documents, 1960,* no. 154. For details see *Bulletin,* November 7, 1960, pp. 722-723, and *United Nations Review,* November 1960, pp. 52-55 and 99.

34. *New Times,* no. 41, October 1960, pp. 33-39; U.N. Document A/4502.

35. Resolution 1569 (XV), December 18, 1960; details in *United Nations Review,* January 1961, p. 62.

36. Speech of Senator Wayne Morse, October 14, reported in *New York Times,* October 15, 1960.

37. Resolution 1542 (XV), December 15, 1960; details in *United Nations Review,* December 1960, pp. 19-23 and 42.

38. Resolution 1514 (XV), December 14, 1960, in *Documents, 1960,* no. 156. For details see *Bulletin,* January 2, 1961, pp. 21-28, and *United Nations Review,* January 1961, pp. 6-9 and 37-40.

39. *New York Times,* December 16, 1960; *Bulletin,* January 2, 1961, pp. 26-27; *Documents, 1960,* no. 157.

40. Cf. Section 30.

41. *New York Times,* December 13, 1960.

42. *Documents, 1959,* pp. 528-535. Cf. *The United States in World Affairs, 1959,* pp. 391-393; also statement by Herman Phleger, June 14, 1960, in *Bulletin,* July 11, 1960, pp. 49-52; Robert D. Hayton, "The Antarctic Settlement of 1959," *American Journal of International Law,* April 1960, pp. 349-371; and Howard J. Taubenfeld, "A Treaty for Antarctica," *International Conciliation,* no. 531, January 1961, pp. 245-322.

43. *New York Times,* October 22, 1960; *Bulletin,* November 21, 1960, p. 805.

44. Statement of Arthur H. Dean to Senate Foreign Relations Committee, January 20, in *Bulletin,* February 15, 1960, pp. 259-261.

45. For details see same, pp. 251-261, and *The United States in World Affairs, 1958,* pp. 411-413.

46. *New York Times,* April 27, 1960. For background and details see Arthur H. Dean, "The Second Geneva Conference on the Law of the Sea: The Fight for Freedom of the Seas," *American Journal of International Law,* October 1960, pp. 751-789.

47. G. Zhukov, "Space Espionage Plans and International Law," *International Affairs* (Moscow), October 1960, pp. 53-57; cf. *New York Times,* November 14, 1960.

48. Resolution 1472 (XIV), December 12, 1959, in *Documents, 1959,* pp. 536-537; cf. *The United States in World Affairs, 1959,* pp. 393-395.

49. *Bulletin,* October 10, 1960, pp. 554-555; *Documents, 1960,* no. 151.

50. *Bulletin,* January 25, 1960, pp. 117-118; *Documents, 1960,* no. 1; for details cf. *Bulletin,* February 15, 1960, pp. 227-232.

51. *New York Times,* March 30, 1960.

52. Eisenhower speech, August 29, in *New York Times,* August 30, 1960; Herter speech, September 1, in *Bulletin,* September 19, 1960, p. 438.

53. *New York Times,* October 13 and 21, 1960.

54. *Bulletin,* September 19, 1960, p. 438.

55. *United Nations Review,* December 1960, p. 86.

56. *New York Times,* October 18, 1960.

57. *Bulletin,* October 10, 1960, p. 553; *Documents, 1960,* no. 151.

58. *New York Times,* December 11, 1960; Resolution 1529 (XV), December 15, 1960.

59. *United Nations Review,* November 1960, pp. 88-89; same, December 1960, p. 94; same, February 1961, pp. 46-48; *Bulletin,* November 7, 1960, pp. 731-732.

60. *New York Times,* December 20, 1960.

61. Same, November 26 and 27, 1960.

62. Resolution 1521 (XV), December 15, 1960. See *United Nations Review,* January 1961, pp. 24 and 51; also *New York Times,* December 7, 1960, and U.N. Document A/4648, December 14, 1960.

63. Resolution 1522 (XV), December 15, 1960; cf. *United Nations Review,* January 1960, pp. 25, 51, and 55; same, January 1961, p. 51; and U.N. Document A/4648, December 14, 1960.

64. *Bulletin,* October 10, 1960, p. 554; *Documents, 1960,* no. 151.

65. Resolution 1496 (XV), October 27, 1960, in *Documents, 1960,* no. 155. For details see *Bulletin,* November 21, 1960, pp. 798-801; *United Nations Review,* December 1960, pp. 14-18, and February 1961, p. 4.

66. For a brief summary of world population statistics see same, October 1960, pp. 2-3.

67. *Bulletin,* January 18, 1960, p. 90.

68. Cf. Section 37.

69. *Bulletin,* August 15, 1960, pp. 254-258; same, March 13, 1961, pp. 386-389.

70. Same, June 27, 1960, p. 1046, and July 4, 1960, p. 15.

71. Public Law 86-648, approved July 14, 1960; cf. *Bulletin,* August 8, 1960, p. 219.

72. *United Nations Review,* December 1960, pp. 43-46; see also *Bulletin,* November 21, 1960, pp. 801-803 and 804-805.

73. *United Nations Review,* January 1961, p. 21.

74. *New York Times,* November 15, 1960. For details of the four articles adopted in 1960 see *United Nations Review,* December 1960, p. 90, and January 1961, p. 36.

75. *The United States in World Affairs, 1959,* p. 402; *United Nations Review,* May 1960, p. 43; same, January 1961, pp. 36 and 52.

76. Cf. Chapter IV, note 35.

77. Section 35.

78. *Bulletin,* December 5, 1960, p. 877; see also *United Nations Review,* February 1961, pp. 20-22.

79. *Bulletin,* October 17, 1960, pp. 617-618; *United Nations Review,* November 1960, pp. 4-5, and February 1961, p. 3; Department of State, *Foreign Policy Briefs,* January 6, 1961. Cf. also Section 5.

80. *United Nations Review,* November 1960, pp. 2-3; *Bulletin,* January 16, 1961, pp. 90-91.

81. For details cf. *Bulletin,* June 27, 1960, pp. 1033-1036, and December 12, 1960, pp. 894-897.

82. For details cf. Honoré M. Catudal, "The 1960-61 GATT Tariff Conference," *Bulletin,* February 22, 1960, pp. 291-299; also *Bulletin,* September 19, 1960, pp. 455-456.

83. *New York Times,* November 22, 1960. On U.S. participation see *Bulletin,* October 24, 1960, pp. 664-665, and December 19, 1960, pp. 941-945.

84. *New York Times,* December 13, 1960.

85. Same, November 19, 1960.

86. Same, July 2, 1960; for background cf. *Bulletin,* January 18, 1960, pp. 94-98.

87. *New York Times,* May 20, 1960.

88. Same, December 13, 1960; cf. also *Bulletin,* January 16, 1961, pp. 92-94.

89. *New York Times,* September 21-October 1, 1960, *passim.*

90. *Bulletin,* October 10, 1960, p. 557; *Documents, 1960,* no. 151.

CHRONOLOGY OF WORLD EVENTS

JANUARY 1-DECEMBER 31, 1960

N.B. Italicized references are to relevant sections of the text.

THE UNITED STATES

Major Treaties and Agreements

Entered into force:
June   11—Treaty of Amity, Economic Relations, and Consular Rights with Muscat and Oman (signed Salalah, Dec. 20, 1958.)
June   23—Treaty of Mutual Cooperation and Security with Japan (signed Washington, Jan. 19, 1960). *Sec. 41.*
Sept.   24—Articles of Agreement of the International Development Association (done at Washington, Jan. 26, 1960; signed by U.S., Aug. 9, 1960). *Secs. 5 and 58.*
Dec.   21—Convention of Establishment with France (signed Paris, Nov. 25, 1959).

Ratified:
Aug.   —The Antarctic Treaty (signed Washington, Dec. 1, 1959; U.S. ratification deposited Aug. 18, 1960). *Secs. 4 and 57.*
Aug.   29—Treaty of Friendship and Commerce with Pakistan (signed Washington, Nov. 12, 1959).

Senate advice and consent to ratification given:
May   26—Convention on the Territorial Sea and the Contiguous Zone; Convention on the High Seas; Convention on Fishing and Conservation of the Living Resources of the High Seas; Convention on the Continental Shelf (done at Geneva, Apr. 29, 1958). *Sec. 57.*

Signed:
June   21—Agreement for the Establishment of the Caribbean Organization (signed Washington). *Sec. 50.*
Dec. 14—Convention on the Organization for Economic Cooperation and Development (signed Paris). *Secs. 19 and 23.*

Congress

Jan. 6-Sept. 1. The 86th Congress holds its Second Session and adopts the following major legislation relating to foreign affairs (with Public Law numbers and dates of presidential approval):

P.L. 86-472, May 14 (H.R. 11510)—Mutual Security Act of 1960. *Sec. 5.*

P.L. 86-565, June 30 (H.R. 11001)—Providing for U.S. participation in the International Development Association. *Sec. 5.*

P.L. 86-592, July 6 (H.R. 12311)—Amending the Sugar Act of 1948. *Sec. 47.*

P.L. 86-601, July 7 (H.R. 11998)—Defense Department appropriation for Fiscal Year 1961. *Sec. 4.*

P.L. 86-610, July 12 (S.J. Res. 41)—International Health Research Act.

P.L. 86-648, July 14 (H.J. Res. 397)—Enabling U.S. to participate in resettlement of certain refugees. *Sec. 59.*

P.L. 86-651, July 14 (H.R 12740)—Supplemental Appropriation Act, 1961, appropriating $73,667,700 for the International Development Association. *Sec. 5.*

P.L. 86-678, Aug. 31 (H.R. 11666)—Departments of State and Justice, Judiciary, and related agencies appropriations, Fiscal Year 1961.

P.L. 86-704, Sept. 2 (H.R. 12619)—Mutual Security and Related Agencies Appropriation Act, 1961. *Sec. 5.*

P.L. 86-722, Sept. 8 (H.R. 13161)—Second Supplemental Appropriation Bill for Fiscal 1961, including an additional $65 million for the Mutual Security Program. *Sec. 5.*

P.L. 86-735, Sept. 8 (H.R. 13021)—Authorizing $600 million in economic aid to Latin America. *Secs. 5 and 49.*

Political Developments

Feb. 22-Mar. 7. President Eisenhower visits Puerto Rico, Brazil, Argentina, Chile, and Uruguay. *Sec. 46.*

May 14-20. President Eisenhower visits Paris for the summit conference, returning by way of Portugal. *Secs. 3 and 13.*

June 12-26. President Eisenhower visits Alaska, the Philippines, Taiwan, Okinawa, Korea, and Hawaii. *Secs. 39 and 40.*

July 13-14. Senator John F. Kennedy and Senator Lyndon B. Johnson are nominated as Democratic candidates for President and Vice-President respectively. *Sec. 4.*

July 27-28. Vice-President Richard M. Nixon and Ambassador Henry Cabot Lodge are nominated as Republican candidates for President and Vice-President respectively. *Sec. 4.*

Sept. 7. Ambassador James J. Wadsworth succeeds Ambassador Lodge as Permanent U.S. Representative to the United Nations.

Sept. 19-Oct. 13. Soviet Premier Khrushchev visits New York for the U.N. General Assembly session. *Secs. 7, 16, and 53-56.*

Sept. 22. President Eisenhower addresses the U.N. General Assembly. *Secs. 54 ff.*

Nov. 8. Senator Kennedy is elected 35th President of the U.S., for a four-year term starting Jan. 20, 1961. Senator Johnson is elected Vice-President, and Democrats retain control of both houses in the 87th Congress. *Sec. 7.*

Economic Developments

Jan. 4. Agreement is reached on a new contract settling a 116-day steel strike. *Sec. 1.*

Nov. 16. The President orders comprehensive measures aimed at reducing the balance-of-payments deficit. *Sec. 8.*

Military Developments

May 10. The nuclear-powered submarine U.S.S. *Triton* completes a 41,500-mile underwater voyage around the world.

May 20. An Atlas intercontinental missile is test-fired 9,000 miles to a point in the Indian Ocean. *Sec. 2.*

July 20. Two Polaris missiles are successfully test-fired over a 1,000-mile course from the nuclear submarine *George Washington*. *Sec. 4.*

Sept. 30. Gen. Lyman L. Lemnitzer succeeds Gen. Nathan F. Twining as Chairman of the Joint Chiefs of Staff.

Nov. 15. The nuclear submarine *George Washington* puts to sea with 16 operational Polaris missiles. *Sec. 8.*

Space Exploration (Sec. 4)

Earth satellites placed in orbit include the following:

Apr.   1—Tiros I weather satellite.
Apr.   13—Transit I-B navigation satellite.
May   24—Midas missile defense alarm satellite.
Aug.   12—Echo I communications satellite.
Nov.   23—Tiros II weather satellite.

Other developments:

Aug.   11—Successful recovery of a space capsule ejected from the Discoverer XIII satellite.
Aug.   19—Recovery in mid-air of the instrument capsule of Discoverer XIV.

EAST-WEST RELATIONS

Jan. 12-May 12. The tripartite Conference on the Discontinuance of Nuclear Weapons Tests continues in Geneva. *Sec. 10.*

Mar. 15-Apr. 29. The Ten-Nation Disarmament Committee meets in Geneva. *Sec. 11.*

May 7. Khrushchev discloses the capture of the pilot of the American U-2 aircraft shot down over the U.S.S.R. May 1. The pilot is sentenced Aug. 19 to ten years' loss of liberty. *Secs. 3, 13, and 14.*

May 16. The "Big Four" heads of government hold a preliminary session to the summit conference in Paris.

May 17. The three Western heads of government note that substantive discussions at the summit have been made impossible by the attitude of Khrushchev. *Secs. 3 and 13.*

May 27-Aug. 22. The conference on nuclear weapons tests continues in Geneva. *Sec. 14.*

June 7-27. The ten-nation disarmament conference resumes in Geneva but is terminated by the walkout of the Soviet bloc delegates. *Sec. 14.*

July 11. The U.S.S.R. discloses the shooting down of an American RB-47 aircraft, assertedly in Soviet Arctic waters. *Secs. 4 and 14.*

Sept. 27-Dec. 5. The conference on nuclear weapons tests continues in Geneva. *Sec. 17.*

THE WESTERN COMMUNITY

North Atlantic Treaty Organization

Feb. 26. Admiral Robert L. Dennison (U.S.) succeeds Admiral Jerauld Wright (U.S.) as Supreme Allied Commander, Atlantic.

May 2-4. The North Atlantic Council holds its spring ministerial session in Istanbul and approves Western plans for the summit conference. *Sec. 21.*

Sept. 20-30. NATO commands conduct a triennial series of land, sea, and air training exercises. *Sec. 24.*

Dec. 16-18. The North Atlantic Council holds its regular ministerial session in Paris and discusses a NATO nuclear deterrent. *Sec. 24.*

Economic Affairs

Jan. 12-13. A Special Economic Committee of the O.E.E.C. meets in Paris to discuss coordination of economic effort within the Western community. *Sec. 19.*

May 3. The seven-nation European Free Trade Association comes into being with the deposit of ratifications of the convention initialed Nov. 20, 1959. *Sec. 19.*

May 13. The Council of the six-nation European Economic Community agrees on an accelerated program of tariff adjustments starting Jan. 1, 1961. *Sec. 19.*

July 1. A second 10 per cent reduction in internal tariffs among "the six" and an additional 20 per cent reduction in internal tariffs among "the seven" become effective. *Sec. 19.*

Dec. 14. The 20-nation convention establishing the Organization for Economic Cooperation and Development is signed in Paris. *Sec. 23.*

United Kingdom

Mar. 28-30. Prime Minister Harold Macmillan confers with President Eisenhower at Camp David and Washington. *Sec. 10.*

July 27. The Earl of Home succeeds Selwyn Lloyd as Foreign Secretary. *Sec. 22.*

Sept. 25-Oct. 5. Prime Minister Macmillan attends the U.N. General Assembly and confers with President Eisenhower Sept. 27 and Oct. 2. *Sec. 16.*

France

Jan. 24. European extremists in Algiers engage in armed demonstrations against the government. The revolt collapses Feb. 1. *Secs. 18 and 28.*

Feb. 13. The first French nuclear explosion takes place in the Sahara. Further explosions take place Apr. 1 and Dec. 27. *Secs. 20 and 24.*

Mar. 23-Apr. 3. Premier Khrushchev visits France. *Sec. 12.*

Apr. 22-26. President Charles de Gaulle visits Washington. *Sec. 20.*

The Federal Republic of Germany

Mar. 15. Chancellor Konrad Adenauer confers informally with President Eisenhower in Washington. *Sec. 12.*

Italy

Feb. 24. The cabinet of Premier Antonio Segni (Christian Democrat, approved Feb. 15, 1959) resigns. An all-Christian Democratic cabinet headed by Attilio Tambroni is sworn in Mar. 26 and receives final confirmation Apr. 29.

July 19. The Tambroni cabinet resigns and is replaced July 27 by an all-Christian Democratic cabinet under Amintore Fanfani. *Sec. 22.*

Benelux

Nov. 1. The Benelux economic union of Belgium, the Netherlands, and Luxembourg comes into force.

Belgium

Sept. 2. Premier Gaston Eyskens (Social Christian; assumed office Nov. 6, 1958) forms a new coalition cabinet to deal with the situation resulting from the Congo crisis. *Sec. 22.*

Denmark

Feb. 19. Premier H. C. Hansen (Social Democrat; appointed Feb. 1, 1955) dies. Viggo Kampmann (Social Democrat) is appointed Feb. 20 to head the coalition government.

Oct. 11-14. King Frederick IX and Queen Ingrid make a state visit to Washington.

Nov. 15. The Social Democratic party gains seven seats in parliamentary elections. Premier Kampmann forms a new coalition government Nov. 18. *Sec. 22.*

Iceland

Aug. 1. President Asgeir Asgeirsson (assumed office 1952) is inaugurated for a third four-year term after having been unopposed for reelection.

Portugal

May 19-20. President Eisenhower visits Lisbon.

Austria

June 30-July 8. Premier Khrushchev makes a state visit to Austria. *Sec. 22.*

Oct. 22. The coalition government of Chancellor Julius Raab (People's party; inducted July 16, 1959) resigns. A new coalition government headed by Chancellor Raab is inducted Nov. 3.

Finland

Sept. 2-4. Premier Khrushchev visits Finland. *Sec. 22.*

Nov. 20-24. President Urho K. Kekkonen visits Moscow. *Sec. 22.*

Sweden

Sept. 18. The Social Democrats increase their strength in elections to the lower chamber of the Riksdag.

Canada (Sec. 22)

Feb. 16-17. The Joint U.S.-Canadian Committee on Trade and Economic Affairs holds its fifth meeting in Washington.

June 3-4. Prime Minister John Diefenbaker confers with President Eisenhower in Washington.

July 12-13. The Canada-U.S. Ministerial Committee on Joint Defense holds its third meeting at Montebello, Quebec.

Sept. 26-27. Prime Minister Diefenbaker addresses the U.N. General Assembly and confers with President Eisenhower in New York.

Sept. 28. An agreement is reached with the U.S. on joint development of the Columbia River basin.

THE COMMONWEALTH OF NATIONS

(See also regional headings.)

Feb. 2. *Australia*—Viscount Dunrossil succeeds Field Marshal Sir William Slim as Governor-General.

May 3-13. The Commonwealth Prime Ministers hold their tenth postwar meeting in London.

July 1. *Ghana* becomes a republic within the Commonwealth. (See "Africa.")

Aug. 16. *Cyprus* achieves independence as a republic within the Commonwealth, with Archbishop Makarios as President and Dr. Fazil Kutchuk as Vice-President. *Sec. 22.*

Oct. 1. *Nigeria* achieves independence within the Commonwealth. (See "Africa.")

Oct. 2. *Australia*—Premier Robert Gordon Menzies confers with President Eisenhower and Prime Minister Macmillan in Washington. *Sec. 16.*

Nov. 26. *New Zealand*—The National party wins a majority in general elections. Keith J. Holyoake (National party) becomes Prime Minister Dec. 12, succeeding Walter Nash (Labor party; took office Dec. 11, 1957).

THE COMMUNIST WORLD

Feb. 4. The Political Consultative Council of the Warsaw Treaty Organization meets in Moscow and issues a declaration on East-West relations. *Secs. 12 and 21.*

June 24. Representatives of 12 ruling Communist parties meet in Bucharest and reaffirm the 1957 Moscow declaration on peaceful co-existence. *Sec. 14.*

July 24. Marshal Andrei A. Grechko succeeds Marshal Ivan S. Konev as commander-in-chief of the combined armed forces of the Warsaw Treaty states.

July 30. The Council for Economic Mutual Assistance (Comecon) concludes a four-day meeting in Budapest.

Nov. 7-Dec. 1. Leaders of 81 Communist parties discuss ideological issues in Moscow. A declaration embodying the results is issued Dec. 6. *Sec. 17.*

The U.S.S.R.

Jan. 14. Premier N. S. Khrushchev tells the Supreme Soviet that the U.S.S.R.'s armed forces will be reduced from 3,623,000 to 2,423,000 within the next year or two. *Secs. 2 and 11.*

Jan. 21. A space rocket launched in the U.S.S.R. is claimed to have struck within less than two kilometers of its Central Pacific target after a flight of 12,500 kilometers. A second successful test is announced Feb. 1. *Sec. 2.*

Feb. 11-Mar. 5. Premier Khrushchev visits India, Burma, Indonesia, and **Afghanistan.** *Secs. 15, 34, 35, and 39.*

Mar. 23-Apr. 3. Premier Khrushchev visits France. *Sec. 12.*

May 5. Aleksei N. Kosygin becomes a First Deputy Premier and Frol R. Kozlov is shifted from First Deputy Premier to the secretariat of the Communist party Central Committee as part of a general shake-up of the government and party leadership.

May 7. Leonid I. Brezhnev succeeds Marshal Kliment Y. Voroshilov (elected Mar. 15, 1953) as Chairman of the Presidium of the Supreme Soviet.

May 14-19. Premier Khrushchev visits France for the summit conference. *Secs. 3 and 13.*

May 15. A space ship carrying a dummy space man is placed in orbit. *Sec. 15.*

July 5, 7. Moscow announces two further successful rocket tests in the Central Pacific. *Sec. 15.*

Aug. 19. A second space ship (Sputnik V) is launched with a cargo of two dogs and other animals whose successful return to earth is announced Aug. 20. *Sec. 15.*

Sept. 2-4. Premier Khrushchev visits Finland. *Sec. 22.*

Sept. 9-Oct. 14. Premier Khrushchev is absent to attend the U.N. General Assembly in New York. *Secs. 7, 16, and 54-56.*

Dec. 1. A five-ton space ship carrying two dogs and other animals is orbited but burns out Dec. 2. *Sec. 17.*

Bulgaria

Mar. 14. Diplomatic relations with the U.S., broken in 1950, are restored with the presentation of credentials by U.S. Minister Edward Page, Jr. *Sec. 17.*

Czechoslovakia

June 12. Elections are held to the National Assembly and the Slovak National Council.

July 11. A new constitution for the "Czechoslovak Socialist Republic" is adopted.

Poland

July 16. An agreement in settlement of U.S.-Polish nationalization and other financial claims is signed in Washington.

July 21. An agreement covering the sale to Poland of $60 million in U.S. surplus farm products is concluded in Washington. *Sec. 17.*

Rumania

Mar. 30. An agreement for a financial settlement with the U.S. is signed in Washington. *Sec. 17.*

Dec. 9. A cultural exchange agreement with the U.S. is signed in Washington. *Sec. 17.*

The "German Democratic Republic"

Sept. 7. President Wilhelm Pieck (first elected Oct. 11, 1949) dies. The Presidency is superseded Sept. 12 by a 23-man Council of State with Walter Ulbricht as Chairman.

Yugoslavia

Sept. 22. President J. B. Tito addresses the U.N. General Assembly and confers with President Eisenhower in New York. *Sec. 7.*

Dec. 7. Plans are announced for a major currency and foreign trade reform based on $275 million in international credits. *Sec. 17.*

AFRICA

General

June 14-24. The second Conference of Independent African States is held in Addis Ababa.

Dec. 23-24. The President of Ghana, Guinea, and Mali meet at Conakry and announce a union of their countries. *Sec. 30 (3).*

Algeria

Jan. 24. See "France."

May 27-29. Elections to departmental general councils produce majorities favorable to President de Gaulle's Algerian policy. *Sec. 28.*

June 25-29. Emissaries of the Algerian "Provisional Government" make contact with French representatives at Melun. *Sec. 28.*

Nov. 4. President de Gaulle predicts the emergence of an Algerian republic. *Sec. 30 (3).*

(See further "The United Nations: General Assembly.")

Morocco

May 20. The government of Premier Abdallah Ibrahim (established Dec. 24, 1958) is dismissed. King Muhammad V announces May 23 that he will exercise the administrative power through the intermediary of Crown Prince Moulay Hassan.

Sept. 1. France agrees to evacuate its military bases by March 2, 1961 and its remaining air force facilities by the end of 1963. *Sec. 30 (3).*

Libya

Oct. 17. Muhammad ben Othman heads a new cabinet, succeeding Abdel Majid Kubar (inducted May 26, 1957).

Ethiopia

Dec. 14. An unsuccessful military coup against the Emperor Haile Selassie I is carried out in the name of Crown Prince Asfa-Wossen. *Sec. 30 (3).*

Liberia

Jan. 4. President William V. S. Tubman (True Whig party; inaugurated 1944) is inaugurated for a fourth four-year term.

Ghana

Apr. 21. Premier Kwame Nkrumah is elected President in a nationwide vote in which proposals for a republican constitution are approved.

July 1. Ghana becomes a republic within the Commonwealth as the new constitution goes into effect and Premier Nkrumah is inaugurated as President. *Sec. 30 (1).*

Sept. 22. President Nkrumah confers with President Eisenhower in New York during his attendance at the U.N. General Assembly. *Sec. 30 (1).*

Guinea

Sept. 6-8. President Sékou Touré visits the U.S.S.R.

Sept. 10-13. President Touré visits Communist China and signs a friendship treaty and a 100 million ruble loan agreement. *Sec. 30 (1).*

Oct. 5-18. President Touré attends the U.N. General Assembly in New York.

Cameroun

Jan. 1. The trust territory of Cameroons under French Administration achieves independence as the Republic of Cameroun. Amadou Ahidjo (Cameroon Union party) remains as Premier and is elected President in May following adoption of a new constitution. *Sec. 25.*

Togo

Apr. 27. The trust territory of Togo under French Administration achieves independence as the Republic of Togo. Sylvanus E. Olympio remains as Premier. *Sec. 25.*

Somalia

July 1. The trust territory of Somaliland under Italian Administration achieves independence as the Republic of Somalia and unites with former British Somaliland. Aden Abdallah Osman is elected President. *Sec. 25.*

The Congo

Feb. 20. Agreement to establish an independent Congo state to succeed the Belgian Congo is announced at the conclusion of a Brussels round-table conference. *Sec. 25.*

June 30. The former Belgian Congo becomes independent as the Republic of Congo, with Joseph Kasavubu (Abako party) as Chief of

State and Patrice Lumumba (Mouvement National Congolais) as Prime Minister. *Sec. 29 (1)*.

July 11. The new government asks U.N. military assistance following a revolt of the Congolese armed forces. The province of Katanga under Premier Moise Tshombe declares itself independent. *Sec. 29 (1)*.

Sept. 5. President Kasavubu dismisses Premier Lumumba and names Joseph Ileo to succeed him, but Lumumba denounces the action as illegal and declares Kasavubu ousted on Sept. 6. *Sec. 29 (3)*.

Sept. 14. Col. Joseph Mobutu, Army Chief of Staff, announces that the army is taking power until Jan. 1. On Sept. 20 he appoints a College of High Commissioners under Justin Bomboko to supervise the administration. *Secs. 29 (3) and 30 (2)*.

Nov. 8-24. President Kasavubu attends the U.N. General Assembly in New York. *Sec. 30 (2)*.

Dec. 2. Ex-Premier Lumumba is arrested by the Congolese Army. *Sec. 30 (2)*.

(See also "The United Nations: Security Council" and "General Assembly.")

The French Community

June 20. The Mali Federation of Senegal and Soudan declares itself fully sovereign. Similar declarations are issued by the Malagasy Republic (June 26), Republic of Dahomey (Aug. 1), Republic of Niger (Aug. 3), Voltaic Republic (Upper Volta) (Aug. 5), Ivory Coast (Aug. 7), Republic of Chad (Aug. 11), Central African Republic (Aug. 13), Republic of the Congo (Aug. 15), Gabon (Aug. 17), and Mauritania (Nov. 28).

Aug. 20. The Federation of Mali is dissolved as the Republic of Senegal declares its independence of Soudan. *Sec. 30 (1)*.

Sept. 23. The Republic of Soudan renames itself the Republic of Mali and annuls its agreements with the French Community. *Sec. 30 (1)*.

Nigeria

Oct. 1. The Federation of Nigeria achieves independence within the Commonwealth. Sir Abubukar Tafawa Balewa is Prime Minister. *Sec. 30 (1)*.

Oct. 6. The Prime Minister attends the U.N. General Assembly and confers with President Eisenhower in Washington Oct. 8. *Sec. 30 (1)*.

Nov. 16. Dr. Nnamdi Azikiwe is inducted as Governor-General.

Union of South Africa

Jan. 12. Charles R. Swart is inducted as Governor-General, succeeding the late Ernest G. Jansen.

Mar. 21. Eighty-nine are killed in Sharpeville and elsewhere as police fire on Africans demonstrating against the pass laws. *Sec. 26*.

(See also "The United Nations: Security Council.")

Apr. 9. Premier Hendrik F. Verwoerd is seriously wounded by a white assassin. *Sec. 26*.

Oct. 5. White South Africans declare for a republic in a nationwide referendum. *Sec. 30 (3)*.

THE MIDDLE EAST

Central Treaty Organization

Apr. 28-30. The CENTO Ministerial Council holds its eighth session in Tehran with Secretary of State Herter representing the U.S. *Sec. 34.*

Turkey

May 27. The government of President Celal Bayar and Premier Adnan Menderes (Democratic party; in office since May 22, 1950) is overthrown by a military group headed by Lt. Gen. Cemal Gursel, who becomes President and Premier in a provisional government May 28. *Sec. 34.*

Iran

Aug. 3-20. Parliamentary elections produce a victory for the Nationalist party. *Sec. 34.*

Aug. 28. Premier Manouchehr Eghbal (inducted Apr. 3, 1957) resigns amid criticism of the elections and is succeeded Aug. 29 by Jaffar Sharif-Imami. *Sec. 34.*

United Arab Republic

Jan. 9. Construction of the Aswan High Dam begins.

Aug. 27. Agreement on a 900 million ruble Soviet credit for the second stage of the Aswan High Dam is concluded in Moscow. *Sec. 32.*

Sept. 23-Oct. 4. President Gamal Abdel Nasser attends the U.N. General Assembly and confers with President Eisenhower and Premier Khrushchev in New York. *Sec. 36.*

Lebanon

May 14. The government of Rashid Karami (appointed Oct. 14, 1958) resigns in favor of a caretaker cabinet headed by Ahmed Daouk.

June 12, 19, 26, July 3. Parliamentary elections are held.

Aug. 1. Saeb Salaam forms a new cabinet.

Sept. 22. Premier Salaam confers with President Eisenhower in New York.

Iraq

Apr. 8-16. Soviet First Deputy Premier A. I. Mikoyan visits Iraq. *Sec. 32.*

Jordan

Aug. 29. Premier Hazza Majali (inducted May 6, 1959) is killed in a bomb explosion. Bahjat Talhuni heads a new cabinet. *Sec. 32.*

Oct. 7. King Hussein confers with President Eisenhower in Washington after addressing the U.N General Assembly Oct. 3. *Sec. 36.*

Saudi Arabia

Dec. 21. King Saud accepts the resignation of the cabinet headed by Crown Prince Faisal, who was granted full powers Mar. 24, 1958. *Sec. 37.*

Israel

Mar. 10. Premier David Ben-Gurion confers with President Eisenhower in Washington. *Sec. 33.*

SOUTHERN ASIA

Afghanistan

Mar. 2-5. Premier Khrushchev visits Afghanistan. *Sec. 34.*

Aug. 26. A treaty of friendship and nonaggression with Communist China is signed in Kabul. *Sec. 34.*

Sept. 23. Deputy Premier Muhammad Naim confers with President Eisenhower in New York.

Pakistan

Feb. 17. President Muhammad Ayub Khan (assumed office Oct. 27, 1958) is sworn in as elected President following endorsement Feb. 14 in a special referendum of village councillors. *Sec. 34.*

Aug. 1. Rawalpindi replaces Karachi as the official capital.

India-Pakistan Relations

Sept. 19. A treaty and related agreements regulating the use of Indus River waters are signed in Karachi. *Sec. 35.*

India

Feb. 1. An anti-Communist coalition wins a majority in Kerala state elections.

Feb. 11-16. Premier Khrushchev visits India. *Sec. 35*

Apr. 19-26. Premier Chou En-lai visits India but fails to reach agreement with Prime Minister Jawaharlal Nehru on the Sino-Indian frontier dispute. *Sec. 35.*

May 4. A four-year agreement covering sale of 17 million tons of surplus grain for the equivalent of $1,276 million is signed in Washington. *Sec. 35.*

June 20-July 5. President Rajendra Prasad visits the U.S.S.R.

Sept. 25-Oct. 9. Prime Minister Nehru attends the U.N. General Assembly and confers with President Eisenhower in New York Sept. 26. *Secs. 7, 16, and 36.*

Nepal

Mar. 11-22. Premier B. P. Koirala (inducted May 27, 1959) visits Communist China. A border agreement and a $21 million economic aid agreement are concluded Mar. 21. *Sec. 35.*

Apr. 26-28. Premier Chou En-lai of Communist China visits Nepal for conclusion of a treaty of peace and friendship. *Sec. 35.*

Apr. 27-29. King Mahendra and Queen Ratna visit Washington. *Sec. 35.*

Sept. 22. Premier Koirala confers with President Eisenhower in New York.

Dec. 15. King Mahendra dismisses the Koirala government, jails the ex-Prime Minister, and personally heads a new cabinet inducted Dec. 26. *Sec. 37.*

Ceylon

Mar. 19. The United National party wins 50 out of 151 elective seats in elections to the House of Representatives. *Sec. 35.*

Mar. 20. The government of Wijayananda Dahanayake (Freedom party; took office Sept. 26, 1959) resigns. A cabinet headed by Dudley S. Senanayake (United National party) is sworn in Mar. 23. *Sec. 35.*

July 20. The Sri Lanka (Freedom) party wins 75 of 157 seats in new elections to the lower house. Mrs. Sirimavo Bandaranaike (Freedom party) becomes Prime Minister July 21 and forms a Freedom party cabinet. *Sec. 35.*

SOUTHEAST ASIA

The Colombo Plan

Nov. 14-17. The Colombo Plan Consultative Committee holds its 12th ministerial meeting in Tokyo. *Sec. 36.*

Southeast Asia Treaty Organization

May 31-June 2. The SEATO Ministerial Council holds its sixth annual meeting in Washington. *Sec. 39.*

Burma

Jan. 24-29. Premier Ne Win (inducted Oct. 29, 1958) visits Communist China and signs a treaty of friendship and mutual nonaggression and a boundary agreement. *Sec. 39.*

Feb. 6. The "Clean" faction of the Anti-Fascist People's Freedom League (A.F.P.F.L.) wins a majority in parliamentary elections. *Sec. 39.*

Feb. 16-18. Premier Khrushchev visits Burma. *Sec. 39.*

Apr. 5. U Nu (A.F.P.F.L.) resumes the premiership, succeeding Gen. Ne Win. *Sec. 39.*

Apr. 15-19. Premier Chou En-lai visits Burma. *Sec. 39.*

Oct. 1. A treaty defining the boundary with China is signed by Premier Nu in Peking. *Sec. 42.*

Indonesia

Feb. 18-Mar. 1. Premier Khrushchev visits Indonesia and promises a Soviet credit of $250 million. *Sec. 39.*

Mar. 5. President Sukarno suspends the Parliament elected in 1955. An appointed Parliament of 283 members is installed June 25.

Aug. 15. President Sukarno names a 609-member Provisional People's Congress (installed Sept. 16) and a governing council of the National Front.

Oct. 6. President Sukarno confers with President Eisenhower in Washington after attending the U.N. General Assembly. *Sec. 54.*

Philippines

June 14-16. President Eisenhower visits the Philippines. *Sec. 39.*

Thailand

June 28-July 2. King Phumiphol Aduldet and Queen Sirikit visit Washington. *Sec. 39.*

Malaya

Apr. 1. Tuanku Abdul Rahman, Paramount Ruler since 1957, dies and is succeeded Apr. 14 by Sultan Sir Hisamuddin Alam Shah.

July 31. The emergency proclaimed in 1948 is formally ended. *Sec. 39.*

Sept. 1. The new Paramount Ruler dies. His successor, elected Sept. 21, is Putra Ibni al-Marhum Syed Hassan Jamalullail, Raja of Perlis.

Oct. 25-27. Prime Minister Tunku Abdul Rahman confers with President Eisenhower and other U.S. authorities in Washington. *Sec. 39.*

Republic of Vietnam

Nov. 11-12. An unsuccessful military coup takes place against the government of President Ngo Dinh Diem. *Sec. 44.*

"Democratic Republic of Vietnam"

July 15. President Ho Chi Minh is elected to a new presidential term by the National Assembly.

Laos

Jan. 8. A new coalition government is inducted under Kou Abhay (nonparty). *Sec. 39.*

Apr. 24, May 8. Leftist candidates are heavily defeated in elections to the National Assembly. *Sec. 39.*

June 2. Prince Tiao Somsanith forms a government drawn principally from the Paxasangkham (Youth) party. *Sec. 39.*

Aug. 9. A neutralist group headed by Capt. Kong Le overthrows the government in a military coup. A neutralist government under Prince Souvanna Phouma assumes office Aug. 17. *Sec. 43.*

Sept. 10. A counterrevolutionary movement is launched by Gen. Phoumi Nosavan and Prince Boun Oum. *Sec. 43.*

Dec. 9. Premier Souvanna Phouma flees to Cambodia in face of imminent leftist and rightist attacks on Vientiane. A successor government under Prince Boun Oum is formed Dec. 12 and takes control in Vientiane Dec. 18. *Sec. 43.*

Cambodia

Apr. 3. King Norodom Suramarit (acceded Mar. 2, 1955) dies.

Apr. 12. The cabinet of Premier Prince Norodom Sihanouk (invested July 10, 1958) resigns. Pho Proeung is confirmed Apr. 18 as head of a new government.

May 5-9. Premier Chou En-lai visits Cambodia. *Sec. 39.*

June 20. Prince Norodom Sihanouk is installed as Chief of State.

Sept. 25. Prince Norodom Sihanouk heads Cambodia's delegation to the U.N. General Assembly and confers with President Eisenhower in New York September 27.

Nov. 28-Dec. 25. Prince Norodom Sihanouk visits the U.S.S.R. and Communist China. *Sec. 44.*

EAST ASIA

Republic of China (Formosa)

Mar. 21. The National Assembly elects President Chiang Kai-shek (assumed office May 20, 1948) to a third six-year term starting May 20. *Sec. 40.*

June 18-19. President Eisenhower visits Formosa. *Sec. 40.*

"People's Republic of China"

Nov. 5-Dec. 8. Government Chairman Liu Shao-chi attends the Moscow celebration of the 43rd anniversary of the Bolshevik Revolution and the subsequent conference of Communist party representatives. *Sec. 44.*

"Mongolian People's Republic"

May 31. A treaty of friendship and mutual assistance and a five-year economic aid agreement with Communist China are signed in Ulan Bator. *Sec. 42.*

Sept. 9. An agreement on a Soviet credit of 615 million rubles in aid of Mongolia's five-year economic plan for 1961-65 is concluded in Moscow. *Sec. 42.*

Japan

Jan. 17-20. Premier Nobusuke Kishi (Liberal Democrat; assumed office Feb. 25, 1957) visits Washington for the signature Jan. 19 of a new treaty of mutual cooperation and security with the U.S. *Sec. 41.*

June 16. Premier Kishi announces the postponement of President Eisenhower's intended visit to Japan because of internal opposition. *Sec. 41.*

June 21. Japanese ratification of the security treaty is completed, and instruments of ratification are exchanged June 23 (Tokyo time). *Sec. 41.*

July 15. The Kishi government resigns. A new government headed by Hayato Ikeda (Liberal Democrat) assumes office July 19. *Sec. 41.*

Sept. 27-29. Crown Prince Akihito and Princess Michiko visit Washington.

Nov. 20. The Liberal Democratic party improves its position in parliamentary elections. *Sec. 44.*

Republic of Korea

Mar. 15. President Syngman Rhee (Liberal party; assumed office Aug. 15, 1948) is reelected for a four-year term starting Aug. 15. Lee Ki Poong (Liberal party) is elected Vice-President. *Sec. 40.*

Apr. 18-19. At least 115 are killed and 777 injured in demonstrations protesting the conduct of the elections. *Sec. 40.*

Apr. 27. President Rhee offers his resignation as antigovernment riots continue. Foreign Minister Huh Chung becomes *de facto* head of state. *Sec. 40.*

June 19. President Eisenhower visits Korea. *Sec. 40.*

July 29. The Democratic party wins majorities in both houses in parliamentary elections held under a new constitution. *Sec. 44.*

Aug. 12. Yoon Bo-sun (Democratic party) is elected by the National

Assembly to a five-year term as President and inaugurated Aug. 15. Dr. John M. Chang (Democratic party) is approved as Premier Aug. 19. *Sec. 44.*

"Korean People's Democratic Republic"

Oct. 13. Two agreements providing for a Communist Chinese loan of 420 million rubles are signed in Peking. *Sec. 44.*

INTER-AMERICAN AFFAIRS

General

Feb. 6. An economic association treaty among Guatemala, Honduras, and El Salvador is signed in Guatemala. *Sec. 49.*

Feb. 18. A treaty establishing a seven-nation free trade area in Latin America is signed in Montevideo. *Sec. 49.*

June 21. An agreement to establish a Caribbean Organization to replace the Caribbean Commission established in 1946 is signed in Washington by the U.S., U.K., France, and the Netherlands. *Sec. 50.*

Aug. 16-21. The American Foreign Ministers hold their Sixth Meeting of Consultation in San José and adopt a resolution condemning the Dominican Republic for aggressive acts against Venezuela. *Sec. 48.*

Aug. 22-29. The Seventh Meeting of Consultation of American Foreign Ministers in San José condemns threats of extracontinental intervention in American affairs. *Sec. 48.*

Sept. 5-13. The Special Committee to Study the Formulation of New Measures for Economic Cooperation (Committee of Twenty-One) holds its third meeting in Bogotá and approves the Act of Bogotá, a program for social development. *Sec. 49.*

Oct. 1. The Inter-American Development Bank begins operations in Washington. *Sec. 49.*

Dec. 13. A Treaty of Central American Integration among Guatemala, Honduras, Nicaragua, and El Salvador is signed in Managua. *Sec. 49.*

Argentina

Feb. 26-29. President Eisenhower visits Argentina. *Sec. 46.*

Mar. 27. The governing Intransigent Radical party is seriously set back in congressional and provincial elections.

Bolivia

June 5. Víctor Paz Estenssoro (National Revolutionary Movement— M.N.R.) is elected to a four-year term as President, succeeding Hernán Siles Zuazo (M.N.R.; inaugurated Aug. 6, 1956). *Sec. 50.*

Brazil

Feb. 23-26. President Eisenhower visits Brazil. *Sec. 46.*

Apr. 21. The capital is officially transferred from Rio de Janiero to Brasília.

Oct. 3. Jánio da Silva Quadros (National Democratic Union) is elected to a five-year presidential term starting Jan. 31, 1961. *Sec. 50.*

Chile

Feb. 29-Mar. 2. President Eisenhower visits Chile. *Sec. 46.*

May 21-27. Earthquakes and tidal waves kill an estimated 5,000 to 10,000 persons.

Colombia

Mar. 20. Elections to the House of Representatives are held without major incident.

Apr. 5-8. President Alberto Lleras Camargo visits Washington. *Sec. 50.*

Cuba

Feb. 4-13. Soviet First Deputy Premier Mikoyan visits Cuba and concludes agreements Feb. 13 embodying a $100 million credit and five-year sugar purchase commitments. *Sec. 47.*

May 9. Cuba and the U.S.S.R. announce the resumption of diplomatic relations, interrupted in 1952. Relations are restored Aug. 22.

July 23. A five-year trade and credit agreement with Communist China is signed in Havana. *Sec. 48.*

Aug. 7. Premier Fidel Castro announces the expropriation of all U.S.-owned companies in Cuba. *Sec. 48.*

Sept. 18-28. Premier Castro attends the U.N. General Assembly in New York. *Sec. 51.*

Oct. 19. The U.S. embargoes most exports to Cuba. *Sec. 51.*

(See also "Inter-American Affairs: General" and "The United Nations: Security Council.")

Dominican Republic

Aug. 3. President Héctor Bienvenido Trujillo Molina (inaugurated Aug. 16, 1952) resigns and is succeeded by Vice-President Joaquín Balaguer. *Sec. 48.*

Aug. 26. The U.S. severs diplomatic relations pursuant to the San José resolution of Aug. 21. *Sec. 48.*

Ecuador

June 5. José María Velasco Ibarra (Independent) is elected to a four-year presidential term starting Sept. 1, succeeding Camilo Ponce Enriquez (elected 1956). *Sec. 50.*

Mexico

Oct. 24. President Adolfo López Mateos meets President Eisenhower at Ciudad Acuña. *Sec. 50.*

Panama

May 8. Dr. Roberto F. Chiari (Liberal party) is elected to a four-year presidential term starting Oct. 1, succeeding Ernesto de la Guardia, Jr. (inaugurated Oct. 1, 1956). *Sec. 50.*

Peru

July 28. The extension of two U.S. credits totaling $53.2 million is announced in Washington. *Sec. 49.*

El Salvador

Apr. 24. The Revolutionary Party of Democratic Unification wins all seats in elections to the Legislative Assembly.

Oct. 26. The government of President José María Lemus (assumed office Sept. 14, 1956) is supplanted by a six-man military-civilian junta under Col. César Yanes Urías. *Sec. 51.*

Uruguay

Mar. 1. Benito Nardone (National party) succeeds Martin R. Echegoyen (National party) as President of the National Council.

Mar. 2. President Eisenhower visits Uruguay. *Sec. 46.*

Canada

(See "The Western Community.")

THE UNITED NATIONS

Membership

U.N. membership is increased from 82 to 99 as the following 17 states are admitted to membership by vote of the General Assembly:

Sept. 20—Cameroun, Togo, Malagasy Republic, Somalia, Republic of the Congo (Leopoldville), Dahomey, Niger, Upper Volta, Ivory Coast, Chad, Republic of the Congo (Brazzaville), Gabon, Central African Republic, Cyprus. *Sec. 30 (1).*

Sept. 28—Republics of Senegal and Mali. *Sec. 30 (1).*

Oct. 7—Federation of Nigeria. *Sec. 30 (1).*

Security Council

Following is a list of major Security Council decisions, with votes:

Jan. 26—Recommending Cameroun for U.N. membership. (Unanimous.)

Apr. 1—Deploring recent violence in South Africa and requesting the Secretary-General to consult with the South African Government. (9-0-2.) *Sec. 26.*

May 26—Rejecting a Soviet proposal to condemn U.S. intelligence flights. (2-7-2.) *Sec. 13.*

May 27—Asking renewed talks on disarmament. (9-0-2.) *Sec. 13.*

May 31—Recommending Togo for U.N. membership. (Unanimous.)

June 23—Requesting Israel to make reparation to Argentina for the abduction of Adolf Eichmann. (8-0-2.) *Sec. 33.*

June 28—Recommending the Federation of Mali for U.N. membership. (Unanimous.)

June 29—Recommending Malagasy for U.N. membership. (Unanimous.)

July 5—Recommending Somalia for U.N. membership. (Unanimous.)

July   7—Recommending the Republic of the Congo (Leopoldville) for U.N. membership. (Unanimous.)

July   14—Calling for the withdrawal of Belgian troops from the Republic of the Congo and authorizing the Secretary-General to provide the Congo with military assistance. (8-0-3.) *Sec. 30 (1)*.

July   19—Referring Cuban charges of economic aggression and interference by the U.S. to the Organization of American States. (9-0-2.) *Sec. 48*.

July   22—Calling on Belgium to withdraw its forces speedily from the Congo (Unanimous.) *Sec. 30 (2)*.

July   26—The U.S.S.R. casts its 88th and 89th vetoes to defeat resolutions calling for international investigation in the shooting down of a U.S. aircraft July 1 (9-2) and envisaging Red Cross contact with survivors (9-2). *Sec. 14*.

Aug.   9—Calling on Belgium to withdraw its forces immediately from the Katanga Province of the Congo. (9-0-2.) *Sec. 29 (2)*.

Aug.   23—Recommending Dahomey, Chad, Niger, Upper Volta, Ivory Coast, Congo Republic, Gabon, and Central African Republic for U.N. membership. (Unanimous.)

Aug.   24—Recommending Cyprus for U.N. membership. (Unanimous.)

Sept.   9—Taking note of the San José decision of the American Foreign Ministers regarding the Dominican Republic. (9-0-2.) *Sec. 48*.

Sept.   17—The U.S.S.R. casts its 90th veto to defeat a resolution supporting the U.N. effort in the Congo. (8-2-1.) The Council calls an emergency special session of the General Assembly. (8-2-1.) *Sec. 29 (3)*.

Sept.   28—Recommending Senegal and Mali for U.N. membership. (Unanimous.)

Oct.   7—Recommending Nigeria for U.N. membership. (Unanimous.)

Dec.   4—The U.S.S.R. casts its 91st veto to defeat a recommendation of Mauritania for U.N. membership. (8-2-1.) *Sec. 30 (1)*.

Dec   14—The U.S.S.R. casts its 92nd veto to defeat a Western-supported resolution on the Congo. (7-3-1.) *Sec. 30 (2)*.

General Assembly

Sept. 17-20. The Assembly holds its Fourth Emergency Special Session in New York and adopts the following resolution:

1474 (ES-IV), Sept. 20—Supporting the U.N. action in the Congo. (Vote: 70-0-11.) *Sec. 29 (3)*.

Sept. 20-Dec. 21. The Assembly holds the first part of its Fifteenth Regular Session in New York under the presidency of Frederick H. Boland of Ireland, adopting the following resolutions among others (with votes):

1476 (XV)-1489 (XV), Sept. 20—Admitting 13 African states and Cyprus to U.N. membership. (Unanimous.) *Sec. 30 (1)*.

1490 (XV) and 1491 (XV), Sept. 28—Admitting Senegal and Mali to U.N. membership. (Unanimous.) *Sec. 30 (1).*

1492 (XV), Oct. 7—Admitting Nigeria to U.N. membership. (Unanimous.) *Sec. 30 (1).*

1493 (XV), Oct. 8—Postponing discussion of Chinese representation. (42-34-22.) *Sec. 42.*

1495 (XV), Oct. 17—Urging constructive steps to reduce world tensions. (Unanimous.) *Secs. 16 and 56.*

1496 (XV), Oct. 27—Authorizing a plan for use of food surpluses. (Unanimous.) *Sec. 58.*

1497 (XV), Oct. 31—Urging Austria and Italy to resume negotiations on the South Tyrol dispute. (Without objection.) *Sec. 22.*

1498 (XV), Nov. 22—Accepting the credentials of the Kasavubu delegation from the Congo. (53-24-19.) *Sec. 30 (2).*

1514 (XV), Dec. 14—Declaration on the Granting of Independence to Colonial Countries and Peoples. (89-0-9.) *Sec. 56.*

1521 (XV), Dec. 15—Favoring a U.N. capital development fund. (71-4-10.) *Sec. 58.*

1542 (XV), Dec. 15—Requesting Portugal to report on nine overseas territories. (68-6-17.) *Sec. 56.*

1568 (XV), Dec. 18—Deprecating application of *apartheid* in South West Africa. (78-0-15.) *Sec. 30 (3).*

1569 (XV), Dec. 18—Approving an independence plebiscite in Western Samoa. (81-0-10.) *Sec. 56.*

1573 (XV), Dec. 19—Recognizing the right of the Algerians to independence. (63-8-27.) *Sec. 30 (3).*

1579 (XV), Dec. 20—Recommending postponement of elections in Ruanda-Urundi. (61-9-23.) *Sec. 30 (3).*

1583 (XV), Dec. 20—Establishing a separate financial account for the Congo. (46-17-24.) *Sec. 30 (2).*

Other decisions:

Dec. 5—Electing Felix Schnyder to succeed Dr. Auguste R. Lindt as U.N. High Commissioner for Refugees. (Unanimous.) *Sec. 59.*

Dec. 9—Electing Chile and the United Arab Republic to two-year terms, and Turkey to a one-year term, on the Security Council. *Sec. 55.*

—Electing five new members of the Economic and Social Council. *Sec. 55.*

Dec. 20—Electing Liberia to a one-year term on the Security Council. *Sec. 55.*

Other developments:

Sept. 22—President Eisenhower addresses the Assembly. *Secs. 7, 16, 54, 57, 58.*

Sept. 23—Premier Khrushchev addresses the Assembly. *Secs. 7, 16, 54, 56.*

Trusteeship System

Jan. 1. The trusteeship agreement for Cameroons under French Administration is terminated as the territory becomes the independent Republic of Cameroun. *Sec. 25.*

Apr. 27. The trusteeship agreement for Togoland under French Administration is terminated as the territory becomes the independent Republic of Togo. *Sec. 25.*

July 1. The trusteeship agreement for Somaliland under Italian Administration is terminated as the territory becomes the Republic of Somalia. *Sec. 25.*

Disarmament Commission

Aug. 16-18. The Commission meets in New York and urges the early continuance of disarmament negotiations. *Sec. 14.*

Other Activities

Mar. 17-26. The Second U.N. Conference on the Law of the Sea meets in Geneva. *Sec. 57.*

June 30. The World Refugee Year 1959-60 is officially concluded. *Sec. 59.*

Aug. 31. The U.N. Korean Reconstruction Agency established in 1950 passes out of existence.

International Court of Justice

Nov. 16-17. Six new justices are elected by the General Assembly and the Security Council. *Sec. 57.*

Specialized Agencies

May 3-20. *W.H.O.*—The Assembly of the World Health Organization holds its 13th session in Geneva. *Sec. 60.*

June 1-23. *I.L.O.*—The International Labor Conference holds its 44th session in Geneva.

July 1. *F.A.O.*—The Food and Agriculture Organization opens a five-year "Freedom from Hunger" campaign. *Sec. 60.*

Sept. 26-30. *I.B.R.D.-I.M.F.*—The Boards of Governors of the International Bank for Reconstruction and Development, International Monetary Fund, and International Finance Corporation hold their 15th annual meeting in Washington and formally establish the International Development Association effective Sept. 24. *Sec. 60.*

Nov. 14-Dec. 13. *UNESCO*—The 11th General Conference of the U.N. Educational, Scientific and Cultural Organization is held in Paris. *Sec. 60.*

OTHER INTERNATIONAL ORGANIZATIONS AND CONFERENCES

International Atomic Energy Agency

Sept. 20-Oct. 2. The I.A.E.A. holds its fourth General Conference in Vienna. *Sec. 60.*

General Agreement on Tariffs and Trade

May 16-June 4. The Contracting Parties hold their 16th session in Geneva. *Sec. 60.*

Sept. 1. A tariff bargaining conference opens in Geneva. *Secs. 6 and 60.*

Oct. 31-Nov. 19. The Contracting Parties hold their 17th session in Geneva. *Sec. 60.*

INDEX